Religion in Multicultural Education

A volume in
Research in Multicultural Education and International Perspectives
Series Editor: Farideh Salili and Rumjahn Hoosain

Research in Multicultural Education and International Perspectives

Farideh Salili and Rumjahn Hoosain, *Series Editors*

Religion in Multicultural Education

Farideh Salili
and
Rumjahn Hoosain
The University of Hong Kong

INFORMATION AGE
PUBLISHING

Greenwich, Connecticut 06830 • www.infoagepub.com

Library of Congress Cataloging-in-Publication Data

Religion in multicultural education / edited by Farideh Salili and Rumjahn Hoosain.
    p. cm. – (Research in multicultural education and international perspectives)
 Includes bibliographical references and index.
 ISBN 1-59311-489-3 (pbk.) – ISBN 1-59311-490-7 (hardcover)
 1. Multicultural education–Cross-cultural studies. 2. Religion–Study and teaching. I. Salili, Farideh. II. Hoosain, R. (Rumjahn) III. Series.
 LC1099.R435 2006
 370.117–dc22

                                   2006005238

ISBN 13:

  978-1-59311-489-3 (pbk.)
  978-1-59311-490-9 (hardcover)

ISBN 10:

  1-59311-489-3 (pbk.)
  1-59311-490-7 (hardcover)

Printed in the United States of America

CONTENTS

PREFACE

Religion is an increasingly dominating force in global affairs and conflict, even though Francis Fukuyama declared *the end of history* in 1992. One might expect religion to be a central topic in discussions of multicultural education. Yet curiously, as noted by Subedi, Merryfield, Bashir-Ali, and Gunel in this volume, there is no chapter on religion in the *Handbook of Research on Multicultural Education* (Banks, 2004). Similarly, the *Encyclopedia of Multicultural Education* (Mitchell & Salsbury, 1999) only has an entry on religious freedom. A related facet of the lack of discussion of religion in multicultural education is what Christine Clark, in another contribution in this volume, referred to as a discomfort with open discussion of Christian privilege in American society. For example, the religious right would rather expend its energy on issues at a different level, such as that of intelligent creation versus evolution. This discomfort ties in with the idea of the melting pot, although with the increasing role of globalization there is discussion about whether the melting pot still works and talk of reinventing the melting pot (e.g., Jacoby, 2004).

What then should be a focus for discussion of religion in multicultural education? The National Association for Multicultural Education in Washington, D.C., listed a number of issues that the school curriculum should address with reference to multicultural education, including racism, sexism, classism, linguicism, ablism, ageism, heterosexism, and religious intolerance. It is noteworthy that of all these issues, religion is about the only one that throughout history people are willing to die for, although whether what is at issue is really religion or other things such as territory is another matter. It is also interesting that all the others have *isms* in their names but religious issues are characterized by intolerance. Perhaps we should try to understand this intolerance and look at what steps might help to alleviate it.

However, while intolerance might seem a simple thing, understanding what is behind it and how it plays such a crucial role in religion requires what we refer to in the Introduction chapter as a multifaceted approach at

Religion in Multicultural Education, pages vii–x
Copyright © 2006 by Information Age Publishing
All rights of reproduction in any form reserved.

multiple levels. It is not enough just to try to dispel stereotypes of followers of other religions, or to point out commonalities in world religions. We should, for example, try to understand and appreciate how adherents of other religions try to answer questions regarding their adaptation to the contemporary environment. It is through understanding how different religions coexist side by side at various levels that we truly come to learn about religion in multicultural education.

In the second chapter, Wilson provides us with an example of empathetic teaching of world religions, with accounts of how major world religions, including Hinduism, Buddhism, Confucianism, Judaism, Christianity, Islam, and Sikhism, teach about the treatment of other people. They all have variations of the theme about doing unto others as we would have done to ourselves, often called the golden rule of religions. The understanding of how believers of different versions of the golden rule and their related teachings could harbor intolerance and worse, and the role that multicultural education could play to change this, should be a goal of multicultural education.

The next three chapters approach the topic of religion and multicultural education from different perspectives. Michael Merry points out that parents choose comprehensive religious schools hoping that they will help maintain their children's cultural and religious identities. He gives us an account of the Islamic philosophy of education and the problems it has in trying to educate and socialize Muslims in Western societies. He perceives deep-rooted issues between Islamic educational ideals, aspirations of school administrators, and the manner in which Islamic schools are operated, and contrasts *education for cultural coherence* with multicultural education.

Moving from the focus of a single religious group, Franklin and Van Brummelen look at religious diversity in Western Canada, where multiculturalism instead of the melting pot, as well as a liberal worldview in education is presumed. Apart from historical and sociopolitical perspectives, the personal experiences of school administrators, parents, and teachers are discussed. The authors argue that there should be a balance between minority religious rights and the needs of all citizens to contribute to a compassionate, just, and equitable society.

Gerald Fry takes us to a different geographical and cultural environment, Thailand—with its Buddhist majority and a sizable Muslim population, particularly in the south. Five case studies are described, including the work of the Islamic College and the International Cooperative Learning Project, pointing to the benefit of reciprocal learning of values and traditions, at the same time verifying Allport's social contact theory, which suggests that social and personal contact with people of different cultural and racial backgrounds reduces prejudice, stereotypes, and misunderstanding.

The remaining chapters all deal with various issues in the American context. Some are more concerned with the negative aspects of religious issues, and some are more concerned with regional issues rather than the general picture, but they all inform us regarding religion in multicultural education. Rossatto and Hampton note that religious doctrines often induce fear of the *Other* mentally to promote their own faith, and describe the impact of religious and political manipulations in education in communities near the Mexican border. On the other hand, Conde-Frazier points to the task of changing the negative image of *others* in religious traditions, in the context of transforming people's perspectives when they relocate from religiously intolerant societies to one that promotes religious freedom. She makes use of the history of Latino Catholic and Protestant tensions as the case study, and suggests that the insights gained can be applied to the greater dialogue regarding relationship with more diverse religions. Christine Clark presents us with the case of the University of Maryland's Office of Human Relations Program to build a religiously and secularly inclusive community. She relates Christian privilege to white supremacy, and gives us an account of strategies to understand these challenges arising from Christian privilege in the public education and work context.

Subedi, Merryfield, Bashir-Ali, and Gunel explore how teachers' beliefs, experiences, and perspectives influence their instruction and interaction with students. A number of interviews provide insights into how teachers respond to religious stereotypes and how religious identities intersect with racial and gender identities. Kujawa-Holbrook is more concerned with the education of theology students in the face of an increasingly diverse society. She emphasizes cultural competence and describes a change process to enhance cultural competency, correlating with a framework based on appreciating diversity, reducing prejudice, power analysis, visioning, and implementing the new vision.

Finally, Curry and Houser propose the notion of moderate secularism after a review of the history of religion in education. The debates about religion in education in America has come to polar extremes, between those who fear that teaching particular religious beliefs would eventually divide the country by religion and those who fear that replacing religion with *secular humanism* would lead to development of an immoral society. The proposed moderate secularism involves balanced inquiry into spiritual issues without supporting any privileged orientation, based on inclusion, plurality, egalitarianism, inquiry, and authenticity. However, with the ruling by the U.S. Supreme Court that secular humanism is a religion (in the case *Torcaso v. Watkins*, 1961), how this can be included in the curriculum needs to be considered together with the question of the separation of church and state (see the Introduction).

—Farideh Salili
Rumjahn Hoosain

REFERENCES

Banks, J. A. (Ed.). (2005). *Handbook of research on multicultural education.* San Francisco: Jossey-Bass.

Jacoby, T. (Ed.). (2004). *Reinventing the melting pot: The new immigrants and what it means to be American.* New York: Basic Books.

Mitchell, B. M., & Salsbury, R. E. (Eds.). (1999). *Encyclopedia of multicultural education.* Westport, CT: Greenwood Press.

CHAPTER 1

INTRODUCTION

Dimensions of Religion
in Multicultural Education

Rumjahn Hoosain and Farideh Salili
The University of Hong Kong

With the increasing significance of religion in world affairs on the one hand, and seeming lack of discussion of the role of religion in multicultural education (see the Preface to this volume), we wish to outline a framework in which discussion and practice of this important component of multicultural education can proceed. The emphasis is that many discussions and practices should be multifaceted or on multiple levels. We can take the example of multicultural literacy.

RELIGION IN MULTICULTURAL LITERACY

Knowledge goes hand in hand with an inquiring and open mind. A person who cannot tell a Sikh from a Taliban (one is reported to have killed a Sikh in the street, thinking that he looked like a Taliban, soon after September 11) is unlikely to accept a pluralistic view of culture and religion. People like that are also more prone to accept the negativity and stereotypes purveyed by the popular media, such as the entertainment industry in Holly-

Religion in Multicultural Education, pages 1–8
Copyright © 2006 by Information Age Publishing
All rights of reproduction in any form reserved.

wood (see Shaheen, 2001). Quite a few authors in this volume have emphasized the importance of countering such stereotyping and also the need for knowledge about different religions. There is little question that many of our students do not have any deep knowledge about other cultures and, in particular, religions other than their own.

Some examples of the negative stereotyping prevalent about Islam include the ways it treats women, jihad and the use of violence, and the lack of democracy. An empathetic and open-minded discussion of such issues should include drawing a distinction between the original tenets of a religion and how some societies following the religion have evolved practices specific to their own sociopolitical history. For example, the original tenet might regard only dressing modestly, and there are dress codes for practitioners of other religions in specific situations too. A more in-depth discussion of the issue should involve tracing the historical background to their development. Regarding the popularly purveyed picture of jihad and the *jihadist*, we should note that a certain amount of reference to violence can be found in the scriptures of most religions, reflecting the historical background of the time, such as in the early chapters of the Old Testament. We should also note the deeper meaning of jihad as a personal struggle in the path of Allah, not necessary involving violence. The popular notion of the lack of democracy in Islamic countries should be tempered with historical reviews of how democratically elected governments have been undermined by western *democratic* states for selfish economic reasons, while other autocratic states have been shored up for the same reasons. The above is not a justification for negative or undesirable practices of some religions, but a plea for a more open-minded understanding of the multifaceted nature of religion and people of different religions in their historical environment. For example, an enlightening discussion of how people of different religions interact with each other in historical context could concern whether for centuries Jewish people had been treated relatively better by Moslems than by Christians up to World War II.

At the higher levels of religious hierarchies, there appears to be an awareness that the perpetuation of prejudices and negative stereotypes is undesirable. For example, the Office for Non-Christian Affairs at the Vatican, resulting from the Second Vatican Council, published Orientations for a Dialogue between Christians and Muslims calling for "a critical examination of our prejudices" and admitted to "out-dated image inherited from the past, or distorted by prejudice and slander" (see Bucaille, 1979, p. 111). It is up to the teacher at the grassroots level to devise ways to counter the prejudice and negative stereotypes, through in-depth discussions rather than just stating that one or the other stereotype is wrong.

Dispelling negative stereotypes is one aspect of an open-minded attempt to understand. Looking for the common positive aspects of religions, such as Wilson's effort in this volume to portray how major religions teach adherents how to treat their neighbors, as exemplified in different versions of the golden rule, is another. Similarly, we can point out other positive aspects of religious teachings, such as the reference to Jews and Christians in the Koran.

However, to pursue understanding of other religions, these are not enough. To be really empathetic, we need to appreciate how other religions and communities holding different religions evolve and attempt to adapt to the contemporary world. This gives us a better appreciation of each other, as our own religion should be similarly attempting to adapt (e.g., in trying to deal with issues of abortion and women priests) and foster the feel for our common humanity, although we practice different religions. An example would be questions posed by intellectuals like Tariq Ali about "why did Islam, once so pluralistic and intellectually progressive, ossify and withdraw to such a degree that it wound up isolated from the continent (Europe) it helped civilize" (Foran, 2005, p. 82)? There is something to be learned, in a multicultural education program, in trying to understand how Islam was pluralistic and intellectually progressive and what happened.

We could also include discussions of critics of differing religions as well as debates within religions. For example, Michael Merry in this volume discusses the need to problematize Islamic knowledge, so that knowledge can be divorced from its interpretation. Also, just as there are debates within Christianity and Judaism between more conservative or fundamentalist and more reformed-minded adherents, there are Moslems who advocate a more literal interpretation of Islam and those who are more reformist (cf., Jacob, 2005).

The religion component in multicultural literacy should include more than just an outline knowledge of the tenets of major religions and how stereotypes are wrong, but an appreciation of the trials and tribulations as well as triumphs of different religions.

IS RELIGION IN MULTICULTURAL EDUCATION ADDITIVE OR SUBTRACTIVE?

The question of whether religion in multicultural education is additive or subtractive finds a parallel in bilingual or multilingual education. There, the question is whether the learning of more than one language might have a negative effect on the learning of another, although the influence is usually thought of as from the native language to the second or the additional language. In psychology of learning terms, the concern is with negative instead of positive transfer of learning (e.g., Gredler, 2005). Thus, a child who migrates to a second language environment might end up speaking the native language with a slight accent (although a more common concern is that native language structures might affect the learning of a second language with significantly different structure, such as from a native language with few inflections to one with many). In the case of religion in multicultural education, there is some unsaid concern that with exposure to other religions we could be opening the door to questioning of the original faith, even substituting one truth with another (Nieto, 2000) or encouraging proselytism.

There is not much evidence for subtractive bilingualism. The language features that a bilingual learner finds difficult, such as inflection, are also features that the native learner has to work on to acquire. In particular, retroactive negative transfer (affecting the native language) seldom occurs. The child mentioned above who migrates and speaks a new language simply has not kept up with the learning and use of the native language. Many others become more accomplished persons with the bilingual or multilingual experience. Religion in multicultural education is not meant to replace the student's personal or familial religious experience. Neither is it meant to dilute the student's feeling and commitment for his or her own religion. As pointed out by many authors in this volume and elsewhere (e.g., Nieto, 2000), diversity in multicultural education is used to enrich the entire learning process. The nonpartisan way in which multicultural education is conducted invites the student to ponder the complexity of religious experience, resulting in a deeper appreciation of the experience. Proselytism occurs for as many reasons as there are personal lives, with or without multicultural education. Religion in multicultural literacy, just as multilingualism, is a desirable attribute in the global village.

SEPARATION OF "CHRUCH" AND STATE

The relation between religion and government has increasingly become an issue in the forefront of political discussion, in a whole spectrum of countries including those where the relation is thought to have been decided a long time ago, where it has been changed not too long ago, and where it is right now being decided. One debate in Iraq regarding the constitution and governance is the role of religion, with about 60% of the population being Shi'a Moslems, and a significant Sunni minority. There is also debate about whether Iraq might become a theocracy. At the other end, the United States has clear constitutional separation of the church and state. However, Gerald Fry in this volume noted that the legalistic separation of church and state makes discussion of religion and multicultural education in the United States problematic. How is it that in both theocracies and nations with constitutional separation of church and state, there could be concerns about difficulty of open discussion of religion in a multicultural education context?

It could be that both extremes are in their own ways dogmatic and not conducive to open, pluralistic discussion. The insistence of separation of church and state itself could be a form of intolerance that is referred to by the National Association for Multicultural Education (2003) in its advocacy for a school curriculum conducive to religious tolerance. Historically in the U.S., it can be considered an attempt to protect the church from the state. But historically too the church was often taken to mean one's own Christian denomination. With the ruling by the Supreme Court in the case of *Torcaso v. Watkins* in 1961 that Buddhism, Taoism, and secular humanism among others are also religions, church becomes more like religion in a multicultural context. What might be more important in the modern context is to revise the original notion of separation of church and state to one of ensuring a level playing field, with no religious denomination or point of view being in a privileged position. We do need to discuss spirituality and religion in multicultural education if not the practice of organized religion itself. Perhaps the time has come to go beyond the yoke of history and discuss a program for religion in a multicultural context.

Discussion of difficulties faced in the spectrum of countries with varying relations between church and state could itself be a useful part of the curriculum for religion in multicultural education. There is probably no one perfect relation for everybody. What is the best system for each nation depends on its own history and the makeup of its people and culture. What is more, the relation should not be static but adapted to circumstances, and again discussion about what are these circumstances and what changes might be appropriate should form part of our understanding of religion in multicultural education. This is another facet for us to appreciate how people in different cultural and religious environments make sense of their situation.

PYCHOLOGICAL ASPECTS OF RELIGION

As part of the suggestion of the multifaceted and multilevel approach to studying religion in multicultural education, we move on to the psychology of religion, whether at the personal or social level. Psychological understanding of the religious experience can involve the person, providing us with insight into the experience itself, as well as the dynamics of prejudice and stereotype and other social psychological aspects. At the personal level the basic question is why do people believe in a supernatural power and engage in rituals with reference to that power. We present a general view of how psychology of learning considers the learning of religion as an example of human functioning, and then a more specific model to account for the psychology of religion provided by Beit-Hallahmi and Argyle (1997).

Psychological Views on How Religion is Learned

Psychology generally considers the learning of religious behavior as similar to that of other behaviors or skills. How religion is taught and the content of teaching can influence one's religious beliefs and experiences. Through exposure to formal and informal teaching at home and in school, individuals learn religious behaviors and beliefs. With repeated practice, knowledge of how to perform religious rituals become automatic and difficult to change (McCallister, 1995). Constant exposure to religious events and religious environments serve to expand religious self-schema. Returning to a familiar religious setting (e.g., a church or a mosque) can bring back memories of past events and activate the individual's religious self-schema (McCallister, 1995). Religious music or chanting used in many religious contexts can create mood congruence. This in turn may activate religious self-schema, directing the individual toward religious material and self-reflection (Brown & Taylor, 1986; Snyder & White, 1982).

Self-focus increases the devotee's awareness of other people's views about religious materials. By identifying one's self-schema with those of the wider religious self seen in other participants, one's religious self-schema may be enhanced during the ritual (Markus & Nyrius, 1986). Other people can therefore function as possible self, and provide incentives for what the individual might become.

Psychology provides a good explanation of how individuals develop religious schema and why some people become devotedly religious and resistant to change. It explains the process by which young children acquire religious belief, learn to perform religious rituals, and can even fanatically follow what they have been taught. The content and context of religious teaching and the extent to which the individual is exposed to religious experience can shape religious beliefs and behaviors.

The Model of Beit-Hallahmi and Argyle

The model has three components, with hypotheses regarding the origin, maintenance, and consequence of religious behavior. The origin of religious behaviors includes the role of hard-wired neurological structure, cognitive need, cognitive style of individuals, different adjustments to anxiety, fear of death, early childhood experience, projection such as Freud's father projection view (or Schoenfeld's [1962] suggestion of God being a mother projection), and sublimation of sexual impulses. Maintenance includes a social learning hypothesis based on the observation that religion is socially acquired, maintenance of identity and self-esteem, deprivation hypotheses linking religious activity to deprivation and suffering, and personality hypothesis surrounding the question about religious personality. It is clear from this one model that psychology has a lot to shed light on religious behavior, and should be a part of any unbiased, pluralistic understanding of religion in a multicultural context. It might be possible to relate the distinctive characteristics of different religions to aspects of the psychological model. For example, Gerald Fry in this volume related the policy of Thailand toward both sides in World War II to its dominant Buddhist religion, with principles of nonviolence and reverence for life. Also, some instances of proselytism could have been the result of new-found attraction between the personality of the individual and features of the new religion.

CONCLUSION

We suggest that discussion of religion in multicultural education should be multifaceted and at multiple levels. We should use all the tools and knowledge of the social sciences and other fields of knowledge to grasp the various issues. Once we open up the discussion to beyond dogmatic reassertion of established positions, we should not be afraid, for example, to ask empirical questions and look for reliable empirical answers to guide our action. We have asked a few such questions in this chapter, such as whether multicultural education in religion is additive or subtractive. Does it make a student more or less committed to his or her religion, or religion as such? Reliable answers would help dispel fear of any open, pluralistic discussion. We hope that this volume would foster such discussion.

REFERENCES

Beit-Hallahmi, B., & Argyle, M. (1997). *The psychology of religious behaviour, belief and experience.* London: Routledge.

Brown, J., & Taylor, S. (1986). Affect and the processing of personal information: Evidence for mood activated self-schemata. *Journal of Experimental Social Psychology, 22,* 436–452.

Bucaille, M. (1979). The Bible, the Quran and science (A.D. Pannell & M. Bucaille, Trans.). Indianapolis, IN: American Trust Publications.

Foran, C. (2005, July/August). A civilizing influence. *Walrus.*

Gredler, M.E. (2005). *Learning and instruction: Theory into practice.* Upper Saddle River, NJ: Pearson.

Jacob, R. (2005, September 3-4). Fabulist takes on the literalists. *Financial Times*.

Markus, H., & Nyrius, P. (1986). Possible selves. *American Psychologist, 41*, 954–969.

McCallister, B. J. M. (1995). Cognitive theory and religious experience. In R. W. Hood (Ed.), *Handbook of religious experience*. Birmingham, AL: Religious Education Press.

National Association for Multicultural Education. (2003). *Resolutions and position papers: Advocates for educational equity and social justice*. Adopted by the NAME Board of Directors on February 1, 2003.

Nieto, S. (2000). *Affirming diversity: The sociopolitical context of multicultural education*. New York: Longman.

Shaheen, J. G. (2001). *Real bad Arabs: How Hollywood vilifies a people*. New York: Olive Branch Press.

Snyder, M., & White, P. (1982). Moods and memories: Elation, depression, and the remembering of the events of one's life. *Journal of Personality, 50*, 460–467.

CHAPTER 2

THE *OTHER*/NEIGHBOR IN WORLD RELIGIONS

An Exploration from a Multicltural Education Perspective

H.S. Wilson
Lutheran Theological Seminary

ABSTRACT

In the contemporary world of increasing multicultural situations, historic world religions have the potential of contributing to the welfare of all humans by appropriately recapturing their traditional visions and values. Multicultural education can facilitate this by empathetic teaching and learning of world religions as part of human heritage and history. The essay specifically deals with the perception of the *other*/neighbor in Hinduism, Buddhism, Confucianism, Judaism, Christianity, Islam, and Sikhism.

Religion in Multicultural Education, pages 9–40
Copyright © 2006 by Information Age Publishing
All rights of reproduction in any form reserved.

INTRODUCTION

Some of the following assumptions have shaped this chapter. World religions and their founders were great visionaries about the well-being of all humans. There are elements of inclusiveness in all religions. The misuse of the teachings of these religions at different stages of human history has caused tremendous harm to various sections of humanity, at times casting doubt about the value of religion in human affairs. However, the resurgence of religions are a fact of time, and have the potential of recapturing the vision of their founders. Multicultural education is a means of achieving that object, as societies around the globe are increasingly becoming multifaith communities. Empathetic teaching and studying of world religions (Nord, 1995, p. 215) as part of the human heritage and history can contribute to the goals of multicultural education.

RELIGION AND EDUCATION

Religions and education are intertwined in more than one way in accompanying their respective objectives even though their projected goals may seem to differ considerably. Historic world religions as well as the enterprise of education are neither neutral nor apolitical. Both in varying degrees are shaped by the values, methods/practices, interests, and goals of their promoters and sponsors. Like a subject matter of education, contents, values, and practices of a given religion are taught and transmitted from generation to generation by making use of pedagogical tools and methods chosen by its promoters. At the same time insights gained from religions and the knowledge acquired through education have tremendous potential of germinating new positive values depending on the creativity and ingenuity of their adherents and recipients.

While religions and the task of education have the primary goal of imparting knowledge, information, beliefs, and practices to their adherents and students; their larger goal is the well-being of the recipients and their community, and through them the well-being of the entire humanity and the whole of creation. When individuals are educated, the assumption is that they will in turn become sources of enrichment to their respective communities and to society at large. Often such goals may not be apparent and well pronounced in all cases. Therefore, the study of religion cannot be narrowly confined to mere training in one's tradition. At the same time, education is not just imparting knowledge of the subject that is taught. The implications of these, religious and secular knowledge, for one's engagement in the larger society need to be carefully discerned as part of teaching/learning. The present reality of greater interdependence and interconnectedness of humanity demands this for ensuring quality of life for all.

The religious founders and their immediate followers were often great educators. The faith they wished to promote would not have survived without their charismatic leadership and leaving behind a community with a commitment to transmit the faith through rites, rituals, customs, institutions, teachings, and appropriate pedagogical arrangements. In fact in the early stages of human history, education both religious and others were imparted in religious communities, institutions, and centers of worship like temples, ashrams, monasteries, cathedrals, catechetical schools, synagogues, mosques, and *gurdwaras* (Sikh places of worship) and continues even today in some circumstances. Religious communities and "orders" were often pioneers in the establishment of public educational facilities like schools, colleges, and universities.

In recent history, human societies have gone through a process of separating religious from secular education, and for a period certain secular forces systematically worked toward the demise of any trace of religion in human affairs, like the Communist societies. Now that such a type of antagonism has diminished, a number of secular states, international organizations, and local communities are back to recognizing the positive role that religions play in preserving moral values, and enhancing the quality of life. In a world that is becoming increasingly multicultural and multireligious, the positive role that world religions can play would have a determinative impact on human relations. I use the term *multicultural* as an inclusive term that embraces multiracial, multiethnic, multicolor, multilinguistic, multireligious, multicaste, multitribal, class, and gender differences. However, my focus in this chapter is to discuss what a multireligious ethos can contribute to multicultural education.

Some scholars are of the opinion that multicultural education should focus primarily on worldviews, which encompasses a broader outlook on life than religious worldviews. Perry L. Glanzer (2004) states, "Worldviews have expressions in religion (e.g., various forms of Christianity, Islam, Judaism and Hinduism) as well as philosophical or political outlooks (e.g., existentialism, pragmatism, Marxism, postmodernism, hedonism)" (pp. 3–4). However, according to Emile Lester (2004):

> Religions are treasure troves of advice for a wide variety of endeavors accumulated through generations of reflection. They instruct us not only about philosophy and metaphysics, but about political and economic justice, professional ethics, family relationships, and the ideals and purposes or art. (p.76)

In spite of some possible limitations, religious worldviews have the potential of contributing to several crucial life-affirming and community-building issues of our time along with the secular worldviews, as about 70% of humanity still relates to religions in one way or the other. Therefore it is important as Glanzer (2004) has stated that "Educators must become conscious of the influence of secular as well as religious worldviews on education, knowledge and themselves" (p. 8).

RELIGIOUS PLURALISM

In the last several decades with the increased mobility of people around the globe, human communities in most places have become multicultural. When people and communities move around they carry with them their histories—ethnicity, customs, languages, and so on—creating a multicultural situation in places that were hitherto monocultural or had only one or two dominant communities. Multicultural ethos has become a reality in many countries of the world and it is here to stay (Banks, 1993; Wilson, 2004, pp. 172–173).

Isolated living is not a possibility for the majority of humanity today. That has challenged communities around the globe, some more than others, to address the issue for the sake of helping people to deal with the multicultural phenomenon. Multireligious environment is one of the contributing factors to the multicultural ethos of a community. To promote a healthy religious pluralistic attitude in communities, which hitherto were shaped mainly by a single religious culture, single ethnic community, single language, or solo tradition, is a very demanding task. Coping with multiple religions, with each of them making truth claims, needs careful attention in a community if it's existing experience has been only with a single religion. Such a challenge has an implication for the activities of various institutions of a community, including the schooling and education of children and adults.

We are in a historic time where we have the advantage of learning from the wealth of information about past accomplishments and mistakes. Human history is full of accounts of atrocities that have been committed by religious and religiously affiliated bodies through their intolerance of others. Many a times such intolerances were primarily shaped by the narrow understanding of the teaching of one's own faith and the misunderstanding of the other. Comparing the best of one's tradition with the least of the other, claiming superiority on this false comparison, and arriving at such conclusions without any genuine engagement with the *other*. The multireligious situation in a given community challenges its members to make some hard choices of either welcoming and appropriately incorporating the newcomers and their religious traditions and practices, or resisting them and thereby creating a conflicting environment for all.

Many a time innocent religious followers have become victims to the interpretation of their heritage by individuals and groups who made use of religions as a tool of hatred, harming themselves and their neighbors. While such possibilities of misuse of religions may not be totally irradiated, taking precaution is a responsibility of every concerned individual. Minimizing the possibilities of misunderstandings between religious groups has to be a top priority to any community, as world communities are witnessing religious pluralism in a scale that was not seen before. The appropriate knowledge and greater appreciation of other religions is needed for the healthy existence of communities.

It is not that religions have to be updates and that aspect of generous embrace of others has to be somehow added to the teachings of any world religion. In fact such visions are embedded in all of the world religions. In the interreligious dialogues carried out informally or through organization and institutions like the Parliament of World's Religions and the World Conference for Religions and Peace, it is clear that the attitude of well-being toward the other as a fellow human being regardless of that person's ethnicity, race, color, caste, gender, and even religion is enshrined in all historic world religions. The unfortunate truth is that such attitudes toward others were not often lifted up and celebrated. The past several decades of intense interreligious dialogues and engagements have permanently put the concern of better understanding and cooperation between religious followers, both in the local and international agendas.

However, besides the formal religious dialogues, a more systematic way of decimating greater understanding between religious people through multicultural education, formal and nonformal, is required in shaping the attitude of people. A multicultural education that will positively use religious diversity in the total teaching and learning process is a crucial necessity (Gollnick & Chinn, 1998, p. 330). What Gollnick and Chinn (1998) are describing about the United States, is also the reality or the becoming of reality in many countries and regions of the world.

> Educators should never underestimate the importance that Americans place on religion. For some individuals, their religion takes precedent over all other micro-cultures. People have been willing to die for their religions; some have been willing to inflict great pain on others because of their beliefs. We live in a society that has become increasingly diverse. Along with increasing ethnic diversity has come increasing religious diversity. (p. 220)

Resurgence of Religion

Religions are alive and are shaping the lives of people and communities around the globe. Sociologist Peter Berger (1999) categorically states, "The world today is massively religious, is *anything but* the secularized world that had been predicted (whether joyfully or despondently) by so many analysts of modernity" (p. 9). Modernity has failed to provide the certainties religions have been providing for centuries. According to Gilbert Sewall (1998), since religions provide systems by which to live, people will "defend or denounce them more passionately than mere facts and ideas." So their "affect on the working of a community and the quality of public life" is inevitable (p. 83).

Religion provides a framework for the individuals' lives as well as communities' life. Religion is an important source of identity (who and what they are) for many people and is a source of legitimacy for actions they can support or oppose in their personal and societal life (Fox and Sandler, 2004, p. 176). "The resurgence of religions can (also) be seen in the growing saliency of religion in the politics of countries throughout the world" (Thomas, 2000, p. 112).

Religion plays a double role in most communities. On the one hand, it provides what Peter Berger calls a *Sacred Canopy.* It provides meaning for life with references to higher powers going beyond the appeal, to the uniqueness of humans in creation and the freedom they enjoy in relation to the rest of creation. On the other hand, for the sake of peace and harmony, it encourages obedience to authority and adherence to rules and regulations to maintain healthy bonds within the community. Thus religion *permeates and decisively affects* the lives of a majority of people. Religions are a fundamental force in human life of a large section of people, whether that person be a nuclear physicist in India, business magnate in Singapore, military commander in the United States, ranch owner in Argentina, or a political leader in South Africa. In the world we live, religions matter. The issue therefore is how religions can be better used for building a better society.

The new millennium started with a significant gathering of religious leaders of the world from August 28–31, 2000, summoned by the United Nations in New York City just before the millennium assembly of the heads of states and governments. Probably this was the first time the United Nations took such an initiative. More than 1,000 leaders from around the globe took part in the so-called Millennium World Peace Summit of Religious and Spiritual Leaders.

At the end of the summit the participants unanimously adopted a "Commitment of Global Peace," affirming their role in peace and justice at this critical junction in human history, in cooperation with the United Nations stating, "[W]e declare our commitment and determination: To collaborate with the United Nations and all men and women of goodwill locally and globally in the pursuit of peace in all its dimensions (*Millennium*, 2000, p. 1).

In some sense the outcome of the summit actualized what the United Nations Secretary General Kofi Annan had envisaged about the religious and spiritual dimension of the work in the United Nations:

> The United Nations is a tapestry, not only of suits and saris but of clerics' collars, nuns' habits and lamas' robes; of miters, skullcaps, and yarmulkes.... There is a basic affinity between the teachings of the great religions of the world and the values of the Charter of the United Nations. (*Millennium*, 2000)

The Summit was a recognition by the world political leaders and statesmen/women that people belonging to historic religious faith traditions have a positive role to play in global peace and justice, especially in the contemporary situation of a multicultural environment of human society.

Fox and Sandler (2004), in their book *Bringing Religions into International Relations*, state that the resurgence of religions especially outside the West is compelling scholars to give serious consideration to religions in the international relations theories and recognize their social and political influence. According to them, religions were rarely given the attention they deserved in most major theories of international relations. "In the few cases where it is addressed directly, 'religion tends to be characterized as fundamentalist, extreme, radical or militant' rather than as a normal element of political process" (p. 9).

In the changed world situation, paying appropriate attention to and promoting religious values in international relations is unavoidable. The challenge is to discern which values are to be promoted and celebrated.

Loving and Caring for One's Neighbor

When we look at the teachings of historic faith traditions, all of them have clear teachings on caring and even loving one's neighbor, often called as the "golden rule" of religions. Here are a few examples from the list compiled by Leonard Swidler (1998):

> Zoroastrianism: *That which is good for all and any one, for whomsoever—that is good for me ...what I hold good for self, I should for all.*
>
> Confucianism: *Do not to others what you do not want done to yourself.*
>
> Jainism: *A man should wander about treating all creatures as he himself would be treated.*

Buddhism: *Comparing oneself to others in such terms as "Just as I am so are they, just as they are so am I," he should neither kill nor cause others to kill.*

Hinduism: *Do not others what you do not wish done to yourself; and wish for others too what you desire and long for yourself—this is the whole of Dharma; heed it well.*

Judaism: *You shall love your neighbor as yourself.*

Christianity: *Do to others just what you want them to do for you.*

Islam: *Noblest Religion is this—that you should like for others what you like for yourself; and what you feel painful for yourself, hold that as painful for all others too.*

Bahai: *He should not wish for others that which he doth not wish for himself, nor promise that which he doth not fulfill.* (pp. 19–21)

Sikhism: *Don't create enmity with anyone. God abides in every heart. It is your duty to treat one and all with respect.* (Johar, 1977, p. 153)

The "golden rule" alludes to a vision that loving a neighbor in some sense is an extension of ones' love toward God and the whole of humanity. Safety and security of life is at threat when love and care is not the governing principle in human relations.

The golden rule probably may have evolved in different societies as a guiding principle for survival, and eventually became part of the teachings of the world religions. World religions highlighted and made use of the golden rule, as their context demanded it. So there is often debate about the similarities and differences, especially comparing the "merit of the positive formulation versus negative one." In spite of their different origin and diverse use, the contemporary multireligious situation demands utilizing the golden rule as a symbol of human kinship. Jeffery Wattles (1996) expounds this as follows:

> The golden rule, happily, has more than a single sense. It is not a static, one-dimensional proposition with a single meaning to be accepted or rejected, defended or refuted. Nor is its multiplicity chaotic. There is enough continuity of meaning in its varied uses to justify speaking of the golden rule. My own thesis is that the rule's unity is best comprehended not in terms of a single meaning but as a symbol of a process of growth on emotional, intellectual, and spiritual levels. (pp. 4–5)

The golden rule gives us both the option of reviewing the attempts of the past and at the same time moving beyond, with the vision needed for the present time.

Communitarian political ethos proponent Amitai Etzioni (1996) explains the functioning of the traditional golden rule as follows. The golden rule "contains an unspoken tension between what ego would prefer to do to others, and that which the golden rule urges ego to recognize as the right course of action" (p. xviii). Etzioni's concern is that in our time there is a need for "a new golden rule," which should read: "Respect and uphold society's moral order as you would have society respect and uphold your autonomy" (p. xviii). As societies and communities around the globe are becoming multiethnic, multilinguistic, multiracial, multicolored, and multireligious, it may be appropriate to highlight these positive affirmations of neighbors (golden rules) enshrined in the world religions and promote them for greater harmony among peoples in the increasingly evolving pluralistic world society. It can function as a basic device of moral education, community building, and as a first step toward an expanded vision and commitment as Amitai Etzioni proposes.

Unless these significant religious values are incorporated into the daily affairs of the people and are carefully nurtured, conflicts among religious followers can instantly crop up like the recent incident of the murder of Theo van Gogh, a controversial filmmaker (often referred as the Michael Moore of the Netherlands) in the Netherlands. He was shot and stabbed in broad daylight in Amsterdam on November 2, 2004. Mohammad Bouyeri, the 26-year-old suspect killer, dressed in Moroccan robe (as an affirmation of his Islamic identity) was apparently taking revenge for Theo van Gogh's controversial documentary on Muslim women, *Submission*. The note pinned to van Gogh's chest warned of similar attacks on public personalities who ridiculed Islam. The killing set off a wave of verbal slander against Muslims and Islam sympathizers, and retaliatory attacks on mosques, churches, and Muslim primary schools, shaking the foundation of healthy religious tolerance built in the Netherlands for several decades. Committed and concerned persons immediately started working on a renewed relationship through a process of forgiveness and reconciliation. Part of the success of such attempts greatly depended on earlier relationships and education.

WORLD RELIGIONS

Religions are very intricate and can be a highly subjective matter. According to Leonard Swidler (1998), "Normally all religions contain the four 'C's': Creed, Code, Cult, Community-structure, and are based on the notion of the Transcendent" (p. 1; see also Nord & Haynes, 1998, p. 49). Religions thus shape all the aspects of human life depending on one's receptivity. However, for our purpose we will limit our discernment to some basic teachings about humans and their responsibility to care and love their neighbors—in each of the following world religions: Hinduism, Buddhism, Confucianism, Judaism, Christianity, Islam, and Sikhism. These religions embrace the major section of the human community today. Even though these religions have emerged in different contexts and periods, in one form or another, in all of their teachings there is a mandate to the followers to respect the "other" belonging to different communities and religions, and treat them with humane attitudes for the sake of greater good for all.

The founders of these great world religions were sensitive to the multi-cultural context of their time. The communities they lived and served had issues related to ethnicity, gender, class, race, language, and religious differences. Their keen sense allowed them to see the discrimination that has been practiced and enshrined in societal norms by making use of these differences. So as visionaries they made clear pronouncements denouncing negative attitudes and showed ways to overcome them. That involved at times questioning the prevailing religious and social practices; challenging the custodians of the practices; and showing alternative ways for better human and community relations, which often resulted in the founding of a new religious community.

Since these religious leaders were prophets, preachers, philosophers, reformers, and teachers, they believed in accomplishing their goals by means of persistence, persuasion, and education. The persons and communities that were willing to follow their teachings were led to adopt new ways of personal and community living. We turn now to these religions and identify some key teachings about the ways one is expected to live and to relate to one's neighbor as a member of a respective faith community.

Hinduism—Commitment to Dharma

Hinduism is about a total way of life, a righteous living. That is why its authentic name is *Sanathana Dharma* (eternal way). The truth of Hinduism is not revealed or taught by a single teacher (*guru*). Not a single central authority, single scripture, or a set of dogmas bind Hindus together, even though there are shared beliefs and practices among its followers. Its prime concern is a holistic relation of an individual with one's own being/self (*atman*), with the supreme Being/Self (*Brahman*), as well as with fellow humans and with all the living beings in creation. Therefore, one's well-being is integrally interconnected with the well-being of the other. The attitude toward others, including one's adversaries, should be that of *ahisma* (nonviolence), popularized by Mahatma Gandhi.

According to Hinduism the Divine encountered humanity and creation through a number of incarnations to preserve good and eliminate the evil needed at a particular time. Harmony and order (*rta*) is important for the cosmos to move on. Harmony and order is ensured by every human adhering to *dharma*, a comprehensive term that includes righteousness and duty, right conduct that is tested and handed down through the ages. Fulfilling or flouting *dharma* has a consequence to an individual and the whole of the humanity. *Karma* is consequences of one's action that impacts life not only for an individual but also the community he or she is part of. *Dharma* and *karma* in that sense interlocks one another and the whole of creation.

Hindus have no difficulty in relating to people of other religions. They accept that others have the right to what they believe and worship, on their own terms. God is one and free to manifest in many ways. *Truth is one, sages call it by various names (Rig Veda). I am the same towards all beings; to me none is hateful or dear (Bhagvad Gita* 9:31). So there is no compelling sense of mission toward people of other faiths apart from the interest of communicating the truth of Hinduism. According to T.N. Madan (2005), "conversion from other religions" is a relatively new "modern times" phenomenon in Hinduism (p. 67). Encounters with Christianity and Islam and the passion in these world religions for conversion would have certainly influenced Hinduism even though one of its most revered sons, Mahatma Gandhi, was against any religious conversions (Chandra, 2005).

Even though the central teaching of Hinduism is that all humans possess the same *atman* derived from and connected to Brahman, inequalities between male and female and between castes (*varna, jati*) still prevail in daily practice, which is a great social barrier to equality. The plea to accept the caste distinction primarily as a division of labor (as did by Mahatma Gandhi) emerged at the formation of the society, promote healthy coexistence between persons of different castes, does not condone the atrocities done by the upper castes on the lower and the societal life shaped by caste superiority and inferiority, as long as they last. Even the liberal explanation that one is truly Brahmin (upper caste) not just because of one's birth, but rather, one is Brahmin because he or she follows the *dharma* is not a very convincing argument to weaken the caste rigidity. The way forward is a commitment on the part of all, Hindus and the others shaped by Hindu ethos, for a careful introspection and evaluation of the forces that perpetuate caste discriminations, and preventing future occurrences by addressing the causes and promoting ways of *dharma*.

The past conversion of Hindus to Islam and Christianity and similar attempts today is a point of contention among these religious followers. Invoking the historical memory of the division of the Indian subcontinent on a religious basis, and some community practices like consumption of beef by Christians and Muslims, creates hurdles for healthy relations. Periodic clashes between Hindus and Muslims and occasional tension between Hindus and Christians should not be treated lightly either, but introspected with courage and the vision of *ahimsa* should be promoted with commitment of all the religious parties involved. Many centuries of prejudices are not going to wither away that easily. Formal and informal multicultural education incorporating interreligious study and programs associated with social reform is a way forward in creating a multicultural spirit in the community.

Buddhism—Compassion (Karuna) Toward All Beings

Hinduism and Buddhism share many religious teachings like *dharma, karma, nirvana,* and *ahimsa.* However, Buddhism as a heterodox movement within Hinduism does not subscribe to priestly privileges and caste hierarchy. Loving kindness is an important aspired component in human relations. Buddhists are called to shun all forms of hatred.

The root cause of all evil is ignorance. As far as attitudes toward other religions are concerned, Buddhism teaches an attitude of goodwill toward all. While cherishing and affirming the truth found in Buddhism, it will not make any exclusive claim for possession of truth. All people are equally endowed with Buddha nature (nature of enlightenment) but often it may not be apparent to one because of ignorance. Therefore, in spite of different personalities and individualities, every human is somewhere on the path to enlightenment.

The perceived differences of color, race, nationality, social position, or intelligence are in the end impermanent and caused by illusion. Among the key teachings of Buddhism as far as relating to neighbors are concerned are genuine expression of kindness in human relations and a commitment not to harm any living being. Buddhism's teachings unabashedly points that, it is the elated ego and self-centeredness that puts a person into bondage and disrupts relations with others. But a way out is possible through one's own effort, guided by the teaching of Buddha and teachers.

First of all one has to develop an awareness of what is going on in one's mind and heart in their relations with others, and in the world in general. Knowing the truth about the way things are is the prime concern in Buddhism. Therefore, ignorance (*avidya*) is an issue to be tackled. Ignorance creates illusion and contributes to arrogance. Arrogance contributes to the bondage to life circle (reincarnations) as a consequence of *karma* (actions), resulting from improper words, deeds, and thoughts of an individual. *Karma* has not only individual but also communal consequences.

The goal of life is the attainment of wisdom (*prajna*), being cognizant of four Nobel truths and eightfold paths taught by Buddha. The four noble truth are: Life is suffering (*dukkha*), desire is the cause of suffering, suffering can be ceased, and following the eightfold path leads one out of suffering. The eightfold paths are: right understanding (of impermanence of all), right thought, right speech, right livelihood, right effort, right mindfulness, and right concentration. Ordering one's life following the eightfold path has the consequential result of developing right relationships with neighbors and with the environment as a whole. As one thinks and acts as a selfless person, the barrier between one and others, and with the world itself, disappears. The disappearance of egoism and selfishness means that people are connected and concerned about each other as about themselves. Thus the surfacing and cultivation of an attitude of compassion (*karuna*) toward all life is a key quality upheld in Buddhism.

Buddhism is often referred to as a "middle way" between two extremes of strict austerity and irresponsible living. Whatever material means are needed to live a dignified life has to be acquired through proper vocation. But excess accumulation and attachment to one's possession creates bondage. This is applicable for both householders and members of the monastery (*sangha*). The middle way frees one from greed and self-mortification of any extremity. In that sense it is a nonattached life with a right attitude toward material possession. Therefore, generosity (*dana*) is one of the most important Buddhist virtues. It is an indication of guarding against unhealthy attachment to wealth and possessions.

Among world religions pacifism is a hallmark of Buddhism. The practice of pacifism is based on respect for all life. Nonviolent ways of pursuing one's goal, personal or societal, has been made popular through the decades-long struggle of Tibetans under the leadership of the Dalai Lama, attracting attention of many around the globe. Such a nonaggressive attitude in engaging with others holding different views, has made it easier for Buddhists to engage in interfaith relations with the followers of other world religions.

Confucianism—Shu "Reciprocal Care of Others"

Confucianism has the distinction of equally being considered a religion and ethic. It is one of the oldest religious and ethical traditions still engaging a vast majority of people in Asia and Asians the world over. Confucius (latinized), Kung Fu-tzu (b. 551 BCE), or Kung the Master is revered by Chinese as a great teacher, as the one who consolidated the ancient wisdom of Chinese culture as a guidance for a wholesome personal, communal, and societal living. Traditionally, Confucianism has the reputation of providing a balanced ethical premise for the proper ordering of personal lives and organizing of societal functioning. The pursuit of self and public interest are to be complementary. Fusan Zhao (1998) expounds this as follows. Serving the self as necessitated by self-preservation was considered a valid virtue. But such self-preservation had to be pursued without causing any damage to public interest or well-being (p. 148).

Confucianism is alive and active in spite of periodic opposition and critical evaluation of its historical role and contemporary significance. Leonard Swidler (2004) comments that New Confucianism was revived in 1920s with the objective of revitalizing its role in Chinese society, which "wants to remake the Confucian tradition into living, creative dialogue partner for the West and the Rest, bringing its own distinctive contribution as one of many human partners in this Age of Global Dialogue" (p. 12).

In Confucianism one sees dual emphasis, first on personal formation through moral education and the second on social and political cultivation through ethical discernments and engagements. In that sense it has personal, spiritual, and moral goals and harmonious social and political goals. Human beings as social creatures are related to each other through *jen*, a term variously rendered as "human-to-human-ness," or "human-heartedness," or simply "humanity" (Smith, 1995, p. 110; Zhao 1998, p. 148). The potentiality of *jen* is enhanced or diminished depending on the nature and intensity of relationship between humans. Hans Kung (2002) points out that "Humanity according to Confucius is to be understood as 'reciprocal care of others' *(shu)*, mutual respect. As he explains in the Golden Rule, 'What you do not wish for yourself, do not impose on others'" (*Analects* 15:24) (pp. 100–101).

As far as relating to others is concerned, the level of one's social engagements determines its breadth. The narrow focus of self (egoism) defuses when one gets committed to the welfare of family; family preoccupation (nepotism) gives way when community interest is embraced, when the interest of nation is embraced it helps to overcome communal parochialism; when one is drawn to the well-being of humanity the national chauvinism recedes to the background. Thus:

> Becoming fully human involves transcending (sequentially) egoism, nepotism, parochialism, ethnocentrism and chauvinistic nationalism…(and) transcending self-sufficient humanism as well. In its fullness humanity *"forms one body with Heaven, Earth, and the myriad things."* (Smith, 1995, pp. 114, 117; original emphasis)

Confucianism has a place for autonomy of the individual conscience. But that autonomy has to be exercised within the context of promotion of harmonious human relations. The ethical norms and imperatives that have come down from the past, a gift of ancestors, must be preserved. The autonomy and selfhood has to be accomplished within the framework of Five Constant Relationships that constitute social life. *The Book of Rite (Li-chi)* of Confucianism expounds this as follows:

> Kindness on the part of the father, and filial duty on that of the son; gentleness on the part of the elder brother, and obedience on that of the younger,

righteousness on the part of the husband, and submission on that of the wife; kindness on the part of the elders, and deference on that of juniors; with benevolence on the part of the ruler, and loyalty on that of the minister. (Shih 1981, pp. 199–200)

Thus for the sake of an enriched life for all, humans are expected to relate in a humane way toward themselves, toward others, and toward nature (Kung, 2002, p. 101). Confucianism as a great narrative with an influence on a great section of humanity has penetrated all sections of human enterprise, including education.

Judaism—Welcome the Strangers

Even though Judaism has been the predecessor of two of the world's largest religions, Christianity and Islam, Judaism still continues to be a vibrant faith with a small number of followers as compared to Christianity and Islam. In Judaism historical events and historical personalities have an important role to play in the faith formation of the community.

Judaism as a religious community draws its sustenance from the Torah, the first five books of the Hebrew Bible. A large portion of Torah is law, and contains 613 rules or commandments for living (Lawton, 1996, p. 154). Through the law, the stability of society and protection of individuals is ensured. The purpose of the law is also meant to "encourage spiritual life and awareness" of individuals and the community (Lawton, 1996, p. 155). Therefore, commandments given to the community must be passed on from generation to generation. Religious education therefore is the duty of the parents and the elders of the community. "Teach them [commandments] to your children, talking about them when you are at home and when you are away, when you lie down and when you rise" (Deuteronomy 11:19; 6:7).

As far as relating to others, especially to strangers, Judaism has a high standard drawing on its own history of being strangers amidst other communities, including being slaves in Egypt. The Torah categorically stipulates that people in need and having difficulty should be given all assistance. "Throughout Torah; more than twenty times the Jews are admonished in one context or another to care for the strangers" (Lawton, 1996, p. 152). "You shall not deprive a resident alien or an orphan of justice; you shall not take a widow's garment in pledge. Remember that you were a slave in Egypt" (Deuteronomy 24:17; Exodus 23:9).

Caring for the other/non-Jewish is very much a core affirmation of the Jewish religion. This is because as per the Torah caring for the chosen as well as all humans is an important characteristic of God. "For the Lord your God is God of gods and Lord of Lords,...who executes justice for the orphan and the widow, and who loves the strangers, providing them food and clothing" (Deuteronomy 10:17–18). Rabbi Sacks (2003) categorically states that:

> *We encounter God in the face of a stranger.* That, I believe, is the Hebrew Bible's single greatest and most counter intuitive contribution to ethics. God creates difference; therefore it is in one-who-is-different that we meet God. (p. 59, original emphasis)

The Jewish creation story upholds the unity of humanity in spite of the multiple tribes and clans among them. God is the creator of all people with differences they posses for the good of the world. All humans are descendents of common ancestral parents Adam and Eve, and are endowed with the image of God. In the sight of God all people are equal and as such every human being has to be respected and honored as God's creatures. The human differences have to be handled with care promoting the positive and containing the negative consequences of these differences. Therefore the notion of justice plays a predominant role in Judaism. Commitment to justice is very much central to the covenantal relationship between God and the community. "You must not distort justice; you must not show partiality;...Justice, and only justice, you shall pursue" (Dueteronomy 16:19–20). Denise and John Carmody (1988) state that, "In many biblical contexts, *justice* is virtually synonymous with *holiness, mercy,* and *grace.* Thus, some Jewish ethicists go so far as to say that 'virtually the entire spectrum of ethical values is comprised in the notion of justice'" (p. 30). All human beings will be held responsible for the good and evil they do on the Day of Judgment.

So, even though Judaism teaches about two classes of religious people, Jews and gentiles, they do recognize that God has His own way of dealing with people of other faiths and traditions. The self-understanding of Jews as God's "chosen people" speaks more about their responsibility than superiority. Therefore, all the people are to be treated as equals and Jews have to be a model for good living.

Judaism is not a pacifist religion. When it is appropriate, engaging in conflicts and wars to preserve the religious as well as the communal integrity was part of Jewish history. However, a constant theme through Jewish history is a longing for peace (*shalom*), as peace is considered a great blessing from God. *Shalom,* the phrase used for greeting fellow Jews and outsiders, is a reminder of the significance of peace in human interactions and relations (Carmody and Carmody, 1988, p. 32).

Christianity—Love Your Enemy

The key affirmation of Christianity is: *"For God so loved the world that he gave his only Son (Jesus), so that everyone who believes in him may not perish but may have eternal life"* (John 3:16). The central message of Jesus was that the "reign of God" (Mark 1:15) is at hand, and that people can embark on a new life through forgiveness of their sins (made possible through Jesus Christ) and part take in a new humanity through the power of the Holy Spirit. The teachings and ministry of Jesus brought about a new religious community, Christianity. The members of this community had a special sense as a new humanity with a strong positive relationship between themselves and with the God they worshipped.

From inception, the good news of Jesus (the gospel) was meant to be a transethnic and transcultural message. Two farewell commands of Jesus to disciples signify this. *Go...make disciples of all nations* (Matthew 28:19). And *You will be my witnesses in Jerusalem, in all Judea and Samaria and to the ends of earth* (Acts 1:8b). In the very initial years of its existence, circumcision for the new non-Jewish converts became an issue. The very first council in Jerusalem (Acts 15) resolved not to impose circumcision on new converts to guard its inclusive spirit and to be open to be a multicultural and multiethnic community.

Among his various teachings Jesus affirmed *love* as a key ethical principal in human relations. *I give you a new commandment, that you love one another. Just as I have loved you, you also should love one another* (John 13:34–35). Jesus extends this command of love even beyond his circle of disciples with a radical proposition of including everyone. *You have heard that it was said, "You shall love your neighbor and hate your enemy." But I say to you, Love your enemies and pray for those who persecute you* (Matthew 5:43–45; Luke 6:36).

However, in Christianity the pacifists and nonpacifist traditions coexist, depending on the ethical stands of denominations and groups. St. Paul, one of the early prominent converts from Judaism, elaborates the dynamics of that love in an affectionately called hymn of love. *Love is patient; love is kind; love is not envious or boastful or arrogant or rude.... Love never ends.... And now faith, hope and love abide, these three: and the greatest of these is love* (I Corinthians 13).

Christianity as a new faith community strived toward unity amidst diversity. St. Paul writes, *There is no longer Jew or Greek, there is no longer slave or free, there is no longer male and female; for all of you are one in Christ Jesus* (Galatians 3:28). Thus Christianity is not tied to any race or nation. *From one ancestor, he [God] made all nations to inhabit the whole earth* (Acts 17:26). So all are equal in God's sight and equally loved by God.

In his teachings and ministry Jesus showed a special concern for the poor, marginalized (because of physical ailment or other social ostracization), foreigners, and the neglected. In a parable about the last judgment, Jesus related the service done to these least and neglected as a service done to him. *I was a stranger and you welcomed me, ...Truly I tell you, just as you did it to one of the least of these, ... you did it to me* (Matthew 25:32–40). As per this parable, if people genuinely relate to the others, transcending humans created barriers, they are considered as being faithful to the teachings of Jesus.

The writer of the book of Revelation in the Bible records that at the end of time when all of humanity is brought together it will be an inclusive community. *After this I looked, and there was a great multitude that no one could count, from every nation, from all tribes and peoples and languages* (Revelation 7:9). They are brought together for what they have done with their lives toward the well-being of humanity, than their humanly defined traits. Such an inclusive divine plan has been a strong motivating force for many Christians to engage with people of other faiths and traditions in search of a greater kinship among peoples with diverse cultures.

Islam—*Salam,* Peace to and with Everyone

The Islamic confession of faith (*shahada*) is clear and straightforward: *There is no god but Allah (God) and Muhammad is the prophet of Allah.* For Muslims, Islam is a total way of life. It demands total obedience to One God (*Allah*) and a commitment to a way of life according to Holy Quran, the depository of God's revelation through Muhammad, the final Prophet. Muhammad was not only the prophet, but also a political and religious leader. Accordingly, civil and religious life is intertwined in Islam. Therefore, Muslims prefer to live in an Islamic state, which follows the Islamic law known as *Shariah,* emerged from the teachings of Quran, the life example of Prophet Muhammad and the interpretations of these teachings by religious scholars (*ulama*). Living in non-Islamic countries and remaining faithful to the tradition is a challenging task to the Muslim communities, especially in the post–September 11, 2001, developments.

All Muslims, regardless of their race, tribe, ethnicity, nationality, and class, are considered members of *ummah* (house of Islam), a worldwide community of believers. *Ummah* is the universal social order to nurture, support, and promote the wholesome life among Muslims. Along with the oneness of God and oneness of Islamic community, Islam also emphasizes oneness of humanity, as all humans are the creation of God, created in the divine image of God. *O mankind! We have created you from a single (pair) of a male and a female, and made you into nations and tribes, that you may know each other not that you may despise each other* (Quran 49:13). Therefore, humans are to honor the diversity of humanity within its overall unity (Alley, 1996,

p. 252). The difference that matters in God's sight are the spiritual and moral qualities of people. During *hajj* (pilgrimage) to Mecca Muslims are expected to wear a simple white garment to reinforce a sense of their equality before God. Similarly, the corpse is shrouded with such simple garments affirming equality of humans (Alley, 1996, p. 253).

The Quranic teaching on the unity of humanity makes it necessary for Muslims to deal with non-Muslims kindly and justly, and the Islamic states to guarantee safety of all those who live within its borders. However, Jews and Christians and all those who believe in one God were given a special status in Quran (2:62) along with Magians, Sabians, and Zoroastrians. According to Mashuq ibn Alley (1996), "The main concern for Islam is that Muslims live in cooperation, not competition, with fellow human beings, whether they are of the same or different faith, race, culture and status" (p. 228).

Islam requires Muslims to be kind and caring toward the poor and the weak, widows, orphans, slaves, and the needy. To that end, Muslims are encouraged to share their wealth. Being rich is not detested but being selfish about it and neglecting the poor and needy is against the spirit of Islam. All the wealth ultimately belongs to God, one who created them all. Human beings as trustees have to properly use and share their wealth as an act of thanksgiving and worship to God. From that perspective, miserliness and hording of wealth is condemned. *Woe to every (one)... who piles up wealth ...thinking that his wealth would make him last for ever!* (Quran 104:1–3).

Zakat (almsgiving) and *sadaqah* (freewill offering) are two well-known ways of sharing wealth in Islam. *Zakat* is a social tax. Every Muslim is required to pay *zakat*, which is $2\frac{1}{2}$ % of their cash wealth to the poor. In case of land and other assets this contribution may go up to 10%. This is not a voluntary act of charity, but an expected obligation to address the needs of the less fortunate in the community. It is part and parcel of faith. Quran states, *"Have you thought of those who defy religious duty? It is those who turn away the orphan and have no urge to feed the poor... who make a show of piety but withhold contributions from the destitute"* (Quran 107; Phipps, 1996, p. 128). Mintjes (1977) notes that:

> Many are convinced that with Islam's "*zakat*" the treatment of the poor was for the first time in the history of mankind drawn out of the sphere of charity.... *Zakat* means solidarity with and consideration for one's fellow man... "a golden loan" to God. (pp. 21, 27; Quran 30:38–39)

Sadaqah, on the other hand, is a "voluntary contribution, out of altruism, given by individuals over and above the payment of the compulsory *zakat* to relieve the problems and sufferings of fellow human beings," Muslims and non-Muslims (Alley, 1996, p. 242).

While Islam has positive attitudes toward trade and commerce, illegitimate enterprises are prohibited, as it will hurt fellow human beings. Islam also prohibits (*riba*) lending money on interest, as it exploits those who are in need and eliminates the sense of responsibility of those who possess the means of wealth (Mintjes, 1977, p. 27f). *Allah will deprive usury of all blessing, but will give increase for deeds of charity: for He does not love ungrateful and wicked creatures* (Quran 2:276).

Islam strongly endorses Last Judgment on Resurrection Day when all the faithful are held accountable for their deeds on earth, and accordingly they will be rewarded and punished in the coming world. The Quran declares:

> Then, he whose balance (of good deeds) will be (found) heavy, will be in a Life of a good pleasure and satisfaction. But he whose balance (of good deeds) will be (found) light will have his home in a (bottomless) Pit. (Quran 101:6–9)

Sikhism-Seva, Service to Others

Sikhism was born in India in the context of Hindu and Muslim religions. It was influenced by the Hindu *bhakti* (devotion) and Sufi traditions of Northern India. In that sense it has a bicultural ethos. According to Arnold Toynbee (1960) "To have discovered and embraced the deep harmony underlying the historic Hindu-Muslim discord has been a noble spiritual triumph; and Sikhs may well be proud of their religion's ethos and origin." Therefore, he described Sikhism "as a vision of this Hindu-Muslim common ground" (p. 10). As per prominent Sikh writer Khuswant Singh (1963), "Sikhism was born out of wedlock between Hinduism and Islam after they had known each other for a period of nearly nine hundred years" (p. 17).

The Sikh faith is based on the revelation that was received by *gurus* beginning with Guru Nanak (1469–1539 CE) to Guru Gobind Singh (1666–1708). Guru Nanak (even though born a Hindu), through the revelation he received, declared that God is neither Hindu nor Muslim. God is One Supreme Formless being and the proper approach to God is through "self-abnegation." *Adi Granth,* containing the teachings of the founding Gurus, is the principal Sikh scripture and is revered as the living Guru by Sikhs.

All authority belongs to God. The historic Gurus hold a unique place as communicators of divine truth and are revered as the ultimate human authority. "There is one God, Eternal Truth is His name; ... By the grace of the Guru, made known to humans" (Radakrishnan, 1960, p. 28). Sikhs recite this opening creedal statement of the *Adi Granth* daily. Sikhs do not deny similar discloser of God to others. On the contrary, they respect religious traditions of others and as such do not engage in proselytism even though they are happy to share their religious tradition with others. Offending others' faith is against the spirit of Sikhism.

Sikhism does not teach renunciation of the world. Sikhs are expected to engage in a decent livelihood and lead an honest life. They are called to take their secular and political responsibilities without compromising their spiritual life. They are expected to be like a lotus that grows and lives in a water pond without getting drenched or drowned. Guru Nanak has articulated it as follows. "As the lotus lives in water detached, as the duck floats without drenching, so does one crosses the ocean of life" (Johar, 1977, p. 155).

As a religion shaped in the context of Hinduism, Guru Nanak and his successors proclaimed the irrelevance of caste (a dominant feature of Hindu social order) for its followers. Sikhism is a very egalitarian religion. It recognizes the existence of the same divine light in every human being. So every person is accepted as equal and the *gurdwara* (place of worship) is open to all, irrespective of caste, class, creed, color, race, gender, and nationality. The continuation of the institution of *langar* (free common messing), offering a free meal to all the visitors to the *gurdwara* started by Guru Nanak, accomplishes this vision of equality of all in a more demonstrative way. The rule of *langar* requires all the participants in the meal to sit in common rows and partake in the same food without demonstrating any social divisions and prejudices. The institution of *langar* was meant to be a model for Sikhs and others who care to learn, to transcend social barriers that normally divide people and build healthy human solidarity. Every Sikh is encouraged to participate in this community meal and contribute toward its expenses.

Seva, service to all humanity regardless of color, caste, class, and creed, is a central aspect of Sikh social ethics. Service to others enhances the feeling of kinship with fellow humans and generates love and concern toward others. It helps a Sikh to cultivate an attitude of equality by transcending one's social status. In the sight of God, all are equal, both the poor and the rich. Therefore, humans need to relate to each other as siblings. Service can take different avenues. It may involve primarily helping the poor and the needy, reaching out to those who are in distress and trouble, and protecting those who are facing danger. Besides such acts of personal involvements, all Sikhs are required to contribute generously, at least a tenth of their earning, to charity and for any noble welfare programs (Johar, 1977, pp. 151–155).

Complimentary Religious Visions in Multicultural Context

From the above narration it is clear that historical world religions are not the same. However, one can discern some commonalities amidst different answers/solutions they offer to overcome human problems. The noble ethical imperatives in each of these religions—like *dharma* (righteous living), *karuna* (compassion), *shu* ("reciprocal care of others"), caring for the strangers, love toward enemies, *salam* (peace with all), and *seva* (service)—all stand in complimentary relationship as far as making earthy human life a dignified venture for everyone. Related to these ethical imperatives is the need to promote them through practice and teaching and through appropriate pedagogy is a common concern in all of these religions. The multireligious global situation of the present time and the concern to promote moral and spiritual values in secular education (Nord & Haynes, 1998; Purple, 1989) gives an appropriate opportunity to incorporate teaching of religions into school and college curricula, in a spirit promoting greater interreligious understanding where it is not done already.

The above descriptions of select religious teachings have primarily focused on positive teachings in world religions. It is such positive teachings that need to be promoted in multicultural education for promoting better understanding and greater solidarity among humans. From an elementary look at the teachings of these world religions, regarding the proper attitudes toward outsiders of their faith tradition, one can discern the two following common complimentary visions among their teachings. First, *a religious person is a perpetual learner/student* drawing inspiration, encouragement, support, stimulation, motivation, insight, illumination, enlightenment from the teachings of one's faith, and striving to shape one's life and the life of one's community according to the precepts of that faith. For example, the name Sikh literally means a learner (Nesbitt, 1996, p. 99); a disciple (of Jesus Christ) means the one who follows the examples and instruction of the teacher; and Islam means a total submission at all times to Allah and to the Quranic percepts.

Concurrently, learning from the positive virtues and values of other religions and communities and benefiting from them is encouraged as long as one remains faithful to one's faith and community. The multifaith and multicultural interest are not alien to religions, at least in their formative years as they were born in interaction with the then-prevailing faith traditions and practices. Second, *a religious person is mandated to genuinely relate to the "other"/neighbor with love, compassion, care, and kindness*. Relating especially to those who have been despised and ostracized by the existing sociopolitical, economic, and cultural systems/practices, both within a faith tradition and outside it, are to be given priority for such an expression of love, compassion, care, and kindness. This mandate is not a call for a passive tolerance of one's neighbor. Rather, it is a mandate to be proactive in making a change in one's perception of the other and reorienting oneself for the sake of the well-being of the other. It is also a part of one's devotion and love to one's God, Creator, or Source of life. It is an evaluative criteria of ones love toward God. The process begins when one starts to evaluate and question one's overt preoccupation with oneself, one's ego, and selfish and narcissist tendencies. Such an attitude might have been caused by sin, ignorance, arrogance, or by nonenlightened or reflective status of an individual. Interestingly an awakening to the reality of the transitory nature of all created life and developing a spirit of consciously celebrating the interconnectedness and interdependence of life is often perceived by religions as a beginning of one's authentic spiritual and faith journey.

From these common visions enshrined in world religions we can conclude that multicultural concerns are not a recent phenomenon. Religious founders/teachers were aware of them. The notion of stranger, foreigner, alien, and enemy over friend, ally, neighbor, and partner are common in most communities. When a community is under threat from outsiders, negative categorization of them becomes very pronounced. "However, in normal circumstances, if these caricatures are used as tools of exclusion, opposition, domination, or oppression, they curb the spirit human solidarity" (Wilson, 2003, p. 175).

Besides sociohistorical factors, taking shelter in biology is not feasible after what Richard Dawkins has established in his seminal book *The Selfish Gene* (1970). Dawkins, after researching on the biological nature of selfishness and altruism, has affirmed that:

> Our genes may instruct us to be selfish, but we are not necessarily compelled to obey them all our lives.... [E]ven if we look on the dark side and assume that individual man is fundamentally selfish, our conscious foresight—our capacity to stimulate the future in imagination—could save us from the worst selfish excesses of the blind reflectors. (pp. 3, 215)

FACING MULTICULTURAL CHALLENGES

The steady escalation of intensity of tension witnessed between race, caste, class, color, and ethnicity in most of the our societies today is largely the product of modern migration and is closely associated with the European colonial enterprise, which began 500 years back and continues today through the phenomenon of *globalization.* Temporary and long-term relocation, voluntary and forced displacement, and migration of a sizeable section of the world's population within a nation-state and across continents is a common contemporary phenomenon. People move across cultural and political borders for various reasons: "political and military upheavals, economic inequalities, intellectual quests, natural disaster, and sheer wanderlust" (Gonzalez, 1999, p. 4). It is hard to predict the migration pattern of the distant future. However, right now no reversal of this trend is in sight.

The claim of European supremacy (race, religion, civilization, etc.) and the validation of it by developing supportive rationale through different disciplines like anthropology, sociology, history, religions, psychology, and so on, and other communities around the globe that divided people into various gradations of superiority and inferiority, makes it necessary that multicultural issues be once again given proper attention both for dismantling the myth of cultural superiority of Europeans and others (who make similar claims) for promotion of a healthy attitude toward people of all cultures and traditions.

The recognition of the positive role the diversity among human communities play and its enriching role in human heritage is a well-established factor today. The *UNESCO Universal Declaration on Cultural Diversity* (2002) proclaims that cultural diversity is "as necessary for humankind as biodiversity is for nature. It affirms, that culture should be regarded as the set of distinctive spiritual, material, intellectual and emotional features of society or a social group" (p. 5).

The *Declaration* (2002) has several well thought out recommendations to member states and others to protect and promote cultural diversity and to nurture them in their respective countries and communities. A number of suggestions touch on multicultural education in accomplishing objectives by:

1. Encouraging linguistic diversity—while respecting the mother tongue—at all levels of education, wherever possible, and fostering the learning of several languages from the earliest age.

2. Promoting through education an awareness of the positive value of cultural diversity and improving to this end both curriculum design and teacher education.

3. Incorporating, where appropriate, traditional pedagogies into the education process with a view to preserving and making full use of culturally appropriate methods of communication and transmission of knowledge (p. 8).

Mass education and literacy of its citizens is the aspired goal of almost all the countries. What is entailed in such an aspiration? The principle aspiration is the quality of life it can bring to an individual and through individuals to the whole community and possibly to the entire globe. Having narrated above the potentialities world religions possess in contributing to this goal, I suggest that the core values of all these religions, that is affirming the sanctity of all life and dignity of human life, be included in the school curricula and education programs along with other subjects with similar goals. Care must be taken that these core values of religions not be taught as exclusive dogmas and doctrines but as values that have the potential to benefit humanity as a whole.

For effective results, it is best if core values of each of the faith traditions are taught by one of its adherents, or one who has sufficient personal knowledge of that faith, in a spirit of promoting interfaith relations. Incorporating some experiential components into teaching, like participation in worship, festivals, and ceremonies, will have lasting good results (Fraser, 1999, p. 232). When dealing with religions, being sensitive to intra- and interreligious dynamics is crucial, as persons of faith operate with certain fundamental theological perspectives based on their religious worldviews or *transcendental narratives* (Nash, 1999). Robert Nash, with years of teaching experience, has classified possible intra-Christian perspectives into four—Fundamentalist, Prophetic, Alternative Spiritualities, and Post-Theist narratives—and has showed relative strengths and weaknesses of each of them from the perspectives of multicultural education (Nash, 1999). As a Christian theologian, in relation to these narratives, my chapter has leaned more toward the prophetic perspective with certain openness to alternative spiritualities.

As historical residues of suspicion of each others' religions are still operating in the minds of many individuals and communities, the task is not going to be easy. But the only way to overcome this historical suspicion is to venture into new understanding and relations and the one way that is easily available is the prevailing education network.

TEACHING/LEARNING RELIGION WITHIN THE CONTEXT OF MULTICULTURAL EDUCATION

For ensuring a healthy multireligious relationship, promotion of multicultural education that addresses the diversity of religions along with other diversities found in a society is absolutely necessary. It is possible that a multireligous situation in a given society may be due to the existence of multiethnic, multiracial, and multilinguistic communities. The possibility of the promotion of multireligious learning very much depends on the commitment of a community for multicultural education. There are excellent resources on multicultural education (e.g., Banks, 1993; Diaz, 1992; Gay, 2003; Gollnick & Chinn, 1998; Grant, 1995; Nieto, 2000; Salili & Hoosain, 2003; Sleeter & McLaren, 1995). These scholars cover a wide range of concerns that are addressed by multicultural education.

According to Gollnick and Chinn (1998), "Multicultural education is a means for positively using cultural diversity in the total learning process. In the process, classrooms should become models of democracy and equity" (p. 330). As per Sonia Nieto (2000):

> Multicultural education is a process of comprehensive school reform and basic education for all students. It challenges and rejects...(*all*) forms of discrimination in schools and society and accepts and affirms the pluralism (ethnic, racial, linguistic, religious, economic, and gender, among others) that students, their communities, and teachers reflect. (p. 305)

Multicultural education is not subtracting and adding components of cultures to the existing curriculum. It is more than such a mechanical approach. It is being attentive to the breadth of diversities in a community and relating to them with integrity. Thus, "Multicutural education is a philosophy, a way of looking at the world, not simply a program or a class or a teacher" (Nieto, 2000, p. 313). James Banks (1993) envisages even a wider goal: "A major goal of multicultural education is to help students to develop the knowledge, attitudes, and skills needed to function within their own microcultures,... macroculture, other microcultures, and with the global community" (p. 25).

Looking at the world of religions and learning about them would involve dealing with narratives of each of the religions with an empathetic spirit. "To understand a religion," comments Nord (1995), "is to be able to look out on the world and human experience and see and feel it from the viewpoint of the categories of that religion" (p. 214). Religions, therefore, should be taught in such a way that students are helped to appreciate the various sociocultural elements that have shaped their own and others' religious lives, and their historic and contemporary significance (Nash, 1999, p. 191; Nord & Haynes, 1998, p. 56). From a pedagogical perspective, the spirit of multireligious learning is not going to be different than what Sonia Nieto (2000) suggests of multicultural education.

> A multicultural perspective does not simply operate on the principle of substituting one "truth" or perspective for another. Rather, it reflects on multiple and contradictory perspectives to understand reality more fully. In addition, it uses the understanding gained from reflection to make changes. (p. 317)

The purpose of this chapter is not to argue that world religions have to be taught as part of the universal school curriculum as a panacea for all contemporary human predicaments. The concern that I am alluding to is that multicultural education has to equally address the reality of religious plurality and diversity in the society. The cultural pluralism that is experienced by communities around the globe invariably involves religious plurality as well. As indicated above, religion is one of the significant components of cultural identity for most of the peoples. Therefore, when multicultural education deals with cultural plurality, it is invariably drawn into appropriately addressing religious diversities in communities.

Introducing students to different religions in a nonpartisan way is a problematic issue for anyone, educators and others. If one of the objectives of multicultural education is to inculcate a proper understanding and appreciation for diversity and thereby minimize the scope of using the differences among peoples to build barriers, then to find a proper pedagogical method of appreciation of religions other than one's own will be an inevitable task of multicultural education. As far as the process such a pedagogical methodology will involve, I find Sonia Nieto's comprehensive proposal quite challenging. Sonia Nieto (2000) identifies four levels of engagement in accomplishing multicultural education that will lead to embracing pluralism and cultivating an openness to diversity. They are (1) tolerance, (2) acceptance, (3) respect, and (4) affirmation, solidarity, and critique (pp. 353–357). At the *tolerance* level, cultural differences are recognized and permitted in spite of it being unpalatable and unpleasant, but inevitable to avoid in a culturally diverse society. The second level is *acceptance* of differences, and acknowledging their reality and importance. As a result of this acceptance, the community may open up to celebrating cultural events and programs. The third level is *respect.* At this level of multicultural education, the diverse cultural values and experiences are used to help the learners develop multicultural awareness. The forth is *affirmation, solidarity,* and *critique.* Affirmative results happen by the utilization of cultural diversity as a source of learning. Such learning also results in reflecting and critiquing the contributing cultural segments for building cohesive human community with equity and justice (Lewis, Cram & Lee, 1997). Where such a process of educational engagement is applied to the study of religions, at the entry level, great care must be taken to avoid issues that have historically divided or contemporarily contested between religions, to build a certain level of trust and ensure some initial success. It will be helpful to begin with positive aspects of each of the religions like the "golden rule." Better understanding between religions, affirming common values and visions they hold for the welfare of humanity, is a greater service to multicultural communities. It will be a positive alternative in a world of exclusive claims by religious communities.

The contribution of religious leaders like His Holiness Dalai Lama and Professor Hans Kung in promoting a common *global ethic* involving the member religious bodies of the World's Parliament of Religions has great consequences to multicultural relationship and education if promoted appropriately. Professor Kung (2002) has succinctly articulated the noble vision behind this project as follows:

> No peace among the nations without peace among the religions. No peace among the religions without dialogue between the religions. No dialogue between the religions without global ethical standards. No survival of our globe without a global ethic. (p. 266)

Promoting such a *global ethic* engaging religions and cultures is a big challenge for religious bodies. It can only be accomplished in collaboration and cooperation with all other human institutions; a paramount is educational enterprises of every community, society, and nation-state.

Those who are interested in pursuing much more nuanced debates in comparative religious ethics may benefit from *four curricula paradigms in teaching comparative religious ethics* identified by Summer Twiss (1998).

CONCLUDING REMARKS

Like any other new venture, the success of incorporating multireligious study to multicultural education will require a long-term sustained effort. Challenging the still prevailing system of monoculture education with firmly established supporting structures and benefactors is going to be daunting task. The hopeful sign is that diversity among human communities and its enriching role is already well recognized. For example, the clause in *Declaration* (2002) of UNESCO that "cultural diversity is as necessary for humankind as biodiversity for nature" (p. 5) and Hans Kung's (2002) observation that there is "No peace among the nations without peace among the religions" (p. 266), are well-crafted visionary statements that express this sentimentality. Who will dispute such insights? But to intentionally promote them requires overcoming several hurdles. The existing multicultural efforts and discourses on cultural pluralism are certainly bringing the vision into fruition. The stories of experimentations and accomplishments by educationists in the United States and in some countries across the world (Gay, 2003; Nieto, 2000) are encouraging. It is creating healthy ripples around the globe. Concerned persons can gain insights and develop strategies from these stories.

Multicultural education is going to be a collaborative venture. Besides the students who are willing to go though multicultural education, others' committed involvement is also crucial, like that of parents, teachers, administrators, and management. In the day-to-day encounters with students the role of teachers is pivotal. Consequently, their professional preparedness and personal commitment is paramount for the success of multicultural education. Sonia Nieto (2000) has challengingly expressed it as follows. *"Becoming a multicultural teacher, therefore, means first becoming a multicultural person* (p. 338, original emphasis). Teachers' competence and confidence in multicultural education is an important determining factor. The necessity of personal and professional commitment is articulated by Geneva Gay (2003) is as follows: "Multicultural education, like other kinds of teaching, is a moral enterprise that requires deep personal engagement, commitment, advocacy, and agency from those who participate fully and genuinely in the enterprise" (p. 6). By replacing *teacher* in the two preceding quotations form Nieto and Gray by religious personalities like *bhikku*, guru, imam, lama, mullah, rabbi, *sant*, priest, and preacher, we can demonstrate the equally important role religions have to play in facilitating multireligious learning and thus contributing toward multicultural education.

To a certain extent the task of the religious teachers is tougher than the secular educationists, as the issues they deal with are not limited to daily mundane concerns. They have to address peoples' ultimate concerns and quests. Those questions and concerns go deeper than making it through life. The meaning and existence of life now and hereafter; one's appropriate relation to transcendent realities be that is God, Spirit (good and evil), or Truth. Religious people normally relate common concerns like justice and equity addressed in multicultural education to divine plans and schemes. As all good emerges from the divine, that reference is significant for them. Therefore, the phenomenon religious teachers have to deal with will be much wider than that of secular educators. So, besides an egalitarian and democratic spirit, they need to inculcate a convincing grandeur vision of the Ultimate, and the role each religion will have within it. Virgilio Elizondo (1997), who has ministered for decades in promotion of multicultural ethos within Christianity in the United States, as graphically articulated one such vision as follows:

> Ultimate and absolute truth is like a massive puzzle. Each cultural expression of truth, together with its religious expression, is like a large piece of the complete puzzle of God and humanity. But no one piece alone gives us the complete picture. A more complete picture of the true, the good, and beautiful comes through when all pieces are together in their proper interconnectedness. Yet the fullness of the mystery of God and of humanity will still lie beyond our human understanding. . . . In the puzzle all pieces are of equal importance. Only when they are joined together does the whole make sense. This model does not ask who is the best or the most important. It asks how each one fits into the rest for the benefit of everyone. (p. 398)

Learning religions from the perspective of each being "a large piece of humanity" brings global dimension to multicultural education, as religions have become global with the movement of people between nations and continents (Lynch, 1989).

Even in the present time tensions relating to religious issues continue, especially when a religious group is a minority in a community or a nation-state. It may be as simple as focusing on a religious observation or practice like the appropriateness of Sikhs wearing turbans; Muslim women wearing head coverings, *hijab* to school; or securing time off from work or holidays for observation of holy days and festivals. However, with the greater consciousness about rights of individuals and communities; interventions of religious organizations and concerned nongovernmental organizations committed to equity and justice and involvement of concerned professionals belonging to various guilds like legal, educational, parliamentarian, noble laureate, several changes have been brought to resolve conflicting issues amicably. Sustained advocacy programs, educational arrangements, and networking of bodies committed to multicultural ethos will help in overcoming religious and cultural disputes, clashes, and conflicts that emerge in different parts of the world at a steady phase. Such an existential reality itself provides a good reason for including the study of religion in the curriculum. Therefore, Martin Marty's (2000) advice is that "If educators aspire to teach a fairly accurate picture of the world around us, it is both necessary and good to have religious themes included in secondary education" (p. 7). The same sentiment is voiced strongly by Nord and Haynes (1998), stating, "One can't be an educated human being *at the present time* without understanding a good deal about religion and its role in human affairs" (p. 35, emphasis added).

REFERENCES

Alley, M. (1996). Islam. In P. Morgan & C. Lawton (Eds.), *Ethical issues in six religious traditions* (pp. 220–263). Edinburgh: Edinburgh University Press.

Banks, J. A. (1993). Multicultural education: Characteristics and goals. In J. A. Banks & C. A. M. Banks (Eds.), *Multicultural education: Issues and perspectives* (2nd ed., pp. 3–28). Boston: Allyn & Bacon.

Berger, P. L. (Ed.). (1999). *The desecularization of the world: Resurgent religion and world politics.* Grand Rapids, MI: William B. Eerdmans.

Carmody, D. L., & Carmody, J. T. (1998). *How to live well: Ethics in the world religions.* Belmont, CA: Wadsworth.

Chandra, S. (2005). Denial of plurality: Thinking of conversion through Gandhi. In J Malik & H. Reifeld (Eds.), *Religious pluralism in South Asia and Europe* (pp. 184–215). New Delhi: Oxford University Press.

Dawkins, R. (1977). *The selfish gene* (2nd ed.). New York: Oxford University Press.

Diaz, C. (Ed.). (1992). *Multicultural education for the 21st century.* Washington, DC: National Education Association.

Elizondo, V. (1997). Benevolent tolerance or humble reverence? A vision for multi-cultural religious education. In B. Wilkerson (Ed.), *Multicultural religious education* (pp. 395–409). Birmingham, AL: Religious Education Press.

Etzioni, A. (1996). *The new golden rule: Community and morality in a democratic society.* New York: Basic Books.

Fox, J., & Sandler, S. (2004). *Bringing religions in to international relations.* New York: Palgrave Macmillan

Fraser, J. W. (1999). *Between church and state: religion and public education in a multicultural America.* New York: St. Martin's Griffin.

Gay, G. (Ed.). (2003). *Becoming multicultural educators.* San Francisco: Jossey-Bass.

Glanzer, P. L. (2004) Taking the tournament of worldviews seriously in education: Why Teaching about religion is not enough. *Religion and Education, 31*(1), 1–19.

Gollinck, D. M., & Chinn, P. C. (1998). *Multicultural education in a pluralistic society* (5th ed.). Upper Saddle River, N.J: Merrill.

Gonzalez, J. L. (1999). *For the healing of the nations: The Book of Revelation in an age of cultural conflict.* Maryknoll, NY: Orbis Books.

Grant, C. A. (Ed.). (1992). *Research and multicultural education: From margins to the mainstream.* London: Falmer Press.

Grant, C. A. (1995). *Educating for diversity.* Boston: Allyn & Bacon.

Johar, S. S. (Ed.). (1977). *Handbook on Sikhism.* Delhi: Vivek Publishing.

Kung, H. (Ed.). (1996). *Yes to a global ethic.* New York: Continuum.

Kung, H. (2002). *Tracing the way: Spiritual dimensions of the world religions* (J.Bowden, Trans.). London: Continuum.

Lawton, C. (1996). Judaism. In P. Morgan & C. Lawton (Eds.), *Ethical issues in six religious traditions* (pp. 220–263). Edinburgh: Edinburgh University Press.

Lester, E. (2004). Religious autonomy and world religious education. *Religion and Education, 31*(2), 62–82.

Lewis, L. B., Cram, R. H., & Lee, J. M. (1997). Curriculum and multicutural religious education. In B. Wilkerson (Ed.), *Multicultural religious education* (pp. 323–391). Birmingham, AL: Religious Education Press.

Lynch, J. (1989). *Multicultural education in a global society.* London: Falmer Press.

Madan, T. N. (2005). Religions of India: Plurality and pluralism. In J Malik & H. Reifeld (Eds.), *Religious pluralism in South Asia and Europe* (pp. 42–76). New Delhi: Oxford University Press.

Marty, M. E. (2000). *Education, religion and the common good.* San Francisco: Jossey-Bass.

Millennium World Peace Summit. (2000). www.millenniumpeacesummit.com.

Mintjes, H. (1977). *Social justice in Islam.* Amsterdam: Free University.

Nash, R. J. (1999). *Faith, hype and clarity: Teaching about religion in American schools and colleges.* New York: Teachers College Press.

Nesbitt, E. (1996). Sikhism. In P. Morgan & C. Lawton (Eds.), *Ethical issues in six religious traditions* (pp. 99–134). Edinburgh: Edinburgh University Press.

Nieto, S. (2000). *Affirming diversity: The sociopolitical context of multicultural education* (3rd ed.). New York: Longman.

Nord, W. A. (1995). *Religion in American education.* Chapel Hill: University of North Carolina Press.

Nord, W. A., & Haynes, C. A. (1998). *Taking religion seriously across the curriculum.* Alexandria, VA: Association for Supervision and Curriculum Development.

Phipps, W. E. (1996). *Muhammad and Jesus: A comparison of the prophets and their teachings.* New York: Continuum.

Purple, D. (1989). *The moral and spiritual crisis in education.* Granby, MA: Bergin & Garvey.

The Quran. (2002). (9th U.S. ed.). (A.Y. Ali, Trans.). New York: Tahrike Tarsile Qur'an, Inc.

Radakrishnan, S. (Trans.). (1960). *Selections from the sacred writings of the Sikhs.* London: George, Allen & Unwin.

Sacks, J. (2003). *The dignity of difference: How to avoid the clash of civilizations.* London: Continuum.

Salili, F., & Hoosain, R. (Eds.). (2003). *Teaching, learning and motivation in a multicultural context.* Greenwich, CT: Information Age.

Sewall, G. T. (1998). Religion and textbooks. In J. T. Sears, with James C. Carper (Eds.), *Curriculum, religion, and public education* (pp. 73–84). New York: Teachers College Press.

Shih, J. (1981). The Chinese way and Christian way. *Studia Missionalia, 30,* 191–205.

Singh, K. (1963). *A history of the Sikhs: Volume I. 1469–1839.* London: Oxford University Press.

Sleeter, C. E., & McLaren, P. L. (1995). *Multicultural education, critical pedagogy, and the political difference.* Albany: State University of New York Press.

Smith, H. (1995). *The illustrated world's religions: A guide to our wisdom traditions.* New York: Harper.

Swidler, L. (Ed.). (1998). *For all life: Toward a universal declaration of a global ethic. An interreligious dialogue.* Ashland, OR: White Cloud Press.

Swidler, L. (2004). Confucianism for modern persons in dialogue with Christianity and modernity. *Journal of Ecumenical Studies, 15*(1-2), 12–24.

Thomas, S. (2000). The global resurgence of religions and the changing character of international politics. In M. L. Stackhouse, with D. B. Obenchain (Eds.), *God and globaliztion: Vol. 3. Christ and the dominions of civilization* (pp. 110–138). Harrisburg, PA: Trinity International.

Toynbee, A. (1960). Forward. In S. Radakrishnan (Trans.), *Selections from the sacred writings of the Sikhs* (pp. 9–11). London: George, Allen & Unwin.

Twiss, S. B. (1998). Four paradigms in teaching comparative religious ethics. In S. B. Twiss & B. Grelle, *Exploration in global ethics: Comparative religious ethics and interreligious dialogue.* Boulder, CO: Westview Press.

UNESCO Universal Declaration on Cultural Diversity. (2002). Paris: UNESCO.

Wattles, J. (1996). *The golden rule.* New York: Oxford University Press.

Wilson, H. S. (2003). Globalization for global community: A challenge to ministerial formation. *Currents in Theology and Mission, 30*(3), 173–179.

Wilson, H. S. (2004). Multicultural Christian community—A bouquet of multiple flowers. *Word & World, 24*(2), 171–181.

Zhao, F. (1998). For dialogue on a global ethic: A Confucian/Taoist view. In *For all life: Toward a universal declaration of a global ethic. An interreligious dialogue* (pp. 145–153). Ashland, OR: White Cloud Press.

CHAPTER 3

ISLAMIC PHILOSOPHY OF EDUCATION AND WESTERN ISLAMIC SCHOOLS

Points of Tension

Michael S. Merry
Beloit College

ABSTRACT

In this chapter, I elaborate an idealized type of Islamic philosophy of education and epistemology. Next, I examine the crisis that Islamic schools face in Western societies. This will occur on two fronts: (1) an analysis of the relationship (if any) between the philosophy of education, the aspirations of school administration, and the actual character and practice of Islamic schools; and (2) an analysis concerning the meaning of an Islamic curriculum. To the first issue, I argue that there exists a disjuncture between Islamic educational ideals (as expressed by Muslim philosophers of education), the aspirations of school administrators, and the manner in which Islamic schools operate in practice. Concerning the second item, I argue that Islamic schools, notwithstanding their own insistent claims, must struggle to define what an Islamic education entails that is uniquely distinctive to Islamic

Religion in Multicultural Education, pages 41–70
Copyright © 2006 by Information Age Publishing
All rights of reproduction in any form reserved.

schools. Finally, I argue that Islamic educators need to encourage open-minded discussions concerning issues on which there is no settled opinion. I illumine this discussion by drawing upon minority Muslim voices that encourage further dialogue and debate. Above all else, this chapter is an attempt to highlight the challenges that Muslim educators in the West face as they aim to reconcile an idealized caricature of Islamic philosophy of education with the on-the-ground needs of Muslim children socialized in a non-Islamic society.

[The] culture of a traditional society is dominated by harmony and unity; all branches of social life are deeply integrated. Education is an integral part of life and so are philosophy and knowledge, and these are deeply interrelated.

—Hadi Sharifi (1979)

INTRODUCTION

Multiculturalists usually endeavor to respect the educational needs of each child according to their cultural orientation; similarly, multiculturalists are keen to promote equal educational opportunities. This includes incorporating curricular perspectives missing from the Western canon, attuning students to the underlying assumptions and biases that inform knowledge constructions and enabling students to think and act as empowered citizens. Yet there remain problems with this approach, including the manner in which multicultural curricula often resort to stereotypical and reductionist depictions of non-European cultures and ways of life. It has been claimed that these depictions only increase—or at the very least, solidify—the inequalities suffered by ethnic and cultural minorities whose interests multicultural lessons are meant to promote. Consequently, parents are increasingly choosing comprehensive religious schools for their children, which they hope will do a better job in maintaining their cultural and religious identities. Islamic schools are an important example of this trend, and as their numbers in Western countries climb there may be reasons to think that their aims replicate those of multiculturalism, albeit within the private educational sphere.

In what follows, I attempt to provide an overview of the general philosophy behind Islamic education. What I describe is a highly condensed version of Islamic philosophy of education, followed by a brief account of Islamic epistemology, as provided by some of Islam's finest scholars. Such philosophy is necessarily *theology*, inasmuch as all considerations of human endeavor in Islam have God as their point of reference. In my account of an Islamic philosophy of education, I render an undifferentiated consensus view, one that would appear to contradict the internally diverse *ummāh* as well as the experiences of Western Muslim educators. Therefore, much of what I describe is an ideal type. *The synthesized ideas I will lay out do not exist anywhere in reality.* This is because the reification of abstract ideas necessarily requires interpretation and varied application according to need, organization, competence, and circumstance. It remains to be seen whether Islamic school educators in the West will develop a philosophy of education rooted in the experiences of practitioners.[1]

The incongruence between an ideal type of philosophy of Islamic education and the heterogeneous body of Muslims and Islamic schools in the West is admittedly an antinomy of sorts. In part, this tension exists because virtually all Islamic philosophy of education derives from the so-called Muslim world (e.g., Pakistan, Malaysia, Indonesia, Saudi Arabia), while this study focuses on Islamic schooling in a Western context. This disjuncture poses a serious quandary for anyone attempting to understand the philosophical ideas that inform practice, particularly when a distilled, decontextualized stereotype emerges to inform the highly specific, context-specific practices in Islamic schools. In many ways, this chapter is an attempt to highlight the challenges that Muslim educators in the West face as they aim to reconcile an idealized caricature of Islamic philosophy of education with the on-the-ground socialization needs of Muslim children in a non-Islamic society.

Following an idealized description of Islamic philosophy of education, I describe what Islamic schools aim to provide. Islamic schools are as diverse as the individuals who establish, work, and study in them. It is therefore impossible to describe what an Islamic school, in any pure sense, looks like. The synthesized and ideal description I give is based largely on accounts provided by Western Muslim educators in Europe and North America—diverse in their own right—but I supplement these reports with interviews conducted with Islamic school principals, teachers, and former students from four Midwestern states in North America. My account focuses on what Islamic schools in the West *have in common*, allowing for different degrees of emphasis and implementation.

In my assessment of Islamic schools, I will examine the crisis that Islamic schools face in Western societies. This occurs on two fronts: (1) an analysis of the relationship (if any) between the philosophy of education, the aspirations of school administration, and the actual character and practice of Islamic schools; and (2) an analysis concerning the meaning of an Islamic curriculum. To the first item, I argue that there exists a disconnect between Islamic educational ideals (as expressed by Muslim philosophers of education), the aspirations of school administrators, and the manner in which Islamic schools operate in practice. Concerning the second item, I argue that Islamic schools, notwithstanding their own insistent claims, must struggle to define what an Islamic education entails that is uniquely distinctive to Islamic schools. Finally, I argue that Islamic educators need to encourage open-minded discussions concerning issues on which there is no settled opinion. I illumine this discussion by drawing upon minority Muslim voices that encourage further dialogue and debate.

Islam versus the West?

Though changes in thinking are afoot, a majority of Muslims[2] and non-Muslims continues to cast the opposition of Islam versus the West rather sharply. One commonly encounters the paradigm, infamously advanced by the likes of Samuel Huntington (1996) and Bernard Lewis (1993) some years ago, of two incompatible cultures.[3] The voice of Noura Durkee is not atypical:

> [Religiously-minded Americans] could become Muslims. They might be among the best of us. They have, in general, lived through and come out of the frantic quest for money pursued by most Americans, born or immigrant. They have lived richly and poorly and don't care so much anymore. They do see the poverty in secular humanist materialism. But instead of becoming Muslim, they proceed to invent humanitarian causes like "World Hunger Day," "LiveAid," "Save the Whales." Why? Because Islam is something they know less than nothing about. They live in the Jahiliyyah [state of ignorance, idolatry, and anarchy]. Some of them are Hanif [believers in the One God]. Some of them know they are waiting for something. All of them are misinformed. (1987, p. 56)

Western values, many Muslims allege, assume a secular starting point, operate on the pretense of neutrality, unduly emphasize rationalism—and are accordingly limited by empiricism. Neutrality, Yusuf Waghid argues, "separates practice from theory, theory from fact, and fact from value" (1996, p. 44). Islam, conversely, posits the dual nature of humanity. Human beings possess not only a body and a mind but also a spirit (*rûh, nafs*). While Western scientism acknowledges the human heart as a muscle that pumps blood through the body and sustains its biological functions, the heart (*qalb*) in Islam denotes the core reality of humankind (Sharifi, 1979); its reality is not, ultimately, of this world but lies in union with God so that one may attain *adab* or the inculcation of goodness, leading to the "perfect human" (*al-insān al-kāmil*). Religious faith (*īmān*) is not a separate compartment unattached to one's daily experience; rather, Islam purports to be a total way of life (*Dīn wa Dunya*). Islamic education, then, reposes in a transcendent reality and recognition of this leads to wisdom (*hikmah*).

The perceived antagonism between Western and Islamic educational goals is subsumed within the familiar dichotomy of the abode of Islam (*dār-al-Islām*) versus the abode of war (*dār al-harb*), though both are increasingly believed to be outmoded expressions (Khan, 1998; Ramadan, 1999) and neither is to be found in the Qur'ān or the *Sunnah*.[4] Some Muslims describe Western societies as *dar al-Kufr*, or the abode of unbelief, where

Islam is neither the dominant religion nor are Muslims under special treaty relations with the state. Yet, obvious difficulties immediately arise; a country like the United States, for example, cannot be understood as an abode of unbelievers. Indeed, a majority of its inhabitants would be classified, in Islamic nomenclature, as People of the Book (*ahl-al-Kitab*). Yet acknowledging this does not prevent some Muslims living in the West from conceptualizing this opposition, often for polemical purposes.

Proponents for Islamic schools, joining the thousands of other denominational schools, sometimes echo this belief. Islamic educational ideals hold a great deal in common with, for example, Evangelical Protestant and conservative Catholic and Jewish schools. Each in its own way offers an alternative pedagogical vision to the materialist, secularist, and careerist impulses that permeate Western society generally. Each of these traditions recognizes that humans possess a physical and spiritual self. Islamic education aims to address this whole self, guiding the student along a path conducive to righteousness by integrating faith and spirituality into one's entire life. Increasingly, though, Muslims in Western contexts express skepticism concerning the ability to maintain this spiritual ideal. While democratic liberals will typically view a secularist political apparatus as nondiscriminatory and fair, Muslims are more likely to see secularism as an uncompromising force "sweeping the world in all matters of public life" (Hewitt, 1996, p. 72), an agenda set on relegating religious values to the private sphere. Secularism in public life is itself believed by some (Yousif, 2000) to be discriminatory. Muslims who view their situation in Western societies in this way are endeavoring to vanquish the secular foe, and they will seek to do so in a resolute, confrontational manner (Bleher, 1996). Thus Maulana Abul Hasan Ali Nadwi writes:

> The only way to combat this evil is to make arrangements for the widest possible dissemination of the Islamic *Da'wah* [witnessing to the faith], the spiritual-moral teachings of Islam through good healthy literature and journals propagating ethical norms and the awe of God in public dealings. If necessary, laws should be enacted for the purpose and those found offending these rules of conduct should be punished. (Husain & Ashraf, 1979, p. 21)

Thus, though Western countries operate explicitly or implicitly on moral axioms and policies originally framed around religious arguments, there is the impression—from within and without the Islamic community—that the West operates on principles *opposed* to religious faith.

Islamic Philosophy of Education: Aims and Objectives

At the center of Islamic education is complete submission to the will of God. This is what it means to be a Muslim. The curriculum in an Islamic school, both explicit and hidden, ought to reflect an Islamic orientation. This is because Islamic education is an all-encompassing project, one not reserved for Muslims only. The surest educational proposal for an Islamic education, Muhammad Qutb posits, requires that one make "Allah's doctrine rule supreme" (Husain & Ashraf 1979, pp. 28–29). Islamic education, like most other forms of religious education, is concerned with the whole person. Its ambit includes the spiritual as well as the intellectual student. Syed Muhammad al-Attas explains it this way:

> The training imparted to a Muslim must be such that faith is infused into the whole of his personality and creates in him an emotional attachment to Islam and enables him to follow the Quran and the Sunnah and be governed by the Islamic system of values willingly and joyfully so that he may proceed to the realization of his status as [vice-regent] to whom Allah has promised the authority of the universe. (al-Attas, 1979, pp. 158–159)

In Islamic theology, one encounters the idea that humans are born in a state of *fitrah* (*by decree*), that is, the innate capacity for worship (*'ibādah*) and obedience (*ta'ah*) to the will of God.

Muslim educators are occupied with the need to combat a materialist mindset that fails to place Allah at its center. Islamic education seeks to overturn this materialist thinking by laying the stress on purpose and unity in the universe. Underlying this is the concept of *tawhīd,* the oneness of God that permeates all aspects of life. *Tahwīd* entails the complete integration of all that one does; it includes the physical as well as the spiritual. No dichotomy of sacred and profane exists, for all of life is called to submit to the divine will. All separation between science and spirituality is therefore believed to be a Western secular innovation (*bid'a*).[5] Harmony between faith and empirical work, between knowledge and values, must be maintained so that individuals participate in the noblest achievements of Islamic society. Even class differences are rejected inside the Islamic school, and complete equality among all students is the ideal (Ahmed, 1990).[6]

If there is an explicit purpose to Islamic education, it is this: to "teach us how to worship God and so fulfill our task of *Khalifah* [vice-regent] on earth" (Mohamed, 1991, p. 15). An Islamic education will bring up children according to their developmental needs and provide the student with

> the creative impulse to rule himself and the universe as a true servant of Allah not by opposing and coming into conflict with Nature but by understanding its laws and harnessing its forces for the growth of a personality that is in harmony with it. (al-Attas, 1979, p. 159)

This vice-regency is not to be seen as being in conflict with one's civic responsibilities. The society in which one lives, and not only an Islamic society, is one's *ummāh*. Islamic schoolteachers frequently discuss civil rights, civic responsibilities, and encourage their students to engage actively in the democratic process, though *da'wa* is usually the motive. Some believe that *da'wa* denotes active proselytizing of unbelievers in the community through interfaith alliances; for others, *da'wa* entails a life of prayer and pious living, that is, living one's faith. Either way, the goal of *da'wa* is to testify to the truth of Islam as the best way to enjoy inner peace and spiritual satisfaction.

Islamic education is impossible unless one has first accepted the revelation (*Wahi*) of God to humanity through the angel Jibrā'īl (Gabriel) to the last of the prophets, Muhammad. Without these premises, there can be no Islamic education. Beyond this prerequisite, Ghulam Sarwar (1996) elucidates the objectives of Islamic education:

1. Prepare and train the future generation to work as agents of *Allāh* on Earth.

2. Ensure the promotion of *Ma'rūf* (good) and the prevention of *Munkar* (evil) in a society.

3. Ensure the balanced growth of the total personality of a person.

4. Promote spiritual, moral, cultural, physical, mental, and material development in children in preparation for the responsibilities, experiences, and opportunities of adult life.

5. Develop all the faculties to realize the full potential of people.

6. Develop the skills required to enable people to face real-life situations with a clear consciousness about their responsibility and accountability in the *Ākhirah* [life after death].

7. Prepare people to work toward the economic and material growth of a society with a strong sense of the unity of the human race and ensure equitable distribution and proper use of wealth.

8. Develop a sense of social responsibility for the efficient use of resources to eliminate wastage, avoid ecological damage, and safeguard the well-being of all created beings.

9. Encourage competition in good things to promote excellence and the highest achievements for the greater welfare of people and society.

10. Ensure that children grow up with a strong belief in sharing opportunities, equity, justice, fair play, love, care, affection, selflessness, honesty, humility, integrity, and austerity (pp. 13–14).

The dichotomy mentioned earlier between "Islam" and the "West" (both are presented as undifferentiated) surfaces here again: the West dichotomizes while Islam harmonizes; the West, the argument runs, compartmentalizes disciplines, while Islam situates learning within its proper point of reference, which is revelation (*Wahi*). Islam, also, purports to synthesize the various disciplines together neatly into a unified whole (*tawhīd*).

Again, it must be stressed that the above description of an Islamic philosophy of education captures an oversimplified, decontextualized "essence" as expounded by particular Muslim scholars, mainly from predominantly Muslim cultures, and not the diversity of the Muslim *ummāh* or the variety of practices that individual Islamic schools evince in the West. Most Islamic educators in the West are very keen to develop an Islamic philosophy of education that does not eschew liberal democratic values but incorporates them into an Islamic framework. While the details of this symbiotic relationship have yet to be worked out, it can be said of progressive Muslim educators that they wish to:

> Advocate a modern educational system, which is inclusive [of] a clearly defined religious curriculum, that enhances the child's development as a Muslim, in addition to his/her development as an intellectual capability. [This] approach to religious education as a foundation of an Islamic moral code, behaviorism and way of life is essential within [this] understanding of a comprehensive body of education. (Saadallah, 2004, p. 48)

Therefore, for most Muslim educators in the West, Islam is not so much guided by the abstract theology of intellectuals from the Muslim world but from the on-the-ground needs of Muslims struggling to retain their identity in an environment indifferent, and in some cases hostile, to Islam.

ISLAMIC EPISTEMOLOGY

Modern epistemology, many Islamic pedagogues insist, minimizes the knowledge one derives from revelation (*Wahi*) and thus reduces knowledge to a material realm wholly dependent on reason. In other words, they continue, Western thought assumes a secular starting point (al-Attas, 1979, 1991; Barazangi, 1990, 1991; Husain & Ashraf, 1979; Nasr, 1987; Sarwar, 1996). Knowledge (*ilm*) from an Islamic point of view must take all of life into account; learning cannot be separated from belief in God. "Seeking knowledge is the duty of every Muslim," reads a famous *hadīth*. Indeed, belief in God is the key to true knowledge and understanding, for all knowledge comes from God. Knowledge must guide the Muslim "towards a high ultimate destiny in the Hereafter" (al-Attas, 1979, p. 157). The combination of knowledge with the spiritual discernment that recognizes and distinguishes truth from falsehood is called *'aql* and it can be used synonymously with "heart" (*qalb*). Real knowledge, however, is the balance between knowledge (*ilm*) and practice (*'amal*), and its purpose is the cultivation of goodness.

The Qur'ān, as the final authority on Truth (*haqq*), provides the basis for all knowledge claims. These knowledge claims then provide the basis for proper action (*lim*), spirituality (*iman, nur* and *huda*), ethics (*ulama*), and wisdom (*hikma*) (Hilgendorf 2003, p. 65). The point of an Islamic education is to grow and mature according to the wisdom of the tradition. Possessing true wisdom means being able to "effect correct judgments as to the proper place of things" (al-Attas, 1979, p. 20). Islam considers all intellectual and scientific learning and achievements to be an expression of wisdom derived from one's Creator. All inquiry and creativity are means to a greater end, that is, to reflect upon the greatness of Allah or to gain deeper insight into the meaning of the Qur'ān, and not as ends in themselves (Surty, 1989). While Islamic epistemology recognizes all levels of learning and perception, all are subordinate to the edicts of the Qur'ān, believed to reflect God's will. This is the idea behind *Tarbiya*, the goal-orientedness of an education, the nourishing of the whole person, in which no aspect of the individual is left untouched by faith (*īmān*). As an act of worship (*ibadāh*), Islamic education is preeminently concerned with cultivating and sustaining faith.

Whereas Western epistemology acknowledges both sensory and intellectual perception, Islam posits that yet another level of perception—namely, the spiritual—realizes the highest level of discernment and it is only through spiritual insight that all learning assumes a meaningful composite. Manzoor Ahmed explains:

> The aim of acquisition of knowledge in the Islamic system is not merely to satisfy an intellectual curiosity but to train rational and righteous individuals for the moral and physical good of their families, their people and for the entire mankind [*sic*]. The Islamic system of education strikes a balance between the need for individual excellence and the requirements of the society. (1990, p. 6)

There are differences of opinion concerning the degree to which one may blend imitation (*taqlīd*) of tradition with independent knowledge based on reason (*ijtihād*)[7] in areas where the Qur'ān and the *hadīth* are silent.[8] Additional knowledge can be gained, for example, from experimentation and observation of the material world, but all knowledge must be carefully integrated into an Islamic frame of reference (Yusuf, 1992). In a word, all learning must be *Islamicized*, that is, brought into conformity with the foundation, theory, and principles set forth in the Qur'ān.

A popular turn of phrase with earlier theorists such as Ismail al-Faruqi (1982), the "Islamization of knowledge" entails an interpretation of school subject matter that coincides with an acceptable orthodox understanding. The urgent task of Islamizing knowledge, for many Muslim educators, will "immunize" Muslim pupils from inevitable moral decline as they are confronted by secularist ideologies and practices. Take, for example, the following quote from Allama Kazi:

> Islamic education [means] instruction to lead a life at the period of evolution initiated by the Quran. Anything that is detrimental to this progress at this stage is un-Islamic. Anything that defeats the purpose that the Quran has introduced to be achieved by humanity is bad education, wrong education, un-Islamic education—education that leads man [*sic*] from light to darkness. (1989, p. 84)

A correct understanding of the Qur'ān is believed to provide the Muslim with the tools to make sense of the modern world. Definitive answers are accessible to those who apply the "science" of revelation to all modes of inquiry. Those who wish to establish their interpretations as authentic and "orthodox" may avail themselves of the views of other Muslims who are in agreement (Stenberg, 2000).

Islamic education recognizes two types of knowledge, those acquired (*tahsīlī*) and those revealed (*Wahi*). Those acquired include the human sciences, the natural sciences, the applied sciences, and the technological sciences. In addition to these, one might add the following: comparative religion, Western culture and civilization, linguistic sciences, and Islamic history. Muslim educational scholars encourage the "Islamization" of each discipline. This entails "the elaboration of a prior constituted Islamic conceptual framework to convincingly meet the challenges of modern society" (Mohamed, 1991, p. 18). The former takes priority over the latter and becomes the criteria by which all learning is judged. Yasien Mohamed further differentiates the two types of knowledge: "The revealed sciences [Qur'ān, *Sunna, hadīth*] provide human beings with permanent objective truths which are important for their guidance, the acquired sciences provide the knowledge of sensible data necessary for daily practical use" (Mohamed, 1991, p. 19). To the extent that the acquired sciences usurp the place of revelation, the Muslim, it is said, will be alienated from the tradition and its eternal truths.

WHAT ISLAMIC SCHOOLS PROVIDE

Islamic schools may organize around Sunni or Shi'a understandings, but they are united in the five pillars or duties of the faith. These duties begin with the profession of faith (*Shahāda*), espousing that there is no God but Allah and Muhammad is his messenger. To sincerely pronounce these truths in front of two witnesses is to become a Muslim. Other pillars of the Islamic faith include obligatory prayer (*salāh*) five times a day, *zakāh* or almsgiving,[9] *sawm* or fasting during Ramadan, and the *hajj* or pilgrimage to

Mecca. To these pillars the following may be added: a belief in the oneness of God,[10] a belief in angels (except for Shi'a), a belief in the prophets,[11] a belief in the day of judgment (*Yaum al-Dīn*), and a belief in God's sovereignty over all things. Many also add *jihād*, or spiritual struggle against darker impulses.[12]

Despite the many different types of Islamic schools, including varying degrees of orthodoxy, strictness, and ethnic affiliation, many overlapping similarities unite them. To begin with, Islamic schools promise to unite the spiritual with the material in the children's' education. An awareness of Allah in all that children do and learn is central to Islamic education. One cannot visit an Islamic school without hearing repeated references to God: *Al-Hamdilullah* (thanks be to God) or *insha'Allah* (if God wills) infuse the speech of teachers and staff throughout the day. The God-consciousness (*taqwa*) promoted by all of the Muslim staff is thought to foster student development that maintains a balance between the spiritual and the material, but this God-consciousness is also believed to lead to justice (*'adl*) and the witnessing to the truth of Islam (*da'wa*). The Muslim who spreads the true faith must first be mindful of God in all that he or she does; put another way, he or she must maintain equilibrium between the physical and spiritual realms. *Taqwa*, then, is best understood as a "conscious balance between the individual, the society, and the limits set by Allah or God as the source of value and knowledge" (Barazangi, 2000, p. 30).

Prayer times in Islamic schools are routine—though each school varies slightly in the time it sets apart for prayer—and space is provided for students to carry out ablutions (*wudu*) either in an adjoining mosque (*masjid*) or in the school itself. Gender separation is a common practice in most Islamic schools, at least prior to the onset of puberty. Only in smaller classes, as a practical necessity, does one find blending of boys and girls, and even then self-segregation tends to happen. Physical education, assuming it is provided, is usually segregated according to sex, except in the most liberal Islamic schools. Because Islam compels modesty, dress codes are usually strict. Beyond a certain age (most schools begin in the third or fourth grade), it is characteristic for girls to wear a headscarf (typically *hijāb*), as a show of inward as well as outward modesty, and a loose-fitting robe (*jilbab*). Makeup is strictly forbidden. Boys also wear uniforms, usually navy blue pants and white shirts. Hair is kept neat and trimmed. Art classes are sometimes available, provided there is funding and staff, but depictions of persons and animals are strictly forbidden because of the sanctions against idolatry. Music classes are only available in a few schools, but many (particularly stringed and wind) instruments are forbidden. Drums (*tabla*), however, are often part of Arabic culture, as are certain kinds of cultural dance (*dabka*). All Islamic schools celebrate the two important feasts in the calendar: the Festival of Sacrifice (*Eid al-Adha*) and the Festival of the

Breaking of the Fast (*Eid al-Fitr*). Many schools also take a day off for the birthday of the Prophet.

As it concerns the curriculum, one finds important differences to other religious schools. Certainly there is Qur'ānic instruction (with recitation), including studies of the life of the Prophet (*sira*) and the period of the first four Caliphs. The moral example of the Prophet Muhammad, whose deeds are collected in the *Sunna*, and whose attributed sayings are collected in the *hadīth*, provides a reliable moral guide. For older students, there is also study of jurisprudence (*fiqh*), including consideration of Islamic law (*sharī'āh*). From these are derived judgments concerning that which is either approved (*ma'ruf*) or morally intolerable (*munkar*). Islamic history is taught, as are various cultural studies that reflect the different ethnic compositions of schools. Most importantly, perhaps, is the fact that issues of faith can be broached in the classroom, openly and unabashedly. Examples include discussions in literature, social studies, and even science. Children and teachers often use their personal experiences as Muslims for instructive examples in classroom discussion. Many Islamic school staff members have considerable teaching experience in other public and private schools, some for many years. Their ability to contrast previous teaching experience is an advantage in their facility to assess Islamic schooling, though some have only the worst public school experiences to compare with. These messages are sometimes passed along to students in Islamic schools (i.e., that public schools are *ipso facto* unsafe, academically undemanding, promiscuous, materialistic places to be).

Several Islamic schools actively participate in interfaith exercises with the high school students, though the interaction is usually rather tame.[13] Students explain their faith while the others respectfully listen; each group—Jewish, Lutheran, Catholic, etc.—takes turns. While participants are exposed to different beliefs, challenges to one's faith are not likely to occur at these exchanges. Other teachers try to involve their students in academic competitions with a range of public and private schools, though some claim that other children have not always been kind.

Many schools are host to children whose parents and families are known to the entire school staff. (This is not always the case, of course, because many families drive long distances to reach the school.) Thus accountability is high, and respect toward adults is expected. Moreover, owing to the stronger formal relations that usually exist between school board members and teaching and administrative staff, there is usually a stake in the performance of the school, as well as the well-being of the students. In a number of Islamic schools, school board members are also part of the teaching staff. Accordingly, Islamic schools strive to provide an atmosphere conducive to higher student achievement.

Critical to the purpose of Islamic schools is their aim to maintain a school culture that operates according to particular values and norms. Often these values and norms are believed to be opposed to the norms of other schools, including the larger society. This value coherence is extended to the general climate in Islamic schools and not just to the dress code, prayer times, and a religiously sanctioned diet. Especially from curriculum developers and school principals one hears that Islam offers a structural advantage over Western forms of education, owing to its integration in all aspects of living. There is, generally, very little "clericalism" among those running Islamic schools; school administrators encourage their students to read and interpret the Qur'ān within certain reasonable limits, and critical discussion for the most part is encouraged.

ASSESSMENT

In attempting to assess Islamic education I have two items in mind: (1) The relationship (if any) between Islamic philosophy of education, the aspirations and goals of school administrators, and the actual practices of Islamic schools; and (2) the precise meaning of an Islamic education. Taking the first item, Muslim philosophers of education doubtless hope their objectives will filter down into practice. Reality, however, can offer up less agreeable testimony. Although there is inevitably some degree of confluence, it may appear to the observer that there is an unclear relationship between the ideals of Islamic education, the aspirations of school administrators, and the manner in which Islamic schools operate in practice. Concerning the second item, Islamic school educators are challenged to defend what is essentially Islamic about the education they promote. Generally, attempts to describe what an Islamic education is remain imprecise. On both counts, I base my assessment on a small empirical literature (mainly from self-reporting articles in Islamic magazines) and the testimony of both Islamic school teachers (not all of whom are Muslim) and former students.

Philosophy of Education

Muslim philosophers of education, most of whom write from contexts outside of the West, aim to provide Islamic school educators in the West with a vision of Islamic education. I have already proffered a condensed version of this pedagogical vision above. Entailed in this vision is Divine Revelation, the dual nature of human beings, the spiritual realm that permeates all that Muslims say and do (and, pertinently, *learn*), the submission of all knowledge to the authority of the Qur'ān, and the Islamization of education. None of this is possible without faith (*iman*), a disposition that unfolds within a community of believers and is witnessed to by the *shahāda*. This disposition is concretized in specific acts of worship and moral duty, including fasting, prayer, and charity. The meaning of Islamic education, if a precise meaning can be properly distilled, is to remember (*dhikr*) and worship (*ibadāh*) God in all that one does. It is to be mindful of the Last Day and to treat others with the dignity and respect they deserve. To bring all elements of one's life within the jurisdiction of the Divine is both to submit to God and to realize one's true self.

Muslim philosophers of education continue, with few exceptions, to stress how an Islamic education differs *fundamentally* from education offered by other—ostensibly conflicting—philosophical bases. I elaborated in the first part of this chapter how the Islamic vision of education is believed to be at odds with the values and norms of Western culture. However, it must be stressed again that this vision remains idealistic and decontextualized; moreover, these lofty aims, inasmuch as they take little account of the actual practice of educators in schools on the ground, approach something akin to a stereotype.

School Mission

Islamic schools and their managers aspire to the best education possible for their students. Their goals in many ways match those of Muslim philosophers of education, though the level of specificity often differs because of the incredible diversity among Muslims themselves but also because of the variety of concrete practices different Islamic schools adopt. Nevertheless, an impressive uniformity exists, as school mission statements from across North America make abundantly clear. Thus from the American upper Midwest we learn of one Islamic school where the mission is to have their students understand *tawhīd*, to develop a strong moral character, develop a strong sense of responsibility, interact with the community and global issues with an Islamic frame of mind, and recognize Islam as the only viable solution to life's problems and challenges. Another school in western Canada states that it seeks to provide a superior standard of education, to foster academic achievement, and to cultivate an Islamic spirit in each student. Its leaders also expect a high standard of academic achievement, commitment, and integrity, combined with respect, self-discipline, and a code of conduct based on Islamic teachings. On the East Coast, an Islamic school announces its intention to "help Muslim children excel in learning and compete with their counterparts in passing the Standards of Learning as mandated by the Department of Education." Finally, from another school in New England, the goals of an Islamic education are expressed as follows:

The academy guides the children to lead decent contemporary lives, enrich their families, serve their community, tolerate differences, think critically, promote collaboration and respect others. School activities help the children develop individual talent, self-esteem and leadership characteristics and offer an outlet for demonstrating creativity. The entire school community provides high learning and practice standards preparing the students to live in a complex, technological and multi-cultural society as proud practicing Muslims. (http://www.iane.org/)

Those who manage Islamic schools, unlike most Muslim philosophers of education, recognize the importance of training children to simultaneously identify both as Muslims and as citizens of the West. Much of the language that Islamic schools adopt to convey their mission is therefore unsurprisingly Western in origin. This includes using the best academic resources (i.e., texts, pedagogical tools and teaching methods). It extends further. One school includes in its mission the aim to "interact effectively with people who follow other faiths, to tolerate differences of opinion within [one's] own community, and to keep [the students'] minds receptive to knowledge from all sources." Yet what remains unclear is the degree to which Muslim students are encouraged to interact with the belief systems of others in that world in which it is hoped they will succeed.

While all Islamic schools seek to cultivate Islamic virtues and character, many Islamic schools also endeavor to equip their students to succeed in a relentlessly competitive world, including being appropriately trained in the technological sciences. Earlier I pointed out that Islamic schools provide opportunities for their students to interact with others outside the school; the mission of each school is to train students for success in the marketplace. There are real tensions here. Perhaps as a direct consequence, school principals and administrators are frequently placed in the position of mediator between the values—many of them cultural—and expectations of parents and the realities facing children growing up in a society manifestly different from their parents' homeland.

School Practice[14]

Just as one might find in other small religious schools, it is impossible to miss the zeal and commitment among Islamic school staff and teachers. Little can deter those who have put aside other priorities and focused on the education of the youth according to a specific rule of faith. Islamic school staff work tirelessly to provide the highest levels of instruction while attending to the personal and developmental needs of children. Islamic school educators clearly recognize the advantages Islamic schools provide, including the feeling of security, acceptance and affirmation of one's faith, and the integration of this faith with learning. One does not have to look far to hear stories of students whose Muslim identities grow stronger as a result of Islamic schooling. For these students, this translates into a stronger sense of self and a surer set of beliefs when it becomes necessary to confront non-Islamic customs and values.[15]

Nevertheless, teachers learn very quickly that Islamic schools promise many things that they cannot deliver (cf. Amri, 2000).[16] Some consider the idea of an "Islamic curriculum" unhelpful. This is hardly surprising when one considers that the majority of Islamic schools continue to borrow heavily from public and other private school curricula and textbooks. Most would rather talk about ways to help develop character. Many Islamic school teachers attest to Islamic schools not developing that special character, let alone managing to nourish a strong Muslim identity. To the contrary, many describe their school as very much like a typical public school, only with Islamic elements added on. Aside from the staff and resource shortages, few are unaware that their schools use the same textbooks as their public and private school counterparts. Moreover, the goal of becoming accredited in American schools means that Islamic schools aim to be as much like other state-approved schools as they can. In several European countries, curricular requirements (and hence degree of conformity) are even stricter still. Furthermore, many Islamic schools find it difficult to recruit Muslim teachers, calling into question the possibility of fostering an 'Islamic ethos' in the school.

PROBLEMATIZING ISLAMIC KNOWLEDGE

While Islamic schools encourage an Islamic approach to knowledge, many object to the suggestion that knowledge can be divorced from specific interpretations or constructions of it. Most readily agree that interpretation cannot be a *neutral* endeavor, for it involves incorporating specific attitudes that arise out of particular social rules and historical conditions (Waghid, 1996). Yet, directives pointing to Islamic history or the Islamic tradition pose myriad difficulties for students if they are not invited to join a conversation that questions the habit of imposing a monolithic structure from a previous age onto a new set of experiences (e.g., biotechnology) not faced by previous generations (Dahlén, 2002; Kazmi, 2003; Khan, 2004).

The reader may remember that the *Islamization of knowledge* concerns making all acquired knowledge conformable to an acceptable understanding of Islam. Yet not only is an *acceptable* view not disclosed, but the claim casts the meaning of Islamic education in rather stark contrasts: truth versus falsehood, orthodoxy versus heterodoxy. The truth as revealed in the Qur'ān, according to this view, is presented as unambiguously obvious in its message. This somewhat static view of knowledge as propounded by numerous Muslim scholars has managed to drown out more progressive voices (Safi, 2003). These voices beckon Muslims to see knowledge as dynamic and unfolding. Syed Sajjad Husain (1996), for example, warns:

> [Muslims] stand more or less where the Christian world in Europe stood at the end of the mediaeval period when any interpretation of dogma which deviated from the teaching of the Church Fathers was condemned as heretical.... Human knowledge is a constantly changing process in the humanities as well as the sciences; nothing the source of which is man [*sic*] can ever stand still.... Every new generation of Muslims must be prepared to re-examine knowledge in the light of their understanding to keep pace with advances outside the community. Torpor and stagnation will confront us with the same dilemma in every age. (p. 50)

Unless new situations and intellectual challenges give rise to new interpretations (*ijtihād*), critics worry that the idealized, "pristine" projection of Islam will only alienate those who strive to adapt the norms of the Qur'ān and the *Sunna* to modern life. Without this creative and critical approach to the Islamic tradition, several unfortunate consequences are likely to occur. At a minimum, students will feel overly constrained to address contemporary issues with an outmoded and useless vocabulary on the mistaken hunch that the interpretations and rulings (*fatāwā*) issued by Islamic scholars in particular times and places will be adequate to the task in all other circumstances. Today, Muslim youth are looking for interpretations and adaptations of Islam that are relevant to their lives.

Many Muslim teachers and former students also express frustration with the lack of discussion within Islamic schools *vis-à-vis* cultural issues (e.g., the manner in which males and females relate to one another) that have taken on a prominent religious significance. This means that even when students are hearing many different opinions about specific issues, they are often uncertain about the way one ought to believe or think about them chiefly because many are reluctant to question the "follow the rules" custom. Yet again this is unsurprising when one considers that it is commonplace for adolescents generally to vacillate in this manner. Furthermore, Muslim scholars stress submission (*aslama, islam*) of one's volition to the doing of justice (*'adl*) and that which is good and beautiful (*ihsan*) as modeled by the prophets and revealed in the holy Qur'ān. To fail in this endeavor (i.e., to mistreat others or to stray from the right course) is to wrong one's own soul and to "deviate from what is right and to repudiate the truth and suffer loss" (al-Attas, 1979, p. 27). The devout Muslim will do only that which he or she believes is permitted by God; well-being depends on divine favor.

Freedom as understood in Islamic education is more typically about the *limitation* of one's desires and passions. It is an ascetic freedom. This freedom does not seek to fulfill one's own aspirations and needs apart from the needs of one's family or one's community. The ordering of one's life according to divine law (*shari'ah*) is the ideal to which devout Muslims aspire. True spiritual growth is suitably guided by the *shari'ah*.[17] Yet freedom will bring inner peace and happiness only by pursuing that which brings one into harmony with one's essential nature and his or her Creator. This kind of freedom, grounded in a life of prayer, aims to liberate the believer. Given these spiritually directed inhibitions, coupled with the range of opinions within each Islamic school—that is, a variety of Islamic traditions and no central authority—not a few students (again, like adolescents elsewhere) complete their schooling unsure about what to think beyond a few core Islamic beliefs. This seems as much an asset as a liability. On the one hand, this uncertainty might lead to greater awareness of diversity and an appreciation for a more complex epistemology. On the other hand, this might lead other students to feel that no right answers are to be found on certain topics, thus undermining one of the core purposes of Islamic schools.

Islamic schools promise to provide an *Islamic orientation* or perspective throughout one's schooling, and this is certainly the case as it concerns a few core beliefs and practices. Nevertheless, few schools, including well-staffed Islamic schools, find it desirable (or possible) to provide a uniformity of beliefs.[18] Instead, Islamic schools will usually follow either a specific traditional interpretation, or the opinion of the local imam concerning various controversial issues, for example, the place of music or art in the school curriculum, whether women ought to be allowed to pray publicly at the mosque, or perhaps even the regard one should have for the local community as opposed to Islamic causes (e.g., Middle East conflict) abroad. However, each of these issues is handled differently from place to place,[19] and increasingly young Muslims resort to chat rooms and other informal channels to arrive at opinions concerning challenges they face (Schmidt, 2004).

LOOKING AHEAD

Islamic schools are one manifestation of the multicultural age. Indeed, they are providing the means whereby Muslim children are being nurtured into a highly specific cultural and religious way of life. Yet points of tension remain. Norma Tarazi (2001), for instance, writes: "Muslims have their own philosophy of education, a middle road" between Christians, Jews, and secular variants. This claim is consistent with the highly idealized, decontextualized understanding of Islamic education I reviewed earlier—one untouched by the diverse reality of particular Islamic schools and the broader Muslim *ummāh*. Notwithstanding this caricatured depiction, there is no discernibly single Islamic pedagogy; nor is there a single approach to governing Islamic schools. A comprehensive guide to Islamic education in the West has yet to be written. It is precisely here that Islamic schools in the West, driven by educational entrepreneurs (Susan Douglass is a fine example), are pregnant with promise. Little wonder, then, that there has been a sharp rise in the number of Islamic schools in several Western countries during the past 15 years, notably in the United Kingdom and throughout North America.

Aware of the different conditions facing their students, the safety and academic and religious freedoms to pursue knowledge for both girls and boys,[20] Islamic schools are uniquely positioned to forge an identity well suited to speak to the needs of Muslim youth living in Western societies. However, one may still question, given the motivations of many Muslim parents and the general orientation of Islamic philosophy of education, whether Islamic schools can succeed in promoting authentic critical inquiry without delimiting the inspirational sources to non-Western ones. But if Muslim educators are to meet one of their desired aims, which is to promote a strong Muslim identity in tandem with an active citizenship in the West, they will look for ways to promote uninhibited inquiry and reform fully consonant with one's fundamental commitments within the Islamic tradition(s). Western-born Muslims, Mustafa Malik says, "are challenged daily to find Islamic answers to existential questions that underscore the urgency of Islamic reforms" (2004, p. 80).

Islamic school teachers are often eager to discuss the role citizenship education plays in the curriculum. "I'm always trying to encourage my students to think outside of their immediate surroundings," one teacher explains. Citizenship, another teacher elucidates, "has to do with respecting others; it concerns getting along with others, working in cooperation." Even where there is clear evidence of sheltering—particularly as it concerns issues involving strong moral opinions—students are reportedly well disposed to handle the crisis. Furthermore, Islamic school administrators are usually aware of the criticisms detractors make against Islamic schools. It is not, after all, only liberals who worry about the sheltering of children; many Muslims do as well. It is therefore not surprising to learn that a significant number of Islamic schools are seeking to prepare their students to live in a society in which they are a distinct minority. Education of this kind, as A. S. Abdullah explains,

> is concerned with developing the unique characteristics of the human being so that he will be able to *adapt* [to] the standards of the society that shares

with him the very same ideals. Such harmony is the first characteristic of Islamic education aims. (1983, p. 129)

But pedagogy is only one dimension of Islamic schooling, for the internal diversity within the Muslim community also means that the social and political aims of Islamic education remain unclear. Thus, it remains a challenge for Islamic schools to "work together to define a unified social, religious, [and] political role for themselves" (GhaneaBassiri 1997, p. 184). This challenge is not, however, cause for dismay. After all, there is—as I've stressed throughout this chapter—incredible diversity among Muslims. Whether or not it is an explicit objective, Islamic schools participate in as well as contribute to a variety of projects, and seek to have an impact on public life. For some the local community is a priority. Here, the aim is to sew "Islamic values" in the midst of a secular society through either public service or *da'wa*. Others prioritize promoting awareness of Muslims in other countries (Chechnya, Bosnia) where their plight goes unnoticed by the rest of the world. The majority appears to foster tight local networks contained by familiar family ties. Perhaps Islamic schools can accommodate each of these. Nevertheless, defining what "true" Islam is continues to challenge any and all notions of what an Islamic education must look like.

Islamic philosophy of education in particular continues to be problematic to the extent that its aims are largely defined by scholars living outside of the West. In particular, the anti-Western flavor of much Islamic philosophy of education continues to create obstacles for Islamic schools eager to depart from secular models of education. To admit to the need to become more self-critical of one's core commitments, including adopting different attitudes and perspectives, is seen by some as an abrogation of an Islamic identity. But this seems more a *betrayal* of Islam.

Muslim educators may think that in teaching a more open approach to matters involving Muslim identity they will be inviting division and disunity, a particularly uninviting prospect to face when so much vilification against Islam already thrives in the West. But it is crucial to the health and survival of Islam as a religion that it be able to confront challenges facing the next generation in ways that are open-minded and transparent. The community of believers (*ummāh*) instantiated in the Islamic school (inasmuch as it is true to the revelation witnessed to by the Prophet) will need to do justice to the day-to-day experiences of its members. Doing so only fosters trust and respect. Having a group of believers divided over a particular issue seems preferable to having a body of conservative clerics insisting that there will be no discussion at all. There is, Tamara Albertini (2003) reminds us, a long tradition within Islam that celebrates the *adab al-ikhtilāf*, or *ethics of disagreement* concerning different schools of interpretation.

The issues facing Islamic schools in the West confront *all* religious groups but they are arguably more pronounced for the Islamic community in the West because of the negative press they routinely receive (Abu-Laban, 1983; Noakes, 1998; Pitts, 2004). Issues like domestic violence[21] and clinical depression are only beginning to be openly discussed in some Muslim communities, while cultural divisions,[22] the acceptability of fine arts, arranged marriages, and the relationship of Muslims to public education remain largely undecided topics desperately in need of further discussion. The West is providing the space and the freedom to organize and develop strategies to respond to the needs of the Muslim community, in many ways better than other so-called Islamic countries do (Abdul-Rauf, 1983; Malik, 2001, 2004; Ramadan, 1999). Nevertheless, the resolution of Muslim educators to grapple with issues such as these will determine the health and sustainability of Islamic schools in the generations to come. If predetermined principles win out over continued reflection and interpretation, if open discussion about controversial issues is met with denunciations of "*bid'a!*" or "*haram!*" (i.e., unlawful), one can expect a certain measure of cynicism among many Muslim youth, who consider the Islamic schools to have nothing to say to their lived experience.

Yet whatever the failings of Islamic schools, they are not lacking able and eloquent defenders. So to the question, "What makes an Islamic school unique?" one is likely to hear that the students feel at peace, that the Islamic school fosters better character, and aligns the actions of students with God's will. School staff continues to provide abidingly strong support, even when the precise mission of the school is unclear and dire shortages in resources and faculty persist in those countries where direct government funding is unavailable.

What is more, there are rewards. So, for instance, one may hear how much better behaved Islamic schoolchildren are compared to other schools. This the staff attribute to a school philosophy built on *tarbiyah,*[23] a life guided by prayer, morality, and God-consciousness (*taqwa*). Academic excellence, too, is a feature every Islamic school wants to promote, especially to parents eager to see their child(ren) succeed in an intensely competitive environment. It is also not uncommon to hear from teachers and former Islamic school pupils (some of whom return to teach at their alma mater) that a feeling of unity prevails among the student body. This is the case especially as it concerns the dress code, prayer times, eating *halal* food, and celebrating Islamic holidays. Other items include a higher degree of adult supervision and concern, fewer cliques, and more self-confidence among the student body. In short, well-being is enhanced.

CONCLUDING REMARKS

In this chapter, I have elucidated the main themes in Islamic philosophy of education and in particular I have drawn attention to the fact that the individual, seen against the backdrop of an epistemology of faith, possesses a dual nature. In Islam, education does not merely serve the purposes of intellectual growth; rather, learning is part of what it is to be a created subject toward a larger cosmic purpose. Contrary to the Western custom of reasoning by way of doubt and uncertainty, Muslims—while encouraged to be critically minded—are called to an education built on the premise of faith in a divine order. Freedom to exercise one's intellect, on this understanding, must be restrained by an awareness of one's finitude. Furthermore, knowledge claims can only be predicated on the understanding that acquired knowledge is not likely to conflict with revealed knowledge as given in the Qur'ān and the *Sunna*. The curriculum in Islamic schools affirms the identity of the students in a way that the state and private schools systematically do not. Whether it is the role of Arabic scholarship in transmitting and enhancing valuable Greek education to the West or the different perspectives that attend social studies lessons, one's cultural identity and contribution is not degraded or ignored in Islamic schools; rather, it is affirmed, elaborated, and celebrated (at least for the majority ethnic group in a particular school).[24] This is not a multicultural education so much as it is an education for cultural coherence.

Though there are exceptions, in most cases Islamic schools follow the standard educational practices found in public and other private schools. They also insist upon a very high moral ethos. Teachers are expected to live up to the values that they teach, and accountability is highly regarded. At the same time, Muslim parents, like most parents, desire that their children attain high academic and vocational achievement. It remains an open question whether material competitiveness *an sich* is at loggerheads with the spiritual aims of Islamic education.[25]

The aims of Islamic education continue to be a challenge to Islamic educators in Western societies; to wit, locating the precise meaning of an Islamic curriculum and ascertaining how to integrate one's faith into a way of life that largely excludes Islam from the public sphere. Whether Islamic schools can successfully navigate this route, cultivating strong Muslim identities while at the same time aiding students in the integration process so essential to their identity as citizens of a liberal democracy, is still being assessed. Many Muslims claim that living in an environment in which they must interact daily with others who are unfamiliar with Islam or, more likely, have serious misconceptions about it, strengthens their faith.

This is as much an argument against Islamic schools as one for them. For those who opt for Islamic schools, the challenge of interpreting the

Islamic tradition remains. Muslims in the West are arguably better placed than anywhere in the world to give attention to interpretive polyvalence, to the benefits of democratic pluralism, and to the relevance of human experience to a living faith. Still, many teachers recognize that literal readings of the Qur'ān and the *sharī'āh* remain a problem.

Be that as it may, it cannot be denied that Muslim educators are seeking to have a fruitful parley between Western and Islamic norms. Yet this relationship to Western educational norms continues to divide most Muslim educators into two camps. The first camp plays host to those who are keen to locate commonalities with Western discourse and believe that many Islamic norms are in fact culturally based and must be jettisoned in deference to context-specific reinterpretation. Those in this camp will also see the *ummāh* as broader than the Islamic world, namely, to include the immediate space in which one dwells. As one *hadīth* says, "Loving one's country is a portion of one's faith." Those in this camp will also strongly oppose the blending of Islam with state building and instead liken the diaspora of Muslims in Western countries to Muhammad's own *hijra* or migration from Mecca to Medina. Yet many in this camp would also not send their own children to an Islamic school because they believe that it is only in "the world" that one comes to understand the meaning of living out one's faith.

Conversely, the second camp includes those who would seek to dissociate themselves from the corruption of Western ideas, inhabiting the *abode of apostasy* (*dar al-kufr*) and replacing them with normative Islamic ones. For the time being, the second camp is winning on the level of rhetoric and theory. But it is the first group that is prevailing in practice. The significance of this disjuncture augurs continued struggle for Islamic school educators.

Despite an overlying philosophical unity concerning the purposes of Islamic education, a great deal of diversity manifests itself in the practical realm. Indeed, Islam is every bit as much an internally conflicted religious community (Bilgrami, 1992) as any other. Therefore, inasmuch as Islamic schools seek to promote and emulate behaviors and beliefs that reflect a *true Islam*, it is necessary to distill its meaning and specifically to examine instances where conflicting notions of what it means to be a Muslim—of the sort I discussed above—can be found. A self-critical approach to Islamic education will allow Muslim students to openly question prohibitions on beliefs and practices even when it is widely believed that the Qur'ān has spoken definitively on the matter. Notwithstanding the tremendous assets one is likely to find in Islamic schools, there continue to be enormous challenges associated with the meaning of Islamic education. Further discussion, including a continued appeal to jurisprudence (*fiqh*),[26] both appropriate to Western contexts and sensitive to contextual considerations, must be sought after if Islamic schools are to have the efficacy and relevance needed to build strong Muslim character capable of tackling new challenges. This will entail moving beyond binary oppositions of *dar al-Islam* versus *dar al-harb* and will necessitate taking into account the freedoms, protections, and opportunities of Muslims to participate in society to a degree almost not found in the Islamic countries themselves. This attitude will avert a defensive posture against Western societies, naively believed by so many to be devoid of moral principles. Moreover, it will also facilitate a much-needed discussion among ordinary Muslims concerning different ways of appropriating the religious sources.

How Islamic schools in the West will address these challenges remains to be seen. Yet the fact remains that many Muslims are calling out for fresh reexaminations of their conceptual models and terminology. The formidable influences of popular culture, purveyed through various media and the hidden curriculum[27] (including children taken out of the state school system and placed in comprehensive religious schools), will exert considerable influence on a child's thinking. Simplistic moralizing and Islamic prohibitions, to which many immigrant Muslim children are exposed in after-school and weekend Qur'ānic classes, will not suffice to counter these influences, nor will they likely to appeal to the Muslim child without more culturally sensitive lessons that take account of non-Muslim societies.[28] There is no better time than the present for Islamic schools to begin tackling the challenges Muslim youth face with frankness and honesty. The alternative is waiting another generation when the controversy will be passé and acceptance, minus the standard vestigial resistance, will have become mainstream. Is it only the most reactionary Muslim voices that will have a say in this matter? Has all truth been settled once and for all in Islam? If Islamic education entails the cultivation of wisdom (*hikma*) (and possessing true wisdom, according to al-Attas, is being able to effect correct judgments as to the proper place of things), surely it is the Islamic school in the West that is best equipped to take up the charge of having this conversation.

NOTES

1. All italicized non-English words are in Arabic unless otherwise specified. Thanks to Safaa Zarzour for his careful checking of Arabic transliterations. Thanks also go to Jeffrey A. Milligan and Adam Nelson for reading and commenting on a previous draft.

2. It is necessary to distinguish between those who attempt to practice Islam and those, mainly in the West, who only see themselves as Muslim by virtue of their ethnic or national origin. Devout Muslims would likely assert that those I have just described are not really Muslims; however, many from either grouping do not see their Muslim identities as incompatible with

Western values. Secularism among Muslims can take two forms: (1) Islam is nothing more than the cultural forms (including music, dance, dress, and manners) that comprise one's identity, or (2) Islam is to be confined to the private sphere and not to be mixed with politics. Secularists, as well as many progressive believing Muslims, are also willing to recognize man-made laws, democratic institutions, and embrace education in its modern and secular forms. See S. Saadallah (2004) for a more elaborate discussion.

3.   Increasingly there are voices, notably Tariq Ramadan, who have incisively argued for the abrogation of this paradigm. Ramadan argues that this binary model fails to take account of different political arrangements today that make the practice of the Islamic faith, for instance, more possible in Western contexts than is to be found in many Islamic countries, where the governments are often hostile to all religious freedom. See T. Ramadan, *To be a European Muslim* (1999).

4.   The *Sunna,* a collection of the deeds of the Prophet Muhammad, serves as the model *par excellence* of morality for Muslims.

5.   This alleged scientific hostility to religion is a very narrow reading of the history of scientific inquiry. Many scientists then (Galileo, Faraday, Newton, etc.) as now (Polkinghorn, Einstein, Hawking) were interested to address questions having to do with human purpose and meaning.

6.   Here is an example of an ideal aim that is not reflected in reality. Most Islamic schools appear to track their students into different academic levels. This becomes more obvious in Islamic high schools, where one finds regular, accelerated, and advanced placement classes. These graded levels of difficulty in Islamic school classrooms would seem to facilitate—rather than downplay—inequalities among students.

7.   *Ijtihād* is the third arm of Islamic jurisprudence (the other two being the Qur'ān and the *Sunna*), though it is usually thought that only the jurist (*mujtahid*) or legal expert (*mufti*) is qualified among the leaders (*ulemā*) to make decisions according to *shari'āh* where the other sources are silent. The difficulty remains, however, because there are several traditional schools of law (*madhāhib*), including Shāfi'ī, Hanbalī, Mālikī and Hanafī. One's position with respect to *Ijtihād* will determine a great deal about one's position as an Islamic traditionalist, modernist, fundamentalist, etc. Traditionalists and fundamentalists (not to be confused with Radicalists) will incline toward the view that all truth for Muslims was canonized prior to the 13th century and thus no *ijtihād* is acceptable. All authority lies, therefore, in the period of the four major schools of interpretation and application of these canonized truths are limited to the *ulema* or clergy.

8.   Even when there is silence in the Qur'ān, there may be varying degrees of agreement.

9.   Sometimes *zakah* is translated as "poor tax."

10.   The Muslim God is an undifferentiated monad, with whom there can be no "associators." The notion of *šurik* or associating anything or anyone with God has its origins in the repudiation of the Christian doctrine of the Trinity. Many of the debates between Christians and Muslims ca. 700–950 CE focused on this doctrine.

11.   The prophets, of whom Muhammad is the last and final seal, are said by some to number 125,000. The Qur'ān mentions: Adam (the first Muslim), Ibrahīm (Abraham), Nûh (Noah), Musa (Moses), Ishaq (Isaac), Ya'qûb (Jacob), Dawûd (David), Yusuf (Joseph), Sulayman (Solomon), Idris, Ayyûb

(Job), Dhu l-Kifl, Hûd, Salih, Shu'ayb, Yûnus (Jonah), Zakariiyya (Zechariah), Yahya (John the Baptist), and Isa (Jesus). Jews and Christians will recognize most of these.

12. Of course, *jihād* carries a secondary meaning (one appropriated by militants) of "holy war" (i.e., armed struggle).

13. Many parents also continue to object. The events of 9/11 have removed much of this opposition, as more and more Western Muslims see the absolute necessity of conveying a positive image to a society that consumes only stereotypes concerning Islam.

14. I base many of the following comments on interviews I conducted during 2003–2004.

15. But this is not the case for everyone, and many children succumb to the same peer pressures that ordinary children do.

16. For these individuals, an encounter with the world outside of the Islamic school had not occurred to a significant degree before attending high school, and for those who attended an Islamic high school, this "awakening" often did not occur until university, where many students struggle to interact in coed situations, or to accept the lifestyle options of others. Some former Islamic school students confess that they believe public schools do a better job helping young people adjust to the "real world," and even many of the most eager proponents of Islamic education lament the absence of music in the curriculum, the social awkwardness of adolescent youths with the opposite sex, and the gendered nature of certain school activities. Many Muslim teachers acknowledge the shock that their graduates experience as freshmen in university. Open discussion about abortion, same-sex marriage and child adoption, euthanasia, depression, etc., catches many students unaware. Rejoinders to media reports from the Middle East can sometimes elicit impassioned knee-jerk reactions. Still, one former student explains, "After I recovered from my shock to hear certain topics being discussed so openly, and I paused to listen to what others had to say, I found that I was well equipped to handle it." Now she declares herself friends with many people with whose lifestyles and opinions she does not agree. Many former students admit that they wished they had been better prepared to anticipate challenges facing them in society, but most do not give the impression that they feel cheated by their Islamic education and typically speak highly of it (i.e., with considerable pride).

17. Free will (*qadariyyah*) exists, otherwise there would be no responsibility and human destiny would be predetermined (*taqdīr*).

18. Kambiz GhaneaBassiri writes, "The fact that Muslims do not have the same understanding of Islam prevents them from being able to unite behind [various] issues. What kind of Islam [will] be taught at school? Whose definition of Islam will be presented to non-Muslim Americans?" (1997, p. 185). Following the events of 9/11, a considerable amount of internal division among Western Muslims abated. This was likely the case in order that Muslims might combat Islamic stereotypes and profiling as well as to communicate their faith in a positive light to other Westerners.

19. To take one example, the issue of music and art in the curriculum of Islamic schools continues to be extremely contentious. There are those who would argue that music and depictions of animal or human faces in drawing or painting are strictly forbidden. Others take a more lenient view. Some Islamic schools, for example, allow paintings of persons as long as the facial

features are—in a kind of "impressionist" way—blurred. Perhaps a majority of Western Muslims considers music acceptable if one's intentions do not stray from basic Islamic principles, though one is likely to find many Muslims espousing a position publicly opposed to instruments in school while privately seeing to it that their own children receive lessons in the home. Consequently, with the exception of *a cappella* choirs, very few schools will venture to include instruments or musical appreciation into their curriculum. The same can be said for most cinema, photography, sculpture, and drawing. The various proscriptions are based on literal readings of the Qur'ān concerning verses that speak to those who craft objects "in competition with God." Moderate interpreters maintain that these references regard idol worship. (Much of Islamic aesthetics, accordingly, has been limited to architecture and calligraphy.) These issues are even more intractable to the extent that Islamic schools remain embroiled within *masjid* politics. If structural and administrative independence is established in relation to the mosque authorities, Islamic schools stand a much better chance of exercising the sort of critical role I have called for in this chapter.

20. In many so-called Islamic countries the illiteracy rates can reach 70% and even higher for girls. In many of these countries, for a variety of reasons, education is not a national priority.

21. Of particular concern is the Qur'ānic verse (4:34) that gives husbands permission to "beat" their wives if they fail to measure up to conjugal expectations. A great deal of debate surrounds the interpretation of this verse, but its very presence in the Qur'ān remains a formidable obstacle.

22. Cultural and denominational divisions can run so deep that many Muslims would rather their children marry a Christian or Jew than a Muslim of a different cultural or denominational background.

23. Tarbiyah, according to the Sufis, is concerned primarily with an individual's inner excellence.

24. This continues to be a problem within individual Islamic schools. Schools with, say, a majority of Palestianian or Pakistani students will in all likelihood cater to the cultural and political concerns of those respective groups (though they are seldom evenly divided; one is likely to find a school with a clear majority). Consequently, the cultural and political concerns of, say, the Bosnian or the African American are often ignored or neglected.

25. Certainly material prosperity within religious traditions has many precedents. Within Protestantism, the Calvinist work ethic gave credence to the idea that material gain was a sign of God's blessing. Examples can also be found in the Jewish scriptures and high-caste Hinduism and various schools of Buddhism (e.g., Sokka Gakkai).

26. This practice, *usūl al-fiqh*, continues to be a contested domain. Most Muslims believe that only those with a sophisticated knowledge of the Qur'ān, the *Sunna* and the Arabic language can qualify as a *mujtahid* (i.e., an individual capable of rendering prudent interpretations of the sources in order to issue sound advice or rulings [*fatāwā*]). While this opinion has the most defenders and is wise, considering the spurious claims to authority in issuing *fatāwā* (witness Khomeini's *fatwā* against Rushdie or bin Laden's *fatāwā* against American civilians, both of which were denounced by Muslim jurists), *usūl al-fiqh* remains problematic inasmuch as others, wishing to challenge traditional readings of the sources, are dismissed as amateurs and unable to understand the sources in their "true intent." The same line of argument was

used by the Catholic hierarchy against the laity for centuries. Only in the mid-20th century were Catholic biblical scholars allowed to openly contest traditional readings of the Christian sources (patristic, liturgical, and biblical), though many did so at great risk to their careers in the Church. Even so, few could question their knowledge of the Greek and Latin sources. Slowly, the same debate is beginning to unfold among Muslims.

27.   The hidden curriculum, for my purposes here, will refer to the *implicit* messages conveyed to schoolchildren through the attitudes and actions of school staff, one's peers, and materials used in classrooms.

28.   In a comparison with Irish Catholics and Ashkenazi Jews, Mustafa Malik argues that secularization in both groups was inevitable, owing to (1) interaction with coworkers and neighbors, thus eroding their sense of religious certainty; and (2) the rise of industrialization and technology, thus permitting them to rationalize the outcome of human actions (2004, p. 75).

REFERENCES

Abdullah, A. S. (1983). *Educational theory: A Qur'ānic outlook.* Makkah: Educational and Psychological Research Center.

Abdul-Rauf, M. (1983). The future of the Islamic tradition in North America. In E. H. Waugh, S. M. Abu-Laban, & R. B. Qureshi (Eds.), *The Muslim community in North America* (pp. 271–278). Edmonton, AB, Canada: University of Alberta Press.

Abu-Laban, B. (1983). The Canadian Muslim community: The need for a new survival strategy. In E. H. Waugh, S. M. Abu-Laban, & R. B. Qureshi (Eds.), *The Muslim community in North America* (pp. 75–92). Edmonton, AB, Canada: University of Alberta Press.

Ahmed, M. (1990). *Islamic education: Redefinition of aims and methodology.* New Delhi: Qazi.

Al-Attas, S. M. N. (1991). *The concept of education in Islam: A framework for an Islamic philosophy of education* (2nd ed.). Kuala Lumpur: International Islamic University.

Albertini, T. (2003). The seductiveness of certainty: The destruction of Islam's intellectual legacy by the fundamentalists. *Philosophy East and West, 53*(4), 455–470.

Al-Faruqi, I. (1982). *Islamization of knowledge: The problems, principles and the workplan.* Islamabad: National Hijra Centenary Committee of Pakistan.

Amri, N. (2000, May/June). Students speak out: Students discuss pros and cons of Islamic and public schools. *Islamic Horizons 7.*

Barazangi, N. H. (1990). The education of North American Muslim parents and children: Conceptual change as a contribution to Islamization of education. *American Journal of Islamic Social Sciences, 7*(3), 385–402.

Barazangi, N. H. (1991). Islamic education in the United States and Canada: Conception and practice of the Islamic belief system. In Y. Y. Haddad (Ed.), *The Muslims of America* (pp. 157–164). New York: Oxford University Press.

Barazangi, N. H. (2000, May). The equilibrium in Islamic education in the US. *ISIM Newsletter,* p. 30.

Bilgrami, A. (1992). What is a Muslim? Fundamental commitment and cultural identity. *Critical Inquiry, 18,* 821–843.

Bleher, S. M. (1996). A programme for Muslim education in a non-Muslim society. In *Issues in Islamic education* (pp. 61–65). London: Muslim Education Trust.

Dahlén A. (2002, October). Towards an Islamic discourse of uncertainty and doubt. *ISIM Newsletter,* p. 22.

Durkee, N. (1987). Primary education of Muslim children in North America. *Muslim Education Quarterly, 5*(1), 53–81.

GhaneaBassiri, K. (1997). *Competing visions of Islam in the United States: A study of Los Angeles.* Westport, CT: Greenwood Press.

Hewitt, I. (1996). The case for Muslim schools. In *Issues in Islamic education* (pp. 72–78). London: Muslim Education Trust.

Hilgendorf, E. (2003). Islamic education: History and tendency. *Peabody Journal of Education, 78*(2), 63–75.

Huntington, S. (1996). *The clash of civilizations and the remaking of world order.* New York: Simon & Schuster.

Husain, S. S. (1996). Islamising university education: Problems and prospects. In *Issues in Islamic education* (pp. 44–50). London, Muslim Education Trust.

Husain, S. S., & S. A. Ashraf (1979). *Crisis in Muslim education.* Jeddah, Saudi Arabia: Hodder & Stoughton.

Kazi, A. (1989). *On education.* Karachi, Pakistan: Royal Book Company.

Kazmi, Y. (2003). Islamic education: Traditional education or education of tradition? *Islamic Studies, 42*(2), 259–288.

Khan, M. A. M. (1998). Muslims and Identity Politics in America. In Y. Y. Haddad & J. Esposito (Eds.), *Muslims on the Americanization path?* (pp. 87–101). Oxford: Oxford University Press.

Khan, M. A. M. (2004, May/June). Rediscover knowledge. *Islamic Horizons,* 51–52.

Lewis, B. (1993). *Islam and the West.* New York: Oxford University Press.

Malik, M. (2001). Islam in Europe: Quest for a paradigm. *Middle East Policy, 8*(2), 100–115.

Malik, M. (2004). Muslims pluralize the West, resist assimilation. *Middle East Policy, 11*(1), 70–83.

Mohamed, Y. (1991). Knowledge in Islam and the crisis in Muslim education. *Muslim Education Quarterly, 4,* 13–31.

Nasr, S. H. (Ed.). (1987). *Islamic art and spirituality.* Albany: State University of New York Press.

Noakes, G. (1998). Muslims and the American press. In Y. Y. Haddad & J. Esposito (Eds.), *Muslims on the Americanization path?* (pp. 285–299). Oxford: Oxford University Press.

Pitts, L. (2004, September 27). An unfair question, but one that Muslim-Americans face all the time. *Wisconsin State Journal,* A6.

Ramadan, T. (1999). *To be a European Muslim.* Leicester, UK: Islamic Foundation.

Saadallah, S. (2004). Islam, religious orientations and education. In H. Daun & G. Walford (Eds.), *Educational strategies among Muslims in the context of globalization* (pp. 37–61). Leiden, The Netherlands: Brill.

Safi, O. (Ed.). (2003). *Progressive Muslims: On justice, gender and pluralism.* Oxford: Oxford University Press.

Sarwar, G. (1996). Islamic education: Its meaning, problems and prospects. In *Issues in Islamic Education* (pp. 7–23). London: Muslim Education Trust.

Schmidt, G. (2004). Islamic identity formation among young Muslims: The case of Denmark, Sweden and the United States. *Journal of Muslim Affairs, 24*(1), 31–45.

Sharifi, H. (1979). The Islamic as opposed to modern philosophy of education. In S. M. N. Al-Attas, *The concept of education in Islam: A framework for an Islamic philosophy of education* (pp. 76–88). Kuala Lumpur, Malaysia.

Stenberg, L. (2000, June). Science in the service of God: Islamizing knowledge. *ISIM Newsletter,* p. 11.

Surty, M. I. (1989). Muslim response to knowledge, *Muslim Education Quarterly, 4,* 17–22.

Tarazi, N. (2001, July/August). Who is teaching your child? *Islamic Horizons, 13.*

Waghid, Y. (1996). Why a theory of Islamic education cannot be epistemologically neutral. *Muslim Education Quarterly, 13*(2), 43–54.

Yousif, A. (2000). Islam, minorities and religious freedom: A challenge to the modern theory of pluralism. *Journal of Muslim Minority Affairs, 20*(1), 28–40.

Yusuf, S. (1992). Islamisation of knowledge: A workplan for Islamic nursery education, *Muslim Education Quarterly, 2,* 34–45.

CHAPTER 4

RELIGIOUS DIVERSITY IN WESTERN CANADIAN EDUCATION

Presumptions, Provisions, Practices, and Possibilities

Kimberly Franklin and Harro Van Brummelen
Trinity Western University

ABSTRACT

This chapter outlines how Canada's provisions for education have dealt with religion and religious issues within a multicultural, multireligious context. It examines current legal and political provisions for religious diversity in Canadian schooling, with an emphasis on the situation in Canada's westernmost provinces. Nine school administrators, teachers, and parents of various religious backgrounds respond to questions about their experiences with religious diversity in government public schools. The chapter teases out some common themes in their reflections. It then concludes by probing possibilities for providing a school system where stakeholders can express and uphold their religious identity without fear of reprisal, while at the same time

Religion in Multicultural Education, pages 71–99
Copyright © 2006 by Information Age Publishing

balancing such individual needs with the need of all citizens to contribute to a compassionate, just, equitable, and democratic society.

THE BACKDROP TO CULTURAL AND RELIGIOUS DIVERSITY IN CANADIAN SCHOOLING

One of the first formal schools in Canada and the first in Montreal was established by Marguerite Bourgeoys in 1658. A devout Catholic Christian, she had dedicated her life to imitating the life of Mary, the mother of Jesus. While at first she taught the children of French settlers, her passion to overcome poverty led her in 1676 to begin teaching reading, writing, arithmetic, and vocational skills to Aboriginal children as well as to older Aboriginal women—while also transmitting the Christian faith to persons who had a very different spiritual tradition (Clarke, 1998; Wilson, Stamp, & Audet, 1970).

Later, in the 19th century, education in English-speaking Canada was characterized by a fierce struggle about whether the (Anglican) Church of England should be the predominant influence in its public schools. Egerton Ryerson, often called the father of English-speaking public Canadian schools, was a convert from Anglicanism to Methodism. In 1846, upon becoming the chief superintendent of schools for Upper Canada (the province of Ontario), he resolved this dispute by founding a public school system that was generically Protestant Christian in its orientation. Ryerson never did succeed, however, in convincing Catholics, both French-speaking and English-speaking (many of the latter hailing from Ireland), to send their children to one unified *common* school system. In an 1857 letter to the press, the rector of the Catholic cathedral in Toronto wrote:

> Yes, a Catholic parent, who values his faith above all worldly advantages, and who rightly considers religion as the basis of all education, and the life of man upon earth, would rather doom his child to the horrors of the most degrading ignorance, than permit him to drink in the common Schools the poison of infidelity or heresy along with the pure draught of useful knowledge. (reprinted in Prentice & Houston, 1975, p. 140)

As a result of such strongly held views, a separate but publicly funded Catholic school system developed in Ontario alongside Ryerson's favored common structure. Later, the 1896 Canadian federal election was fought mainly on the issue of the rights of Catholics, most of whom were French-speaking Canadians, to establish their own publicly funded schools in the province of Manitoba. However, what became clear is that provincial governments rather than the federal one had the right to regulate schooling as long as they did not override some general constitutional provisions. As a result, this issue was not resolved until the late 1970s when Manitoba provided some funding for all religiously based independent schools.

The French–English and Catholic–Protestant disputes were not the only multicultural and religious conflicts that shaped Canadian schooling, however. Canada has a sad legacy of forced assimilation of Aboriginal children in residential schools. Furthermore, in 1898 the Superintendent of Education for the North West Territories (including what are now the provinces of Alberta and Saskatchewan) complained about colony schools having difficulty "assimilating" 12 different European cultural groups because they tended to settle in rural colony "blocks" and sometimes used teachers whose English left something to be desired: "If these children are to grow up as Canadian citizens they must be led to adopt our viewpoint and speak our speech"—"our" meaning Anglo-Protestantism (*Report of the Superintendent of Education*, 1898; reprinted in Prentice & Houston, 1975, p. 216). Anglo-Canadians feared religious influences in ethnic groups even though their own clergy did exercise influence on education through church-related groups (Jaenen, 1979). In the late 1970s, a survey showed that the British and the French cultures were still the main ones depicted in Canadian social studies curricula, with minority groups often portrayed as outsiders who clashed with the majority cultures despite being indebted to them (Tomkins, 1986).

These examples make clear that religious and multicultural diversity and concomitant issues have been part and parcel of Canadian society and its schools during most of its recorded history. However, a number of factors has led to a broader scope and increased recognition of cultural and religious pluralism. While immigration in the 1940s and 1950s was primarily from Europe and predominantly Christian, today the majority of immigrants come from various parts of Asia, representing many different ethnic and religious backgrounds. At the same time, within Canada a growing proportion of persons have adopted nonreligious or nontraditional spiritual positions. Moreover, there has been a renaissance of Aboriginal culture and religion. As well, in the 1970s Canada's federal government declared cultural pluralism to be a fundamental characteristic of Canadian society, although in practice the accommodation of difference still took place within the dominant liberal cultural perspective (Ghosh & Abdi, 2004; Tomkins, 1986).

During the past 50 years, the preponderance of European immigrants has faded away, with most immigrants now arriving from Asia and the Caribbean. This has resulted in the school population in major Canadian cities representing an increasing multiplicity of religious backgrounds (in 2006 Canada's 33 million inhabitants are expected to include about 850,000 Muslims and 350,000 adherents of each of the Jewish, Buddhist, Hindu, and Sikh faiths (Statistics Canada, 2005). The largest city on Canada's west coast, Vancouver, is one of the most ethnically and religiously diverse cities in the world. For more than half of its elementary and secondary students English is not their first language. Their religious backgrounds include all the major world religions as well as Aboriginal spirituality. In Surrey, a large Vancouver suburb, a significant number of schools have only a small minority of students with a Christian background, with students of the Sikh, Muslim, and Buddhist faiths being strongly represented. Furthermore, the number of students in nonpublic schools in British Columbia has steadily increased and now represents more than 10% of the total school population. Most of these schools are religiously based because of parental dissatisfaction with the trend in Canadian society and in public education to banish religion to the private sphere of life. These schools, until recently exclusively Catholic, Protestant, and Jewish, now embrace a growing number of Islamic, Sikh, and Baha'i schools as well. Add to this mix the view often expressed by previously marginalized minorities that Christians have endeavored to maintain their historical dominance in Canadian culture, it is understandable that debates and conflicts about the place of religious faith in Canadian schools have been widespread.

In this context a key issue becomes how schooling in Canada can be conceptualized and provided so that it finds support among the various sectors of its multicultural, multireligious society. Such schooling needs to respond respectfully to the religious diversity represented by all stakeholders. It must allow children of all religious backgrounds to be free to develop as whole and healthy individuals. However, schools also need to prepare children to become contributing members of Canadian society—a society that will be able to thrive only on the basis of shared common values that provide the cement for a compassionate and robust democratic society. Teachers, at the same time, should not feel inhibited by their own religious beliefs, while, particularly in public school classrooms, they must allow their students to explore their spirituality without imposing their own beliefs. This chapter, therefore, investigates provisions for and experiences of religious diversity in Canadian education, emphasizing the British Columbia context.

THE PRESUMPTION OF A LIBERAL WORLDVIEW IN CANADIAN EDUCATION

The Council of Ministers of Education of Canada (1992) recognized and lent support to cultural, linguistic, and religious diversity in education:

> Canada is a highly diversified country in every respect. Linguistic, racial, cultural and religious differences, within and among provinces and territories,

are a fundamental characteristic of its people. We view this pluralism as a source of great richness for the country, and believe that its strength lies in maintaining a profound respect for differences. (p. 1)

Yet, a gulf exists between this statement and the reality in many Canadian schools where "some important differences between Canadians are barely tolerated, let alone accepted or celebrated" (Badley, 2000, p. 55). Badley describes how the Canadian Muslim population, for instance, rejects the neutrality of Canadian public schools, claiming that they are devoid of the sense of the Sacred and as such impose a secular Western conception of knowledge that is diametrically opposed to their view that the hand of Allah is on all of life. This is a reason why some Muslim parents send their children to Christian schools when Islamic ones are unavailable. Moreover, Badley continues, by and large Canadian curricula give only minimal attention to Aboriginal epistemology. Even schools controlled by Aboriginal bands, according to Aboriginal leaders, indoctrinate their children with a worldview inimical to traditional Aboriginal spirituality. These leaders object to the narrow focus of the mission statement of British Columbia's public schools that emphasizes that schools must "enable learners to develop individual potential and to acquire the knowledge, skills and attitudes needed to contribute to a healthy society and a prosperous and sustainable economy" (British Columbia Ministry of Education, 2005, p. 1).

In British Columbia one reason is that its *School Act* states that its public schools "must be conducted on strictly secular and non-sectarian principles" (2002, par. 76 (1)). The interpretation of this clause has meant that almost all religious and spiritual concerns have been excised from consideration in British Columbia's public schools. For instance, science curriculum guides in British Columbia warn teachers that no religious beliefs or theories based on beliefs may be presented in the course of instruction, including reference to intelligent design, despite the fact that such questions often arise in research in cosmology (British Columbia Ministry of Education, 1996). A compulsory grade 10 course that deals with life, career, and health issues has only one brief reference to religion, suggesting that students could make a poster or collage to illustrate the interconnectedness of physical, intellectual, emotional, spiritual, and social health (British Columbia Ministry of Education, 2004). Even for historical periods when religion played an important role, social studies curriculum guides almost neglect its role. For instance, only one of 28 learning outcomes for the years 1500–1815 A.D. mentions religion: "Assess how identity is shaped by a variety of factors including family, gender, belief systems, ethnicity, and nationality" (British Columbia Ministry of Education, 1997, p. 24).

These examples illustrate that British Columbia's public schools attempt to be religiously neutral by banishing nearly all discussion of religious and spiritual issues from their programs and by minimizing its relevance for life and culture. Yet by so doing, rather than remaining neutral, the public school system restricts real freedom of religion in schools. It does not allow students to explore what for many is a way of contemplating and encountering the underlying mysteries and issues of life in the universe. Such deliberate exclusion endorses at best a passive ignorance of religious meanings, and at worst creates hostility and intolerance of religious perspectives in society. School programs have, as such, contributed to acceptance of the view held by many Canadian political and societal leaders that religious beliefs may not affect the consideration of issues debated in the public square.

Philosopher Hendrik Hart (2000) has shown that liberalism as a theory of society, together with its conception of tolerance, has been a main factor in establishing freedom and democracy in the West. But he also argues that liberalism is ideologically intolerant in that its domination of public policy has curtailed what may be considered *public*. In other words, while liberalism holds that the highest good is for humans to be free and autonomous, it favors the separation of religion from politics and public policy. Therefore, in practice it does not allow religious views to influence society and de facto curtails the role of religion in life. Thus it has prevented a more radical freedom and democracy where persons and communities are allowed to practice their spiritual passion publicly within a compassionate civic ethos. The question that arises is whether the epistemic privilege of Western Enlightenment liberalism ought to be or even can be sustained in a multicultural, multifaith society. Liberalism, in the view of those who believe that their religious faith is the foundation of their life's praxis, trivializes religious differences, takes away the meaning of particular religions by forcing their removal from the public realm (Marshall, 2000).

This general societal issue leads to educational questions. Legitimate questions have been raised about the restricted view of spirituality in government-mandated programs. How can Canadian society provide schooling where persons of religious minorities will feel that their voice is heard and taken into account? How can a society disagree with the religious views of others and yet show true tolerance by allowing such views to have a legitimate place in Canadian schools? While schools cannot be neutral, is it possible for public education to be impartial and fair to the diverse points of view in a multireligious society? Is it right for the state to impose a school system designed to espouse only what Holmes (1990) calls low-doctrine values such as the right to determine what each person believes or does?

True tolerance, many claim, means that we must support school choice on philosophical and religious grounds, and make this possible financially both within and outside of the public system. Others respond that provision for publicly funded schools of choice leads to the fragmentation of a society and the eventual undermining of democratic principles and human rights. They hold that it is desirable for children of all cultural groups and religions to attend a neighborhood school that forms a cohesive learning community. But the (limited) research suggests that schools with a homogeneous philosophical and religious base are more successful in nurturing young adults who are tolerant and become more involved in contributing to the social and political life of a nation (Cooper, 1972; Erickson, Macdonald, & Manley-Casimir, 1979; Godwin, Ausbrooks, & Martinez, 2001; Smith & Sikkink, 1999). The reality in the two westernmost Canadian provinces is that stratification of the student population by cultural background—and hence also by religion—is already occurring, particularly in major population centers. This has resulted from ethnoreligious groups settling in certain neighborhoods, from parents having the right to choose which public school their children will attend, from the increasing number of alternative programs in both public and independent schools, and from Aboriginal people increasingly establishing schools that will sustain their cultural and spiritual ideals. The liberal ideal of one homogeneous, common school system may well be fading.

THE LEGAL CONTEXT OF RELIGIOUS DIVERSITY IN CANADIAN SCHOOLING

Canada has never had an established church, but neither has it had the American history of a strict division between church and state. Section 93 of the 1867 British North America Act, Canada's original constitution, assigned exclusive control of education to the provinces, subject only to conditions regarding existing publicly funded denominational schools. Because of provincial control of education, provisions for religious diversity in Canadian schooling have varied widely. On the east coast of Canada the state-funded schools in the province of Newfoundland until 1998 were operated by various church denominations. On the other hand, in British Columbia the public schools were legislated to be nondenominational from their inception in 1872, and for more than a century there was no provision for government financial support of religiously based schools. That does not mean that the schools were religiously neutral: British Columbia's first prescribed textbooks assumed a literal interpretation of the Bible and promoted a belief in orthodox Christian doctrines. However, in accordance with the shifting prevalent views of political and educational leaders, gradually the links to Christian faith waned and morality was severed from its religious roots (Van Brummelen, 1986).

Until the passing of Canada's 1982 *Constitution Act,* which incorporated *The Canadian Charter of Rights of Freedoms,* Canadian courts were reluctant to intervene in the provincial political regulation of education. A 1971 court decision quoted the Chief Justice of the Supreme Court of Canada as saying that "it is necessary for good administration, municipal or school, that those who are charged with it... are not hampered in the exercise of their duty by the intervention of the courts of justice except by grave reasons" (*Ward v. Board of Blain Lake School Unit 57*, 1971). Thus, when, for instance, the Doukhobors in British Columbia refused to send their children to public schools because of their religious beliefs, the Court upheld the local school board's insistence on attendance. It also incorporated a liberal worldview by declaring that it "absolutely rejected" the contention that tenets such as opposition to war and materialism can "take on a religious colour" (*Perepolkin v. the Superintendent of Child Welfare of B.C.*, 1958).

Before 1982, most provinces mandated or allowed schools to be opened with Christian prayer and the reading of passages from the Christian Bible. The courts did uphold the rights of parents to withdraw their children from religious observances and instruction, as in the case when a Quebec public school expelled some Jehovah Witness children for refusing to participate in Catholic Christian religious exercises (Guldemond, 1990). After the *Charter of Rights and Freedoms* was enacted, the courts became more active and made a number of decisions relating to religious diversity in schooling. Above all, the Courts have construed the *Charter* to mean that public schools must be secular. As Justice Sopinka of the Supreme Court of Canada put it, "The reason why the public school system is not acceptable to the [Adler parents] lies in its secular nature. This secular nature is itself mandated by 2.2(a) of the *Charter* as held by several courts in this country" (*Adler v. Ontario*, 1996, par. 705). Thus when an Ontario court dismissed a request of Muslim parents to close predominantly public schools on two Muslim holy days, the court defended its decision by arguing that closures on Christmas, Good Friday, and Easter Monday were secular and not designed to observe Christian celebrations (*Islamic Schools Federation of Ontario v. Ottawa Board of Education*, 1997).

However, the courts have not been entirely consistent in their interpretation of the meaning of secular. Courts in several provinces have ruled that religious exercises in public schools infringe on the freedom of religion and conscience guaranteed by the *Charter* since Christian practices are no longer acceptable to some citizens. Courts in Ontario have gone one step further. In *Bal v. Ontario* (1994), parents argued that by offering only a secular program, public schools are coercive and undermine their religious values. Therefore, they should have an "opting-in" possibility of religious instruction in their own faith. The court disagreed, not only holding that the public school system is secular, but also that "secularism is not coercive, it is neutral." What that has meant in practice is that the previous existence of several alternative Christian schools within the public system in Ontario could not continue. More broadly, in order to protect minority groups from mandatory rules relating to religion, the court effectively said that religion has no place in Canada's public schools. In other words, freedom *of* religion was equated with freedom *from* religion, without considering the possibility "that freedom of religion might require an accommodation of all religions in the public school system" (Brown, 2000, p. 592).

Nevertheless, recent Supreme Court of Canada decisions indicate that its conception of secular does not hold that religion must be totally banned from the public square, including education. In a recent case involving the use of books depicting same-sex parent families with young students in public schools, the Supreme Court said that "the Board must act in a way that promotes respect and tolerance for all the diverse groups that it represents and serves.... The requirement of secularism ... simply signals the need for educational decisions and policies, whatever their motivation, to respect the multiplicity of religious and moral views that are held by families in the school community" (*Chamberlain v. Surrey School District No. 36,* 2002, par. 25 & 59). Similarly, courts have ruled that the *Charter* prohibits public schools to instruct in any particular religion, but allows them to educate students about various religions as long as they avoid promoting that students conform to any one belief.

Even so, uncertainty exists about what role persons with deeply held religious faith commitments can play in Canada's public schools. Canada's Supreme Court has ruled, for instance, that graduates of a Christian teacher education program should receive certification to teach in a public school since "freedom of religion is not accommodated if the consequences of its exercise is the denial of the right of full participation in society" (*Trinity Western University v. The British Columbia College of Teachers,* 2001, par. 43). Yet it added that while "tolerance of divergent beliefs is a hallmark of a democratic society, acting on those beliefs ... is a very different matter" (*TWU v. BCCT,* 2001, par. 37). On the one hand, the Court made clear that religiously based organizations as well as individuals can hold religious beliefs while participating in the public square. On the other hand, the Court's ruling contained an implicit warning that acting on those religious beliefs may have detrimental consequences. Indeed, the Court, by deciding not to deal with a more recent case, implicitly upheld the suspension of a Christian teacher by the British Columbia College of Teachers for writing letters in a local paper that questioned the wisdom of promoting a homosexual agenda (*Kempling v. The British Columbia College of Teachers,* 2004 and 2005). Even though no members of the school community complained about the teacher's writings, lower courts ruled that his actions might lead to controversy within the school system that would disrupt its proper functioning. The teacher is filing a formal complaint with the United Nations Commission on Human Rights, believing that free speech for religious minorities has been compromised (Jason, 2006). The study in this chapter suggests that teachers with religious convictions may already conceil or "veil" their religious beliefs in public schools since they find it difficult to walk the fine line between belief and conduct. The *Kempling* decision will no doubt result in increased innate as well as external suppression of religious views in Canadian public schools.

PROVISIONS FOR RELIGIOUS DIVERSITY IN BRITISH COLUMBIA'S SCHOOLS

Many of British Columbia's early schools were religiously based. However, in the 1860s both leading newspaper editors (both future premiers of the province) campaigned for nondenominational public education in order to prevent Anglican domination and to promote a more unified society. After British Columbia joined Canada in 1871, most class- and denominationally based schools were replaced by free and public schools that were to be "conducted upon strictly non-sectarian principles" (British Columbia Government, 1872, par. 85). While the separation of church and state was never formally adopted, British Columbia's public school system has been guided by the American interpretation of this principle in education.

The first superintendent of public schools in British Columbia, John Jessop, was a former student and admirer of Egerton Ryerson. He outdid Ryerson, however, in fulfilling what had been Ryerson's dream: the establishment of one common system without a parallel separate, publicly funded Catholic school system. Predictably the opposition to this came mainly from the Catholic and Anglican communities. In 1881, for instance, the Catholic bishops petitioned the provincial legislature for the funding of denominational schools, claiming that public schools favored "only the sect of irreligionists" and that "the absence of religious instruction in school does generally bring forth immoral youths, and consequently is a source of evil" (Prentice & Houston, 1975, pp. 159–160). However, the government rejected the appeal. By 1887, all Anglican church schools had collapsed, and by the end of the century almost all independent schools were unregulated Catholic ones (Van Brummelen, 1996).

Several factors militated against the rapid growth of religiously based schools. First, during the first century of British Columbia's existence as a province, its leaders held that only common public schools could nurture and sustain a unified and tolerant society. Until 1977 they therefore withheld using public funding to support nonpublic schools. Also, until the 1940s small one- and two-room public schools were the only realistic educational possibility outside B.C.'s few urban centers (Van Brummelen, 1996). Nevertheless, four developments resulted in nonpublic school enrollment accelerating after World War II. First, several groups of immigrants, notably Dutch Calvinists and Mennonites (and more recently Sikhs and Muslims), felt that public school attendance would weaken the faith of their children. They saw religiously based schools as a means to preserve their religious identity. Also, more parents, particularly in the evangelical Christian community, perceived public education to be failing to instill strong morals, discipline, and standards, and saw the legal removal of Christian religious exercises from the schools as an affront to their faith. Simultaneously, official endorsement of multiculturalism meant increasing tolerance of pluralism, including the acceptability of educational alternatives to neighborhood public schools. Finally, government funding of nonpublic schools began in 1977 and for religious schools is now usually half of the operational costs of public schools. Tuition fees decreased, but, just as importantly, the schools gained legitimacy through government inspections and classification (Van Brummelen, 1996).

Today, religiously based nonpublic schools comprise about 8% of B.C.'s total school enrollment, and include Catholic and Evangelical Protestant Christian schools as well as Jewish, Sikh, Islamic, and Baha'i ones. While the funded schools must meet the Ministry of Education's basic prescribed curriculum outcomes, there are few restrictions on schools teaching curriculum content within their own religious and philosophical framework other than that their students must participate in the provincial Foundation Skills Assessment Tests and high school diploma examinations. What is still an open question is whether these schools have prepared their graduates to address the problems of modern life within the religious, ethical, and social worldview that they propound, or whether their students tend to conform to society as much as their public school counterparts.

In the last 25 years, there has also been parental pressure for schools of choice within the public system. As a result, parents can send their children to French immersion, Japanese immersion, fine arts, environmental, and traditional schools. While so-called traditional and fundamental schools are popular and maintain Judeo-Christian values, the schools by law must remain secular and nonsectarian. This is unlike the neighboring province of Alberta where a significant number of private Christian schools have become Christian alternatives within the public system. Of the 203 schools in the 80,000-student Edmonton Public School System, 80 schools have one or more program specialties. Half of those are immersion and bilingual language and related cultural programs (including Arabic, Mandarin, and Ukrainian). Just as significantly, there are programs that maintain Aboriginal and Jewish culture and traditions, and 12 Christian ones that "help students examine and understand a biblical perspective when studying the curriculum...[and] learn to demonstrate knowledge, skills and attitudes that reflect Christian teachings and principles" (Edmonton Public Schools, 2005, p. 19).

The Edmonton Public Schools, like others in Alberta, have opened their doors to communities with diverse worldviews and perspectives that previously have not found a home in public education. The popularity of the wide range of alternatives indicates that parents, teachers, and students favor cultural and religious choices in education, particularly when there is little or no additional cost. In British Columbia, however, parents with deep religious commitment must make different choices. Some accept that the education of their children will marginalize what they hold to be most important in life. Others pay tuition fees to independent religiously based schools that cover about half the cost of their children's education. Still others challenge the public system, trying to influence it to become more open to religiously held views. Teachers with a deeply held faith commitment also face a dilemma. In British Columbia's public school setting, they may not promote their faith in any way or form. The values they uphold must be those that are generally accepted by society's leaders, and not necessarily what they believe themselves. They may, for instance, be required to participate in actions that oppose their beliefs (e.g., participate in a strike). Yet by teaching in independent religious schools, where their faith may permeate their praxis, their salary and benefits will likely be less and they may well feel marginalized from the mainstream of education. How do religious parents, teachers, and pre-service teachers respond to playing their roles in British Columbia's public schools? That is the focus of the next section.

EXPERIENCING RELIGIOUS DIVERSITY IN BRITISH COLUMBIA'S PUBLIC SCHOOLS

In order to gain insight about current experiences related to religious diversity, we asked 11 individuals active in public education in various parts of British Columbia to complete an open-ended questionnaire. The participants were chosen for their varied viewpoints about public education and their diverse spiritual identities. They included parents, teachers (both experienced and beginning), and school administrators. We asked the participants to characterize their spiritual identities, and for the purpose of this chapter we will identify the nine that responded as follows: Administrator, Humanist (AH); Administrator, Jew (AJ); Parent, Muslim (PM); Experienced teacher, Agnostic (ETA); Parent, Christian (PC); Beginning teacher, Christian (BTC); Experienced teacher, Christian (ETC#1); Experienced teacher, Christian #2 (ETC#2); and Administrator, Christian (AC). The five self-identified Christian participants represent a denominational range that is helpful in understanding varied experiences and understandings.

The participants responded by email to 10 research questions (listed at the end of the chapter). They reported that the questionnaire took approximately 2 hours to complete. The small number of participants limits the conclusions that can be drawn. However, we expect that their varied experiences and understandings will resonate to some degree with other participants in public education. While we did not include direct student voices, several participants did speak of their experiences as public school students. The responses will, we hope, provoke additional inquiry.

All respondents except ETA saw their motivation for participating in public education as clearly connected with their spiritual identity and strongly focused on the greater good of society rather than on public education itself. ETA, also outwardly motivated, highlighted his appreciation for young people and his ability to help them find their path. Some viewed the system as already *best* for children in bringing about a greater good for society (AH, AJ, ETA, PM). However, others wanted to effect change within the system in order to transform society (PC, BTC, ETC #1, ECT#2, AC). ECT#1 gave an ambivalent response. She did not necessarily choose the public system, but wanted to "bloom" where God had planted her. PC expressed a very direct desire to reach the world for Christ: "The chief motivating factor is the realization that people need Jesus and without Him, they will spend eternity forever separated from God." BTC also expressed an additional motivation arising out of personal experience:

> Another central motivation for teaching comes from the way religion was dealt with when I was a student. Growing up in the public system, I always felt a sense of shame because of my faith. By teachers and peers, my faith was seen as an emotional, nonintellectual aspect of me....This mindset almost destroyed my motivation to pursue purpose in my life....Therefore, one other motivation to teach comes from my desire to help students understand that spirituality is central to who we ALL are as human beings. It is a very real part of our history, who we are now, and who we have the potential to be.

The second question asked respondents to consider how their spiritual identity impacts their role in public education. All indicated that their spiritual identity had a direct even if implicit connection to how they act, especially with respect to the teaching of values and morals (AJ, PM, ETC#2) or the choosing of methods and resources (ETC#1). AH said that simply acting within public education and supporting its purpose was the living out of his spiritual identity. On the other hand, AC (an ordained Anglican deacon), said that his spiritual identity enhanced his role as administrator. He called his work a ministry in which he became a respected bridge between the church and world.

> During my years as a member of my local school administrators' association, I was the unofficial chaplain and was called on for prayers on many

occasions.... In my early years of teaching, I co-sponsored "Tuesday Club," a ministry sponsored by Inter Varsity Christian Fellowship. My English students also know that I have drawn upon my worldview in teaching literature and stimulating class discussion. My Christian commitment also motivated me to develop a course in comparative religions for grade 11 students.... As an ordained deacon, I have participated in or conducted weddings and funerals for colleagues and their family members.

PC also viewed her role as "bridge building" in bringing the presence of God and His principles into a world separated from him.

Had the respondents ever concealed their spirituality while acting within the public education system? AH, AC, ECT#1, and ECT#2 had never made the conscious choice to conceal their spirituality, although ECT#2, while never concealing her Christian identity, did make conscious choices to remain silent when a reaction clearly rooted in her spirituality would not be welcome. AJ discussed her need to initially conceal her spirituality due to concerns about anti-Semitism. These concerns became real in interactions with students at the beginning of her career:

In my first teaching job, one of my grade 7 students told me someone had "jewed him down." I pointed out that this was an inappropriate thing to say. He countered by telling me it was alright because his dad said it all the time. I did not tell him I was Jewish.

While she had less need to conceal when working within schools with a number of Jewish children, AJ again made a conscious choice not to be open about being Jewish when she applied for an administrative position:

Initially, I believe my appointment was blocked by an associate superintendent who knew I was Jewish and made oblique allusions to this. She suggested that I list the church groups I worked with on my administrative application. When she retired, I got a vice-principalship. A few years later I became the first Jewish principal in the district. Once I was appointed to administration, I did not conceal my religion. I don't believe there were negative consequences to my "disclosure" after this point.

Others also made choices to consciously conceal their spiritual identity. In order to avoid a confrontation about his concerns about the celebration of Halloween, PM had his daughter stay home from school for 2 days. However, he mentioned that he now does things differently, calling his initial choice unwise. "I am there in the system and give my input." PC recorded that she made a number of conscious choices to conceal her spirituality. Active in parent committees, she disagreed at times, on a spiritual/moral basis, with the committee's actions. She would choose to argue her view on secular grounds, recognizing the greater potential for success. For instance, she had a decision changed about a fortune teller being secured at a school fund-raiser based on financial reasoning. BTC spoke about her choice to suppress her personal spirituality when answering student questions:

> One student asked another why his father did not want to celebrate Christmas. This grade 2 student...struggled with the fact that his friend's father wouldn't want to believe in the "Christmas spirit." I explained to this boy that we celebrate Christmas for another important reason as well—the birth of Christ. He asked quite a few questions, especially regarding the truth of the story of Christ. I simply said that many people believed it and it was very important to them (nondirectly asserting my own beliefs). I told him that he should ask his mom what his family believes....I admit that it was hard for me to not jump and say, "Yes, all of this is true—it's eternal life you're talking about here!" But my goal as a school teacher is not to evangelize....I see my role as showing children that faith is a very real, influential, life-changing part of many people's lives.

ETC#1, unlike her actions as a teacher, did mention that as a student teacher she had concealed her spiritual identity based on her perceptions about her institution's reputation in regard to Christians.

The next question asked the reverse: Had the respondents ever deliberately revealed their spirituality in the public school setting? Only one participant (AH) had never done so. After she became an administrator, AJ made it known when she began work in a new school. That, she believed, affected the school's celebrations of religious holidays. While her revelations caused some controversy, it also increased sensitivity and understanding. PM also felt that his "proper explanation" helped to remove barriers to understanding. During a religious celebration, his request to support his child's need to fast was met with "full understanding and support." ETA revealed his spiritual upbringing when students would bring up the issue of spirituality, in part to help to build rapport or understanding. BCT mentioned making similar choices. She tried to ensure that "other children do not feel alienated because they do not go to church or share the same faith" since her role was to educate and empower every child. ETC#2 did not "advertise" her Christianity, focusing mainly on acting as a Christian. However, she did feel that parents should know there are Christians on staff "so that they can make requests for their children to be (or not to be) in certain classrooms." When appropriate, she did not hesitate to openly discuss spiritual issues with parents.

ETC#1 was unique in her unconcealed approach to living out her spiritual identity in a public setting, particularly in regard to speaking vocally about issues related to gay marriage. However, she did mention that being in a school that is highly multicultural (mainly Indo-Canadian and Muslim) helped because the parents' and students' religious views coincided with hers on this issue. While most teachers openly supported issues such as gay marriage and warned her that she might lose her teaching certificate, she added that she treats gay people with respect and has the right to freedom of speech with respect to gay issues, pointing out that students generally support her views: "So far, I have not had any serious repercussions, because I usually say that if I lose my license to my disagreement with the gay issues, then so be it." PC revealed her spirituality when a group of parents requested the establishment of a fundamental school. She felt that the separation of students within the public system was based on a Christian agenda, and she opposed the creation of this school on that basis, revealing her identity so that others would know that not all Christians were "intolerant" of homogeneous public schools.

The fifth question asked if respondents had ever identified religious intolerance while participating in the public education system. AH commented on his vigilance about the purpose of public schools and his desire to protect students:

> I have had to contend with demands for tolerance or recognition of different religious beliefs.... The students of a public school are brought together for a purpose and I was always sensitive to protecting that purpose and those students from elements within the community who wanted access to the "captured" group for one purpose or another that reflected their agenda, and not the agenda of the school and its community.

Other respondents mentioned many specific incidents of perceived intolerance. These included affirming only Christian religious holidays in a public setting (AJ, ECT#1); using a Christian cross as a Remembrance Day symbol (AJ); renaming Christmas as a winter festival (ETA); shunning persons participating in a parent prayer group (PC) and colleagues showing dislike of Christians (BCT); the teaching certification authority taking a teacher education program to Canada's Supreme Court because of its religious stance (BCT); Muslims and Sikhs resenting the Christian content in Canadian history and literature (ECT#1); being "scolded" by colleagues for not decorating the classroom on Halloween (ECT#1); imposing a decision no longer to purchase explicitly Christian literature for the library (ECT#2); a Jewish parent challenging the reading of *The Legend of the Candy Cane* (ECT#2); parents accusing a teacher of expressed favoritism when a student writing sample with a Christian message was put in the school newsletter (ECT#2); being prevented from participating in the parents' prayer group when held on school property (ECT#2); lacking the freedom to discuss religious issues, celebrations, or questions about God without some fear of reprisal (ECT#2); and openly teaching and promoting First Nations culture and religious practices (ECT#2).

AC stated that the only intolerance he observed was from professed Christian teachers who opposed the inclusion of religious practices such as Aboriginal sweet grass ceremonies or places and times for Muslims to pray: "I have had to 'stickhandle' these kinds of attitudes that have reinforced stereotypical pictures of Evangelical Christians as bigoted and intolerant." PM was the only respondent who quite adamantly expressed that he had not observed or experienced any intolerance at all.

Next, all respondents expressed the reality of religious diversity as a feature of public education in Canada that was here to stay. They characterized such diversity as important to build understanding and the ability to live together, but recognized its complexity, requiring ongoing negotiation:

> I believe that religion, especially ethics, should be part of the school system. It needs comprehensive research of what/whose to be accommodated. I wish to see the next generation knows more about others not through media but educational systems. That could benefit individuals and the Canadian society. (PM)

AJ and BCT also expressed concerns that children were not being served well because teachers feel inadequate and insecure about addressing religious issues and therefore avoid it entirely or inadvertently support a hierarchy of religions. ETA thought that courses like Comparative Religions fostered the kind of dialogue needed between people of different faiths. He also emphasized the need for teachers to be quite neutral so that students were able to make their own determination of spiritual identity. PC and ETC#2 saw a trend of increasing intolerance of Christian beliefs, feeling that increased open-mindedness toward plurality might unwittingly limit Christian freedom. This view was shared by ETC#1 who said that the level of accommodation made to please all religions and their holidays may require significant changes in education that are not in harmony with principles of democracy. In contrast, however, AC held that religious diversity opened possibilities for Christians:

> Religious diversity gives opportunity for productive dialogue and community building.... Professionally, educators now enter into dialogue with colleagues of a variety of faiths (or no faith) and those of differing sexual orientations. Christians must be prepared for this exciting opportunity. We cannot claim a privileged position in the public school system—nor can any other religious or faith group. We must find ways ... to be a credible, creative voice speaking with integrity and for the greater public good. We must not be seen as promoting narrow self-interested agendas as has often been the case.

Our seventh question asked if respondents had ever placed demands on the public education system to accommodate religious diversity. AH and

ETA did not recall ever doing this, but AH expressed that many demands had been made on him. ETA thought the system was quite accommodating and rightfully left the religious realm to the individual and their family. ETC#1 expressed that she had never placed a demand, but had and continues to have many placed on her, particularly from the Muslim community. BTC has never yet felt the need to make a request for accommodation, and is currently focused on being as accommodating as possible in relation to the various nationalities and faiths represented in her classroom.

AJ worked for accommodation through discussion about religious holidays and the potential of disenfranchising students when Christianity is presented as the norm; however, she was willing to require compliance if understanding could not be achieved. PC asked the public system to accommodate her desire to provide her children with sex education at home during the primary years. She found the system to be very accommodating at that level, but less accommodating at the secondary level in regard to the same issue. ETC#2 expressed a principle of "being as wise as a serpent, and as gentle as a dove" guiding any demands she has made. She came "close to being demanding" when told she could not pray with the parent prayer group, but eventually chose only to pray with the group when it met off school grounds. AC, on the other hand, actively facilitated dialogue between faiths and accommodations for students of all faiths to be allowed times and places to worship on school grounds.

Our eighth question asked respondents how the law of "secular and nonsectarian" was interpreted in the various public school settings of their experience. The responses indicated a wide range of interpretations, usually based on the leadership and/or the school community. AH defined secular as "not concerned with the religious or spiritual" and nonsectarian as "not concerned with a particular group." His responses to previous questions indicated that his interpretation of the legal phrase had become a guiding principle in protecting the purpose of public schools. In contrast, AC believed that the law was never intended to make spiritual/religious issues a marginalized part of the school setting. Instead the intent was to protect against proselytizing, something he considered inappropriate in the public school context.

AJ believed that the concept of "secular" has "little understanding or recognition." Certainly there is little unanimity in its interpretation. PM interpreted the phrase as meaning "accommodating." ETA was unsure but thought it meant that "we don't promote any religion in school." ECT#1, ECT #2, and PC indicated that the law was interpreted differently at each school according to the leadership in place:

> Some schools have openly allowed the Christian Christmas story to be told, while other schools make no mention of the birth of Jesus. . . . I know of one

school that changed the name of the Christmas concert and break to the Winter concert and Winter break. However, while once visiting the school board office,... the visiting secondary choirs openly [sang] Christian Christmas carols that mentioned the birth of Jesus. (PC)

In some schools even the name "religion" was a dirty word.... All religion was to be kept private, but even in those schools I witnessed a Christian club operating. In my current school there is much acceptance of and accommodation for religion. (ECT#1)

BCT suggested that public schools are more nonsectarian than secular in that secular means "without God or religion." For schools to be truly secular, the role of faith could not be recognized or taught. She added that even though schools attempt to be nonsectarian, aboriginal spirituality often dominates school curriculum and events. She has also seen that "a lot of room is given to teachers to interpret the law as they best see fit." ECT#2 also described the measured freedom given to teachers to interpret this legal phrase, recognizing "windows of opportunity" to include a Christian perspective as long as other perspectives were also included.

Question #9 asked respondents to describe situations that they believed "crossed the line" with respect to public schools having to be "secular and nonsectarian." The respondents gave a number of examples where they felt this had occurred. A math teacher regularly lectured students on his views about religion (AH). A community Youth for Christ pastor went beyond meeting with students in a school to reach out to other students (AH), and a lunch hour Christian youth event that involved "witnessing" and the teaching of small groups of students to "speak in tongues" (AC). Public schools celebrated the sacred aspects of Christmas in public schools (AJ). Other schools began an event with a First Nations prayer (PC), and an aboriginal staff member led students into a meditative state (BCT). Muslim parents asked teachers to teach on Monday what their children missed every Friday due to worship and prayer (ETC#1). Neither PM nor ETA could recall any situations that "crossed the line." ETA would not want students "to be made to feel uncomfortable" by any kind of religious accommodation, while AC felt that the public system provided harmony and appropriate balance.

The final question asked participants to compare the acceptance of religious diversity with acceptance of other forms of diversity within the public education system. Some felt that the public schools accepted religious diversity more so than other forms of diversity, especially when religious diversity was equated with cultural diversity (AJ, PC, AC). AH added:

In my experience there has been considerable change in the recognition of diversity of many sorts in public schools and other institutions in recent years. I have a strong belief in the secular and nonsectarian nature of public schools, but I also understand that public schools need to develop structures of recognition that allow for diverse elements of society to feel at home with public schools. I have concerns about the lack of spirituality in our society, but I would be concerned about the introduction of spiritual rituals and religious beliefs into the public system.

PC pointed to British Columbia's willingness to partially fund religious schools as evidence of society's willingness to accept religious diversity. Yet ETC#1 expressed a perception that Christianity was less accepted than other faiths and described escalating religiously based student conflict in her school between adherents of Sikh and Muslim faiths. ETC#2 thought that acceptance of religious diversity was fair overall in that she had a measure of religious freedom, but that she understood that there may come a time when she would have to seek employment outside of the public school system.

When the responses are considered as a whole, some general themes emerge that may be avenues for further exploration. In our sample of nine individuals there was a significant difference between the administrative responses and the teacher/parent responses. The administrators gave the impression of being more at ease with their spirituality and less in conflict with regard to its impact on their role within the public system. AJ actually mentioned the change in her ability to more comfortably and confidently provide for religious diversity once she had become an administrator, while AC and AH expressed unwavering confidence in the way they were identified and in the way they acted on their beliefs. Their experiences suggest either a maturing process related to identity formation and/or a reduction of fear once a position of stronger power was achieved. Other respondents did mention the impact of leadership on their actions, supporting the notion that power may be an important consideration with regard to the personal expression of religious identity.

A second theme that emerges is a confirmation of some of the presumptions discussed earlier in the chapter. For example, the presumption of a liberal worldview was evident in both AH and ETA who represent the least religious viewpoints in our sample. AH saw his role as clearly protective of the core values represented by a liberal worldview as it is epitomized by public education, even though he admitted that the system could grow in its ability to respond to all forms of diversity. ETA was content with the notion of neutrality and the maintenance of the status quo. There were threads of this same presumption in the PC response with regard to school choice:

I do not believe that Christians should place demands on the public education system to accommodate their religious diversity in so far as they require their own separate school facilities because of philosophical differences in education.... In my opinion such a demand is unjust and immoral on the part of a Christian, because they are refusing to pay for something other than the "standard issue."

However, the presumption of liberalism was not the only presumption displayed. To varying degrees, each respondent assumed that their interpretation of the core values and ethos of the religious diversity in the public education system should be dominant. For example, Christian respondents often presumed that if there was to be a religious hierarchy, the Christian religion should take precedence. Their argument for precedence was usually related to the Christian origins of Canadian society.

Another theme that is worth exploring further is related to gender. Of the sample, four were men (AH, ETA, AC, PM) and five were women. The women's responses often represented actions or choices made that were highly interpretive of the context. They seemed willing to change their actions when the context required or allowed divergence. Although many factors impacted choices and actions, fear of reprisals was more prevalent in the responses of the women. The men, on the other hand, were generally more certain, more open and proactive, and more at ease and protective of the system. Nevertheless, most persons with a deep religious faith displayed some unease with certain situations that occur in public school settings.

With regard to provisions for religious diversity, the respondents indicated varied interpretations of "secular and nonsectarian." Some of the interpretations were strongly connected to the leadership within the school, some to the community of the school, and some to the age of the student. For example, there appeared to be more provision for religious diversity at the secondary than the elementary level, and also in highly multicultural communities where it was expected that everyone had a religious belief. At the same time, the responses varied according to the strengths and nuances of the religious beliefs of the respondents. On the basis of such disparate individual interpretations, we also expect that the diversity of practice found in various schools will be mirrored by a diversity of practice found in various classrooms within schools.

PROBING POSSIBILITIES FOR RELIGIOUS DIVERSITY IN WESTERN CANADIAN EDUCATION

As we have outlined, the scope of religious diversity in Canada has broadened considerably during the past 50 years. This extended pluralism has resulted from a shift in the ethnic and religious backgrounds of immigrants to Canada, from a resurgence of aboriginal spirituality, and from the dominant liberal cultural ideal increasingly distancing itself from anything that is overtly religious. The Protestant Christian hegemony that formerly dominated public education in Western Canada has crumbled. Strong efforts are still made to maintain a uniform school system dominated by liberalism and secularism. However, such attempts are less successful than in the past. Today, there are more educational choices for stakeholders who believe that their faith should have an impact in the classroom, both within and outside of public education. In all four western Canadian provinces, there are provisions for at least partial government funding of independent schools that adhere to basic teacher certification and curriculum stipulations. In both Alberta and Saskatchewan, there are religiously based schools that have become alternatives within the public school system.

Still, religious adherents continue to disagree and even to be apprehensive about exercising their roles within education. Those who support a common public school system that brings students of different backgrounds together nevertheless differ on whether their role is to buttress a system (1) that is homogeneous and will continue to promote Enlightenment liberalism; (2) that provides for diverse programs, including ones of religious choice; or (3) that will revert to emphasizing Canada's traditional Christian heritage—even if that means personally "crossing the line" when that is deemed necessary. Other persons of faith have, in increasing numbers especially in British Columbia, left public education in order to participate in religiously based nonpublic schools, believing that parents and not the government are ultimately responsible for their children's education.

A surprising aspect of recent Canadian conversations about multiculturalism and education is that the place of religion in these discussions has been minimized if not neglected. For instance, the book *Education and the Politics of Difference: Canadian Perspectives* argues that Canada's multiculturalism policies have led to incorporation of minorities into existing institutions, but that the multiculturalism defined by the liberalism of the dominant group still "uses its ideology to obtain the consent of the subordinate groups," and that its "view of equal dignity is blind to difference as an essential component of democracy" and "an assault on the notion of distinctiveness" (Ghosh & Abdi, 2004, pp. 111, 169). Yet the authors discuss distinctiveness and difference only in terms of race, ethnicity, gender, and class. They disregard that religious beliefs often define identity even more strongly than ethnicity, and fail even to consider how the two are often closely intertwined.

Multicultural reality is significant in Canadian education. This actuality is intertwined with the increasing religious diversity of the Canadian population, a difference that cuts across and may supersede other forms of diversity. Therefore Canadian schools, in our view, must allow for religious distinctiveness as they help students to be and become responsive and responsible individuals with a sense of Canadian nationhood, ones who are prepared to participate in and contribute to a compassionate and just society.

This claim does raise a number of complex questions. How we can build a school system that encompasses and promotes national identification while truly honoring religious diversity and identity? How do we balance individual and societal needs with respect to the place of religion in education? How do we create unity within the reality of diversity? At the classroom and school levels, teachers need to be sensitive to and counter systemic factors, curricula, pedagogy, and experiences that may, intentionally or unintentionally, have a discriminatory impact on persons' identity or life activity. While the absence of the study of religion in Canadian schools has resulted in graduates who cannot understand the points of view of people with various religious backgrounds, schools could take steps, for instance, to teach about religion and spirituality in more open and meaningful ways. They can also include multicentered worldviews, perspectives, and experiences that recognize and respect differences (see, e.g., Magsino, 2003; Van Brummelen, Koole, & Franklin, 2004; Zine, 2002).

However, such approaches, while helpful, will not satisfy many of those with deep religious convictions. The University of New Brunswick's John Valk (2002), for instance, writes that teaching about religion in public education in an objective manner "does little to assist the student in making sense of his/her own life" and may "do violence to the very nature of religion itself, particularly as an expression of one's individual identity" (p. 26). David MacBain (2003), an Ontario Baptist pastor, argues that all major subjects in the curriculum must wrestle with big issues as well as with the spiritual and philosophical foundations of education—but seldom do (e.g., "What gives meaning to life?"). Reluctantly, because of his commitment to the common good, he sent two of his children into the public school system after giving them what he considered a sound metaphysical and ontological foundation by home schooling them for 10 years.

What is clear both from these examples and from the survey respondents is that systemically we face difficult problems. First, teaching is "being," to a large degree. And one's religious identity is an integral and often very significant component of that being. If that is so, then classroom teaching and learning cannot but be affected by a teacher's personal identity—and those identities differ greatly in Canada's pluralist society, even among our Christian respondents. Second, while modern culture has experienced a process of secularization, with education having been rationalized by a narrow, positivist expectation of high performance, more parents and educators in North America are once again realizing that religion can help to restore education's transformative edge. Moreover, unlike in the Western world where it is often assumed that religion has become privatized and irrelevant to modern life, globally religion is gaining clout, and Canadians once again have to take into account the role of spirituality and religion in culture and hence in education (Van Brummelen et al., 2004; Wexler, 1996).

A number of reasons can be identified why Canada's federal multicultural policy, in effect since 1971, has made little impact on Canadian education, and none on education's lack of attention to the religious dimension of life. First of all, education in Canada is a provincial and not a federal responsibility, and even the Canadian Council of Ministers of Education has little clout. At a deeper level, however, true pluralism has been undercut by the liberal tendency to marginalize minority worldviews, especially religious ones, while accommodating lifestyle differences.

Furthermore, little discussion has taken place about the fact that in a compassionate and just democratic society there must be limits to tolerance and that the values of some worldviews are unacceptable and cannot be given equal treatment in Canadian public life. For instance, Canadian society rightly does not tolerate female genital mutilation, discrimination against persons of homosexual orientation, or violence against individuals or legitimate societal institutions. Yet, as Joseph Heath (2002) shows, Canadians, probably as a result of wanting to avoid being labelled discriminatory, have suffered from "an excess of timidity" and "skittishness" in rejecting aspects of worldviews that are unacceptable to Canadian society. We should celebrate the fact, he says, that Sikhs want to join our national police force and are allowed to wear turbans instead of the regular uniform caps. He adds, however, that if we do not reject Sikh schoolchildren wearing kirpans in school, we undermine the principle that in Canadian schools we do not permit anyone to carry anything that can be used as a weapon. In other words, our schools must insist on the values that bind us together as a stable and peaceful pluralistic society. At the same time, all schools, public or nonpublic, must acknowledge diverse views and opinions and leave sufficient room for students to draw their own conclusions while helping them develop a defensible worldview and be respectful of views that differ from their own.

Respect for divergent views must also be extended to pluralism in the way Canadians structure their school systems. The province of Alberta has accepted that in a pluralistic society a "one size fits all" school system is problematic. It therefore provides accredited nonpublic schools with funding from general tax revenues that covers close to half of their operating costs. It also fully funds charter schools that have a particular educational philosophy, although not religious ones. Public and fully funded separate Catholic school boards may also enter into arrangements with groups to offer alternative programs, including religiously based ones. One noteworthy alternative is the existence of nine Protestant Christian Logos programs in the provincial capital city of Edmonton. These programs usually operate as wings of regular public schools. On the one hand, the programs, while meeting provincial curriculum requirements, are distinctly Christian in orientation, and they emphasize a strong sense of Christian community. On the other hand, the schoolchildren not only mix with but also participate in special events with children of other backgrounds. This, together with several other culturally based programs, ensures that religious and cultural diversity is recognized in the way the school system is structured. In short, provisions for plurality and multiculturalism in Alberta schools enables religious and cultural communities to preserve their identity within the overall framework of the values guaranteed by the *Canadian Charter of Rights and Freedoms* as well as within the provincial knowledge and ability expectations of sound educational programs.

Canadian society is based on a number of principles that it must uphold in order to function as a pluralistic, democratic society. These include respect for all persons and their dignity, veracity in all dealings, responsibility toward self and others, and justice and compassion for the disadvantaged. Within such contours but recognizing that a democratic society is in a constant state of flux, Canada must continually be willing to deliberate about, experiment with, improvise around, and implement new educational structures and practices. It has to recognize and take into account, for instance, that in Western Canada the lines between public and private or independent education are increasingly blurred and that this dichotomy represents a continuum rather than an either/or position. If we believe that schools are most effective when they are community enterprises, then we have to reexamine whether community schools should be neighborhood schools, or whether they should reflect a plurality of groups within Canadian society, each of whose identity is affirmed through the ability to establish a school.

In a report for the Saskatchewan government (Saskatchewan is one of the four western Canadian provinces), Michael Tymchak (2001) makes the case that effective community schools have a number of characteristics. For instance, they are ones where the culture of the children and the culture of the supporting community are strongly reflected in the school. They are ones in which parents are valued as partners and where they have meaningful involvement in establishing the school's goals and program design. They are ones that view themselves as an integral part of the community. Smith and Sikkink (1999) supplement these features by avowing that such schools are particularly effective when their stakeholders share a moral culture that facilitates solidarity and trust. In this way, a school based on its supporters' ideological cohesion can form a community among communities, recognizing its public role while maintaining its distinctiveness. That public role would include ensuring equal access to good education, ensuring normal human development toward responsible citizenship, encouraging confessional and cultural pluralism, and protecting the rights of children. This approach would empower teachers and parents to define, implement, and support a clear educational vision. It would also allow all of our survey respondents, for instance, to find an educational context that they can fully support—based on a geographical, pedagogical, cultural, or religious identity.

This alternative way of viewing schooling opens doors to the possibility of different school communities working together as unique entities rather than as opposing systems: communities within larger communities. Their freedom to exist as unique but valid members of the public marketplace would encourage them to establish ties and view the success of other distinct schools as a positive sign of a healthy democratic society rather than as competition to be fought or feared. It may help establish the equal footing and individual abilities to articulate moral and civil frameworks that foster deliberation and build the social cohesion and equity that Canadians continue to seek. It opens up the possibility of greater educational justice and equality for minorities that presently feel that their worldviews and beliefs are challenged, marginalized, or undercut by one homogeneous system of public education. An alternative and stronger representation of liberalism, as described by Gray (2000), could be realized:

> Liberalism contains two philosophies. In one, toleration is justified as a means to truth. In this view, toleration is an instrument of rational consensus, and a diversity of ways of life is endured in the faith that it is destined to disappear. In the other, toleration is valued as a condition of peace, and divergent ways of living are welcomed as marks of diversity in the good life. The first conception supports an ideal of ultimate convergence on values, the latter an ideal of *modus vivendi*. Liberalism's future lies in turning its face away from the ideal of rational consensus and looking instead to *modus vivendi*. (p. 105)

In most jurisdictions, such an alternative *modus vivendi* will require a paradigm shift for both public and nonpublic school communities. Canadians will need to recognize that finding a way to live together does not mean imposing a uniform grayness, but, rather, allowing the many colors of the rainbow to flourish and complement each other, for the sake of Canadian children.

REFERENCES

Adler v. Ontario [1996] 3 S.C.R. 609.

Bal v. Ontario (A.G.) [1994]. 21 O.R. (3d) 682 (Ont. Ct., Gen. Div.).

Badley, K. (2000). Indoctrination and assimilation in plural settings. In J. Olthuis (Ed.), *Towards an ethics of community: Negotiations of difference in a pluralist society* (pp. 51–73). Waterloo, ON, Canada: Wilfred Laurier University Press.

British Columbia Government. (1872). An act respecting public schools. In D. Lawr & R. Gidney, *Educating Canadians: A documentary history of public education* (2nd ed., pp. 57–60). Toronto: Van Nostrand Reinhold.

British Columbia Ministry of Education. (1996). *Physics 11 and 12: Integrated Resource Package.* Victoria: Province of British Columbia.

British Columbia Ministry of Education. (1997). *Social studies 8–10: Integrated Resource Package.* Victoria: Province of British Columbia

British Columbia Ministry of Education. (2004). *Planning 10: Integrated Resource Package.* Victoria: Province of British Columbia.

British Columbia Ministry of Education. (2005). "2005/06–2007/08 service plan." Retrieved March 2, 2005, from www.bcbudget.gov.bc.ca/sp/educ/Vision_Mission _and_Values.htm

British Columbia School Act. (2002). Victoria, BC: Queen's Printer.

Brown, D. (2002). Freedom from or freedom for?: Religion as a case study in defining the Charter of Rights. *University of British Columbia Law Review 33*(3), 551–615.

Chamberlain v. Surrey School District No. 36 [2002]. 4 S.C.R. 710.

Clarke, M. (Ed.). (1998). *Canada: Portraits of faith.* Chilliwack: Reel to Real.

Cooper, G. (1972). *Some differential effects of denominational schooling in Newfoundland on the beliefs and behaviours of students.* Unpublished doctoral dissertation, University of Toronto.

Council of Ministers of Education of Canada. (1992). *The mission of education and training in Canada.* Memorandum of agreement, September 1992. Toronto: Author.

Edmonton Public Schools. (2005). *Your guide to superb results: Welcome to Edmonton Public Schools.* Edmonton: Edmonton Public School Board.

Erickson, D., Macdonald, L., & Manley-Casimir, M. (1979). *Characteristics and relationships in public and independent schools.* Vancouver: Educational Research Institute of British Columbia.

Ghosh, R., & Abdi, A. (2004).*Education and the politics of difference.* Toronto: Canadian Scholars' Press.

Godwin, K., Audbrooks, C., & Martinez, V. (2001). Teaching tolerance in public and private schools. *Phi Delta Kappan 82*(7), 542–546.

Gray, J. (2000). *Two faces of liberalism.* New York: New Press.

Guldemond, A. (Ed.). (1990). *Religion in the public schools of Ontario: Progress in the courts.* Ancaster, ON, Canada: Ontario Alliance of Christian Schools.

Hart, H. (2000). Consequences of liberalism: Ideological domination in Rorty's public/private split. In J. Olthuis (Ed.), *Towards an ethics of community: Negotiations of difference in a pluralist society* (pp. 37–50). Waterloo, ON, Canada: Wilfred Laurier University Press.

Heath, J. (2002). Citizenship education and diversity. *Education Canada, 42*(3), 4–7.

Holmes, M. (1990). Choice in Canadian education. In A. Guldemond (Ed.), *Religion in the public schools of Ontario: Progress in the courts* (pp. 93–106). Ancaster, ON, Canada: Ontario Alliance of Christian Schools.

Islamic Schools Federation of Ontario v. Ottawa Board of Education (1997) 145 D.L.R. (4th) 659 (Ont. Gen. Div.) at 681.

Jaenen, C. (1979). Ruthenian schools in western Canada 1897–1919. In D. Jones, N. Sheehan, & R. Stamp, *Shaping the schools of the Canadian West* (pp. 39–58). Calgary: Detselig.

Jason, R. (2006). Kempling statement on Supreme Court decision. *News and Views Newsletter,* January 19. Retrieved from www.christianity.ca/news/national/2006/01.004.html on January 27, 2006.

Kempling v. The British Columbia College of Teachers [2004] BCSC 133.

Kempling v. The British Columbia College of Teachers [2005] BCCA 327.

MacBain, D. (2003). Towards a just peace: Opening our schools to dissenting worldviews. *Education Canada, 43*(1), 26–27, 47.

Magsino, R. (2003). Study of religions: For Citizenship: Why not? *Canadian Diversity, 2*(1), 24–27.

Marshall, P. (2000). *Being Christians in a pluralistic society: A discussion paper on pluralism in Canada.* Markham, ON: Social Action Commission of the Evangelical Fellowship of Canada.

Perepolkin v. the Superintendent of Child Welfare of B.C. [1958] 23 W.W.R. 592-593.

Prentice, A., & Houston, S. (Eds.). (1975). *Family, school and society in nineteenth-century Canada.* Toronto: Oxford University Press.

Smith, C., & Sikkink, D. (1999). Is private schooling privatizing? *First Things, 92*(4), 16–20.

Statistics Canada. (2005). *Population projections of visible minority groups, Canada, provinces, and regions 2001–2017.* Ottawa, ON, Canada: Government of Canada.

Tomkins, G. (1986). *A common countenance: Stability and change in the Canadian curriculum.* Scarborough, ON, Canada: Prentice-Hall.

Trinity Western University v. British Columbia College of Teachers, [2001] 1 S.C.R. 772.

Tymchak, M., & Saskatchewan Instructional Development Unit. (2001). *School-plus: A vision for children and youth.* Final report to the Minister of Education. Saskatoon: Government of Saskatchewan.

Valk, J. (2002). Religion and education: A way forward? *Didaskalia, 14*(1), 17–38.

Van Brummelen, H. (1986). Shifting perspectives: Early British Columbia textbooks from 1872 to 1925. In N. Sheehan, J. D. Wilson, & D. Jones, *Schools in the West: Essays in Canadian educational history* (pp. 17–38). Calgary: Detselig Enterprises.

Van Brummelen, H. (1996, April). Religiously-based schooling in British Columbia: An overview of the research. *Journal of the Canadian Church Historical Society, 38*(1), 101–122.

Van Brummelen, H., Koole, R., & Franklin, K. (2004). Transcending the commonplace: Spirituality in the curriculum. *The Journal of Educational Thought, 38*(3), 237–254.

Ward v. Board of Blain Lake School Unit No. 57 [1971] 4 W.W.R. 161.

Wexler, P. (1996). *Holy sparks: Social theory, education and religion.* Toronto: Canadian Scholars' Press.

Wilson, J. D., Stamp, R., & Audet, L. (Eds.). (1970). *Canadian education: A history.* Scarborough, ON, Canada: Prentice-Hall.

Zine, J. (2002). Inclusive schooling in a plural society: removing the margins. *Education Canada, 42*(3), 36–39.

APPENDIX

Questions to Survey Participants

1. As a practicing _____ (insert your spiritual identity), what motivates you to actively participate in the public education system?

2. In what ways does your spiritual identity impact your role within the public education system?

3. Have you ever made a conscious choice to conceal your spirituality when acting within the public education system? Describe the context of your choice and the consequences.

4. Have you ever made a conscious choice to reveal your spirituality when acting within the public education system? Describe the context of your choice and the consequences.

5. Have you ever observed or experienced religious intolerance while participating in the public education system? Describe the incident and its impact on you.

6. What concerns do you have about religious diversity in the public education system? For you? For the education profession? For students? For Canadian society?

7. Have you ever placed a demand on the public education system to accommodate religious differences? Please describe the demand and the response.

8. How is the law of "secular and nonsectarian" interpreted in the public schools you have been involved with?

9. Have you ever observed a situation in the public education sphere that you believe "crosses the line," or in other words, breaks the law of "secular and nonsectarian"? Describe the situation.

10. In your experience, how does the acceptance of religious diversity compare with the acceptance of other forms of diversity?

CHAPTER 5

BUDDHISM, CULTURAL DEMOCRACY, AND MULTICULTURAL EDUCATION

Gerald W. Fry
University of Minnesota

ABSTRACT

The focus of this chapter is on the relationship among Buddhism, cultural democracy, and multicultural education. The key research questions are: (1) *Why* should religion (in this case Buddhism) be an integral part of multicultural education? and (2) *How* can religion be used to enhance and strengthen multicultural education? The case study approach is particularly appropriate for studying why and how questions. In case study research, it is important to have guiding theories. For this study the key theoretical conceptual frameworks used are cultural democracy, multiple intelligences and the mismeasure of man, and Allport's social contact theory. Five cases from the Kingdom of Thailand provide the major empirical data for the study. The cases are:

- Wat Suan Mokh and Buddhadāsa Bhikku
- Santhira–Dhammasathan and Mae Chee Sansanee Sthirasuta
- The Islamic College of Thailand
- Islam Lamsai Environmental School
- International Cooperative Learning Project

Religion in Multicultural Education, pages 101–119
Copyright © 2006 by Information Age Publishing

101

An analysis of these five cases indicate strong support for the validity of All-port's social contact theory and how religion (in this case Buddhism and Islam) not only can enhance multicultural education, but is central to the development of authentic cultural democracy. Contact with other worldviews represents an important paradigm shift and represents a major revolution in the world. The authentic implementation of diverse religious ideals and the promotion through multicultural education of the deep understanding of other religions and value systems is central to fostering world peace and harmony. Contact with other world views can result in a shift of perspective, along with a concomitant appreciation for the diversity and richness of human beings. This paradigm shift is the kind that one writer has described as "the greatest revolution in the world...one which occurs with the head, within the mind" (Ferguson, 1980, pp. 17–20) (cited in Fantini, 1995, p. 152).

INTRODUCTION

To begin this chapter, I share two inspiring, concrete examples of how religion can contribute to multicultural understanding. The first is about an overseas Vietnamese college student in the United States. He and his immediate family had been boat people fleeing from Vietnam. While at sea, his boat was attacked by Thai pirates. His sisters had been raped and the pirates had stolen their valuables. This particular student had been greatly influenced by the Vietnamese Buddhist thinker and philosopher, Thich Nhat Hanh, who argues that we should always be compassionate, even toward those who have done us harm. After hearing of such a tragic boat incident, Thich Nhat Hanh (1993) stated:

I was angry when I received the news of her death [a 12-year-old raped by a pirate who threw herself into the sea], but I learned after meditation for several hours that I could not just take sides against the pirate. I saw that if I had been born in his village and brought up under the same conditions, I would be exactly like him. (p. 107)

This Vietnamese student was in one of my university classes in which there were three new students who arrived from Thailand. More than any other student in the class, he went out of his way to be helpful to these students and he seemed gently interested in learning more about their Thai culture. He showed no bitterness or animosity toward these Thai students, despite his harrowing experience with Thai pirates. I attribute his actions to his being a serious follower of the teachings of Thich Nhat Hanh.

The second example is from the Middle East. Dr. Malcolm H. Kerr, the president of the American University of Beirut in Lebanon, was assassinated by terrorists in January 1984. He was a distinguished scholar of the Middle East (1975), who had taught at UCLA for many years and worked tirelessly to improve U.S.–Arab relations. The reactions and subsequent actions of his wife, Ann Kerr (1994, 2002), to this personal tragedy is genuinely inspiring. She decided to establish a special foundation to provide scholarships to facilitate U.S. students in being able to study in countries such as Egypt, Syria, Jordan, and Tunisia to learn more about Islam and the Middle East. Funding for such an endeavor was probably facilitated by her son who became a star in the National Basketball Association in the United States. In behaving in this way she reflected the true spirit and teachings of an authentic Christian.

The focus of this chapter will be a case study of Thailand, a country never colonized and in which roughly 90% of the population is Buddhist. The Thai situation is quite distinct from that of the United States where there is such an emphasis on the legal separation of church and state, which makes the discussion of religion and multicultural education in the United States highly problematic. Thailand faces no such constraint. In fact, the three pillars of the Thai polity and society are nation, religion, and king.

BACKGROUND ON THAILAND

Thailand has a long history dating back to the 13th century. Actually, the country was known as Siam until 1939, when its name was changed to Thailand, meaning land of the free. In 1945 after the end of the Pacific War, its name reverted to Siam. In 1949, it became Thailand again, its current name. Integral to the Thai polity is its monarchy, which dates back to the 13th century and its founding King Ramkhamhaeng. Throughout its history, Siam had an openness to outsiders. In the Ayuthhaya period under King Narai in the 17th century, there was an extremely prominent Greek advisor and counselor at the court (Sioris, 1998).

Its current Chakri Dynasty dates back to 1782. The third king in the current dynasty, King Rama III, known as the *Merchant Prince*, had the vision to open Siam to both Western missionaries and migrants from China, which was to have a profound effect on the evolution of Thailand and its multicultural future (see Amyot, 2003; Kim, 1980). In 1833, Siam established formal diplomatic relations with the United States. This was 11 years before the United States had such relations with China and 21 years before relations were established with Japan.

King Rama V (Chulalongkorn), the creator of modern Thailand, traveled throughout Europe and upon his return instituted a policy to send young Thais to study in places such as England, France, Germany, and Russia. This decision was also to have a profound impact on the future of the country.

Thai policy during World War II also was profoundly Buddhist, given its central principle of nonviolence and reverence for life. During the war Thailand cleverly sided simultaneously both with the Axis powers and the Allies. The result was that Thailand suffered the least (both in loss of human life and destruction of cultural heritage) of any countries in the Pacific theatre. In the postwar period, Thailand has tended to be coup-prone but generally such irregular political changes have occurred with minimal violence or loss of life, reflective of the country's Buddhist character.

THEORETICAL CONSTRUCTS UNDERLYING THE STUDY

Cultural Democracy

Cultural democracy is a construct proposed by Latino scholars Manuel Ramírez III and Alfredo Castañeda (1974). They define cultural democracy as: "Cultural democracy assumes that a person has a legal as well as a moral right to remain identified with his own ethnic group, his own values, language, home, and community, as he learns of and accepts *mainstream* values" (p. xi). This important construct has been grossly neglected as a focus on political democracy dominates world discourse and geopolitics. Cultural democracy emphasizes the inclusion of all cultures and world-views without privileging some over others or making individuals feel ashamed of their *unusual* culture. In the United States, for example, people have often looked down on the Amish for being *strange and weird.* The state at times has also used legal means to try to force the Amish into mainstream practices. Polynesian scholar Linda Tuhiwai Smith (1999) has been highly critical of the West and its scholars for their exploitation of indigenous peoples. The late Palestinian scholar Edward Said (Bayoumi & Rubin, 2000) was highly critical of Western scholars for the way they misrepresented other cultures and people, especially in Asia. There has been inadequate appreciation of local culture and wisdom (Champagne & Abu-Saad, 2003; Geertz, 1983). The recent tsumani disaster provides a dramatic example of the power of local wisdom and knowledge. There were Moken people (sometimes referred to as "sea gypsies," a derogatory term) who lived on Surin Island about 40 km out into the sea off the coast of Thailand. They were hit directly by the tsunami before it hit the mainland. Though thousands died on the mainland of Thailand, the Moken people, drawing on centuries of having lived close to the sea, noticed the unusual sea patterns and behavior of animals and immediately fled to higher grounds. Only one Moken perished, an extremely old, paralyzed man.

Related to the ideal of cultural democracy is the importance of developing what Hofstede and Hoftsede (2005) call "software of the mind" (i.e., knowing about many cultures and different value systems). University of Chicago scholar Charles Morris (1973a, 1973b) in his key books *Paths of Life* and *Varieties of Human Value*, emphasizes a similar theme.

Central to the ideal of cultural democracy is the absence of any prejudice or discrimination against individuals based on religion or culture. For example, the common discrimination against the Roma people in various parts of Europe is a sad, concrete example of the violation of cultural democracy (Pogamy, 2004). The strong assimilationist ideology of Samuel Huntington's recent volume, *Who Are We?*, goes directly against the spirit of cultural democracy. His earlier work (1996), emphasizing civilizational and cultural conflicts, is also contrary to the ideal of cultural democracy and has served to legitimize increased military spending to fight "cultural wars" (see also Chomsky, 2005). It is easy to find rankings of countries of the world with respect to economic success, international competitiveness, and other such materially oriented criteria. In contrast, the King of Buddhist Bhutan, with a more spiritual orientation, calls for the measure Gross National Happiness (see Carpenter & Carpenter, 2002). With regard to nonmaterial criteria, we have no rankings of the countries of the world in terms of cultural democracy. Perhaps in terms of cultural democracy, Singapore and Switzerland might rank high, given that both countries recognize multiple national/official languages.

Multiple Intelligences and the Mismeasure of Man

In the West, there has been a common pattern to assess the worth of people based on either their material wealth and/or cognitive skills. The two are often related because of the strong social class influences on educational and occupational opportunities and the pervasive influence of the diploma disease (Dore, 1976; Treiman, 1977). In contrast, Howard Gardner (1993) at Harvard emphasizes the importance of multiple intelligences. Stephen Jay Gould, in his *Mismeasure of Man* (1996), provides a devastating critique of narrow and rigid Western ways of assessing people. Another interesting alternative is presented in Erich Fromm's *To Have or To Be?* (1976). Interestingly, in traditional Latino culture there is an important construct, *una buena educación*, which does not mean a good formal education but refers to an individual's behavior, their moral integrity, and their ability to get along well with others and to be respectful and thoughtful (Villenas, 2001, p. 12). Building on Gardner's work and such scholars as Fromm and Gould, it is important to include cultural intelligence as an important part of an individual's profile (see Earley & Ang, 2003; Landis, Bennett, & Bennett, 2004). A part of cultural intelligence would be a good understanding of comparative religion and an appreciation of and respect for religions different than one's own. Actual instruments have been developed to assess empirically the extent to which individuals are interculturally sensitive (the Intercultural Development Inventory (IDI; Landis et al., 2004) and cultural intelligence (Earley & Ang, 2003). Also central to this concept would to not be defensive about one's own religion and related cultural values in encounters with cultural diversity.

Related to the development of intercultural sensitivity and cultural intelligence is the Protean self construct of the political scientist-psychologist Robert J. Lifton (1993). This construct draws on Greek mythology and the Greek god Proteus, who could easily shift forms from one genre of life to another. The Protean individual has maximal and optimal flexibility in drawing upon diverse cultural values. Anthropologist Ward Goodenough (1963) talks of simultaneously having *multiple operating cultures.*

Allport's Social Contact Theory

The late social psychologist Gordon Allport at Harvard developed the important concept of social contact theory in addressing the important issue of pervasive human prejudice (1954). Under carefully defined scope conditions, Allport hypothesizes that real social personal contact among diverse groups will reduce prejudice, misunderstandings, and stereotypes. Subsequent empirical work by diverse scholars lends strong support to Allport's theory (see, e.g., Johnson 1992; Pettigrew, 1999, 2001; Tomita, Fry, & Seksin, 2000). Allport's theory has direct relevance to the issue of religion and multicultural education. If individuals were to have the opportunity to have an in-depth understanding of major religions of the world, that should definitely reduce prejudice and intolerance. In the west, particularly the United States, there is much misunderstanding of the Islamic religion, fueled by distortions from the media and films (Shaheen, 2001). Even distinguished scholars such as Samuel Huntington at Harvard and Bernard Lewis at Princeton have contributed to negative attitudes toward Islam. Scholars such as John Esposito (2002) at Temple and former nun Karen Armstrong (2000) are to be commended for their attempts to help explain the complexities and diversity of Islam to the West in understandable and empathetic terms.

Methodology and Research Questions

The case study approach is highly appropriate when "how" and "why" questions are being posed (Yin, 2003, p. 1; see also Merriam, 1998; Stake, 1995). In the case of this study, the two key research questions are: (1) *Why* should religion (in this case Buddhism) be an integral part of multicultural education? and (2) *How* can religion be used to enhance and strengthen multicultural education? Given the focus of this research on both why and how religion relates to multicultural education, the case method is utilized. The approach here is multiple cases embedded within the general case of Thailand. The five specific case studies are:

1. Wat Suanmokkh (Garden of Liberation) and Thaan Buddhadāsa Bhikku
2. Sathira–Dhammasathan and Mae Chee Sansanee
3. The Islamic College of Thailand
4. The Islamic Environmental School of Thailand
5. The International Cooperative Learning Project

With respect to the first case study of Wat Suanmokh and Buddhadāsa Bhikku, both phenomenology (Dahlberg, Drew, & Nystrom, 2001; Van Manen, 1990) and participant observation are used, based on my own direct lived experience of having been a monk at Suan Mokh under the tutelage of Buddhadāsa Bhikku.

Wat Suan Mokh and Buddhadāsa Bhikku

Wat Suan Mokh (Garden of Liberation) is located in southern Thailand near Chaiya in Suratthani province. It is a forest monastery and quite different than the vast majority of Thai temples with their often many large and gilded Buddhist images. It dates back to May, 12, 1932, when the monk Buddhadāsa (born in 1906 as Ngueam Phanit of Siamese-Hokkien ethnicity) took up residence at Wat Traphangchik. He renamed the site Suan Mokkhaphalaram ("the garden to arouse the spirits to attain liberation") (Jackson, 2003, p. 13). For the first two years he lived there alone following the tradition of a forest monk. In 1944 Suan Mokh moved to its present location with over 120 acres of forest land adjoining Golden Buddha Hill several kilometers southeast of Chaiya (Warut, 1998, p. 51).

I first became acquainted with Suan Mokh when I went there in the fall of 1969 to be ordained and learn directly about Buddhism. I was urged to go to Suan Mokh to study Buddhism by Phra Panyananda Bhikku, a highly respected Buddhist monk in Bangkok and a former student of Buddhadāsa. The bilingual volume *Chaiya: Suan Mokh* (Warut, 1998) provides many visual images of Suan Mokh with explanatory text. By the time I arrived at Suan Mokh it already had a strong and pervasive international/intercultural character. Almost immediately upon my arrival Phra Nagasena (a monk from India) took me under his wing. In exchange for his teaching me Pali to prepare for my ordination examination, I assisted him with translating one of Buddhadāsa's books into English. This was an excellent introduction to his philosophy and related distinctive and insightful critical approach to Buddhism. Phra Nagasena also introduced me to naturalistic and herbal medicine. A pervasive theme of the setting was respect for life in all its forms, reflecting the major motif in Herman Hesse's (1971) insightful novel about the life of the Lord Buddha. Because of the importance of this principle, Suan Mokh was a haven for a wide variety of flora and fauna, including highly poisonous snakes such as cobras and kraits. In addition to a number of Thai monks, there were also monks from Tibet, Germany, Japan, Korea, and other parts of the world. Buddhadāsa, who had been influenced by Zen, introduced me to the important Zen Buddhist work of Daisetz Suzuki (1970).

The most important physical structure at Suan Mokh is the Spiritual Theater. Inside the Theater, its walls, pillars, and stairways are covered with extensive artwork and visual images reflecting major principles of Buddhism and morality. They are from diverse cultural sources such as Zen, Tibetan, Chinese, ancient Siamese, and even Western. Monks of Suan Mokh in their teaching role explain the art and pictures to visitors from around Thailand, around the world, and from many Thai schools. The Theater represents a powerful example of informal multicultural and moral education. My own stay at Suan Mokh (for approximately three months) was certainly the most powerful informal education I have ever experienced at any point in my life.

Buddhadāsa's life and his approach to Buddhism have been synthesized brilliantly by Australian scholar Peter A. Jackson (2003) in his volume on the monk's approach to Buddhist reform in Thailand. The volume also includes an excellent bibliography of Buddhadāsa's extensive writings (see also Gabaude, 1988). Among his many works are *Dhammic Socialism* (1986), *When Dhamma Rules the World* (1979) in Thai, and *Heartwood of the Bodhi Tree* (2004). Buddhadāsa emphasized a return to the original teachings of the Buddha and the application of Buddhist principles to practical, everyday living. He was highly critical of the growth of materialism in Thailand and emphasized overcoming greed, lust, selfishness, and egotism. He was also deeply concerned about interreligious relations. Buddhadāsa stated, for example:

> Looking on other religions as enemies is the height of stupidity; it is the greatest misunderstanding and the greatest danger to humanity. There is nothing in any religion that need make it an enemy of another religion. That is, if we look at the heart of the thing called religion we will feel that every religion wants to eradicate the feeling called *I—mine*, or strong self-centredness. That is the core of every religion. (Jackson, 2003, p. 253)

Buddhadāsa's three key principles related to interreligious harmony are: (1) Help everyone to realize the heart of their own religion; (2) develop mutual understanding among the religions; and (3) cooperate to drag the world out from under the power of materialism (Warut, 1998, p. 154).

Buddhadāsa is from the southern part of Thailand, where most of its Islamic population lives. His hometown was Phumriang, most of whose population is Muslim. This may be one explanation for his deep commitment to establish and encourage contacts with other religions. He was deeply committed to civilizational and cultural dialogue and Suan Mokh has always been most welcoming to outsiders of any faith. One of his books focuses on Christianity and Buddhism (1977). Buddhadāsa often would mention that the Christian cross could symbolize the negation of *I, me, mine, selfishness,* and *the ego.*

Buddadāsa, because of his strong criticisms of Thai materialism and "Buddhists" who were not committed to the authentic teachings of the Lord Buddha, was a highly controversial figure. At one point, he was accused of being a communist and he wrote about dhammic socialism (1986). The German scholar, Benz (1963), wrote about Buddhism and Communism as alternative future paths for Asia. Despite the controversy concerning Buddadāsa, he had influence on thousands of followers and at the time of his death in 1993 was extremely popular and held in high respect. Among some of the most well known of his followers are the public intellectual and social critic, Sulak Sivaraksa (Chappell, 2003; Ip, 2004); the physician and major political and educational reformer, Dr. Prawes Wasi; Phra Payom, a monk who is well known for his charisma in popularizing Buddhism and promoting innovative civic engagement and environmental projects; and Mae Chee Sansanee, a Buddhist nun whose project is the focus of the next case study.

Santhira–Dhammasathan and Mae Chee Sansanee Sthirasuta

Santhira–Dhammasathan (2005) is known as a learning community for peace and harmony for all, a second home to all (Litalien, 2001). It was founded in 1987 by a Buddhist nun, Mae Chee Sansanee, a remarkable and versatile woman. The seven-acre site, comprised of trees, lotus ponds, winding nature paths, and meditative nooks, is a green oasis of calm in the northeastern part of the hyperurbanized mega-city of Bangkok, one of the world's largest cities.

Before becoming a nun, Sansanee had been a successful model and business woman. However, she decided to devote her life to religion and Buddhist social engagement. Thus, she committed herself to establish a special learning community in Bangkok. Major principles of the community are care, share, respect, and the concept that *simplicity is the essence of life*. Many activities are carried out at her peace abode. One early major activity was to serve as a shelter for abused women. Another major activity is a Buddhist preschool, which emphasizes the development of moral character in children and preparation for ethical leadership. Unlike most preschools in Thailand, Mae Chee's school does not emphasize academic and cognitive training. Alumni of her school have the qualities of *una buena educación* mentioned earlier. They have developed excellent social and people skills. Follow-up research has indicated that, while they may initially be behind academically, they catch up, but clearly demonstrate superior traits in terms of character, leadership, maturity, and social skills. Using systematic tracer study methodology, it will be interesting to do long-term followup of the graduates of the Buddhist preschool. It will be particularly interesting to see how well they do in terms of being multicultural and having high levels of intercultural sensitivity. Given the emphasis of the Buddhist preschool, its graduates should be high in cultural empathy. The community is also the site for many short-term retreats for both students of different ages and diverse adults.

Another talent of Mae Chee Sansanee (2003) is a special black and white painting style known as one-stroke dhamma. Funds from her artwork contribute to the work of the abode. She is active internationally and last year was in Senegal chairing a major international congress on gender issues. Immediately after the tsunami tragedy on December 26, 2004, she went to the south to assist in the relief effort for victims, the majority of whom were international tourists and non-Thais. Her various one-stroke dhamma paintings are often accompanied by religious proverbs. The following are some examples:

> *Find the courage to create no more suffering.*
> *Be calm while living in this messy world.*
> *Your life is too precious to be stressful.*
> *Become happy by giving love, without expecting anything.*

The Islamic College of Thailand

This is actually a Thai public school covering grades 1–12. The use of *college* is a British influence. Given the separation of church and state in the United States, this school would be a total oxymoron there. The school originally was in the main part of Bangkok near the Siam Cement Company in Bangsue, but because of related dust and dirt and urban congestion, it moved to its current site, in the southwest suburbs of the Bangkok metropolitan area across the Chao Phrya River in Thonburi. It has a large campus of 41 rai with 100 teachers and 1,945 students. Two hundred and fifty of its students are boarding school students who live on campus who are from the four predominantly Muslim southern-most provinces of Thailand. The school serves Muslims from those four provinces as well as Muslims from Bangkok and other areas of Thailand. There are also Buddhist students at the school. The school has an excellent reputation and among its many distinguished alumni is the current Minister of Interior. The school appears to be well funded. In addition to regular government funding the school receives donations from prominent alumni and friendly Muslim countries. The school has an attractive Olympic swimming pool. The Muslim girls swim in a segregated fashion, while the Buddhist students may swim co-ed. Buddhist students at the school are expected to learn about Islam and Islamic cultures. Similarly, the Muslim students are expected to learn about Buddhism and Thailand. The Muslim students have areas for their five prayers each day. While those students are practicing Islam, the Buddhist students have areas for them to use to practice Buddhism. On January 19, 2004, I had the opportunity to visit this school and to talk to administrators, teachers, and students. At lunch we were served an Islamic meal and welcomed by three musical performances. The first performance was traditional Islamic. The second performance involved classical Thai dancing and music (Buddhist orientation). The third performance was by a scarfed Muslim female student singing a modern Western song. All the Muslim female students wore head scarfs. Clearly, the goal of the administrators of the school was to have all students develop an appreciation of and respect for Islam, Buddhism, and Western cultures. Though I spent only a day at the school, it appears to be an excellent example of the implementation of cultural democracy and the effective integration of religion and multicultural education. Of the many schools I have visited in past decades in many countries, this one certainly ranks at the top in terms of cultural democracy (see Jurairatna, 2005).

Islam Lamsai Environmental School

This school is also located in the Bangkok metropolitan area in the far western outskirts of the city. The Muslim community in which this private school is located dates back 130 years. The school was built by members of the community on land donated by a Muslim named Abrahim. Ninety percent of the school's students are Muslim. The school has two major foci: the teaching of Islam and its traditions and the importance of environmental preservation, with a strong focus on trees. In fact, the school is named after a canal bounded by banyan trees and a gorgeous 300-year-old tree is the center piece of the school grounds.

The basic philosophy of the school is that the key to life is nature and the school draws heavily on the green aspects of the Koran and Islam, about which few in the West seem to be aware. The natural environment is actively used in the teaching of science at the school. Students are strongly encouraged to plant trees. With so many trees and a forested community, modern air conditioning is unnecessary. The school emphasizes a nonmaterialist philosophy highly consistent with the fundamental teachings of Buddhism and the Thai King's philosophy of *setakit papieng* (economic self-sufficiency) (1997). The school also emphasizes reverence for life. While visiting the school in January 2005, the head of the school board mentioned the following proverb: "Stop shooting and the sounds of birds will come." Birds are seen as a valuable resource in spreading the seeds of trees.

The school has also had a strong tradition of a close relationship between the community and the school in terms of both governance and curriculum development. As part of current educational reform efforts in Thailand, strengthening school–community relations is an important goal. This school is a model of such relationships.

International Cooperative Learning Project (Tomita, Fry, & Seksin, 2000)

With support from the Sasakawa Peace Foundation in Japan, this project was carried out in Buddhist Thailand, Cambodia, Laos, Vietnam, and Japan over an 8-year period, 1993–2001, involving cooperation among key universities in each of these countries and the University of Oregon in the United States. The Asian universities participating were Chiang Mai University (Thailand), the National University of Laos (NUOL), Royal University of Phnom Penh (Cambodia), and the Vietnam National University (VNU)—Hanoi. Also various universities in Nagoya, Japan, such as Nihon Fukushi and Mizuho, participated.

The key goal of the project was to foster multicultural learning among participants from highly diverse cultural and ethnic backgrounds. Usually during the summer, participants would come together in a Southeast Asian field site to do action research and in the later years of the project service in rural settings. The project was conducted in all mainland Southeast Asian countries except Myanmar (Burma). The normal duration of the project was 1–2 months. The average number of participants was 20–30, with participants coming from diverse disciplinary backgrounds, including the humanities, social sciences, and the natural scientists. Among religions represented in the project were Theravada Buddhism, Christianity (a

Karen participant, for example), animism (several Hmong participants), Mahayana Buddhism (some Japanese and Vietnamese participants), and Native American religious traditions (several Oregon participants).

For each field experience (normally during summers), students were broken down into multicultural and interdisciplinary research teams. The basic rule was that no team would have more than one individual from a given culture. The research often focused on rural development problems and issues in countries such as Cambodia, Laos, Thailand, and Vietnam. For example, during one of the Thai programs, participants lived at an orphanage for victims of HIV/AIDS in northern Thailand. In addition to learning about the AIDS problem in northern Thailand, participants actually lived at the orphanage and worked as volunteers while there. Over time such a service learning dimension was added to the project. During a program in Aicihi-ken, Japan, participants, for example, had the opportunity to study and visit homes for the aged, somewhat of an oxymoron in the Asian context. Participants also had the opportunity to live in and study remote, rural, mountainous communities in Japan.

Historically, numerous participants came from cultures and countries where there had been some dramatic historical animosities (e.g., Vietnamese and Khmer, Thai and Lao, Khmer and Thai, Vietnamese and Thai, and Japanese and U.S.). One of the most encouraging and inspiring elements of this project was the intense bonding that occurred among participants from countries that had had historical animosities. A tracer study of former participants and related testimonials collected indicate that for many individuals, this was a genuinely transformative experience (Mezirow, 1990) and intercultural competencies developed have contributed significantly to subsequent career and personal success.

CONCLUSIONS

These five cases help inform answers to the key research questions raised above and provide compelling evidence for both why and how Buddhism can contribute to multicultural learning and genuine appreciation of cultural diversity. All indicate the powerful potential of religion in multicultural education and the promotion of cultural democracy. Traditional Western approaches to education have privileged cognitive analytical learning. Western binary thinking also emphasizes many false and overly simplistic dichotomies, which need to be transcended. The most recent and cutting-edge brain research suggests that emotive and cognitive learning are much more complexly intertwined than previously thought (Edelman, 2004; Marcus, 2004; Ramachandran & Blakeslee, 1998; see also Rung & Fry, 2000).

The case studies described above, particularly of the Islamic College and the International Cooperative Learning Project, also provide solid support for Allport's social contact theory. It is critically important for those of diverse cultural and religious backgrounds to have the opportunity to know each other intimately and study each others' values and traditions. This is a major way to transcend the cultural distortions and misrepresentations emphasized by scholars such as Edward Said (Bayoumi & Rubin, 2000) and Linda Tuhiwai Smith (1999).

These case studies also indicate the potential for training individuals to become more Protean and to practice cultural democracy actively. The authentic practice of various religions such as Buddhism can be a powerful force for peace in the world (Chappell, 1999; Paige & Gilliatt, 1991). Thus, instead of separating church and state, as is the norm in the United States, what is needed globally is enhanced moral education. Central to enhancing moral education is the development of a deeper and authentic understanding of the world's major religions and their related philosophies and worldviews. The past century was one in which there was frequent conflict, including two world wars. In his thoughtful memoirs, Jean Monnet (1978), the man who inspired the vision of the European Union, laments on how the *curse of nationalism* spawned war and violence. Even in the postwar "peaceful" period, 1945–1986, there were 150 wars in 70 countries with deaths of approximately 30 million men, women, and children (Chappell, 1999). Among such conflicts were tragic events in Cambodia (the killing fields) (Maha Ghosananda, 1992), Bosnia, Chechnya, Northern Ireland, Afghanistan, and currently Iraq. Over 1,000 billion U.S. dollars annually are spent for military purposes (Gaadan, 1991, p. 7). Over 3 million died in the U.S. war in Vietnam (Chomsky, 2005). Robert McNamara (1995; McNamara et al., 1999), in reflecting on the war, admits that the tragedy primarily resulted from U.S. ignorance of Vietnamese history, culture, and language.

Montreal psychiatrist Joel Imbrahim Kreps (2005), writing in *Islamica Magazine*, published in Jordan, argues that religion is an important factor in transcending modern depression. University of Wisconsin cognitive scientist Richard Davidson and his colleagues, in studying the brain activity of Tibetan monks, found an apparently powerful relation between their religious orientation and meditation and the development of a "mental state away from destructive emotions and toward a more compassionate, happier frame of being" (Shreeve, 2005, p. 31). Also, Dean Hamer (2005), in *The God Gene*, finds that religious belief and spirituality is consistently associated with lower mortality and enhanced health.

The ideals of Buddhism were significantly realized in the 3rd century B.C., in the enlightened rule of King Ashoka in India, the third monarch of the Indian Mauryan Dynasty and considered to have been one of the most exemplary rulers in world history (see Strong, 1983). Ashoka was a benevolent and compassionate Buddhist-type ruler and tried to appeal equally to his multicultural, multireligious subjects (Mishra, 2004). There have never been Buddhist religious wars. Buddhism—with its emphasis on reason, tolerance, compassion, empathy, reverence for life in all its forms, voluntary simplicity, and understanding the root causes of human suffering—has great relevance to both cultural democracy and multicultural education (Buddhadāsa, 1977, 1979; Mishra, 2004). Genuine multicultural education should expose all students to the world's diverse religions and value systems. As suggested by Ferguson in the opening epigraph of this study, such a paradigm shift in education is *the greatest revolution in the world.* The heart of Buddhist epistemology reflected in the quotation below indicates how strikingly relevant this ancient philosophy is to contemporary education and many educational reforms being promoted around the world:

> Yes, you may well doubt, you may well be uncertain.... Do not accept anything because it is the authoritative tradition, because it is often said, because of rumour or hearsay, because it is found in the scriptures, because it agrees with a theory of which one is already convinced, because of the reputation of an individual, or because a teacher said it is thus and thus.... But experience it for yourself. (Kalma Sutta; Khantipalo Bhikku, 1975)

REFERENCES

Allport, G. W. (1954). *The nature of prejudice.* Cambridge, MA: Addison-Wesley.

Amyot, J. (2003). *I remember Chula: Memoirs of four decades of involvement in a Thai University (1962–2002).* Bangkok: Chulalongkorn University Social Research Institute.

Armstrong, K. (2000). *Islam: A short history.* New York: Random House.

Bayoumi, M., & Rubin, A. (Eds.) (2000). *The Edward Said reader.* New York: Vintage Books.

Benz, E. (1965). *Buddhism or Communism: Which holds the future of Asia?* London: George Allen & Unwin.

Buddhadāsa Bhikku. (1977). *Christianity and Buddhism—Sinclair Thompson Memorial Lecture, Fifth Series* (2nd ed.). Bangkok: Sublime Life Mission.

Buddhadāsa Bhikku. (1979). *Muea thaam khroong look [When Dhamma rules the world].* Chaiya, Thailand: Thammathan Foundation.

Buddhadāsa Bhikku. (1986). *Dhammic socialism.* Bangkok: Thai Inter-Religious Commission for Development.

Buddhadāsa Bhikku. (2004). *Heartwood of the Bodhi tree: The Buddha's teachings on voidness* (Santikaro Bhikku, Ed. & Dhammavicayo, Trans.). Chiang Mai: Silkworm Books. (Original work published 1962)

Carpenter, R. B., & Carpenter, B. C. (2002). *The blessings of Bhutan.* Honolulu: University of Hawai'i Press.

Champagne, D., & Abu-Saad (Eds.). (2003). *The future of indigenous people: Strategies for survival and development.* Los Angeles: UCLA American Indian Studies Center.

Chappell, D. W. (Ed.). (1999). *Buddhist peacework: Creating cultures of peace.* Boston: Wisdom Publications.

Chappell, D. W. (Ed.). (2003). *Socially engaged spirituality: Essays in honor of Sulak Sivaraksa on his 70th birthday.* Bangkok: Sathirakoses-Nagapradipa Foundation.

Chomsky, N. (2005). *At war with Asia.* Oakland, CA: AK Press.

Dahlberg, K., Drew, N., & Nystrom, M. (2001). *Reflective lifeworld research.* Lund, Sweden: Studentlitteratur.

Dore, R. P. (1976). *The diploma disease: Education, qualifications, and development.* Berkeley: University of California Press.

Earley, P. C., & Ang, S. (2003). *Cultural intelligence: Individual interactions across cultures.* Stanford, CA: Stanford University Press.

Edelman, G. M. (2004). *Wider than the sky: The phenomenal gift of consciousness.* New Haven, CT: Yale University Press.

Esposito, J. L. (2002). *What everyone needs to know about Islam.* Oxford: Oxford University Press.

Fantini, A. (1995). Introduction—language, culture and world view: Exploring the nexus. *International Journal of Intercultural Relations, 19*(2), 143–153.

Ferguson, M. (1980). *The Aquarian conspiracy.* Los Angeles: J. P. Tarcher.

Fromm, E. (1976). *To have or to be?* London: ABACUS.

Gaadan, Khambo Lam Kh. (1991). From violent combat to playful exchange of flowers. In G. D. Paige & S. Gilliat (Eds.), *Buddhism and nonviolent global problem-solving: Ulan Bator explorations* (pp. 7–10). Honolulu: Center for Global Nonviolence Planning Project, Spark M. Matsunaga Institute for Peace, University of Hawai'i.

Gabaude, L. (1988). *Une herméneutique bouddhique contemporaine de Thaïlande: Buddhadāsa Bhikku.* Paris: Ecole française d'Extrême-Orient.

Gardner, H. (1993). *Multiple intelligences: The theory in practice.* New York: Basic Books.

Geertz, C. (1983) *Local knowledge: Further research in interpretative anthropology.* New York: Basic Books.

Goodenough, W. (1963). *Cooperation in change: An anthropological approach to community development.* New York: Russell Sage Foundation.

Gould, S. J. (1996). *The mismeasure of man.* New York: Norton.

Hamer, D. (2004). The *God gene: How faith is hardwired into our genes.* New York: Doubleday.

Hesse, H. (1971). *Siddhartha.* New York: Bantam Books.

His Majesty King Bhumipol Adulyadej. (1997). Royal speech given to the audience of well-wishers on the occasion of the Royal Birthday Anniversary at the Dusidalai Hall, ChitraladaVilla, Dusit Palace, December 4.

Hofstede, G., & Hofstede, J. G. (2005). *Cultures and organizations: Software of the mind intercultural cooperation and its importance for survival* (2nd ed.). New York: McGraw-Hill.

Huntington, S. P. (1996). *The clash of civilizations and the remaking of world order.* New York: Simon & Schuster.

Huntington, S. P. (2004). *Who are we? The challenges to America's national identity.* New York: Simon & Schuster.

Ip, Hong Yuk. (2004). *Trans Thai Buddhism: Spirtuality, politically and socially & envisioning resistance: The engaged Buddhism of Sulak Sivaraksa.* Bangkok: Suksit Siam.

Jackson, P. A. (2003*). Buddhasāsa: Theravada Buddhism and modernist reform in Thailand.* Chiang Mai, Thailand: Silkworm Books.

Johnson, R. P. (1992). *Journey with the global family: Insights through portraits & prose.* Cody, WY: World View Art & Publishing.

Jurairatna Pongsapichaat. (2005, January 18). Jerajaa M. Egypt: Put 'Islamsugsaa' laksuut Thaj maatrataan look [Discussions with Egyptian University: Thai Islamic Studies curriculum meets world standards]. *Matichon Raajwan,* p. 30.

Kerr, A. Z. (1994). *Come with me from Lebanon: An American family odyssey.* Syracuse, NY: Syracuse University Press.

Kerr, A. Z. (2002). *Painting the Middle East.* Syracuse, NY: Syracuse University Press.

Kerr, M. H. (1975). *The elusive peace in the Middle East.* Albany: State University of New York Press.

Khantipalo Bhikku. (Trans.) (1975). *Kalama Sutta, Lord Buddha's discourse to the Kalama people.* Bangkok: Mahamakut Rajavidyalaya Press.

Kim, S. I. (1980). *The unfinished mission in Thailand: The uncertain Christian impact on the Buddhist heartland.* Seoul, Korea: East-West Center for Missions Research & Development.

Kreps, J. I. (2005, Spring). Depression. *Islamica Magazine, 12.*

Landis, D., Bennett, J. M., & Bennett, M. J. (2004). *Handbook of intercultural training* (3rd ed.). Thousand Oaks, Ca.: Sage.

Lifton, R. J. (1993). The *Protean self: Human resilience in an age of fragmentation.* Chicago: University of Chicago Press.

Litalien, M. (2001). *Le statut des religieuses (mae-chi/mae ji) dans l'institution Bouddhique contemporaine en Thaïlande: Vers un changement de paradigme.* Master's thesis, Université de Montréal.

McNamara, R., with VanDeMark, B. (1995). *In retrospect: The tragedy and lessons of Vietnam.* New York: Times Books.

McNamara, R., et al. (1999). *Argument without end: In search of answers to the Vietnam tragedy.* New York: PublicAffairs.

Mae Chee Sansanee Sthirasuta. (2003). *Mae Chee Sansanee Sthhirasuta's art book: One stroke dhamma.* Bangkok: Sathira–Dhammasathan.

Maha Ghosananda. (1992). *Step by step: Meditations on wisdom and compassion.* Berkeley: Parallax Press.

Marcus, G. (2004). *The birth of the mind.* New York: Basic Books.

Merriam, S. (1998). *Case study research in education: A qualitative approach.* San Francisco: Jossey-Bass.

Mezirow, J. (1990). *Fostering critical reflection in adulthood: A guide to transformational and emancipatory learning.* San Francisco: Jossey-Bass.

Mishra, P. (2004). *An end to suffering: The Buddha in the world.* Farrar, Straus & Giroux.

Monnet, J. (1978). *Memoirs.* Garden City, NY: Doubleday.

Morris, C. W. (1973a). *Paths of life: Preface to a world religion.* Chicago: University of Chicago Press.

Morris, C. W. (1973b). *Varieties of human value.* Chicago: University of Chicago Press.

Paige, G. D. (Ed.). (1984). *Buddhism and leadership for peace.* Honolulu: Dae Won Sa Temple of Hawai'i.

Paige, G. D., & Gilliat, S. (Eds.). (1991). *Buddhism and nonviolent global problem-solving: Ulan Bator explorations.* Honolulu: Center for Global Nonviolence Planning Project, Spark M. Matsunanga Institute for Peace, University of Hawai'i.

Pettigrew, T. (1999, Fall). Gordan Willard Allport: A tribute. *Journal of Social Issues, 55*(3), 415–427.

Pettigrew, T. (2001, April). *Does intergroup contact reduce prejudice throughout the world?* Paper presented at the 2nd Biennial Congress of the International Academy for Intercultural Research, University of Mississippi, Oxford.

Pogamy, I. S. (2004). *The Roma Café: Human rights and the plight of the Romani people.* London: Pluto Press.

Ramachandran, V. S., & Blakeslee, S. (1998). *Phantoms in the brain: Probing the mysteries of the human mind.* New York: HarperCollins.

Ramírez, M., & Castañeda, A. (1974). *Cultural democracy, bicognitive development, and education.* New York: Academic Press.

Rung Kaewdang, & Fry, G. (2000). *Learning from monkeys at the Monkey Training College, Surat Thani, Thailand* (G. Fry & T. Pongpanich-Fry, Trans.). Bangkok: Amarin.

Sathira-Dhammasathan. (2005). *The learning community for peace and harmony: A second home to all.* Bangkok: Sathira-Dhammasathan. Available at www.sathira-dhammasathan.org

Shaheen, J. G. (2001). *Real bad Arabs: How Hollywood vilifies a people.* New York: Olive Branch Press.

Shreeve, J. (2005, March). Beyond the brain. *National Geographic,* 2–31.

Sioris, G. A. (1998). *Phaulkon: The Greek first counselor at the court of Siam: An appraisal.* Bangkok: The Siam Society.

Smith, L. T. (1999). *Decolonizing methodologies: Research and indigenous peoples.* London: Zed Books.

Stake, R. E. (1995). *The art of case study research.* Thousand Oaks, CA: Sage.

Strong, J. S. (1983). *The legend of King Asoka: A study and translation of the Asokavadana.* Princeton, NJ: Princeton University Press.

Suzuki, D. (1970). *Zen and Japanese culture.* Princeton, NJ: Princeton University Press.

Thich Nhat Hanh. (1993). *The blooming of a lotus: Guided meditation exercises for healing and transformation.* Boston: Beacon Press.

Tomita, T., Fry, G., & Seksin S. (2000). *International cooperative learning: An innovative approach to intercultural service.* Nagoya: Tokai Institute of Social Development for Asia and the Pacific and Aichi Mizuho College; Eugene, OR: Center for Asian and Pacific Studies, University of Oregon.

Treiman, D. J. (1977). *Occupational prestige in comparative perspective.* New York: Academic Press.

Van Manen, M. (1990). *Researching lived experience: Human science for an action sensitive pedagogy.* Albany: State University of New York Press.

Villenas, S. (2001). Latina mothers and small-town racisms: Creating narratives of dignity and moral education in North Carolina. *Anthropology and Education Quarterly, 32,* 1, 3–28.

Warut Thongchua. (Ed.). (1998). *Chaiya: Suan Mokh* [Chaiya: Garden of liberation]. Bangkok: Mental Health Publishing.

Yin, R. K. (2003). *Case study research: Design and methods* (3rd ed.). Thousand Oaks, CA: Sage.

CHAPTER 6

RELIGIOUS RIGHT AND "THE RIGHT RELIGION"

Multicultural and Educational Impacts

César Rossatto and Elaine Hampton
University of Texas at El Paso

ABSTRACT

This chapter seeks to critically uncover religious and political manipulations and their consequences and implications on education from evidence in the context of communities in the United States located near the Mexican border. Relevant examples are used to deconstruct some of these aspects of religion.

The first aspect examined is the fear of the *Other* mentality. Religious doctrines often induce fear of the *Other* to promote their own faith. In the United States today, this practice, in conservative Christian teaching, has political support and is on the increase. The inherent patriarchy in most world religions and its role in marginalizing women are also examined. This patriarchy permeates societies and the schools that serve them, perpetuating the unequal gender power structure. In the third aspect, the authors demonstrate how the standardization of curriculum eliminates the teaching of critical thinking, scientific principles outside of church doctrine, and even basic

Religion in Multicultural Education, pages 121–137

understandings of human sexuality and birth control. The final aspect is the pathological patriotic doctrine that elevated the dominant religious power's control in education through the new doctrine of fear spread by the U.S. administration's *antiterrorism campaign* after the bombing of the World Trade Towers.

INTRODUCTION

Education, by nature, is embedded in many social contexts. The following explores education in the global era in the United States as it is embedded in a political-religious context. Understanding the power of this context assists in the examination of the purposes of schooling and the forces that drive the curriculum. Religion has held sway over education throughout the centuries as a method of maintaining society in accord with the constructs of the dominant religion. In a globalizing world, as societies merge and mingle, the increasingly multicultural and multireligious communities elevate the demand for a critical examination of the role of religions in education. As Richard Shaull says in his introduction to Paulo Freire's *Pedagogy of the Oppressed* (1996):

> There is no such thing as a *neutral educational* process. Education either functions as an instrument that is used to facilitate the integration of the younger generation into the logic of the present system and bring about conformity to it, *or* it becomes "the practice of freedom," the means by which men and women deal critically and creatively with reality and discover how to participate in the transformation of their world. (p. 16)

We acknowledge the richness and contribution of different cultures and their religious perspectives to education; however, a critical analysis is intrinsically necessary to examine the manipulative aspects of religious doctrines. Critical educators are called upon to reexamine their *commitment to social justice* within a hegemonic context and analyze how the influence of religion today, just as in the past, can blind people and mislead them. *Religious supremacy* can be a source of cruelty and an enabler of political monopoly. We seek to critically uncover religious and political manipulations and their consequences and implications to education from evidence in the context of communities in the United States located near the Mexican border. We seek to deconstruct some of these aspects of religion through relevant examples.

The first aspect we examine is the fear of the *Other* mentality. Religious doctrines often induce fear of the *Other* to promote their own faith. This hegemonic conservative religious teaching plays out across the globe in the creation of private conservative religious schools providing separatist shelters from multicultural understanding and multiethnic student bodies. In the United States today, this practice, in conservative Christian teaching, has political support and is on the increase (National Center for Educational Statistics, 2005). Second, we analyze the aspect of the inherent patriarchy in most world religions and its role in marginalizing women. This permeates societies and the schools that serve them, perpetrating the unequal gender power structure. Third, we investigate how the *standardization of curriculum* eliminates the teaching of critical thinking, scientific principles outside of church doctrine, and even basic understandings of human sexuality and birth control. Finally, we examine the new doctrine of fear spread by the current U.S. administration's *antiterrorism campaign* after the bombing of the World Trade Towers, sold under the guise of a *struggle for idealized democratic world ideologies*. This doctrine swelled to the point of a *pathological patriotic doctrine* that elevated the dominant religious power's control in education.

Both authors bring strong religious histories to the study. Cesar, a Brazilian white male, was raised Christian and studied 7 years for the priesthood. He left it after studying critical pedagogy with Nita Freire, Marxist philosophers, and other critical progressive educators. He came to understand that through education it is possible to achieve greater influence on social transformation. To cleanse himself from the guilt induced by formal religious studies, he studied 2 years of university liberation theology. He continues his membership in the critical liberation theology congregation.

Elaine spent most of her life as a conservative Christian in a fundamentalist, patriarchal religion. When she encountered multicultural understanding through readings such as Paulo Freire's *Pedagogy of the Oppressed*, it opened an ongoing critique about which better embodies the words of Christ—fundamentalist religion or critical liberation theory? That question led to her pursuit of advanced education, her embrace of critical feminist studies, and her critique of oppressive educational practices.

A CRITICAL ANALYSIS OF RELIGION

Humans look for spiritual connections with higher or transcendental sources to construct meaning for their existence in the universe. In this search for meaning, however, some become deluded on their journey—inwardly or outwardly. Inwardly, they may lose themselves in false-hearted religious exploitation or fanaticism. Outwardly, they may blind themselves with an idealized paradise post-life with materialistic connotations of lush gardens and jeweled castles—a carnal definition of reward.

We use the term *religion* to speak of the formal social organization, as well as the common doctrines, the members' interpretations of the doctrine, and the hierarchies inherent in the social organizations. In this context, a religion is born and flourishes when a messianic person's ideas become formalized or translated. A circle of believers and followers is formed, a doctrine emerges, and leaders arise. These leaders show to their followers paths to coherent beliefs in their doctrine. Thus, the doctrine has power for good or evil. Unquestioned dogmatic practices can have collective repercussions, such as the mass suicide of the Jones cult in Guiana, the mass suicides at Heavens Gate in California, the subway gassing in Japan, and the armed conflict in Waco, Texas. The deceitful aspects of doctrines cannot go unchallenged, since they can lead to catastrophic consequences.

At its best, the religious doctrine might serve as the channel that guides humans to spiritual experiences, either inwardly or outwardly, connecting them with the universe and what it has to offer and influencing people toward experiences with the divine or higher power that guide them to mystical encounters. But, according to Dalai Lama, it is spirituality, not religion, that enables a deified experience. Spirituality is not a doctrine that can be transmitted. *Spirituality* is a personal experience and religion cannot be the translation of that spirituality (Boff, 2001). In order to demystify oppressive aspects of doctrine and religious controls, religious influence in formal education must be critically analyzed. These analyses can facilitate a discernment of spiritual experiences that free the individual to move beyond the entrapment of manipulated or misleading beliefs.

Within this understanding about religion in our multicultural communities, a rich realm of discourse is born as different cultures bring their variety of religious perspectives to the communities and to the schools. Within this diversity, a critical perspective is intrinsically necessary. Because religion may provide a tenuous grip of hope for many who are oppressed, a *language of critique* must be accompanied by a *language of possibility*, where, on the one hand, critical theorists must denounce injustices or oppression; they must, on the other hand, announce possible alternative solutions.

Context of Patriarchal and Separatist Mentality

Religious organizations are designed by men—only a few exist that are designed by women or with women. These organized religions, throughout history, have had a close association with divisions, conquests, and war. This easy friendship is a manifestation of two embedded components of many religions. First is the belief of supremacy and unique sanctification inherent in most religions, and the second is the *patriarchal history* that forces gender and power divisions in the society the religion influences. These attitudes of sanctimony and patriarchy permeate many world societies and infest public school curricula with practices that are born from them.

Christianity and Judaism are founded on the Old Testament stories of conquest and domination. The stories describe the patriarchal leaders' pride in their conquest of the land called Canaan. The accounts describe the rape, plunder, theft, murder, and human enslavement of the conquest, yet, the Old Testament reports these as Godly deeds—God-ordained and Godly sanctified. This small section of the world population, the Hebrews, considered themselves elite and chosen of God. To make the elite circle even smaller, only men were allowed entrance. The sign of admission was circumcision—the only sign that would exclude all women. The most elite of this man group, the priest class or the Levites, wrote of their belief that their every action was justified because they were the *chosen of God.*

This patriotic mentality plays out in *religious separatist tendencies* that shout discriminatory and exclusionary remarks such as: *We're number one and God says so! God bless OUR country (over and above other countries implied)! If you don't embrace our doctrine (speak our language, look like us, etc.), go back to your own country.* This gives the members of such association consent—holy permission and even holy mandate—to feel justified to inflict evil upon others and outsiders. The theocratic underhandedness impregnates governments and is fueled by the belief that they are chosen by God.

This permeates today's religions, where members believe that as long as they pray to God, whatever they do is sacred. This engenders a belief in a divine right to treat *others*, outsiders, or pagans as they see fit to meet their fanatic views and unchallenged beliefs. This was recently evidenced in the United States in the dearth of Internet and email conversations widely circulated by the political right glorifying President George W. Bush and his unprecedented invasion of Iraq. The messages made it clear that the senders believed that President Bush prayed for God's guidance; therefore, the invasion of Iraq and the subsequent slaughter of thousands were justified and holy. The messages were riddled with claims that the United States was founded in the dominant Christian doctrine, seemingly oblivious to the foundational thesis in the First Amendment to the Constitution prohibiting Congress from making laws about the establishment of religion or prohibiting religious practices. Rift with misquotes, lies, and misinterpretations of historical events and declarations, the consensus of the communications was a sanctified justification of the unilateral invasion.

The economic wealth, comfort, and privileges evident in the membership in the dominant conservative Christian community in the United States are interpreted as gifts from God showing *his* favoritism with the country. Such bias mentality hides from view the obvious questions about fairness, equity, and a God who plays favorites. Christian friends in our border community who accumulate financial success proudly show off their elegant new homes and declare the luxurious facility a special blessing from God. Across the El Paso freeway, clearly visible to everyone, are miles of unpaved roads and very humble dwellings in the sandy foothills on the edges of Ciudad Juárez, in Chihuahua, Mexico. Are these people *unblessed* by God for their location a few yards outside of this *consecrated country?*

This separatist, conquest mentality, boosted by the desire to justify elitism, generates an exclusionary ignorance of Other. Ignorance builds excuses to justify the narrow-mindedness and prejudice. This exclusionary apprehension-based ideology, which dictates that the Other deserve their plot, is interpreted as the Other if it wouldn't fit in anyway, they are not as righteous as we are, they want to harm us, they will take our resources, or they will corrupt our children. From this ignorance is born fear, and this fear stifles multicultural understandings and often swells into violence. It portrays itself in messages such as the one painted on the back window of a car driving down the local freeway, *"Jesus loves you. Allah wants your ass dead."*

The Other is killed softly through marginalization or must be *conquered* (a guise for the terms *murdered or tortured until surrender*). Therefore, the Other cannot become our friend. Taboos are built and political policies enacted to prevent our communities and our children from interacting with or understanding the Other. The taboos enter the schools and find homes in cliques, clubs, church groups, or gangs.

The 2004 reelection of George W. Bush to the presidency in the United States provides evidence of how religious monopoly serves as the institutional apparatus that greases the progress of the dominant doctrine. The campaign's focus on banning abortion and rights for gay men and lesbians provided an agenda that was particularly attractive to the majority conservative Christian religious right and was thus responsible for the narrow victory (Economist.com, 2005; Waldman & Green, 2004). The results of this election confirmed the religious right agenda and provided impetus to attempt cementing a powerful religious doctrine with a national social and educational policy. Emboldened by the victory, religion and politics stepped deeper into the schools. Churches adopted the doctrines and became political pulpits. The confidence led to unprecedented actions such as the June 2005 signing of the state-approved abortion consent bill signed by then Texas Governor Rick Perry in the gym of a Christian school in Fort Worth, Texas.

These historical underpinnings inform today's political agenda and its impact on education. The implication of such historical clumsiness gives grounds for critical educators, multiculturalists, and emerging educators to be better prepared to understand misleading religious and political discourses. Educational access and power are severely and detrimentally affected by the patriarchal and separatist mentality underlying the conservative and dominant U.S. religious doctrine. The Judeo-Christian story is not unique as other religions around the world create their supremacy and sanctification myths. Today, some religions may not make such strong claims to supremacy. However, some do, and this legacy is engrained in human history.

Separatist Mentality and Multiculturalism in Schools

Many uninformed teachers, themselves influenced by religious separatism and political biases, subtly endorse the separation between the students and avoid a *curriculum of multicultural understanding*. The distinct spirit of such tendencies is evident in comments such as these that both authors of this chapter hear regularly in schools: *I don't speak Spanish and they need to learn English. Why should I have to learn sheltered instruction? If they want to speak Spanish, they should go back where they came from. Those people are taking our jobs.*

Teachers whose multicultural views are narrow, intentionally or not, hide choices from their students. A local preacher's wife and public school teacher, Linda, announced that she purposely asks her two daughters to step aside so her son, Josh, can take leadership roles in the home and the church. He leads prayers and makes decisions, and the girls respond in passive adulation. Linda's daughters are socialized away from liberating thought.

The subtle deceit spread to her fourth graders in a school serving mostly Mexican American children. Josh is a star football player in the local high school. Linda wore his jersey to school one Friday and Josh came to visit her class. She showed the newspaper article about his football feats and encouraged Josh to sign autographs for the children. Her lesson for the day—heroes, like white football players, come from the males in her culture group. Choice is a treasured right in democratic society; however, even though choice may be offered, the selection of options is based on the education and understanding of the learner. Linda, representing dominant *malestream* (Harding, 1987) society, subtracts choice from her students by the deceitful portrayal of heroes and their social roles.

Many families in a local conservative Christian church send their children to one of the private Christian schools. The community is about half Mexican Americans and about half white. The church school is 95% white. Church members teach in the school, and parents are active participants in extracurricular experiences. A strong homogeneous community spirit joins the families. The curriculum is strong in traditional content with athletics and religious/classical music dominating the extracurricular activities. The science curriculum teaches creation science and presents evolution as a controversial and unproven theory. There are no classes teaching multicultural understanding or structured around critical issues.

The students' choices to learn are narrow and prescribed; but they are *safe* from multicultural influences.

This reflects a national trend. Enrollment in conservative Christian private schools in the United States is growing faster than enrollment in public schools or enrollment in other private schools (National Center for Educational Statistics, 2005). In addition, private schools enroll significantly fewer minority students (63%) than public schools (77%), and only 13% of private schools serve students identified as *limited English proficient* compared with 54% of public schools serving these children (National Center for Educational Statistics, 2002).

Religious schools with *isolationist curriculum* are not unique to the Christian religion. Isolationism is inherent in religious education. Religions build schools to perpetrate their doctrine, to keep and increase their parishioner membership, and to shelter their youth from the larger society. In the United States, religious schools are institutionalized as a part of the private sector. Those who do not wish for their children to be involved with the larger society can provide for their religious education privately.

At the time of this writing, strong political power was advocating the move to use government funds for private education. In 2003, for example, the U.S. Congress approved H.R. 2765, which created a $10 million *private school voucher program* for students in the District of Columbia (GovTrack, 2004). Florida and Colorado approved statewide voucher programs and they were hotly contested in other states.

Diverting public funds to private education is problematic in the United States since the Judeo-Christian dominant religions provide the great majority of religious education. The Christian school described above is part of a large network of schools and universities. This elite network was strengthened and flourished in the second Bush administration. Public funds were diverted to support the private schools at the expense of public education budgets. Those who overtly or covertly did not want their children in multicultural schools were advantaged in their *choice* of schools (private school vouchering, home schooling, charter schooling). This trend to move to private schools in the United States reserves to parents (usually wealthy parents) the elitist and isolationist educational experience they wish for their children; leaving behind students from other cultures, those in poverty and those who are different. In this setting, the parents ensure that the young are kept away from multicultural and feminist influence that they may not be able to control in public education. They form a paternal support group in which favors are shared, jobs are filled, and elite power circles are maintained.

Curriculum Is Standardized to the Religious and Political Agenda

Perhaps the strongest political force on education in the United States today is the intense focus on high-stakes testing. Because of the revision of the national Elementary and Secondary Education Act of 2002 (commonly called *No Child Left Behind,* or NCLB), all states receiving the federal funds must grade every student and every school on their scores on a single instrument—a short-answer state test. The consequences for failing to meet a set score on the test are severe. Students fail and are denied graduation. Teachers, students, and schools falling below the mark are publicly shamed and sanctioned, and schools may be reassembled. Because of the nature of this powerful instrument to narrow curriculum to test-based content and format, education that involves multicultural thinking is squeezed out and eliminated (Hampton, 2004).

High-stakes *standardized tests* are based in the 1950s paradigm of behaviorist learning. The drill and practice instruction that these tests reinforce is based in early learning theories of association and behaviorism that have been rejected in cognitive psychology. According to the behaviorist theory, higher-order thinking is acquired by breaking learning into small, prerequisite, step-by-step skills. Numerous research studies from the fields of education and cognitive psychology indicate that learning is complex, involving multiple, integrated interactions, and that learning is embedded in contextual and social situations. Assessing learning is also complex and involves multiple strategies and close alignment with the learning environment. It cannot be done with one instrument.

In fact, high-stakes standardized testing was born in racist practices. In the United States in the 1920s, Robert M. Yerkes, a professor at Harvard University, was convinced that psychological testing was a hard science and that human potential could be assigned a number through testing. He used forms of intelligence tests (not designed for this purpose) on 1.75 million army men. The tests were administered in uncontrolled and sometimes hostile environments. Masses of men in crowded rooms were subject to the instruments, and the men in the back could not see or hear. The tests were timed, but the men did not know it. The tests generated tremendous amounts of data, which were interpreted as if they were all accurate and valid (Gould, 1996; Kamin, 1974).

Yerkes published this data in a chart ranking the intelligence of foreign-born men. Those from England, Holland, Denmark, Scotland, and Germany were on the top with high numbers of men scoring A, B, and C. On the bottom were listed *Greece, Russia, Italy, Poland, and countries of nonwhite groups,* with most of these men scoring D (Corbett & Wilson, 1993; Gould, 1996; Kamin, 1974).

Professor C. C. Brigham of Princeton University advocated that these tests measured innate intelligence and concluded that mental test results indicate a genuine intellectual superiority of the *Nordic group* (Kamin, 1974). Professor Brigham became the Secretary of the College Entrance Examination Board and designed and developed the SAT (Scholastic Aptitude Test). The library building of the Educational Testing Service is named in his honor. Brigham's practices are still embedded in the standardized testing culture. He is responsible for the scoring scale, the difficulty rating, and the internally justified item-analysis method still used by the Educational Testing Service in the development of tests (Corbett & Wilson, 1993).

In this era, racial hatred and elitist practices were rampant. Many in power in the United States did not want nonwhite immigrants, and especially persecuted Jews that entered the country. The following quotes are from Brigham's 1923 book, *A Study of American Intelligence:*

> The intellectual superiority of our Nordic group over the Alpine, Mediterranean, and negro groups has been demonstrated. If a person is unwilling to accept the race hypothesis as developed here, he may go back to the original nativity groups, and he can not deny the fact that differences exist. (p. 192)

> Unless we can re-establish geographical isolation of races, we cannot prevent their interbreeding. By rigid laws excluding immigrants of other races, such as they have in New Zealand and Australia, it may be possible for a time to maintain the purity of the white race in certain countries. (p. 206)

The high-stakes testing aspect of NCLB began in Texas in the 1980s as an educational reform movement designed to hold everyone to high standards. Policymakers, bipartisan and uneducated about education, designed an *efficient* system of standards and testing. The simplistic sound bite goes something like this: *We write standards—the same for every school in the state. Everyone receives the same test based on these standards and then we can compare all the schools. Schools that do not score well will be punished. Students who do not score well will fail. It sounds fair to everyone, and students will get busy and will study. No child will be left behind.* This one-size-fits-all mentality has now spread throughout the United States.

The devastating impact of this dictate has been illustrated by hundreds of studies such as those done by Amrein and Berliner (2002), Kohn (2000), McNeil (2000), and Valenzuela (2004). They assert that assessing learners' levels of understanding is extremely complex. It cannot be done with one instrument. Students have multiple intelligences and therefore multiple forms of assessment also must be used. Holding schools or children hostages under this system is unethical and violates their rights as citizens. And yet, U.S. education occurs in an environment fraught with rigid standards and high-stakes tests, where the landscape is altered into one of sameness that chokes children's and teachers' creative potential and crowds out the rich variety of curriculum necessary to prepare students for a complex future. Test preparation and drill dominate the curriculum, shading out the growth of multicultural education, feminist issues, creativity, and critical thought. Children and teachers are distraught. Dropout rates in our community are near the 50th percentile and rising. Many children are being left behind.

Quality curriculum is further reduced by legislation enforcing the dominant religious doctrine. The 15-members of the Texas State Board of Education in the early 2000s was dominated by conservative politics and heavily influenced by right-wing religious thinking. This board selected textbooks for the state. Because of the state's size, textbook publishing companies are heavily influenced by Texas politics. The state-adopted health textbooks presented abstinence as the only birth control and marriage as only between a man and a woman. State history texts were carefully screened for anything that might present multicultural or liberal thought and focuses on facts and dates of traditional content. Phonics instruction dominated the reading texts.

In Texas, and across the country, school boards adopted or attempted to adopt policies to defend their religious doctrine against evolution—one of the foundational explanatory theories in science. (For an update on the ongoing struggles in the United States over the treatment of evolution in the curriculum, see the News Archive at the National Center for Science Education website at www.ncseweb.org.)

With strict controls forcing standardized educational curriculum such as those described above, the conservative forces diminish and eliminate opportunities for citizens to think critically and to see the world from many views through the contributions of other cultures and other thoughts. The purpose of education in this setting is clearly that of reproducing the current social and economic order. The importance of education's role in citizens' actions must be underscored. Near the beginning of the 19th century, the social mindset in the southern United States was that enslaving other people to provide personal economic gain was justified, even sanctified. A century later, the social mindset in Germany was that murdering a group of people because of their ethnicity and historic hatred was justified, even sanctified. Most sadly, public education, infused with dogma, played a significant role in maintaining this social mindset. In settings such as these, clearly society dictated that the purpose of education was to maintain the status quo with its power structures, unfair practices, and resulting atrocities.

How frightening to think that, had any one of us been in one of these communities and had been educated in this curriculum of social maintenance, we might have followed the crowd and participated in these gross injustices. Dream for a moment about what might have been if critical thought had been dominant in school curricula during these most humiliating eras of our histories. Through a transformative (rather than reproductive) curriculum, citizens would have been prepared and poised to counter the atrocities; and a groundswell of critical citizens would have smothered the social atrocities while they were still in conceptual stages.

From the time of Columbus until recent history, the vast majority of North American societies have purposely designed social structures with legislated mandates for inequity and oppressive power structures. Our citizens who remain placated by dominant ideologies today may believe that our societies have achieved social justice and horrors such as those above are a thing of the past. Those who are prepared to think critically and apply multiple perspectives to concepts and actions in their societies understand how easily we can be swayed into false justification of social inequalities. We draw from the following example of recent ideological conflicts escalating into armed conflict and suppression of critical thought.

The New Doctrine of Fear: A Pathological Patriotic Doctrine

In March 2003, the United States and Great Britain, with aid from a few other nations, invaded Iraq. The Bush administration sold the public on the need for the invasion with tales about Iran creating weapons of mass destruction and Iraq's supposed involvement in the bombing of the World Trade Towers. Both of these causes, along with much of the war rhetoric, were later shown to be false (Smith, 2003). Undermined by fear, however, U.S. society was indoctrinated to believe that this invasion was legitimate, even under false assumptions and prefabricated evidence. This mentality was imposed on other countries, thus forcing their permission to invade, control, and dictate U.S. interests to other countries.

This culture of war combined with deviant aspects of religion to impregnate U.S. society, composing a new *doctrine of fear,* a pathological patriotic doctrine. This led to a blatant disregard for the oppositions from many citizens in the United States and other countries. The lack of critical thought was consistent with patterns of indoctrination and a false perception of reality. Millions of conservative and even moderate religious groups bought into the propaganda's ideology and its agenda (Economist.com, 2005).

Why would people embark in such mischievous manipulations? Where do these beliefs come from? And why do people so naively embrace them and act accordingly? Freire's writings credit a lack of critical thinking and critical consciousness. Religions are indeed powerful channels to control the masses, and, as Marx claims, they can serve as the opiate of the people.

Structures and policies created by society, institutions, and dominant groups maintain the supremacy of the wealthy classes. The dominant groups should bear the blame because they have the upper hand in the construction of reality, subjugating those they marginalize. Thus, it is because of the structures and not coincidence that some succeed in education and career options and others do not. Chomsky (2003) stresses that dominant groups are constantly concerned that the *great beast* (masses of people) stay in *their place.* This is why religion, mass media, and educational institutions focus resources on a pathetic divide-and-conquer instruction to coerce people to believe in lies that keep them alienated and ignorant. Thus patriarchal capitalist societies maintain their positions of power and privilege.

Religions contribute to this delusion via covert and overt ways that establish and maintain supremacy. It is not by accident that people in the United States are educated to say devoutly, *God bless America,* forgetting to question the fairness of a God who has preference for one country over another. Why only bless this country and not the others? Wouldn't a fair and just God care for the other countries and their people? It is a major problem to the world when one nation claims superiority over others. People of such a country are educated to believe they are greater than other people. This mentality calls for a special form of *critical pedagogy,* where those who learn to feel superior need to unlearn their false sense of self and relearn to find themselves within a revised sense of collective identity.

To maintain a *religious dogma,* religions must *restrict critical thought.* This is most overtly obvious when religions delude their public via the man-made construct of hell. This ultimate punishment elevates the severity of the doctrines that are made by the leaders who create the dogma. Their doctrines of determinism fuel the ultimately blind fanaticism. In order to maintain the delusion, they must deny to their people the critical education necessary to critique the doctrine. In this context, education must be constricted. The fear of punishment keeps the people from questioning the doctrine's practices. The tranquilized public's mantra goes something like this, *I don't have to question. I'll just obey and then I'll understand it all when I get to heaven.* The leaders themselves are institutionalized in this narrow, placating, unquestioning dogma and then pass it on to others.

Thus, religious movements today also need to be confronted to prevent the educational constrictions described above. For this reason, critical educators, liberation theologians, and well-informed individuals have a responsibility to denounce and deconstruct religion's oppressive practices. At times it is painful to do so, as retaliation often is the norm when the status quo is challenged. Don Helder Camera, a renowned activist bishop from Brazil, led many efforts to challenge the structures. The resistance he felt is evident in his famous comment, *When we fed and clothed the poor, the govern-*

ment applauded us. When we began to ask, "Why are there so many poor?" they called us "communists" and attacked us.

THE LANGUAGE OF POSSIBILITY

In this process of rethinking our politics and religious practices, education has a delicate and arduous task. Undeniably, religions have also contributed positively to society, especially for those most disenfranchised. Religion can provide the hope that sustains through difficult times. Therefore, the language of critique must be followed by the language of possibility (Freire, 1996).

New ways of thinking about education based on notions of solidarity and ethics must challenge postcolonial, postmodern, and poststructural practices. The right-wing conservative rhetoric that induce fear, *silencing*, and *obedience* to standards of *conformity* to the status quo must be replaced by new ethical philosophy of solidarity that fosters critical consciousness, social justice, and inclusion. It is not a rigid set of rules to follow but a dialectic process that empowers citizens to be responsible, to participate, and to commit to community transformation where no one is left behind and everyone becomes a historical agent rather than a hegemonic object of manipulation. Education in this liberating context validates the knowledge students bring with them in order to dialectically generate new understandings.

When we think about religion within the context of education, alternatives to the conservative mentality make a difference in the world. In Brazil, liberation theology and the *comunidades de base* (community grassroots movements) have historically made commitment to oppressed groups.

In Texas, the El Paso Inter-religious Sponsoring Organization (EPISO) operates transformational community work. This group is a nonpartisan, issues-based community association, with activist and critical consciousness raising initiatives that confront injustices encountered in the local neighborhood. They organize local citizens to improve schools and communities, change nonworking school's administration, and transform *colonias'* (communities with underdeveloped infrastructure) inhospitable conditions. Through grants, they have built a fundraising infrastructure to sponsor vocational training and job opportunities. They promote door-to-door political consciousness for people to exercise their political voice through their vote. EPISO's united voice has strong influence over elected officials to abide by their suggestions. They hold political leaders publicly accountable for their promises. Their tremendous commitment to activism and social transformation is evident in their participation in recent marches against standardized testing in Texas and community protests to publicize the unsolved *murders of almost 400 young women* across the border in Ciudad Juárez, Chihuahua, Mexico.

Across the border, a teacher in Ciudad Juárez, Cesar Silva, builds his curriculum around social justice themes. Because of the 350 U.S. factories located in this city, many Mexicans come from the interior to work on the factory lines (for about $6.00 per day). The income is not enough to afford adequate housing. Many of them become squatters in the desert hills surrounding the city, and build homes out of tires, cardboard, or packing pallets on any land that they find available. In 2002, one of the owners of the land where many squatters were located asked for city help in removing the illegal dwellings. The city did provide warning to the immigrants and some assistance in relocating, but city resources were stretched too thin to meet all the needs. In the end, the city brought in bulldozers and tractors to plow down the homes and force the people to relocate.

A high school in one of the low-income communities in Ciudad Juárez was committed to allowing an education founded in social justice and critical thought. Mr. Silva is the communications teacher at the school. He allowed the incident described above to become the curriculum for his writing classes. The students gathered information from many sources and visited the community during the removal processes to interview those who lost their homes. They created their own newspaper accounts and continued the study by searching deeper for the root causes of the conflict from the point of view of the landowner, the city officials, and the squatters.

In an El Paso elementary school, Daniel Heiman also bases his curriculum in critical thought and transformative education. The school administrators denied his fourth graders recess breaks and kept them under watchful eye in the school cafeteria during the 3 days devoted to administering the high-stakes state tests. Because Mr. Heiman had filled his curriculum with opportunities for the students to have their own voices and to critically review just and unjust social practices, the children developed their own letter-writing campaign about their unfair treatment during the test. Letters posted on the school walls eloquently explained, in Spanish and English, to the school community how the sequestering was unfair and actually detrimental to their optimal performance on the tests.

Education based in realities such as those above help abolish structures that oppress people by reinventing the world with schooling for equality, diversity, and humanitarian efforts that dignify the person and the community as a whole. This initiative ought to construct humane values, self-determination, self-affirmation, and self-realization rather than the imprisonment to capitalist exploitation. This new alternative education can smooth the progress of new visions of ethics for teachers who will be able to bring about the best in all students, rather than repressive or recriminatory practices. Instead of working from a disciplinarian's stand and standardized model, teachers will be able to facilitate democratic practices, where both students and teachers construct together new ethical ways of being and new world realities. The uniqueness of each classroom member can flourish, making possible for teachers to be *transformative intellectual leaders* who think with their students and work in their best interest embracing the struggles they go through.

In the words of Cornel West (1997), "... *hope* is not a naive belief, but an evidence based process that sustains a new vision of decency and dignity to never allow inequality, racism, and injustices to set in as a norm." What may be perceived as unprecedented can become reality. The *impossible* is what has never been tried before.

REFERENCES

Amrein, A. L., & Berliner, D. C. (2002). *The impact of high-stakes tests on student performance: An analysis of NAEP results in states with high-stakes tests and ACT, SAT and AP test results in states with high school graduation exams.* Tempe, AZ: Education Policies Study Laboratory.

Brigham, C. C. (1923). *A study of American intelligence.* Princeton, NJ: Princeton University Press.

Chomsky, N. (2003). *Hegemony or survival: America's quest for global dominance.* New York: Metropolitan Books/Henry Holt.

Corbett, H. D., & Wilson, B. (1993). *Testing reform and rebellion.* Norwood, NJ: Ablex.

Economist.com. (2005). *America's religious right: You ain't seen nothing yet.* Retrieved June 23, 2005, from www.economist.com/world/na/displayStory.cfm?story _id=4102212

Freire, P. (1996). *Pedagogy of the oppressed.* New York: Continuum.

Gould, S. J. (1996). *The mismeasure of man.* New York: W.W. Norton.

Gov. Track. (2004). 108th Congress. Available at http://www.govtrack.us/congress/ bill.xpd?bill=h108-2765

Hampton, E. (2004). Standardized or sterilized? Divergent perspectives on the effects of high-stakes testing in West Texas. In A. Valenzuela (Ed.), *Leaving children behind: Why Texas-style accountability fails Latino youth* (pp. 179–200). Albany: State University of New York Press.

Harding, S. (1987). Is there a feminist method? In S. Harding (Ed.), *Feminism and methodology: Social science issues.* Bloomington: Indiana University Press.

Kamin, L. (1974). *The science and politics of I.Q.* Mahwah, NJ: Erlbaum.

Kohn, A. (2000). *The case against standardized testing: Raising the scores, ruining the schools.* Portsmouth, NH: Heinemann.

McNeil, L. M. (2000). *Contradictions of school reform: Educational costs of standardized testing.* New York: Routledge.

National Center for Educational Statistics. (2002). *Special analysis: 2002. Private schools: A brief portrait.* Available online at http://nces.ed.gov/programs/coe/2002/ analyses/private/sa01d.asp

National Center for Educational Statistics. (2005). *The condition of education in brief: 2005*. Available online at http://nces.ed.gov/pubsearch/pubsinfo.asp?pubid =2005095

Smith, S. (2003, September 20). Revision thing: A history of the Iraq war, told entirely in lies. *Harpers Magazine.*

Valenzuela, A. (Ed.). (2004). *Leaving children behind: How Texas-style accountability fails Latino youth.* New York: State University of New York Press.

Waldman, S., & Green, J. (2004). It wasn't just (or even mostly) the "religious right": Catholics and moderately religious voters were just as important as very religious "born agains." Available online at www.NewBeliefnet

West, C. (1997). Restoring hope: Conversations on the future of black America. New York: Beacon Press.

CHAPTER 7

RELIGIOUS EDUCATION AND DIALOGUE WITH THE RELIGIOUS OTHER IN THE LATINA COMMUNITY

Elizabeth Conde-Frazier
Claremont School of Theology

ABSTRACT

This chapter looks at the task of educating persons for living in a multicultural and religiously plural society. It examines the educational dilemma of doing perspective transformation when persons relocate from religiously intolerant societies to a social context that promotes religious freedom. The mission of the religious community and of the public schools is mentioned. The role and resources of the religious educator are identified for carrying out the task of reforming the negative images and beliefs about others that are embedded in religious traditions. Historical Latino Catholic and Protestant tensions serve as the case study for discussing these issues.

Religion in Multicultural Education, pages 139–165

INTRODUCTION

The Immigration and Nationality Act of 1965 in the United States brought persons from all over the world. Each of the new people groups brought with them their religious traditions as a part of their cultural identities. As each group became more established, one could see temples, mosques, and monasteries blending into the architectural horizons. As a previously predominantly Judeo-Christian nation that prided itself in offering religious freedom, the United States has had to accept the emerging challenges of a more pluralistic society. How will we live with these differences? What values guide our vision of democracy in the midst of a growing cultural and religious diversity?

In the United States context, public schools have served the mission of transmitting the values of democracy from generation to generation. They are one of the places where we must engage the important task of maintaining the ideal that free peoples from a variety of backgrounds can live together in a peaceful manner. In this endeavor three things must be recognized: rights, responsibilities and respect. Religious liberty is the right to believe as we choose. It is a part of our freedom of conscience. We are responsible for affirming and defending these rights for all citizens even when this means that we are defending a person's right to have views and beliefs that are at odds with our own. This requires the ability to balance our self-interest with the common good. Lastly, respect is necessary as we engage fellow citizens in conflicts, debates, or the pursuit of the improvement of our communities.

Respect is difficult to sustain without knowledge of the histories, beliefs, or customs of others. The lack of such knowledge may lead to prejudices and stereotypes or to simply trivializing or ignoring those who are different. The knowledge for understanding others includes the study of their religious experiences, doctrines, stories, and rituals. This knowledge may be attained through a public school curriculum that engages in the comparative study of religion where religious beliefs, philosophies, and practices are studied in order to gain an understanding of people's ethical, moral, and ideological commitments and how these have shaped and may continue to improve contemporary society.

While affirming the role that religious traditions play in fashioning worldview, I also want to point to the fact that they may have negative images or beliefs of other religions built into their own self understanding. The process of reforming such views falls under the purview of the spiritual leaders of each religion. Religious educators in the United States have both an insider and outsider role. As outsiders they may serve as consultants and advocates of comparative religious studies in public schools. As insiders they are the spiritual guides in the process of reforming negative images of the religious other in their religious tradition.

The Latino community in the United States context can serve as a case study for looking at how religious educators can reshape the negative images of the religious other with the eventual purpose of uniting with other religious traditions to bring about positive social change in the community.

In order to look at how the Latina community has engaged the principle of Christian harmony and unity known as ecumenism and the contributions of religious education toward this endeavor, one must begin with an understanding of the makeup of the Latina community in the United States and its history of evangelization on both sides of the border. As a predominantly Christian community, this is the background that orients its approach or suspicions about ecumenical and interreligious dialogue.

A religious educator must first look at the construction of the self-understanding that the Protestant and Catholic Latina communities have and the development of their religious traditions in order to understand how to approach the cultivation of relationships between these and other religious communities. One must also seek alternative avenues to the traditional ones such as the places of resistance to the dominant religious expressions of our faith traditions that have contributed to the fashioning of our religious practices and beliefs. At times, it is the commonalities of these expressions, considered marginal by the dominant religious communities that help broker ecumenical and interfaith dialogue.

In this chapter I present the reader with the historical and theological understandings that inform a religious education approach for ecumenical and interfaith dialogue in the Latino community. The theoretical and practical aspects of religious education is interspersed with the historical and theological underpinnings. At the moment there is not a defined religious education for ecumenical or interfaith dialogue that has been written from the Latino perspective. There are potential areas that can be developed. I show a case where dialogue took place due to other ministerial intentions of the religious communities involved. The analysis of how these events took place gives much insight for a religious education approach that fosters dialogue with the religious other. Among the spaces and religious frameworks ripe with possibility for dialogue to be discussed in this chapter are popular religiosity, grassroots movements, *mestizaje*, conversion, and missional praxis. The epistemological underpinnings of these are examined. In that discussion experiential learning and storytelling are some of the methods included.

In order to foster dialogue one must create a process that goes from animosity for the religious other to cultivation of respect and appreciation.

This requires perspective transformation. I describe an anatomy of change and a journey for coming to this transformation.

In my explorations of this topic, I do not seek to prescribe the directions that ecumenism should take in the Latino religious community. Instead, I look at where our ecumenical expressions are currently taking place. I analyze the educational dimensions and their potential for cultivating ecumenical/interfaith relationships and understandings.

HISTORICAL BACKGROUND

Religion is embedded in the many systems and complexes of a cultural context (Berling, 2004). A dimension of the cultural context that has created the relationship between Catholics and Protestants in the Latino community has been one beset by layers of colonial conquest. In these conquests religions were imposed and superimposed upon each other as a way of impressing the worldview of the colonizer among the people colonized. In this reality we must realize that a grounding theological notion such as conversion, for example, is not only about faithfulness to Jesus but also a way that the colonizer uses to ensure loyalty toward the new colonizing system, that is, the set of ideas that takes us out of the grasp of one power into another. It serves as a way of controlling the colonized by having them internalize the ideas such that they assent to live by them. It is inner control rather than a less attractive coercive control from the outside.

However, at the same time, this new religious force contains the very seed of empowerment for the people. Empowerment entails thinking for ourselves, doing a critique of what we have received and what we were asked to leave behind. It invites us to look carefully with our own eyes and not through the lenses of the colonizer. For this we need an understanding of the history and the doctrines and practices involved so that we come to our own insights. These insights will in turn affirm or refashion the present state of our beliefs and practices.

When Spain established its rule in Latin America, Catholicism became the official religion. This was insured as the conquerors brought with them Dominican and Franciscan missionaries. Religion and politics were further wedded to each other through the *patronato*, or right of patronage, that gave the Spanish monarch the right to choose bishops for the episcopacy, ensuring that church leaders would be loyal to Spain. The church became a central part of life in Latin American society by, among other things, controlling education and establishing universities. It wasn't until the 19th century that liberal reformers in Mexico challenged the church's monopoly by taking over church lands and abolishing the special legal status of the church. In spite of this, the influence of the Catholic Church continued to be strong and religious freedom was still not a part of citizens' rights.

This changed in the 20th century when most countries included religious freedom in their constitutions. However, constitutional provisions still recognize the special position of Catholicism as the national religion. The monopoly of the Catholic Church has brought about religious discrimination and even persecution. This has resulted in tensions between Catholics and other religious groups that continue today, even after the Vatican's greater support of democratic ideas in the 1960s with the publication of Pacem in Terris (Peace on Earth, 1963), Dignitatis Humanae (Human Dignity, 1965) and the calling for ecumenical dialogue and improved relations with other faiths. For example, in 1995, at a meeting of the Latin American bishops, they denounced the *sects* (the Pentecostals) for their proselytism of Catholics. The Evangelicals add to this animosity as they argue that the Catholic tradition includes much idolatry. Evangelicals have also refused to recognize Catholics as Christians. It is a rarity to see Catholics and Protestants participating in local ecumenical councils.

This tension migrates to the United States as members of both religious groups relocate. In their booklet on Latino Christian Reformed Identity, Latinos claim:

> We still count among us many martyrs who have suffered and died for their simple attempts to live and preach the gospel in their countries of origin. Still, in many parts of brown America we suffer diverse forms of religious intolerance and social ostracism for belonging to a faith that is not the dominant one. This historical experience continues to shape our theological reflection and the expression of our faith. (Avila, 2004, p. 3)[1]

Protestantism came to the Latino community as part and parcel of manifest destiny. Religious, economic, and political life in the United States during the 18th century was fueled by the notion of a superior race (the Anglo-Saxon race) that was chosen by God to occupy the American continents. This was their *manifest destiny.* This was an ideology whereby the United States was manifestly destined by God to lead the world to progress and freedom. This was reflected in the beliefs of some, such as Caleb Cushing of Massachusetts who was convinced that *Hispanic Americans* were not capable of governing themselves and that this would result in the United States being able to enter and prevail gradually in their territories (Horsman, 1981; Sylvest, 1999).

Eventually, it was by military conquest and purchase of the land that the people of the United States prevailed over Hispanic American territories and imposed political and economic systems as well as introducing a new religious system (Sylvest, 1999, p. 34). At first, however, there was no desire to proselytize Mexicans. The missionary efforts were first directed toward

Anglo-Celtics who crossed the border looking for personal opportunities. Soon Bibles and literature were distributed by the Methodists and Presbyterians among the Mexicans. This was before the authorized work of missions began on the Texas/Mexican border.

However, even the work of evangelizing ministries was done with the spirit of showing *the superiority of the Protestant over the Catholic religion* (Rankin, 1875; Sylvest, 1999). The pioneers formulated theological and racial concepts that explained their own superiority based on the deficiencies of the culture of the existing inhabitants. Daniel Rodríguez-Díaz (1993) notes that on the theological level Mexicans and Native Americans existed outside of God's exclusive covenant of God with the Anglo Americans; as such, they were marginal members of God's kingdom on earth (see also Barton, 1999). Taking their lands was not a crime but part of God's injunction to make the land fruitful. The Protestant denominations also took part in the expansionist program of the nation (Barton, 1999, p. 61).

Schools were organized in Mexico by missionaries from the United States. The organization of such schools became a way to disseminate the Scriptures and other literature to the Mexicans. Ed Sylvest describes the type of values and ideals that characterized that period in the borderland:

> A pattern of Hispanic ministry was established. It manifested Puritan values...that were embedded in a matrix of evangelical piety that developed through the revivals that began in New England. This was especially true of the Methodist Episcopal Church, the Presbyterians, U.S.A., and the Cumberland Presbyterian Church, who sponsored Hispanic Ministry in the Southwest.... Teachers offered the values of Puritan idealism, tinged though it was with the shadow of racist sentiment. (1999, pp. 36–37)

Through this process a convergence of different cultures and their value systems emerged and formed a continuous, evolving border of cultures and peoples. The process of conversion was one where peoples began to be introduced to a sense of self-deficiency and the need to become like the superior other. One's own religion and peoples were seen as inferior. This created a rift in the relationship between the peoples who maintained the current religious system and those who chose the new system. The relationship they will have with one another is henceforth fashioned by this sentiment. The identity of both will be determined by this anti-Catholic/anti-Protestant sense. They will be taught to look at each other's religious frameworks with disdain, promoting the need to convert one another. Name calling and the continuous denigration of each other's beliefs will take place as well as the admonition to distance themselves from each other's places of worship. This will eventually divide even families.

The influence of Roman Catholic Christianity from the United States was also present on the Southwest border. It was a very different expression of Catholicism from that of the Mexican people. The encounter between the new bishops that were assigned to the area with the people can best be described as culture shock.

Orlando Espín (1995) explains some of the causes of the different Catholic expressions of both cultures. He posits that until 1546 "tradition" included the contents of Scripture, the dogmatic declarations of the ancient councils and devotional practices. Between 1545 and 1563 the bishops and theologians assembled as part of the Council of Trent where they separated the different elements of tradition. Trent's theology did not become operative in the Spanish Americas for approximately another century. Catholicism in the Americas was therefore characterized as pre-Tridentine Catholicism. This theological difference was one of the factors that contributed to the culture shock between the bishops and the people.

It is pre-Tridentine Catholicism that first came to the Americas. It came as an evangelization process that first vanquished the people as part of the conquest. The justification for the conquest offered by the Spaniards to the native populations and later to the enslaved Africans was that "the Christian God had sent the Spaniards to them" (Espín, 1995, p. 22). Espín argues that the conquered peoples accepted the religion of the conquerors because their inherited worldviews assumed that divine favor rested upon those who were victors. Furthermore, they believed that it was important to take on the worship and the beliefs of the victor's gods. Refusal to do so would result in more cosmic calamity and punishment in this life (Espín, p. 25).

Popular Religiosity: An Oppositional Epistemology

It is this evangelization of conquest and manifest destiny and not a religious dialogue among equals that has characterized the religious heritage of Latinos and Latin Americans. In the midst of these layers of conquest embedded with a message of the inferiority of the people, the evangelized have fashioned into the dominant religious systems their own expressions and practices, often referred to as popular religiosity. This is a set of experiences, beliefs, and rituals developed by peripheral groups as a way of gaining access to God in ways that are not available through the traditional interpretations and hierarchies of the ecclesial structures (Espín, 1997).

It is through these expressions that the people have maintained the fabric of their true religious experiences. Popular religiosity both Protestant and Catholic reflect the intersections of the different cultures and their worldviews, of the mix of peoples of the Americas, the Native American, the African, the European, and the Anglo American. These expressions come from the people and thus are shaped and formed by them in ways that give meaning to their lives. It is in these that one might find, as a religious educator, the places that could lead to ecumenical and interreligious conversations among Latinos. They are the closest to the people's own theological construction. They are expressions of knowing God that bring together the transcendent and the immanent. Because these practices and beliefs are the *personalismo* of the people in their religious experience, they include stories of faith as expressions of religious resistance of the dominant religion. This is a space where one's consciousness is raised, critical thinking takes place, and an oppositional epistemology begins to form. One may inform this process of critical thinking with the history of the making of the relationships between our religious traditions, thus allowing persons to come to their own conclusions. These conclusions may question and challenge the theological premises for how one's identity has been fashioned in opposition of the religious other for the benefit of the conqueror.

Grassroots Movements: The Beginning of a Dialogue

In recent years due to the sociopolitical issues in Latin America and the United States that have affected the lives of both Latino Catholics and Protestants, these faith communities have reexamined their traditions and rediscovered the strengths of their traditions that have called them to involvement in the social and economic struggles of the people. They are finding themselves working together toward a more just society (González, 1990).

The common struggles of our everyday life have brought together the popular masses. This has emerged as a grassroots ecumenism. Participation in the unionization of farm laborers in California, in the struggle for the independence for Puerto Rico as well as the struggle for more political participation in major cities such as New York and Chicago, have brought us to march together. More recently the struggle for the rights of immigrants has united us. Through these efforts, our understanding of our common religious spaces has been expanded.

Also, Cecil M. Robeck, who has done extensive work in cultivating the International Roman Catholic–Pentecostal dialogue, argues that spirituality can hold common experiences for Roman Catholic and Pentecostal Latinos (1997). He cites how the experience of being filled by the Spirit can be shared between the two communities. He speaks of such experiences in the early 20th century and in the Charismatic movement of the Latino Roman Catholic Church later on in the same century (Robeck, 1997, pp. 48–49). I comment on this in more detail below.

Mestizaje

Another characteristic of the Latina community that has potential for helping to develop a spirit of dialogue is our *mestizaje*. *Mestizos* was the term used for the offspring of the Spanish and the Native peoples. Traditionally it was intended as a pejorative term which made distinction between them and the pure Spaniards or *criollos*. Similarly, once African peoples were enslaved in the Americas, the term *mulatto* was employed to describe the offspring of white and black parents. During the Mexican revolution the Mexican intellectual community gave new and positive meaning to the concept of mestizos and mulattos. The work of Mexican philosopher José Vasconcelos, *La Raza Cósmica: La misión de la raza Iberoamericana* (*The Cosmic Race: The Mission of the Iberoamerican Race*) (1948), was epoch-making. It presents a philosophical basis for pride in the mixture of races. The cosmic race is a fifth race embracing the four major races of the world.

More recently, a theological perspective has been introduced by Virgil Elizondo in his dissertation later published as a book, titled *Galilean Journey: The Mexican American Promise* (1983). Elizondo points to mestizaje as the future of all cultures because ethnic identities evolve rather than remain established. The concept of mestizaje has been extended to all Latino culture and is spoken of by feminist Chicana writer and poet Gloria Anzaldúa as the consciousness where she "continually walks out of the one culture into another because I am in all cultures at the same time" (1999, p. 99). The place where cultures encounter each other and overlap is the borderland. "In these spaces, hybrid significations are created, requiring the practice of cultural translations and negotiations. It is here that we transcend dualistic modes of thinking and come to understand how opposing views can interact with one another" (Conde-Frazier, Kang, Parrett, 2004, p. 176). Certainly the dynamic aspect of mestizaje in our cultures holds possibilities for dialogue across religions.

Each religious tradition has a framework that explains its religious system of thought. As one seeks to converse with a different religious tradition one begins with one's own understanding of religious experience. One must then come to understand the framework of the other and both seek to speak across the two frameworks. For this reason a rich conversation requires that one know one's own tradition well enough to be able to bring to the table the fullness of the gifts one's tradition has to offer. Failure to do this results in an impoverished conversation. It is this framework that can set the boundaries necessary for defining the tradition. It is in it that can also be found the commonalities and spaces where one may engage others across those boundaries.

CONVERSION AS A FRAMEWORK
THAT MOVES US TOWARD THE OTHER

Conversion is a central concept in the religious framework of Latino Protestants. This is a term that refers to a change from one religious belief to another or from lack of faith to belief. Protestant Latino theologian Orlando E. Costas (1979) speaks of conversion as a complex experience. He describes his own conversion as having three dimensions. The first dimension Costas names as a religious conversion to Christ and the second as a cultural conversion to his Puerto Rican and Latin American identity. This, he says, was a consequence of his new identity in Christ. This dimension restores the distorted sense of self created by the process of colonization. The third dimension is Costa's sociopolitical or missional conversion to the world specifically, the world of the poor in society. This phase he describes as an outgrowth of his calling as a follower of Jesus in whom God assumed the identity of a poor person so that the poor became a central reference to God's identity (Costas, 1989, pp. 27–28). This dimension opens our eyes to the other with the purpose of doing justice together. The three dimensions are necessary to the understanding of evangelization in the Latino context.

The first is the experience of encountering and recognizing Jesus in one's life. The experiences of oppression, of being sinned against, cause one to become an oppressor as well. Because inferiority breeds self-hate, we take out our frustrations and sense of inferiority on those who remind us of ourselves. Encountering Jesus initially helps us to get a hold of ourselves, to come into our true selves and to realize who we are becoming. It is the process of self-awareness where we see how we have been objectified. Without such awareness one cannot come to see oneself and others as subject. This is a necessary step in our encounter and understanding of the other. This initial experience is only the beginning of a journey toward empowerment. As we begin to discover ourselves as the recipients of the dehumanization of society, we can then contribute to our liberation—a rebirth of the self.

Awareness of one's situation is not only awakening to our sins but to the world of the oppressor and its unjust structures. Naming those oppressions so as to disclose them, and speaking out against them, reveals them not only to the self but to the general public. It is a process of critical thinking. This leads the person to commit herself to the task of transforming society. Virgilio Elizondo (1980) claims that it is at this point that the person becomes teacher of both the oppressor and the oppressed—the true expression of the pedagogy of the oppressed.

For a U.S. Latino, this awakening needs to be nurtured by an educational process whereby one encounters not only the history of God with humanity but the history of one's own people. Because we have come through layers of conquest and colonization, several imposed worldviews have disrupted the meaning of our lives so that nothing makes sense anymore. This imposition occurs at the levels of customs and traditions, the arts, logic and wisdom, language, and the religions. Elizondo points out that symbols mediate the expressions of the absolute, and thus give us access to God. He states that "They are the ultimate justification of the worldview of the group and the force that cements all the elements of the life of the group into a cohesive, meaningful and tangible world order" (Elizondo, 1992, p. 107). Once the oppressor imposes its own religious symbols, then the worldview of the oppressed comes into confusion and they see themselves through the eyes of the oppressor. The image of the oppressor becomes superior and the image of the oppressed inferior.

Costas documents his own experience of struggle with his identity. As he describes his journey he posits the importance of exposure to one's own history from the perspective of one's own people. Much history has been written from the perspective of the colonizer so that it reinforces the image of the self and the other according to the colonizer. A critical thinking process follows whereby the lack of congruence of the myth of the oppressor about the oppressed is unmasked and the oppressed regain their own image and the image of God created in the oppressed emerges. With this new image, a sense of calling to be a Latino/a for Christ in the world also emerges. There is a sense of *for-otherness* (González, 1990).

This demythologizing also unmasks the forces that fashion the injustices of the reality of the oppressed and the third dimension of conversion takes place. As one follows the call or journey into the mystery of the reign of God it leads to experiences of political praxis and reflection about the mission or the *what for* of the church.

As Latino Protestants we have inherited an apolitical theology. This theology bifurcates the secular and the sacred, the political from the religious. To speak therefore of the social, economic, and political dimensions of the Christian mission is to cause confusion about one's Christian identity. Again, the educational process is one of determining the roots of our theology and of coming to realize how it has shaped the mission of the church as well as the relationships it has with those outside. At this point of conversion, education needs to reinform our theological paradigms. Providing forums for persons to discuss these issues and to do theology is important.

RELIGIOUS EDUCATION: PROVIDING A
THEOLOGICAL PARADIGM AND ANATOMY OF CHANGE

In religious education, where we deal with the renewal of the mind (or theological understandings), attitudes, and behaviors, this journey of conversion entails triggering discomfort and questioning as well as the facilitation of connections between daily life and the radical demands of the gospel. This new appraisal of the situation leads to self-examination, identification with or clarification of the concern. *What is going on here?* is the question that arises from within the person. Deeper encounter with the new may then follow. Allow me to show how this took place with a group of pastors in New England.

A group of pastors shared their experience of immigration with one another and as the religious educator facilitated a process of identifying common themes in their stories, they were able to name the issues that defined the realities of their lives. They then examined these in light of their congregations' programs and activities. This led them to look at the relationships they had with those outside of their faith community. Questions about who these others were and what they might have in common, the possibilities and limitations of the relationships they could forge with others came into the purview of the discussion.

In this process, they explored old and new assumptions, asking themselves *Where might this lead me?* The dialogue with one another provided the support needed to move toward change. It provided a sense of confidence in the scary places of change. The scriptures and their life of the spirit had been central to the reinterpretation and reformulation of a gospel message that became more relevant and life-giving. It also helped them to grieve the sense of security that their old assumptions provided while encouraging each other toward the hope of a not yet fully discovered vision. As they journeyed with each other for a year, continuous questions and challenges were confronted. At this next level, they were able to ask for comments from each other and express new ideas, sensing that the spirit was present in their groping for truth and life.

The religious educator's role was to continue to provide the group with new information so that persons could implement the new. This included theological readings and reflection, different models of ministry and conversation with those whom they never imagined engaging. Slowly the pastors were seeing with new eyes. The process of perception renewal came as they opened themselves to encountering the lives of persons, including other clergy in the community through *pastoral visits.* The stories of those they visited presented a challenge and deepened their understandings of the gospel, which then reshaped the programs and structures of their congregations so that these could address human suffering. These new structures began to include working ecumenically and in one case, working with leaders of faith communities that were not Christian on community projects.

We notice in this progression an anatomy of change that journeys through a variety of conversions and that includes a formation of a new missional praxis or service to others (rather than mission as proselytism).[2] It is within this dimension of their religious framework that ecumenical and interfaith relationships began albeit unplanned. This familiar dimension of their theological framework was able to embrace an element of the unfamiliar and thus sustain it. The pastors engaged in a dialectical relation with their context that invited them to enrich and evaluate their culture, class and group consciousness, and social representations. Had we started with an unfamiliar or untouched dimension of their religious framework it would not have been possible to incorporate the new in the same way. In this manner, the ecumenical and interfaith relationship evolved as a by-product of a process of enrichment of a meaningful aspect of their sense of religious identity.

A Theology of Dialogue: New Directions Toward a Pedagogy of Dialogue

The new life of the spirit that begins through conversion and missional praxis frees persons and congregations to live for others. This means sharing in the common struggles, fears, and hopes of humanity. It implies being open to dialogue with persons of other religious traditions. Costas sees dialogue as part of the journey of conversion. Listening and sharing from the depths of one's commitment is a part of dialogue. Costas defines it as "an attitude of respect and sensitivity to others who may think differently and have other convictions" (1989, p. 127). The basis for our dialogue is both our common humanity and our sensitivity to the divine by way of our unique religious experiences. The pedagogy of dialogue begins with our silence. Our silence is the spiritual exercise of opening our will to listen to others and to the *great other* who speaks through our dialogue partners. The silence and the listening prepare us to speak by making us vulnerable enough to share.

One thing that keeps many Protestant Latinos away from interreligious dialogue is fear of the witness of their neighbor's different experience of God. They are afraid that it may lead to the compromising of central Christian convictions or to syncretism, which is the union of diverse or opposite religious tenets or practices. This originates in the perception of the religious other that was part of the colonization process.

On discussing issues of Christian faith and religious pluralism, Gerald Anderson, who had served as director of the Overseas Ministry Study Center in New Haven, Connecticut, refers to the Chiang Mai statement made in Thailand in 1977 at the World Council of Churches consultation. The statement was made by a man who seeks to make sense of his faith in the religious pluralism of Asia. It views dialogue as Christian service rather than proselytizing. An excerpt of the statement reads as follows:

> Indeed, as Christians enter dialogue with their commitment to Jesus Christ, time and again the relationship of dialogue gives opportunity for authentic witness.... Thus we feel able with integrity to commend the way of dialogue as one in which Jesus Christ can be confessed in the world today; at the same time we feel able with integrity to assure our partners in dialogue that we come not as manipulators but as genuine fellow-pilgrims, to speak with them of what we believe God to have done in Jesus Christ who has gone before us, but whom we meet anew in dialogue. (Anderson, 1988)

This statement both affirms the foundation of the Christian faith while giving consideration to the possibility that our other religious neighbors may hold further truth about God in their faith. It permits and warrants therefore our listening without the motivation that could lead to the manipulative agendas of the past. This recognizes that as Christians we are responsible for helping to bring about trust among those who are in dialogue with one another.

Costas also moves us away from these fears as he claims the witness of the scriptures that state that God has been "working salvation in the midst of the earth (Ps. 74:12)" (1989, p. 128). For Costas, salvation lies in the hands of God, and the church is but a witness to the part of God's truth that it has received. Our knowledge of God through Christ is in bits and pieces. This positions the church in a space of humility that beckons openness in listening to others as their witness may turn out to be a moment of learning for her. This is not an undiscerning moment. The Johannine literature invites us to evaluate all religious truths in light of the revelation we have received in Christ (Jn. 4:1). We are reminded that this revelation is found in the incarnation where the face of God is seen in a poor Galilean who came to bring liberation, healing, and good news to the poor. In this revealed truth, we understand that God identifies with the poor. It is this truth and its implications that we seek to discern and assent to in the witness of others. This theological principle can help to promote dialogue with people of other faiths. It will encourage theological reflection on issues that arise and will help the church discuss the implications of dialogue for her life.

A Relational Epistemology

Our fears and the history of the tense relationship between the Catholic and Protestant churches in Latin America and the Caribbean have not facilitated ecumenical dialogue. Therefore, when it comes to entering into the necessary partnerships for doing social justice, the Protestant Latino churches find themselves groping for the theological paradigms that will guide them. This topic has come up at a variety of different forums, workshops, and conferences where clergy and laypersons have engaged issues of doing social justice, the mission of the church, urban ministry, or the doing of theology.[3] Some of the settings and forums of these discussions have included only Protestant mainliners (Methodists, Presbyterians, Lutherans, Baptists, etc.) or only Pentecostals. Other forums have included Catholics as well.

These discussions point to the fact that the ecumenical interactions and relationships are practical and relational. On the practical side they came about as a result of mergers of smaller congregations that are then sponsored by two or more denominations in a local area. Other manifestations of this practical dimension can be seen when Latinos from various denominational backgrounds attend a congregation because it is closest to home or it best meets their needs. In these cases, denominational affiliation is not the priority. These congregations have had to later work through the different religious expressions and congregational polity that the members bring with them. The other practical dimension is seen above when leaders of congregations expand their missional praxis.

How does this practical and relational dimension inform our epistemology? What is a Latino, theoretical/theological epistemological understanding? I will begin with Daniel Groody's definition of what the heart is in Latino understanding since transformation, and particularly spiritual transformation, cannot be understood without understanding *el corazón*. To us el corazón is "the biological-symbolic site of wisdom and knowledge and a metaphor for the whole of one's conscious, intelligent, and free personality. It integrates and informs all aspects of a person, including the mind, will, and emotions" (Groody, 2002, p. 8). Mujerista theologian Isasi-Díaz speaks of our emotions in relationship to knowing.[4] She states: "Our emotions are central to our knowing and not only our reason and understanding" (2004, p. 110). Our emotions and feelings make it possible for us to hold a relationship with what is to be known such that we can truly claim to know. We know through our experience. Experience is information about what is to be known. It is a history of events in a continuum that are significant and therefore form our habits of response.

As we look more broadly at emotions as part of our intellectual knowing, Michael Stocker posits that "the development of patterns of desire, passions, choice and emotion are part of the development of intellectual character" (1980, p. 325). This is important for perspective transformation, which ultimately brings one to enact or embody knowledge. When we act intellectually our desire is involved as part of our action so that our action is a result of a combination of factors that include beliefs and desires (1980, p. 329). Knowledge therefore involves interaction and one level at which we interact involves responsibility. Isasi-Díaz claims this to be "the ethical component of knowing" (2004, p. 111). Our theological understanding of what to do (an expression of our responsibility) with our religious differences has been translated into a fear of one another, which has in turn been expressed by a distance from one another, debasement, and prejudices about each other's beliefs. It has been created by a system of beliefs and truth claims that emphasize the other's errors of belief so that we have not examined our commonalities and complementarities, thus we have not cultivated a sense of appreciation or a valuing of one another. At times, it even takes the form of violence. This is how we know each other. It is a distorted knowing that drives a wedge of deep distrust between us. The distortion is not only of the knowledge about each other but of the knowledge of the divine. The knowledge of the divine is connected to our knowledge of one another.

The Judeo-Christian understanding of knowledge is relational. It is to know in the practical sense rather than the abstract, referring to persons and things with which we are familiar. To know in this way implies a personal relationship between the knower and the person known. *Yada*, to know in Hebrew, can also be used to designate sexual intercourse. To know therefore implies a degree of intimacy and intensity in a relationship in which an individual stands with the one who is known. In Johannine literature, to know God is to love one's neighbor. Notice that the Christian scriptures do not limit the *other* to persons in our midst but makes it clear that the "other," the distant one, the Muslim, the Catholic, the Buddhist, is our neighbor. To know God is to love our neighbors. Teaching therefore is to bring us to the knowledge of God through the knowledge of our neighbor. This is teaching for neighbor consciousness and has as its purpose the building up of community.

Experiential learning moves one from detached or objective learning to engaged and subjective knowing. Experiential methods can help facilitate coming to such knowledge. These rely on life experiences and involve self-disclosure. They bring together theory, research, personal experience, and practice in ways that are educational and empowering. Personal experiences are used to help persons make sense of new information.

Experience and Storytelling

In the educational field, John Dewey's thinking on the nature of experience is helpful to our considerations of the practical and relational dynamics of our ecumenical expressions. For Dewey, experience is both personal and social. Furthermore, experiences are continuous—one experience grows out of other experiences and leads to further experiences. These experiences are the building blocks of perception formation and change that fashion our worldview (Dewey, 1938).

Our continuum of experiences is usually woven into stories. Educators Clandinin and Connelly (2000) claim that family stories about the world are usually teaching stories that tell the generations listening to the accounts the ways of the world according to the experiences the elders have had. In immigrant communities, intergenerational storytelling is necessary since it is many times the younger generations and not the elders who may be learning and telling about the ways of a new world. In this manner, the stories also help to forge community identity.

When we tell our stories of interaction with our religious other, we are at once building upon the past, creating the blocks for a new future and reinterpreting the ways of our religious world. Because it is our experiences that are shaping our ecumenical understanding, then our narratives or stories are what we most often find as a way of speaking about ecumenism in the church settings. Our oral narratives go beyond concepts, ideas, or abstractions. They speak of that which is tangible and real. They speak of what is alive in our midst and forming the future. It is not surprising, therefore, to find that our scholars also draw from their own narratives. Orlando Costas (1980) and Eduardo Fernández (2001) both use narrative and case study. Carmelo Alvarez (1996) and Justo González (1990) use narrative to flesh out and give texture to their theological reflections on ecumenism.

It is in our stories that we find what James Loder (1981) defines as transforming moments or moments of faith transformation. For Loder, these moments alter our ways of being in the world. A transforming moment is a convictional experience. It disrupts our previous assumptive world by puncturing our previous ways of making meaning and it discloses to us dimensions of being not previously attended to which enables us to reground and realign our ways of seeing and being. These are the moments that are apparent in our stories.

The relational dimensions of our stories have to do with religious and personal encounters at different levels between persons. Although the historical and theological legacy among Hispanics does not easily facilitate ecumenical relations between Protestants, Pentecostals, and Catholics, or interreligious relationships with Jews or Muslims, when persons are in everyday settings where they share their lives, the strength of their relational bonds will create situations for sharing with each other over religious events. When respect dictates these moments, they are not invested with agendas of conversion. Instead, they allow persons to take steps at their own comfort toward knowing the religious other as long as they interpret it as a time to share with their neighbor. When and if such moments are repeated as a tradition between friends or as a routine, then they create an openness for reflecting and learning with respect.

What may be missing from these experiences are the theological frameworks that could enhance the learning. Theological discussions would seek to explore both commonalities and contrary beliefs and paradoxes and would enable persons in the integration process. The goal of this process is to identify the theological significance of one's tradition while honoring the integrity of the tradition of the other. It could eventually lead to ways of working together on common goals. This, however, is not the starting point and comes after the relationship of respect and value of the other's tradition has been established.

An example of this was a quiet revival that took place in New York City during the 1970s. The revival was marked by a charismatic renewal among Catholic, Protestant, and Pentecostal churches. The common experience of the outpouring of the Holy Spirit gave people a point of commonality rather than difference from which to approach each other.[5] It provided a common language, a biblical departure, songs, and a sort of liturgy that was formed among them. Through it, they borrowed different forms of worship and ritual from each other's traditions. It was giving way to a new, ecumenical, popular religiosity. The differences were laid aside for a moment. It created a pause from the animosity and fears that had fashioned the relationship previously.

In this pause, curiosity led us into an honest exploration of the mysteries about each other. For those who were able to resist the temptation to "save" the other from erroneous beliefs, critical reflection took place. The dialogue with the other permitted people to develop a sense of appreciation and respect. It also allowed them to revisit and reinterpret the difficult past that had divided them. As dialogue deepens in these relationships, so does one's faith and faith expressions. Latino Catholics, Pentecostals, and Protestants can then appreciate that which their respective traditions had missed as each one emphasized particular parts of the greater Christian tradition.

Ecumenism as the Progression of Conversion

If we speak of ecumenism as an expression of our continued journey or progression of conversion, then educationally we are looking at a process that takes place in variable units of time. It consists of a period of awareness and decision making.[6]

In the awareness period, one becomes aware of another way of life, behavior patterns or a set of values that are different from one's tradition. This takes place, for example, when Catholics, Pentecostals, and Protestants engage each other's traditions either by attending worship or a family event such as baptism or first communion. This is a place of interaction and cooperation. It is a time of discovery and education.

After this period of engagement or in the midst of it, one begins to ask, *"What will I do with this experience and/or new data?"* The question eventually leads to a time of decision. Decision does not necessarily mean acceptance. One may choose to reject certain beliefs and/or one may make modifications to fit things into one's own structures or patterns of religious life. One may choose to participate in certain rituals and avoid others. One may choose to participate in activities where common values may be lived out while acknowledging that there are other areas that cannot be shared. In this period, differences are discussed and ironed out so that the participants of the encounters are ready to act in unison at some levels.

Finally, there comes a point in these interactions and decisions where one realizes that one is moving through a passage from the old understandings that do not include the religious other, to new reflections and meaningful ways of being together. Ecumenism is no longer an idea or a vague notion but it has become a possibility and a truth that has gained new meaning.

In some contexts, there are opportunities for such encounters as well as structures such as fellowship, Bible study, or community projects that cultivate and sustain these periods of interaction until we become socialized through relationships and shared commitments to the point of incorporating one another into our religious way of life.

Koinonia and Diakonia

We notice that the relational/practical dynamics move us toward koinonia (fellowship) and diakonia (a witness to justice and peace). Koinonia provides the setting for dialogue and for the transforming moments. A part of this is the life of worship that is joyful and inspirational. When we can together experience the spirit's energizing presence connecting us with the life, ministry, death, and resurrection of Christ, we are cultivating a transformative moment. Diakonia provides the what for of our continued commitment, which is defined as being in the service of the mission of Christ. The goal is to contribute to the creation of local communities (barrios) of resistance and hope. For this we need a vision of the catholicity of the church.

For interreligious dialogue koinonia would take the form of sharing around daily life experiences such as neighbors walking children to school or carpooling. The conversations around the common concerns of daily life could lead persons to casually speak about their lives and approaches to life out of their faith. The other can listen from a distance by not commenting on that part of the conversation or may engage more deeply by asking some questions. The conversation's potential lies in the hands of those who engage in it. Diakonia holds more potential as persons may find themselves in the company of the unexpected stranger when dealing with common places of pain or injustice. Diakonia places the focus on the assets that we all bring to problem solving. Faith may become the gift that we learn to share and to respect in that process.

Resistance in the Educational Process

This educational passage has consisted of mutual interaction, dialogue, reflection, koinonia, and diakonia. Its epistemological underpinning defines knowledge as contextual, practical, and relational. The theological assumption is that to follow Christ entails going into new paths that cross new frontiers.

In the educational process one must always take into consideration that because renewal of the mind cultivates the potential for the renewal of one's life, persons resist the process because they resist change. In light of this resistance, one aspect to remember is that there is an educational ecology that includes all of the forces in society that inform and shape our lives—different forms of public education, books, magazines, television, and other cultural media, as well as networks of relationships and the cumulative effects of training and institutional structures.

As a postmodern context, pluralistic expressions pervade us. In the midst of these, there are conservative forces that avoid change as well as catalytic and adopting forces. The Latino church, whether Catholic, Pentecostal, or Protestant, will need to determine the type of agent it wishes to be in society.

Academic Ecumenism

One catalytic force in the Latino church today has been the cultivation and development of a scholarly community that includes Catholics, Protestants, and Pentecostals. At the level of theological education, the spaces for study, fellowship, mentoring, and scholarly endeavors created by the Hispanic Summer program and the Hispanic Theological Initiative have begun to fashion a new generation of church leaders and scholars who are moving beyond the historical divides.[7] Their reflections on this subject include experience, theological and philosophical reflections, new models of ministry for the church in the barrio, and a vision for Latino ecumenism. These point to the fact that we need a journey of transformation. It would not only rework our perspectives but our lifestyle as well.

Lifestyle is about *lo cotidiano*, the daily habits and relational structures that make up our lived realities. Religious education that is working with a relational epistemology may help to create an intentional journey recreating our daily relationships so that these may bear a character of justice. As such, it would move us toward our common points with a vision of improving the life of the *barrios* we live in. This calls for continued dialogue among old and new partners in this greater endeavor. The final goal is not interreligious or ecumenical dialogue but justice for which dialogue is an absolute necessity.

What brings about the transformation of perspective? Sophia Fahs's philosophy of education placed experience and questioning at the heart of such a process. In her book, *Worshipping Together with Questioning Minds* (1965), she speaks about how both experiences and questioning invite us to rethink our old beliefs in light of newly found knowledge. She believed that it is in the light of receiving the enlivening thoughts of others that our prejudiced ideas are brought in the open. Other educators tell us that the learning process for perspective transformation entails a process of socialization in which we see each new context opening up to us values and symbols of culture that we begin to internalize. It is a journey where we learn to reflect on the nature of the relationships in which we engage with persons different than ourselves. As a part of this reflection we ask ourselves: How did this relationship develop? How were conflicts resolved? How did we discover our differences? How did we react to our knowledge of the differences? How did a process of understanding take place? What impeded understanding? This journey of reflection about the relationship is what leads to interfaith sensitivity. Therefore, I would like to introduce and explore five different practices that facilitate this journey of reflection and transformation of perspective. It is a journey that creates new habits of relationship, taking us from hospitality to shalom/salaam.

Hospitality to Shalom/Salaam: A Journey of Reflection and Transformation

This journey is consistent with a relational epistemology. In this journey our first approach to one another is hospitality. Hospitality is a place where we are connected to one another. It is a space that is safe, personal, and comfortable. It is a place of respect, acceptance, and friendship. It is a space where we offer each other a life-sustaining network of relations. The place of hospitality offers attentive listening and a mutual sharing of lives and life stories. It is related to human dignity and respect for persons. In the Christian tradition the theological basis for the recognition of another person is the image of the divine in every person at creation. Also, we were made for others and we depend on others. This is the basic understanding for how we sympathize with the needs and suffering of others. Sympathy comes because we have a common nature.

Hospitality as recognition involves respecting the image of the divine in another and seeing their potential contributions as being of equal value. Valuing is of the utmost importance, for persons who are not valued become socially invisible and their needs and concerns are not acknowledged. This is the foundation for being able to enter into each other's presence for dialogue.

Encounter is the next step. It is where we risk. It is a place for the collusion of two world, for the multiplicity of views. It is where various streams meet. It is the bringing together of a variety of sources that might not often be placed together. It is conjunctive places where we hold together what might be seen as opposite. It is the transfer of the cultural and spiritual values of one group to another. It is straddling the cultures of our faiths. It is a consciousness of the struggle of the border. It is hearing multiple voices, at times with conflicting messages. It is what Asian theologian Jung Young Lee (1995) calls marginality or being "in-both," which restores the balance between the two poles and creates harmony. The tolerance for ambiguity and for keeping opposites in tension allows us to enter into cross-cultural and interfaith dialogue because we can deal with paradoxes.

Our encounters give way to compassion. The origin of the word *compassion* is from the words *cum patior*, which mean to suffer with, to undergo with. It connotes solidarity. Compassion therefore works from a place of the strength of mutuality. Compassion, as part of the journey of perspective transformation, brings us from indifference to care. It also helps us redefine our inner parameters so that we go from blood ties or ties to family and culture to the created family. Compassion is the internalizing of others to where we no longer feel displaced or dislocated when interacting outside of our culture or faith group.

As these connections take place we learn empathy. Empathy makes us aware of the world of our neighbor in the way that our neighbor experiences it. When we have compassion we are able to listen empathetically and to confront or contradict misinformation or injustice because we are seeking the well-being of the neighbor based on our capacity to grasp their experience. In light of this, our understanding of relationships and power are challenged.

Compassion invites passion. After listening to each other's stories and getting to know our diverse gifts, we are connected by a common wound in the place where our two worlds have encountered each other. This brings us into the practice of passion. Passion empowers us to bring life-giving fruits and wisdom to the struggles of our communities. It is a loving entering into the world of the neighbor. This caring disposition moves us to interact with and on behalf of those we love. It is a common pathos and passion that now unites us. Those things that break our hearts and make us angry and that we therefore wish to change are the things that we now hold in common. Our initial connections with one another have now matured and facilitate the building of shalom/salaam together. We are now in a prophetic space.

The way one comes to knowledge through passion is through connected knowing. This type of knowing flows from empathy. It encourages relationship and fosters collaboration among people. It fosters dialogue and solidarity through genuine reciprocity in the exchange of ideas.

The last part of the journey is shalom/salaam. Shalom/salaam is a concept that cannot be captured by a single word, for it includes many dimensions: love, loyalty, truth, grace, salvation, justice, blessing, and righteousness. It is a vision of world history where all of creation is one, every creature in community with every other, living in harmony and security toward the joy and well-being of every other creature. It is therefore a vision of connectedness by and for a whole community.

This journey facilitates a relationship at continuing deeper levels. Our relationships enjoined with the purpose of bringing about justice become the spaces for divine disclosure. They encompass encounter with and insight of the divine.

CONCLUSION

Nurturing and sustaining religious liberty where previously there existed prejudice and intolerance is a matter that must begin to be addressed among the religious groups that are in tension with one another. As was seen with the Latino Catholic and Protestant communities, religious competition is pacified when the religions themselves work at renaming their inner life and rediscover their true missions. In this task, the religious educator's role is that of working from within the religious groups to find the resources they may have for bringing reconciling change and new habits of relationship.

These newly reconciled groups exist within a larger and more pluralistic social context. The educational process of working through their internal tensions can be expanded to bring them to greater dialogue and relationship with more diverse religious groups. The habits of relationship that they learned can now be transferred over to a more religiously diverse context.

The International Association for Religious Freedom posits that:

> Religious education should be conceived as a tool to transmit knowledge and values pertaining to all religious trends, in an inclusive way, so that individuals realize their being part of the same community and learn to create their own identity in harmony with identities different from their own. (Taylor, 2005, p. 1)

In the case discussed in this chapter, we saw this take place as a natural outcome of the encounter of persons of different religious groups. One of these encounters was in the public arena when they were working on common problems related to justice issues. Their work on common issues helped to build their relationships by promoting the positive religious values of justice that they held in common. It also created new habits of relationship between them. These habits of relationship based on common religious values became preventive measures against continued intolerance and discrimination.

World religions contain some of the main resources that we have for humanization. Within the greater educational ecology or configuration these educational resources and processes are congruent with the ones used in public schools for the advancement of democratic values and human freedom. We can conclude that the educational work of promoting the right of religious freedom in a multicultural society consists of religious education carried out internally by the different religious communities to advance their best values in the interest of the rehabilitation of human life in society in tandem with a public school curriculum that includes comparative religious studies. It requires a fruitful partnership between religious educators and public educators as both institutions educate persons for democratic citizenship in a multicultural society.

NOTES

1. "Contamos todavía a múltiples mártires que sufrieron y murieron por el simple hecho de esforzarse por vivir y predicar el Evangelio en nuestros países de origen. Todavía en muchas partes de a América morena se sufre diversas formas de intolerancia religiosa y ostracismo social por pertenecer a una fe que no es la de la mayoría. Esta experiencia histórica ha moldeado muestra reflexión teológica y la expresión de nuestra fe."

2. Missional praxis refers to the church's sense of purpose in the world and service to it. Praxis is the dialectic of action–reflection–action. As the church serves in the world (action) it then reflects on its mission in order to

return with a more informed action. Proselytism is to persuade a person to convert from one religious belief to another.

3. The doing of theology refers to the practice of reflecting on life experiences and where God is revealed in these in the light of the scriptures and the tradition of the church.

4. Mujerista theology is a term that refers to feminist Latina theology. It was coined by Ada María Isasi-Díaz.

5. The outpouring of the Holy Spirit refers to the Christian experience of Pentecost where one receives the spirit of Jesus. This is evidenced in the charisms or the gifts that one receives, such as the ability to speak in tongues (glosalalia), to do miracles, or to prophecy and teach. This is why the group is named "charismatic."

6. Alan R. Tippett (1992) speaks of these units of time as part of a cultural anthropology of conversion. I discuss the educational implications of these units.

7. The Hispanic Summer Program is a floating seminary program carried out each summer on a different site with different Latino professors who teach courses otherwise not offered at theological schools which deal with ministry in a Latino context. This is a residential program where participants live, study, fellowship, and worship together for two weeks. The Hispanic Theological Initiative is a program for fostering doctoral studies among Latinos. One of the activities sponsored by the program is the coming together of seasoned and developing scholars to dialogue and present papers. Both of these programs are carried out ecumenically.

REFERENCES

Alvarez, C. (1996, November). Ecumenism in transition? *Journal of Hispanic/Latino Theology, 4*(2), 60–74.

Anderson, G. H. (1988). Christian faith and religious pluralism. In A. L. Walker (Ed.), *Educating for Christian missions: Supporting Christian missions through education* (pp. 59–71). Nashville, TN: Broadman Press.

Anzaldúa, G. (1999). *Borderlands/La frontera: The new mestiza.* San Francisco: Aunt Lute Books.

Avila, M. (2004). *Lo que significa ser Reformado: Una perspectiva Hispanoamericana.* Grand Rapids, MI: Christian Reformed Church.

Berling, J. A. (2004). *Understanding other religious worlds: A guide for interreligious education.* Maryknoll, NY: Orbis Books.

Barton, P. (1999). Inter-ethnic relations between Mexican American and Anglo American Methodists in the U.S. Southwest, 1836–1938. In D. Maldonado (Ed.), *Protestantes/Protestants: Hispanic Christianity within mainline traditions* (pp. 60–84). Nashville, TN: Abingdon Press.

Clandinin, D. J., & Connelly, F. M. (2000). *Narrative inquiry: Experience and story in qualitative research.* San Francisco: Jossey-Bass.

Conde-Frazier E., Kang S. S., & Parrett, G. A. (2004). *A many colored kingdom: Multicultural dynamics for spiritual formation.* Grand Rapids, MI: Baker Academic.

Costas, O. E. (1979). Conversion as a complex experience: A personal case study. In J. Stott & R. T. Coote (Eds.), *Gospel and culture* (pp. 240–262). Pasadena, CA: William Carey Library.

Costas, O. E. (1980). Ecumenical experiences of an Hispanic Baptist. In W. J. Borey & G. A. Igleheart (Eds.), *Baptists and ecumenism* (pp. 118–124). Valley Forge, PA: Judson Press.

Costas, O. E. (1989). *Liberating news: A theology of contextual evangelization.* Grand Rapids, MI: Eerdmans.

Dewey, J. (1938). *Experience and education.* New York: Collier Books.

Elizondo, V. (1983). *Galilean journey: The Mexican American promise.* Maryknoll, NY: Orbis Books.

Elizondo, V. (1992). Mestizaje as a locus of theological reflection. In A. Figueroa Deck (Ed.), *Frontiers of Hispanic theology in the United States* (pp. 104–123). Maryknoll, NY: Orbis Books.

Elizondo, V. P. (1980). The pastoralist leadership: Conquered...colonized... oppressed. In A. M. Stevens-Arroyo (Ed.), *Prophets denied honor: An anthology of the Hispanic church of the United States* (pp. 214–219). Maryknoll, NY: Orbis Books.

Espín, O. O. (1995). Pentecostalism and popular Catholicism: The poor and traditio. *Journal of Hispanic/Latino Theology, 3*(2), 14–43.

Espín, O. O. (1997). *The faith of the people: Theological reflections on popular Catholicism.* Maryknoll, NY: Orbis Books.

Fahs, S. L. (1965). *Worshipping together with questioning minds.* Boston: Beacon Press.

Fernández, E. (2001, November). Latinos and ecumenism: Compelling servants in a new era. *Journal of Hispanic/Latino theology, 9*(2), 5–16.

González, J. L. (1990). *Mañana: Christian theology from a Hispanic perspective.* Nashville, TN: Abingdon Press.

Groody, D.G. (2002). *Border of death, valley of life: An immigrant journey of heart and spirit.* Lanham, MD: Rowman & Littlefield.

Horsman, R. (1981). *Race and manifest destiny: The origins of American racial Anglo-Saxonism.* Cambridge, MA: Harvard University Press.

Isasi-Díaz, A. M. (2004). *La lucha continues: Mujerista theology.* Maryknoll, NY: Orbis Books.

Lee, J. Y. (1995). *Marginality: The key to multicultural theology.* Minneapolis, MN: Fortress Press.

Loder, J. E. (1981). *The transforming moment: Understanding convictional experiences.* San Francisco: Harper & Row.

Rankin, M. (1875). *Twenty years among the Mexicans.* Cincinnati, OH: Chase & Hall.

Robeck, C. M. (1997). Evangelization or proselytism of Hispanics?: A Pentecostal perspective. *Journal of Hispanic/Latino theology, 4*(4), 42–64.

Rodríguez-Díaz, D. R. (1993, Spring). Los moviminetos misioneros y el establecimiento de ideologías dominantes: 1800–1940. *Apuntes: Reflexiones teológicas desde el margen Hispano, 13*(1), 49–72.

Stocker, M. (1980). Intellectual, desire, emotion, and action. In A. Okensberg Rorty (Ed.), *Explaining emotions* (pp. 323–338). Berkeley: University of California Press.

Sylvest, E. (1999). Bordering cultures and the origins of Hispanic Protestant Christianity. In D. Maldonado (Ed.), *Protestantes/Protestants: Hispanic Christianity within mainline traditions* (pp. 21–37). Nashville, TN: Abingdon Press.

Taylor, J. (2005). Responses to the United Nation's study paper on *The role of religious education in the pursuit of tolerance and non-discrimination*. Retrieved May 26, 2005, at www.iarf.net/REBooklet/UN.htm

Tippett, A. R. (1992). The cultural anthropology of conversion. In H. N. Maloney & S. Southard (Eds.), *Handbook of religious conversion* (pp. 192–208). Birmingham, AL: Religious Education Press.

Vasconcelos, J. (1948). *La raza cósmica: La misión de la raza Iberoamericana*. Barcelona: Agencia Mundial de Librería.

CHAPTER 8

UNBURNING THE CROSS— LIFTING THE VEIL ON CHRISTIAN PRIVILEGE AND WHITE SUPREMACY IN THE UNITED STATES AND ABROAD

Building Multicultural Understanding of Religion, Spirituality, Faith, and Secularity in Educational and Workplace Settings[1]

Christine Clark
University of Maryland

ABSTRACT

Though public education and work spaces are officially secular, subtle religious and quasi-religious messages permeate these environments throughout the year. Generally, these messages come with Christian overtones. In much the same vein as Peggy McIntosh's work on male privilege and white privilege (1988), the goal of this chapter is to identify strategies for creating an inclu-

Religion in Multicultural Education, pages 167–214
Copyright © 2006 by Information Age Publishing
All rights of reproduction in any form reserved.

sive educational and/or work environment that supports and values the identities of Christian *and* non-Christian students and employees, while addressing the overt and subtle forms of discrimination that primarily affect non-Christians. This chapter introduces and discusses the concept of Christian privilege as a form of white supremacy in the United States and abroad. It will undertake a case study examination of the University of Maryland's Office of Human Relations Programs' (OHRP) efforts to confront Christian privilege and build religiously, spiritually, faith-based, and secularly inclusive community within OHRP and across campus, paying special attention to the process through which these efforts were undertaken to ensure that both the confrontation of, and resolution to, Christian privilege honored the complexities of multiple social identities, especially those embedded in a juxtaposition of Christian privilege with race, ethnicity, and socioeconomic oppression. And, it will examine the secularization of Christianity and the impact of this on the perpetuation of Christian privilege and white supremacy, both nationally and internationally, in *Post 9/11* and *Fahrenheit 9/11* political climates.

After Job

I wrestled once with a poem called Forgiveness.
It didn't go anywhere, except to the entire outdoor flea market of Christian wares
where you can buy anything you want except Forgiveness.
It must be in some other booth where God collects.

—Jennie Hair (2004)

INTRODUCTION

Increasing numbers of students and employees: (1) from formal religions other than Christian; (2) from a broad range of *nontraditional*—though historically grounded—spiritual affiliations; and (3) who identify as agnostic, atheist, or, simply, *secular,* are entering public[2] education and employment institutions (Schlosser & Sedlacek, 2001). Approximately 20% of incoming students in public higher education identify as *religious minorities,* either Buddhist, Hindu, Muslim, or Jewish (Schlosser & Sedlacek, 2001). Given these trends, expanding the social justice paradigm to assess the impact of Christian privilege in public learning and working communities is paramount in the ongoing effort to create inclusive and affirming educational and workplace climates.

Even a cursory review of the public academic or employment calendar illustrates the centrality of Christian holidays, despite lip service paid to the legal separation of religion and state[3] in the public sector. Inherent in the organization of the academic calendar in this way is the suggestion that everyone celebrates Christmas in *at least a secular way* (Bayly, 2000). Federal, state, and public institutional policy reinforce this by permitting myriad Christmas and Easter decorations to adorn, and celebrations to occur in public educational and workplace contexts under the auspices of such now being *legally* characterized as *secular* (Bayly, 2000). The laissez-faire attitude that the law takes on these issues creates the perception that even if Christian privilege were acknowledged, it could be easily dismissed as having little impact. But there are measurable consequences of the manifestations of Christian privilege in the public domain. For example, student academic success is linked to class attendance and employee professional success to presence at work, forcing non-Christian students and employees to choose between their educational/professional success and the attentive practice of their religious/spiritual affiliation (Schlosser & Sedlacek, 2001). While jurisprudence requires that *reasonable accommodations* be made for these differences (Bayly, 2000), the practice of this accommodation only serves to reinforce Christian privilege. Non-Christian students and/or employees are required to verify, document, and/or otherwise prove to a person in a position of authority—who is usually Christian—that their absences are associated with the observance of a religious/spiritual event (Schlosser & Sedlacek, 2001). The person in authority has the discretionary power to choose to accept the legitimacy of these absences or not, usually based on their own, often limited knowledge of students'/employees' different communities of faith and corresponding practices, as well as their attitudes toward these (Schlosser & Sedlacek, 2001).

In a recent worst-case scenario example of not only the utter misuse of this kind of discretionary power, but the deliberate abuse of it, it has come to light that cadets at the U.S. Air Force Academy have filed 55 complaints of religious discrimination since 2001 (Mount, 2005). A report of the Americans United for Separation of Church and State concluded that, "both the specific violations and the promotion of a culture of official religious intolerance are pervasive, systemic and evident at the very highest levels of the academy's command structure" (p.1). Complaints filed stated that, "cadets are frequently pressured to attend chapel and take religious instruction, particularly in the evangelical Christian faith; that prayer is a part of mandatory events at the academy; and that in at least one case a teacher ordered students to pray before beginning their final examination" (p. 1).

In a recent poll of the U.S. public, "29 percent said they viewed the United States as 'a Christian' nation; 16 percent see it as a 'Biblical nation, defined by the Judeo-Christian tradition'; 45 percent see it as a 'secular nation.' Still, 84 percent think references to God are acceptable in schools, government buildings and other public settings—if no *specific religion* is mentioned" (Fineman, 2002, p. 24). Clearly, a contradiction exists between these latter two statistics if 45 percent see the United States as secular, but 84 percent of those believe that state-supported references to G–d[4] are acceptable. A related contradiction emerges when the recent decision of the Ninth Circuit Court on the *under God* phrase in the *Pledge of Allegiance* is juxtaposed with the subsequent decision of the U.S. Supreme Court permitting the use of public educational funds in parochial schools through *voucher* or *school choice* programs (Fineman, 2002). The decision in the first instance supports the separation of religion and state, whereas the decision in the second one completely undermines it. These and similar contradictions are becoming increasingly visible in U.S. culture, speaking loudly to the need for increased awareness, knowledge, and understanding to be developed on the totality of concerns relating to Christian privilege.

An area of particular concern that demands immediate attention pertains to Christian fundamentalist exploitation of their children as vehicles of Christian *conversion* of other people's children. As a back-door strategy for bringing fundamentalist Christianity into public schools, the parents of these children have organized them to proselytize to any and all of their non-Christian classmates, no matter how devout these classmates' parents may be in another religious, spiritual, faith-based, or secular direction. "As far as they are concerned, the children of the *unchurched* are ripe for the picking" (Boston, 2004, p. 3). For all the talk about the flight of children of fundamentalist Christians to private and parochial schools, the reality is that 90% of all school-age children in the United States are still educated in the public school system. As such, PK–12 public schools are becoming the ideological battleground for what, increasingly, are beginning to look like modern-day inquisitions (Boston, 2004).

A parallel development exclusive to adults can be seen in the rising popularity of the *Left Behind* series of books coauthored by Jerry Jenkins and Tim LaHaye. As superficial as Harlequin romances, these books articulate an *end times* prophecy, drawing from the authors' quite imaginative *literal* interpretation of the book of Revelations. Arguing not only that this book provides absolute evidence for *an angry God*—one who melts the eyes of enemies (nonbelievers) in their heads, disintegrating their tongues, and causing their flesh to drop off—Jenkins and LaHaye suggest that "liberalism has so twisted the real meaning of Scripture" so as to have "manufactured a loving, wimpy Jesus" (CBS, 2004, p. 2). It should come as no surprise that these authors have chosen the one book of the Bible whose historical origins are most suspect—the one book most religious scholars, as opposed to self-proclaimed ministers, argue may, in essence, be an early version of Ken Kesey's "electric Kool-Aid acid test" (a hallucinogenic rumination inside the head of John)—on which to base their entire book series (Wolfe, 1967). "The message of Revelations is that oppression will be ended. They [the authors] take the message and personalize it to evildoers. They make this an us versus them kind of theology. If you're not with us, you're against us. They forget the message of the Bible is that each person is created in the image of God" (CBS, 2004, p. 4). It is exactly this *us/them* dichotomy that the authors and their Christian fundamentalist counterparts in the White House are seeking to promote to the United States and world populace.

Us/them thinking is, at its very core, anti-intellectual. It discourages critical thinking and the more complex understandings of human behavior that critical thought helps us to garner. But what better way to build support for a political agenda that seeks to undermine all things democratic in service to the economic elite, than under the veil of doing *God's will?* How simple a thing it is to quite literally sell judgment, retribution, even hatred; and how long the road is to walking the talk of compassion. How easy it is to assign blame to others—all too often the racialized and classed *other*—and how monumental the task of accepting responsibility oneself. There is no greater example of the success of this marketing strategy than the outcome of the last presidential election (J. Moore, 2004). Notwithstanding real concerns about the legitimacy of the vote counts in both 2000 and 2004, it is clear that a majority of the U.S. voter population had bought into the dumbed-down, G.I. Joe-ized version of G–d when they cast their votes for the presidency. Though the majority of these citizens have been experiencing extreme financial distress for the last 5 years, they were systematically convinced to vote against their economic self-interest, in favor of not only an angry G–d, but of the extremely wealthy (J. Moore, 2004). Engage the average voter in a discussion of these dynamics and he or she will dismiss such analysis as tantamount to blasphemy. What greater mechanism of social control is required when the people opt themselves out of any process of inquiry—be it based on a qualitative or quantitative methodological approach—that might cause them to question their beliefs? Here, questioning one's beliefs is tantamount to having lost faith, and losing faith is grounds for being *left behind* to *burn in hell on earth* when *the rapture* comes (CBS, 2004). In the U.S. Air Force Academy case, we see, perhaps, the worst consequences of such limited perspectives:

> highly qualified individuals were dissuaded from attending the academy... after learning of the official culture of religious intolerance and hostility toward those who do not subscribe to and practice evangelical Christianity. When the Air Force is denied the service of the country's best and brightest young people because they feel excluded from the academy by religious intolerance, the armed forces and the nation as a whole are weakened. (Mount, 2005, pp. 1–2)

Fundamentalism, then, breeds ignorance and, at best, mediocrity. As if the larger assault on civil liberties represented by the Air Force example was not bad enough, the public school curriculum is once again under attack as well. In high schools debates rage, perhaps with previously unparalleled fervor, as to whether sex education should be a part of the curriculum, and, if it is, whether or not it should include any discussion of birth control beyond abstinence, or of human sexuality beyond heterosexuality (ABC, 2005; Chasnoff & Cohen, 1996; J. Moore, 2004; M. Moore, 2004). At the elementary school level, curricular affirmation of student family configurations where there are two moms or two dads in the home, how gay or lesbian parents might be welcomed as classroom volunteers, as well as whether or not *suspected* or *known* (much less *out*) gay or lesbian teachers should be employed are also at great issue. And although it may seem shocking, the teaching of evolution at all academic levels has been thrown back into the forefront of educational policy debate of late. In a recent exposé on this topic in particular, author David Quammen sums up this debate as follows:

> Evolution by natural selection, the central concept of the life's work of Charles Darwin, is a theory. It's a theory about the origin of adaptation, complexity, and diversity among Earth's living creatures. If you are skeptical by nature, unfamiliar with the terminology of science, and unaware of the overwhelming evidence, you might even be tempted to say that it's *just* a theory. In the same sense, relativity as described by Albert Einstein is *just* a theory. The notion that Earth orbits around the sun rather than vice versa, offered by Copernicus in 1543, is a theory. Continental drift is a theory. The existence, structure, and dynamics of atoms? Atomic theory. Even electricity is a theoretical construct, involving electrons, which are tiny units of charged mass that no one has ever seen. Each of these theories is an explanation that has been confirmed to such a degree, by observation and experiment, that knowledgeable experts accept it as fact. That's what scientists mean when they talk about a theory: not a dreamy and unreliable speculation, but an explanatory statement that fits the evidence. They embrace such an explanation confidently but provisionally—taking it as their best available view of reality, at least until some severely conflicting data or some better explanation might come along.

> The rest of us generally agree. We plug our televisions into little wall sockets, measure a year by the length of Earth's orbit, and in many other ways live our lives based on the trusted reality of those theories.

> Evolutionary theory, though, is a bit different. It's such a dangerously wonderful and far-reaching view of life that some people find it unacceptable, despite the vast body of supporting evidence. As applied to our own species, *Homo sapiens*, it can seem more threatening still. Many fundamentalist Christians and ultra-orthodox Jews take alarm at the thought that human descent from earlier paralleled by Islamic creationists such as Harun Yahya, author of a recent volume titled *The Evolution Deceit*, who points to the six-day creation story in the Koran as literal truth and calls the theory of evolution *nothing but a deception imposed on us by the dominators of the world system*. The late Srila Prabhupada, of the Hare Krishna movement, explained that God created *the*

8,400,000 species of life from the very beginning, in order to establish multiple tiers of reincarnation for rising souls. Although souls ascend, the species themselves don't change, he insisted, dismissing *Darwin's nonsensical theory.*

Other people too, not just scriptural literalists, remain unpersuaded about evolution. According to a Gallup poll drawn from more than a thousand telephone interviews conducted in February 2001, no less than 45 percent of responding U.S. adults agreed that *God created human beings pretty much in their present form at one time within the last 10,000 years or so.* Evolution, by their lights, played no role in shaping us.

Only 37 percent of the polled Americans were satisfied with allowing room for both God and Darwin—that is, divine initiative to get things started, evolution as the creative means. (This view, according to more than one papal pronouncement, is compatible with Roman Catholic dogma.) Still fewer Americans, only 12 percent, believed that humans evolved from other life-forms without any involvement of a god.

The most startling thing about these poll numbers is not that so many Americans reject evolution, but that the statistical breakdown hasn't changed much in two decades. Gallup interviewers posed exactly the same choices in 1982, 1993, 1997, and 1999. The creationist conviction—that God alone, and not evolution, produced humans—has never drawn less than 44 percent. In other words, nearly half the American populace prefers to believe that Charles Darwin was wrong where it mattered most.

Why are there so many antievolutionists? Scriptural literalism can only be part of the answer. The American public certainly includes a large segment of scriptural literalists—but not *that* large, not 44 percent. Creationist prose-lytizers and political activists, working hard to interfere with the teaching of biology in the public schools are another part. Honest confusion and ignorance, among millions of adult Americans, must still be another. Many people have never taken a biology course that dealt with evolution nor read a book in which the theory was lucidly explained. Sure, we've all heard of Charles Darwin and of a vague, somber notion about struggle and survival that sometimes goes by the catchall label "Darwinism." But the main sources of information from which most Americans have drawn awareness of this subject, it seems, are haphazard ones at best: cultural osmosis, newspaper and magazine references, half-baked documentaries on the tube, and hearsay.

Evolution is both a beautiful concept and an important one, more crucial nowadays to human welfare, to medical science, and to our understanding of the world than ever before. It's also deeply persuasive—a theory you can take to the bank. The essential points are slightly more complicated than most people assume, but not so complicated they can't be comprehended by any attentive person. Furthermore, the supporting evidence is abundant, various, ever increasing, solidly interconnected, and easily available in museums, popular books, textbooks, and a mountainous accumulation of peer-reviewed scientific studies. *No one needs to, and no one should, accept evolution merely as a matter of faith.* (2004, pp. 4, 6, 8; emphasis added)

It is exactly this notion of accepting things—everything—as simply a matter of faith that has enabled the Bush administration to take the U.S. citizenry to the cleaners on its way to the bank. Students at a public research institution—ground zero for knowledge production—eschew the efficacy of research integrity, suggesting that "a researcher can make his or her data say whatever he or she chooses." In this way, even *college-educated* U.S. citizens dismiss science and mathematics alike, in favor of personal experience, opinion, belief, and—yes—faith (Clark, 2005).

So what of this practice of child evangelists in public schools and the grossly underfunded No Child Left Behind Act? Is it plausible that this act, hiding in plain sight so to speak, may actually have been designed as a covert evangelical Christian action—a policy of proselytization? Is it possible that in being so grossly underfunded so as to never be effective in actually closing the achievement gap between low-income children of color and middle- and upper-income white children, it may never have been intended to? Questions of this nature beg for the extension of sociopolitically located multicultural education and social justice/action-oriented, multicultural educators into the interfaith and secular realms. We must develop a politics of inclusion—of making the "other" *us* and not *them*, a politics of critical thought, compassion, and collective self-interest (Rorty, 1989). We must reclaim public schools as oppositional spaces in which students, parents, teachers, and administrators come together to fight for equity and justice for all (Clark & O'Donnell, 1999). These are lofty goals that begin with the naming and deconstruction of Christian privilege toward the establishment of interfaith-based and secularly affirming academic and employment settings.

STRATEGIES FOR COMING TO UNDERSTAND, CHALLENGE, AND RESOLVE CHRISTIAN PRIVILEGE IN THE PUBLIC EDUCATIONAL AND WORKPLACE CONTEXT

It is important for multicultural educators to acknowledge the reality of Christian privilege, in the same way that we have acknowledged the reality of white privilege, male privilege, class privilege, and so forth (Clark, Brimhall-Vargas, Schlosser, & Alimo, 2002). But, as is the case with these other forms of privilege, naming Christian privilege as such is not enough. We must develop strategies for coming to understand what Christian privilege is, precisely so that it can be challenged and resolved if we are to develop religious, spiritual, faith-based, and secularly inclusive educational and workplace contexts. In this section, four such strategies are delineated. These strategies involve: (1) defining the terms *Christian* and *privilege*, as well as the phrase *Christian privilege*, (2) offering several examples of Christian privilege; (3) reviewing an example of Christian privilege in the popular culture arena; and (4) using problem-solving scenarios to illustrate how Christian privilege operates, and can be responded to, in academic and employment settings.

Defining *Christian, Privilege,* and *Christian Privilege*

In attempting to define the term *Christian,* even Christians themselves find it difficult to delineate a definition of Christian that is universally acceptable (Clark et al., 2002). It is also difficult for Christians to arrive at a definition of Christian that makes it uniquely distinguishable from other religions and/or faiths, beyond its connection to *The Trinity.* A common problem that arises for Christians in attempting to define Christian can be seen in the question: If proselytization is eliminated as a defining characteristic of Christian, what other defining characteristics remain? Thus, the exercise of merely trying to define the term *Christian* for Christians—as well as for non-Christians conditioned by, or assimilated to, life in a Christian privilege context—is illustrative of the pervasiveness of the privilege associated with it: the fish can't feel the water because it's in it (Lea & Helfand, 2004). This begs the rhetorical question, What is the *water* that is *Christian?*

Defining privilege may seem easier at first; "special access" is the most commonly accepted definition by Christians (Clark et al., 2002). But, as the defining process continues, Christians begin to associate broader definitions of privilege with their experiences of themselves as Christians and object to the critique.

The emergence of this latter dynamic makes seamless the segue between connecting the definitions of Christian and privilege together toward defining the complete phrase *Christian privilege.* Christians often assume one of two dichotomous perspectives: *It is a privilege for me to be a Christian* or *I do not feel that I experience any privilege as a Christian.* Both instances mirror the paradoxical affirmation of superiority and simultaneous denial of advantage often uttered by men and white people in parallel discussions of patriarchy and racism and, correspondingly, male and white privilege (Clark et al., 2002). What makes the Christian privilege definition process so complex is the emergence of the so-called *full gospel* Christian fundamentalist identity. Christians who claim this identity dismiss Christian denominations as limiting their *path to God.* This perspective arises precisely because any connection to a denomination is also a connection to a religious history and tradition—an intellectual connection that mediates the boundaries and balances between reason and faith. Claiming access to the absolute truth through the *literal interpretation* of the *full gospel*—as opposed to one facilitated by an ordained Doctor of Divinity in any one of several long-standing Christian denominations—makes the mere discussion of Christian privilege, much less the comprehensive definition of it, very difficult. At the same time that fundamentalist Christians in particular (though all Christians to lesser extents) enjoy Christian privilege, they argue that, in fact, they are persecuted for their religious beliefs, *as Christ himself was.* While nonfundamentalist Christians will argue that this occurs because of how they are judged by the actions of these extremist Christians, Christian fundamentalists will argue that this occurs because of the blindness—or, worse, sinfulness—of nonbelievers. Historical analysis of Christ's actual persecution as a reformist Jew (not a Christian) or as a social justice activist (the antithesis of a fundamentalist zealot) is largely dismissed. What makes this dismissal particularly challenging is how much of it hails from brown-skinned peoples—people who experience racial discrimination as people of color. In an instant, a profoundly race-conscious African American will act as if such consciousness never existed when asked to adapt it from the race context in order to apply it to the religious one.

Any assumption that having a disenfranchised identity in one context necessarily facilitates consciousness of another person's disenfranchised identity in another context is completely erroneous (Clark et al., 2002). Nonetheless, using the sociopolitically located multicultural education paradigm to continually draw parallels between different kinds of privilege and oppression is, in the long run, the most effective approach for moving Christians and non-Christians alike through the Christian privilege definition process.

Several Examples of Christian Privilege

In the vein of professor Peggy McIntosh's seminal work on male privilege and white privilege, there is a *knapsack* of Christian privilege that also needs unpacking; that is, an invisible set of unearned and unacknowledged benefits with which Christians in the United States walk casually around, as if in a knapsack slung over a shoulder (McIntosh, 1988). To unpack this knapsack is to develop critical consciousness of its presence and impact in the everyday life of both Christians and non-Christians. To facilitate the development of this consciousness, a list of examples of Christian privilege, parallel to McIntosh's *40 Examples of White Privilege* (1988), has been developed (Clark et al., 2002):

1. It is likely that state and federal holidays coincide with my religious practices, thereby having little to no impact on my job and/or education.

2. I can talk openly about my religious practices without concern for how it will be received by others.

3. I can be sure to hear music on the radio and watch specials on television that celebrate the holidays of my religion.

4. When told about the positive aspects of the history of civilization, I can be sure that I am shown people of my religion made it what it is.

5. I can worry about religious privilege without being perceived as *self-interested* or *self-serving.*

6. I can have a *Jesus is Lord* bumper sticker or Icthus (Christian fish) on my car and not worry about someone vandalizing my car because of it.

7. I can share my holiday greetings without being fully conscious of how it may impact those who do not celebrate the same holidays. I can also be sure that people are knowledgeable about the holidays of my religion and will greet me with the appropriate holiday greeting (e.g., Merry Christmas, Happy Easter, etc.).

8. I can assume that there is a universality of religious experience; I can deny Christian privilege by asserting that all religions are essentially the same.

9. I do not need to learn the religious or spiritual customs of others, and I am not penalized for not knowing them.

10. I am largely unencumbered by having to explain why I am or am not doing things related to my religious norms on a daily basis.

11. I am not judged by the improper actions of others in my religious group.

12. If I wish, usually I can be exclusively among those from my religious group most of the time (in work, school, or at home).

13. I can assume that my safety, or the safety of my family, will not be put in jeopardy by disclosing my religion to others at work or at school.

14. It is likely that mass media represents my religion widely *and* positively.

15. It is likely that I can find items to buy that represent my religious norms and holidays with relative ease (e.g., food, decorations, greeting cards, etc.).

16. I can speak or write about my religion, and even critique other religions, and have these perspectives listened to, even published, with relative ease and without much fear of reprisal.

17. I could write an article on Christian privilege without putting my own religion on trial.

18. I can travel without others assuming that I put them at risk because of my religion.

19. It is likely that my religion will not put me at risk from others when I travel.

20. I can be financially successful without the assumption from others that this success is connected to my religion.

21. I can protect myself (and my children) from people who may not like me (or them) based on my religion.

22. Law enforcement officials will likely assume I am a nonthreatening person if my religion is disclosed to them; in fact, disclosure of my religion may actually encourage or incline law enforcement officials to perceive me as being *in the right* or *unbiased.*

23. I can safely assume that any authority figure will generally be someone of my religion.

24. I can talk about my religion, even proselytize, and be characterized as *sharing the word,* instead of imposing my ideas on others or distributing *propaganda.*

25. I can be gentle and affirming to people without being characterized as an *exception* to my religion.

26. I am never asked to speak on behalf of all Christians.

27. My citizenship and immigration status will likely not be questioned, and my background will likely not be investigated, because of my religion.

28. My place of worship is probably not targeted for violence because of sentiment against my religion.

29. I can be sure that my religion will not work against me when seeking medical or legal help.

30. My religion will not cause teachers to pigeonhole me into certain professions based on the assumed *prowess* of my religious group.

31. I will not have my children taken from me by governmental authorities who have been made aware of my religious affiliation.

32. Disclosure of my religion to an adoption agency will likely not prevent me from being able to adopt children.

33. If I wish to give my children a parochial religious education, I probably have a variety of options nearby.

34. I can be sure that my children will be given curricular materials, despite the so-called separation of religion and state that testify to the existence and importance of my religion.

35. I can be sure that when someone in the media is referring to G–d, they are referring to my (Christian) G–d.

36. I can easily find academic courses and institutions that give attention only to people of my religion.

37. My religion and religious holidays are so completely *normal* that, in many ways, they may appear to no longer have any religious significance at all; further, having been legally constructed as *secular,* my religious holidays can be openly practiced in public institutional settings without a thought given to the violation of the separation of religion and state.

38. The elected and appointed officials of my government are probably members of my religious group.

39. When swearing an oath in court or for employment, I am probably making this oath by placing my hand on the scripture of my religion, despite the so-called separation of religion and state.

40. I can openly display my religious symbol(s) on my person or property without fear of disapproval, violence, and/or vandalism.

41. The central figure of my religion is used at the major point of reference for my calendaring system (i.e., B.C. and A.D., as well as B.C.E. and C.E.).

42. I can define the belief system of, and/or its practice by, another group as valid or invalid regardless of my level of knowledge of it.

In reading through this list of Christian privilege examples, it is important to keep four different *lenses* in mind those of: (1) a Christian; (2) a person from another *traditional* faith (Jewish, Muslim, Buddhist, Hindu, etc.); (3) a person from a *nontraditional* faith (Wiccan, Santera/o, Espiritualista, Vodooist, Asatru, Shinto, Yoruban, Druid, Native American, etc.); and (4) an Agnostic or Atheist. In referencing each of these lenses, it becomes clear how differently individuals who represent these lenses will read each item on the list.

While the list was developed *prior* to the events of September 11, 2001, and the release of the critically acclaimed documentary film *Fahrenheit 9/11* (Moore, M., 2004), it takes on new dimensions in their aftermath. Against the backdrop of debate surrounding random security checks of the entire population, or so-called *smart* profiling of those who mirror the identifying characteristics of the people believed to be responsible for this particular crime, the experience of, and procedures for, both domestic and international travel have markedly changed. Despite the ongoing nature of this debate, non-Christians, especially Muslims, bear the brunt of travel-related criminal profiling today. Complicated dynamics have emerged in relationship to these profiling practices.

In one such dynamic, Christian privilege is squarely linked to white supremacy. Evidence of this exists in even just a cursory comparison of the country's differential responses to the Oklahoma City and World Trade Center bombings. This comparison is frequently raised by Muslims and various peoples of color in the discussion of current profiling protocols. Muslims often note that in the wake of the Oklahoma City bombing, there were false reports of *Middle-Eastern-looking* men running from the scene. Yet, when the perpetrators were identified as white supremacist Christian men, no ensuing profiling of whites, of Christians, or even simply of white men took place as a part of the frenzied search for the culprits. Black Americans, Latina/o Americans, Asian Americans, and Native Americans are quick to point out that violent, formally affiliated, white supremacist Christian groups emerged in the United States for the first time simultaneous with the Emancipation Proclamation. Their proliferation, while monitored, is largely unfettered. Whereas generally nonviolent and pro-self-determination (vs. supremacist) groups like the Black Panthers, the Young Lord's Party, and the American Indian Movement were systematically infiltrated and quite effectively dismantled by the FBI relatively soon after their emergence (Takaki, 1994).

In a second dynamic, black Americans, in particular, are asking the question: "Where did Arabs, Arab Americans, Muslims, and/or people of Middle Eastern descent stand on the issue of criminal profiling—largely racial profiling directed at black Americans—*prior* to September 11, 2001?" Many black Americans feel a sense of relief that a group other than theirs is at the epicenter of the law enforcement radar screen. The expression of U.S. nationalistic sentiment—through the display of U.S. flags or Christian privilege-laden bumper stickers that read: *God Bless America*—makes many black Americans feel, some for the first time, like they are connected to, and perhaps better accepted by, *mainstream* or white America, seemingly removing them further (even if only incrementally) from the radar screen. Additionally, many black Americans openly express fear of traveling when people they perceive to be Arab, Arab American, Muslim, and/or of Middle Eastern descent are present. Indeed, such fear is even fodder for several black comedians. In this dynamic we see evidence of what acclaimed author Toni Morrison refers to as *images of whiteness in the black imagination* (Takaki, 1994). While enshrouded in the veil of Christian privilege, these sentiments—expressed in seriousness or in jest—derive from white supremacy. It is the overarching fear of brown-skinned people that creates anti-Arab, anti-Arab American, and anti-Middle Eastern sentiment in the entire U.S. populace—white, black, Latina/o, Asian, and Native American. The anti-Muslim piece of this sentiment is the second category of otherness, not the primary category. If the anti-Muslim piece were central, the picture painted of Muslims by the U.S. media would be more multicolored, more racially representative of the totality of Muslims in the world, especially in the United States. The fear, even black Americans' fear, is of the *brown-skinned* Muslim, not the Muslim, and this fear is mediated by the insinuation of white supremacy into the relationships between and among people of color absent the presence of even a single white person.

A third emergent dynamic exists in the relationship between Muslim and Jewish Americans. It is important to note that Jews have long borne the brunt of Christian privilege, manifest as anti-Semitism, in the United States. But, similar to the experience of black Americans in relationship to those perceived to be Arabs, Arab Americans, Muslims, and/or people of Middle Eastern descent, the experience of Jewish Americans in relationship to Muslim Americans has been altered. Resultantly, there has been a shift in the attitudes of many Jewish Americans; at one time quite progressively minded because of their own experience of discrimination, many now express much more conservative positions in relationship to Muslims in general, as well as Muslim-associated profiling (Takaki, 1994; West, 2005). Furthermore, Jewish Americans tend to express resistance to the suggestion that in taking this position they are perpetrating discrimination. Having been all too painfully on the receiving end of discrimination themselves, it is challenging for them to recognize their role in distributing discrimination to others, especially to Muslim Americans, and to recognize the privilege Israel holds relative to Palestinians in the Middle East. Instead, many Jews paint Israel and Jews as the disenfranchised victims at the hands of Palestinians/Muslims. While this may be individually the case as much as the contrary is, it is at the institutional level that the privilege conversation must take place for the kind of inclusive community at issue to begin to be built. As discussed in relationship to the previous dynamic, white supremacy also lurks in the consciousness of Jewish Americans in their interface with Muslim Americans. Like black Americans, Jewish Americans have also been racialized "others" in the United States. And, like Muslim Americans, Jewish Americans have also been religious "others" in the United States In both of these comparison instances, however, Jewish Americans can, and do, benefit from white supremacy in seeking to be less racially otherized than black Americans, and less religiously otherized than Muslim Americans. While not the favorite connection for most Jewish Americans to make, both mainstream alliances between Christianity and Judaism (through the Judeo-Christian link) against Islam, as well as the wholly misguided alliance between Christian fundamentalists and messianic Jews against Islam, provide insulation for Jewish Americans from the kind of religious otherizing that Muslim Americans are currently experiencing. While that insulation is named as religious, it has increasingly racialized dimensions today. The relationship between black Americans and Jewish Americans forged during the reconstruction era of U.S. history and maintained through the civil rights movement is strained among generations with knowledge of this history in both groups, and largely invisible to the younger populations in each group (Takaki, 1994). While this location is tenuous, at the current historical moment Jewish Americans are both more like Christians than other non-Christians, and more white than other people of color.

When these and other complex dynamics emerge, the challenge is to keep the focus on Christian privilege—especially as it manifests in the United States—despite the tendency for both Christians and non-Christians to direct it elsewhere. This tendency can be read as one of many attempts members of both groups will make to avoid confrontation of the new and uncomfortable topic of Christian privilege. However, it is only through its direct confrontation that the critical consciousness necessary to not only unpack the knapsack of Christian privilege, but to leave the knapsack at home, emerges.

God's Squad Video

Even after reviewing all of the preceding examples of Christian privilege, some Christians still do not *see* the privilege they enjoy at the expense of non-Christians. Perhaps this is because these examples, while based on the real experiences of Christian and non-Christians in the everyday, are still received as abstractions when represented on paper. The *God's Squad* segment of HBO's January 29, 2002, broadcast of *Real Sports with Bryant Gumbel* illustrates even more starkly than the examples, and in a visually interactive manner, how Christian privilege manifests in one *real-world* context. In so doing, it becomes a powerful tool for illustrating Christian privilege as it operates in the everyday, as well as for unpacking the knapsack it resides in on a daily basis.

Briefly, *God's Squad* examines Christian privilege in the workplace context of professional football players. It reports on the experience of several Christians, one Muslim, and one Agnostic against the backdrop of Christian privilege in the NFL's workplace climate, organizational practices, as well as professional development opportunities.

Comparison of the Muslim and Christian experiences in the segment is important. While authoritatively sanctioned, aggressive, evangelical Christian proselytizing by Christian players is positively characterized as *spreading the word of God*, when a Muslim player brings literature explaining the tenets of Islam to a fellow player (who requested it), he is chastised by teammates and team leadership alike for distributing *propaganda*. Likewise, an avowed Agnostic player is characterized as *Pagan, heathen,* and a *devil worshipper* by his Christian teammates.

It is important to problem-pose about the misunderstandings of other religions, formal or informal spiritualities, faiths—especially *nontraditional* faiths—and agnosticism and atheism represented in the segment to encourage more complex views of them as well as of Christianity. In fact, as discussed in the chapter introduction, the view of Christianity put forth by the Christian players in the segment is a view absent critical consciousness about Christianity (as well as other belief systems) and based largely on a sort of cross between Christian fundamentalist ideology and superficial representations of Christianity in popular culture. It is a view that entertains no discussion of different belief systems, whether internal or external to Christianity, in either a positive or simply nonvaluated light. That is, the non-Christian "other"—whoever it is—is unethical and amoral, and is, thus, off *the* path to G–d. Amidst this absolutism, truth is theirs alone. The segment also completely omits mention of, for example, atheism or scientific rationalism, and, in so doing, allows the Christian view of creation to supercede mere discussion of, much less debate on, other explanations of human existence whether based in the divine, the scientific, a combination of both, or something altogether distinct.

In connecting the *God's Squad* example to the public education and workplace context, the following case from the public higher education/ workplace context comes to mind. In the fall of 2000, a major public research institution hired a new Division I head football coach. During his preseason interview with the local television station—conducted at the Catholic student center during their weekly fellowship meeting—the coach affirmed that he was *going to put prayer back into football where it belongs.* Employees of this university who inquired as to whether forced prayer in the football locker room was a violation of the separation of religion and state, as well as the university's policies, discovered that while it was a violation of both, unless an athlete, forced to engage in such practice, objected, no significant action could be taken to stop the practice. That is, there is no violation unless an individual directly negatively impacted by the practice files a grievance. Furthermore, given the fierce competition to play Division I football, realistically, only a star athlete could initiate a challenge, as a less critical player might be cut to silence opposition to the practice.

The view of Christianity put forth in both the *God's Squad* segment and the higher education/workplace example is of the highly conservative bent, from which the most oppressive expression of Christian privilege emerges and takes hold in public education and workplace contexts. As referenced during the discussion of definitions of Christian privilege, many liberal, progressive, left, and/or liberation theology–oriented Christians maintain that this bent of Christianity is not the only one, nor even a historically accurate one, and that all Christians should not be judged by it. While these statements are all correct, the fact remains that all Christians benefit from Christian privilege regardless of the way they express themselves as Christians, in the same way that all white people benefit from white privilege (even white communists engaged in antiracist work), and that all men benefit from male privilege (even black gay men involved in men against violence against women work). In fact, it is precisely this shared benefit that the Bush administration, under the puppeteering prowess of the now infamous Karl Rove, has been capitalizing on in redirecting, in order to resurrect (Christian reference intended) the notion of the United States as *a melting pot* (J. Moore, 2004). Whereas that melting pot originally attempted to belie the Judeo-Christian Eurocentrism embedded within in it (Takaki, 1994), today that Eurocentrism is wrapped in the veil of white supremacy and Christian privilege—a veil that, with the increasingly hostile, racist, anti-Muslim political agenda on the horizon, will eventually be wound so tightly around the heads of all middle- and working-class people in the United States that we will suffocate (as did the German people during World War II) on a fascism borne of our own complicity; a fascism borne of our own indifference to civic engagement, to the erosion of civil liberties, and to the destruction of democracy and justice.

Problem-Solving Scenarios

A final strategy for examining Christian privilege involves the use of problem-solving scenarios. Both scenarios involve a group of people in the planning of an end-of-year celebration. They are identical except that in one scenario the religious, spiritual, faith-based, and secular identities of the group for whom the celebration is to be planned are disclosed (the *revealed* scenario), and in the other it is not (the *unrevealed* scenario).

Unrevealed Problem-Solving Scenario. You, the supervisor of your unit, are planning an end-of-year party for your office. You know almost nothing about the religious and/or spiritual identity of your coworkers. How would you go about planning this party to make sure everyone in the workplace is comfortable attending it? How would you approach people you suspect are religiously or spiritually different from you? What are some assumptions that you are possibly making in the preparation of this party?

Revealed Problem-Solving Scenario. You, the supervisor of your unit, are planning an end-of-year party for your office. The following kinds of people work in your office: a Muslim, an Agnostic, nine Christians from a variety of sects (Catholic, Methodist, Nondenominational, Seventh-Day Adventist, Baptist, etc.), a Wiccan, a Hindu, and two atheists. How would you go about planning this party to make sure everyone in the workplace is comfortable attending it? How would you approach people you know or suspect are religiously or spiritually different from you? What are some assumptions that you are possibly making in the preparation of this party?

DISCUSSION

The planning process, essentially a problem-solving effort, in each scenario can be described as follows: You have this group of people. You need to plan a celebration with them in mind. The celebration needs to be religiously, spiritually, faith-based, and secularly inclusive. How do you make this happen? Two points of conflict repeatedly arise in the problem-solving effort (Clark et al., 2002).

First, rarely does the problem-solving effort in either scenario take into account the idea of *not* planning the celebration for the *end of the year*, read as the end of the Western calendar year. Nor does it even consider what the *end of the year* might mean across workplace contexts (i.e., end of academic year, end of fiscal year, etc.). When this observation is raised, tremendous tension emerges in response. Often Christians vehemently resist the idea of having an inclusive celebration that would *not* occur when Christmas is traditionally recognized. Many non-Christians also express discomfort with not subscribing to this celebration time because of its convenience and/or because of external pressure to do so.

Second, problem-solving efforts routinely avoid: (1) using the knowledge the revealed scenario offers about the members' religious, spiritual, faith-based, and secular identities in the planning process; and (2) the idea of asking the members of the group for whom celebration planning is taking place about their beliefs as a part of the planning process in the unrevealed scenario. That is, the so-called problem-solving efforts avoid taking advantage of what any knowledge of group members' actual religious, spiritual, faith-based, and secular identities and/or practices might mean for an *end-of-year* celebration.[5]

Fear of offending members of the group depicted in the scenarios by asking questions about their beliefs and/or practices is often offered as the rationale for not engaging them in dialogue in the planning process. Tension again arises when this rationale is responded to with the question, What makes you think that excluding or not considering the beliefs and practices of others is less offensive than opening up a conversation with others about their beliefs and practices? Reminiscent of the sentiments expressed by the Christian players in God's Squad, many problem-solving scenario participants suggest that it is unreasonable for those with non-dominant belief systems to expect accommodation in a mainstream educational or workplace context, or that the process of learning about other beliefs is either too overwhelming or too threatening to the unfettered preservation of their own beliefs. In some cases, Christian participants articulate that even learning about others' beliefs is considered blasphemous to their own. That is, because open dialogue with others, even open internal dialogue with oneself (through research or reflective questioning) necessarily leads to the consideration of perspectives different from one's own, many Christian participants consider doing such to be a violation of their practice of Christianity. And this point, perhaps more than any other, is at the crux of Christian privilege in the United States, most starkly manifest as Christian fundamentalism—We're, right, period! Consideration of other perspectives is, therefore, not only futile, but immoral because they're wrong! An obvious contradiction in this perspective is that if one is convinced of the absolute truth of one's beliefs, then exposure to others' would be completely nonthreatening. That such consideration is, indeed, so threatening suggests a fragility of belief—beliefs that may not stand up to exposure to others' ways of knowing.

Clearly, the power of education and/or professional development on this topic cannot be overstated as the fear of dialogue and associated learning illustrates. But, just as clearly, it is only through dialogue-oriented education and professional development leading to new awareness, knowledge, and understanding that a religiously, spiritually, faith-based, and secularly inclusive community can be built.

MULTICULTURAL ORGANIZATIONAL DEVELOPMENT THROUGH THE LENS OF RELIGION, SPIRITUALITY, FAITH, AND SECULAR INCLUSION: A CASE STUDY

What might a religiously, spiritually, faith-based, and secularly inclusive public educational and/or workplace setting look like? What might be involved in creating such a setting? These are questions that the University of Maryland's Office of Human Relations Programs' (OHRP) staff sought answers to on their journey to confront Christian privilege and build a religiously, spiritually, faith-based, and secularly inclusive community within OHRP and across campus (Clark, 2003a). What follows is a case study examination of my experience, as OHRP's Executive Director, of facilitating a multicultural organization change process for my staff—a process in which I was also a participant. This change process was directed toward our creation of a plan of action for a celebration to affirm religious, spiritual, faith-based, and secular diversity. This case study pays special attention to the process through which change efforts were undertaken to ensure that both the confrontation of, and resolution to, Christian privilege honored the complexities of multiple social identities, especially those embedded in a juxtaposition of Christian privilege with race, ethnicity, and socioeconomic oppression.

Background

OHRP is Maryland's version of an office of multicultural affairs. Its point of entry into multicultural affairs work is built from the integration of equity compliance, diversity education, and social justice action. The essence of what this means is that OHRP takes a sociopolitical or progressive approach to multicultural affairs work. Or, said another way, it considers issues of power, oppression, and privilege in seeking to create a multiculturally inclusive and just campus community and, by extension of its students and employees beyond campus boundaries, society.

It is extremely important to note that *even* in this kind of multicultural affairs arena, the issue of Christian privilege and the associated struggle to create religiously, spiritually, faith-based, and secularly inclusive communities is still a relatively new area of diversity-related learning and action (Clark et al., 2002). As such, these areas are treated differently than, for example, those along the lines of race, socioeconomic class, and gender have been. *Differently* in this instance means with less directness, honesty, and confidence. While sociopolitically oriented multicultural and social justice education have long confronted white, class, and gender privilege boldly, openly, and unequivocally, when it comes to Christian privilege, it seems we stutter and stumble, suddenly unsure of what is okay to say or do (Nieto, 2000; Sleeter, 1996). The reason underlying this difference is not monolithic, but three-pronged.

The first part of this difference can be attributed to the influence of the theory of the *hierarchy of oppressions* that has long operated in the left wing of multicultural and social justice education (Adams, Bell, & Griffin, 1997). This theory suggests that some forms of discrimination, namely socioeconomic class-, race-, and sometimes gender-, based forms are more serious than others; such as those related to sexual orientation, disability, and—yes—religion, spirituality, faith, and secularity. In being socially constructed as more serious, especially class- and race-based, forms of discrimination are confronted, almost without apology for the often painful impact of that confrontation on the people whose identities afford them race and class privilege. On the other hand, those socially constructed as less serious forms of discrimination are typically confronted more gingerly, taking into consideration the range of potential outcomes such confrontation might have on those empowered by, say, homophobia, able-body status, and/or Christianity. Clearly, even in describing the hierarchy of oppression theory, its limitations emerge. And, certainly, there has been significant recent backlash against the unabashed confrontation of white privilege as evidenced by the onslaught of legal blows to affirmative action (Milem, 2000). At the same time, it is true that an openly racist comment is likely to be attacked virtually unilaterally in the public sphere as horrible, whereas whether or not Matthew Sheppard's murder or the overt criminal profiling of Muslims is necessarily *all bad* is still fodder for debate in the Christian, privilege-biased media (Adams et al., 1997; Clark et al., 2002). Obviously, the theory of the hierarchy of oppression is difficult to firmly articulate in the abstract, much less delineate in the concrete. Nonetheless, it is a theory that persists within the most sociopolitically engaged quadrants of the multicultural affairs community and, thus, accounts for part of why the topic of Christian privilege has been treated differently even by the OHRP staff—the staff that, perhaps somewhat ironically, provides multicultural and social justice education and corresponding support to the University of Maryland community.[6]

A second part of the difference in how the topic of Christian privilege is confronted in the progressive multicultural and social justice education arena has to do with the fact that virtually everyone who works in this arena is "called" to this work through either a strong religious, spiritual, faith-based, or secular connection to concerns for equity and justice. So, while Christian privilege is another form of privilege that, like white privilege or male privilege, must be interrogated and dismantled in order for religiously, spiritually, faith-based, and secularly inclusive equity and justice to emerge, unlike white privilege and male privilege, with Christian privilege, many Christians are called to equity and justice work—inclusive of the work interrogating and dismantling Christian privilege—because of how they interpret and practice the tenets of Christianity (Clark et al., 2002). The same cannot be said for white people or men; there is no way to interpret and practice the tenets of whiteness or maleness that lead to their interrogation and dismantling (Clark & O'Donnell, 1999). On their face, whiteness and maleness reinforce white and male privilege—to interrogate and dismantle these, white people and men must challenge *all* interpretations and practices of the tenets of whiteness and maleness, and instead reconceptualize their racial and gendered selves as antiracist and antisexist. Obviously, progressive multicultural- and social justice-oriented Christians never become anti-Christian, they become liberation theology-focused Christians, or radical Christians, or leave the Christian faith altogether. While white people and men can politically disidentify themselves from whiteness and maleness by joining *with* people of color and women, and *against* most other whites and men, in the struggles for racial- and gender-based self-determination and liberation, they typically cannot cease to be white or male (Cone, 1970; McLaren, 1999). Thus, related to the limitations in the theory of the hierarchy of oppression, it is clear that while parallels between different forms of oppression can be drawn, there are limitations here as well as each form of oppression is also quite unique (Adams et al., 1997). Understanding the complexity of each form's uniqueness is foundational to its eradication. With the Christian privilege form, the *calling* to equity and justice work, inclusive of those called within OHRP, necessarily limits the ways in which it is confronted.

Related to the second part of the difference, a third part of the difference in how the topic of Christian privilege has been confronted in the progressive multicultural affairs arena—especially OHRP's—has to do with the disproportional overrepresentation of people *called* to equity and justice work among those who also experience psychological disabilities, especially those who experience major depression or bipolar disorder (manic depression) (Clark, 2003a). While members of the OHRP staff are engaged in research to further explore this correlation, preliminary assessments of it suggest that the combination of *calling* and depression may be attributable to multicultural educators being profoundly affected by their awareness, knowledge, and understanding of the suffering of others in the world because of the persistent absence of equity and justice. The outcome of the coupling of *calling* and depression is a self-perpetuating cycle common in multicultural educators: the awareness, knowledge, and understanding of suffering attributable to the absence of equity and justice in the world calls them to the work, a by-product of which is depression (and, often, its outward expression—anger), and the remedy for which is the continued commitment to the work. Here again, then, Christian privilege cannot be confronted in the same way white privilege and male privilege can because the role of Christianity in maintaining a balance in this cycle for some multicultural educators must be acknowledged and respected, at the same time Christian privilege is interrogated and dismantled. This is particularly the case when considering the circumstances of Christian African Americans. Given the role that Christianity, conceptualized as a fundamentalist, mainstream, or progressive religion, spirituality, or faith, has played in the ongoing movement for full and unfettered access to participation in democracy for African Americans over the last 244 years, it is difficult in this instance—to say the least—to locate it in both the white supremacist and Christian privilege contexts. Is it possible that Christianity, viewed through this discrete lens, can cease to function as a vehicle of racial superiority and religious imperialism? The Reverend James H. Cone argues in *A Black Theology of Liberation* (1970) that indeed it is.

> In contrast to this racist view of God, Black Theology proclaims his blackness. People who want to know who God is and what he is doing must know who black people are and what they are doing.... Knowing God means being on the side of the oppressed, becoming *one* with them and participating in the goal of liberation. *We must become black with God!*
>
> ...But *becoming black with God* means more than just saying *I am black*, if it involves that at all. The question *How can white people become black?* is analogous to the Philippian jailer's question to Paul and Silas, *What must I do to be*

saved? The implication is that if we work hard enough at it, we can reach the goal. But the misunderstanding here is the failure to see blackness or salvation (the two are synonymous) is the work of God and not man. It is not something we accomplish; it is a gift. That is why they said, *Believe in the Lord Jesus and you will be saved.* To *believe* is to receive the gift and utterly to reorient one's existence on the basis of the gift. The gift is so unlike what humans expect that when it is offered and accepted, we become completely new creatures. This is what the Wholly Otherness of God means. God comes to us in his blackness which is wholly unlike whiteness, and to receive his revelation is to become black with him by joining him in the work of liberation.

Even some black people will find this view of God hard to handle. Having been enslaved by the God of white racism so long, they will have difficulty believing that god is identified with their struggle for freedom. Becoming one of his disciples means rejecting whiteness and accepting themselves as they are in all their physical blackness. This is what the Christian view of God means for black people.

Professor Peter McClaren builds on Cone's perspective in stating that:

To choose blackness or brownness merely as a way to escape the stigma of whiteness and to avoid responsibility for owning whiteness is still very much an act of whiteness. To choose blackness or brownness as a way of politically disidentifying with white privilege and instead identifying and participating in the struggles of non-white peoples is an act of transgression, a traitorous act that reveals a fidelity to the struggle for justice. (1999, pp. 34–35)

But while Cone's characterization of the Christian view of G–d for black people is compelling in its indictment of white supremacy, it does little to posit any limitations of even a liberatory Christian doctrine; for example, through an interrogation of its inherent patriarchy. God, *the father,* and Jesus, *the son* may be Black, but there is no mention made, for example, of *the Holy Ghost* as woman, nor of a G–ddess (female)/G–d (male) union of opposites deity in any or all three aspects of the trinity. While Cone's later work clearly supports a feminist, even an antihomophobic, view of Christian scripture, it fails to develop this view in the same vein as was done with respect to the black view (Cone, 2000). This is less a critique of Cone and more one of Christianity. While many liberation theologists like Cone choose to interpret this scripture and/or to apply knowledge about Jesus's life to feminist, pro-lesbian, gay, bisexual, transgender, and other social justice struggles, these interpretations and applications are as imperfect in this direction as they are in a fundamentalist one (Daly, 1994; Gutierrez, 1984; Isasi-Diaz & Tarango, 1992). Christianity whether as a reactionary or liberatory vehicle is, in fact, limited by its history. Certainly, this is the case in other walks of life; black/white relationships, though they carry the potential—intermittently realized—to be antiracist, they remain limited by racism. And just as male/female relationships are limited by sexism, gay/ straight relationships by heterosexism, and poor/rich relationships by classism, so too are non-Christian/Christian relationships limited by religionism. With respect to the building of religious, spiritual, faith-based, and secular community, acknowledgment, not only of these limitations, but of the reality that to escape them requires the development and maintenance of an extra-Christian interfaith/secular context, is paramount.

Stage One: Rifts

The impetus for OHRP's confrontation of Christian privilege and, ultimately, its desire to create a religiously, spiritually, faith-based, and secularly inclusive workplace emerged out of an office discussion surrounding the planning of a December holiday party in 2000. At the outset of my tenure as Executive Director in January 2000, I was made aware that there had been some tension around the planning and actualization of the office's annual December holiday party in 1999. This tension emerged because several non-Christian employees had expressed concerns about the party as essentially functioning as a Christmas party despite being called a holiday party. While Christian employees believe that they tried to take into account the concerns of their non-Christian coworkers in putting that party together, the outcome of the party left non-Christian employees angry and Christian employees slightly confused about, but largely oblivious to, what could have been wrong with the way the party turned out.

It is important to mention that OHRP has a 30-year history. For most of that history, the office staffs were all Christian and predominantly African American. The previous director, who was a member of the office for 25 years—first in a staff role and then in the leadership one—had a tradition of inviting the office staff to her home for a Christmas party during which Christmas carols were sung around a piano. In the 5 years prior to my arrival, the office had become increasingly racially—as well as religiously, spiritually, faith-based, and secularly—diverse. Despite this diversity, the interpersonal cultural norms of the office remained largely African American– and Christian-centric, and though the African American–centric part of the office culture was limited by the white male-centric culture of the larger university and society, the Christian-centric part was reinforced by the university's and society's Christian-centricity.

While I was made aware of the December 1999 holiday party tension in January 2000, I failed to address it until December 2000, when the party planning discussion for this year emerged. It is hard to say if planning in advance would have helped our process because it is not clear if Christians in the office would have felt the weight of the concerns of their non-Christian counterparts if those concerns had been raised and addressed at a time of year when Christian celebratory hegemony was not at risk of challenge. That is, what may have allowed the seriousness of the concerns raised by non-Christians to be truly "heard" by Christians was the threat that these concerns posed to the realization of the annual holiday party only a few weeks away. It is likely that a discussion of these concerns in February or June would have been much less contentious, but it is also possible that, in being less contentious, Christian employees may never have been faced with the visceral (and, therefore, uncharacteristically bold, open, and unequivocal) confrontation of Christian privilege for all of the reasons previously articulated. While those reasons did eventually come to bear on the confrontation process—making the confrontation more equivocal—it is likely that no meaningful confrontation, with or without equivocation, would have ever taken place if the initial one had not been pregnant with Christian celebratory expectations and mounting non-Christian defiance empowered by leadership willing to, and to some degree, naively willing to, challenge the prevailing interpersonal cultural norms of the office.

It is crucial for me to acknowledge that although I was raised Christian—the liberatory theology–focused and radical kind—I ended up leaving the Christian faith altogether. I identify as Pagan, in essence, someone who experiences a higher power through the natural world. While I am deeply spiritual, I am not devout in the practice of that spirituality—I do not, by and large, participate in pagan rituals. I am about as disciplined a Pagan as I was a Christian: my spirituality is with me in the everyday, but not in a formal way. I am also white (English or Anglo-Saxon, Dutch, and German). These identities are important to know when considering my willingness to challenge the African American- and Christian-centric interpersonal cultural norms of OHRP. In characterizing my willingness to undertake this challenge as naive, I mean that I am not certain I fully recognized and understood the African American part of the Christian-centrism—their interconnectedness—in the office culture when I began the Christian privilege challenge process. Had I been more aware in this regard, it is highly likely that I, despite my best effort to the contrary, would have been more influenced by the theory of the hierarchy of oppression in deciding, first, if and, second, how to undertake this process. That is, my own fear of being seen as or called a racist if I challenged Christian privilege couched in the African American history and culture of the office (especially given the larger role that Christianity has played and continues to play in African American liberation, notwithstanding its other role in colonization), might have precluded my willingness to engage this process at all. Thus, my limited vision in this regard both allowed and required OHRP to engage this process. Hindsight being what it is, had I known then what I know now, I would have done things differently—more gracefully to be sure—but not necessarily toward a better outcome.

Related to the previous discussions on the theory of the hierarchy of oppression and the parallels between and uniquenesses among different forms of oppression, the interplays of my racial and spiritual identities illustrate how various forms of oppression and, of course, privilege, related to these identities do not exist or operate in a vacuum divorced from one another. On the contrary, all forms of oppression and privilege are interconnected. In this case study, the relationships between oppression and privilege related to race, ethnicity, national origin, socioeconomic class (inclusive of employment status), and language, as well as religion, spirituality, faith, and secularity, are embedded in OHRP's process toward building a religiously, spiritually, faith-based, and secularly inclusive workplace. Thus, it is important for me to delineate not only my own social membership group identities, but also those of the rest of the OHRP staff involved in this building process. These identities are as follows: three African American men, all graduate assistants, two Christian, and one atheist/agnostic; one African American woman, full-time support staff, and Christian; one African (Ghanaian) woman, full-time support staff, and Christian; two Afro-Caribbean (one Guyanese, the other half Barbadian and half Panamanian) women, one full-time support staff and Christian, the other a graduate assistant from a faith-based tradition; one half African American and half Afro-Caribbean (Jamaican) man, full-time professional staff and Christian; one half Latino (Peruvian) and half white (European American) man, full-time professional staff and Wiccan; two white (European American) men, one full-time professional staff and Christian, the other a graduate assistant and atheist/agnostic; one half Chinese and half Korean woman, a graduate assistant and Christian; one Afghan woman, a graduate student and Muslim; one Filipina woman, full-time professional staff and Christian; and, one Indian woman, full-time professional staff and Hindu.

The tensions that emerged in December 2000 came about when an African American, Christian female support staff member, a 30-year veteran of the office, came to me to ask if she should send around an e-mail asking people about how we should organize our annual holiday party. I responded by saying yes, send around an e-mail, but in it ask people how they feel about having this party, and then, based on their response to that, we can look at how we should organize it. Unfortunately, this staff member sent around an e-mail that went straight to the question of how to organize the party. Anticipating a hostile response from non-Christians, I responded to her e-mail by saying words to the effect that if we were to have a party, the party must not be a Christmas party masquerading as a holiday party. That is, it must be sensitive to the celebratory concerns of non-Christians. In retrospect, my e-mail response was *way* too big a hammer for the situation. While I was genuinely concerned about a hostile response from the non-Christians, I was also angry that the employee who sent around the initial e-mail had failed to heed my directions for how to open up the discussion about the party for a number of reasons—her actions seemed deliberately Christian-centrically passive aggressive, and her e-mail forced existing tension relating to the party to escalate and, in so doing, made more work for me. Unfortunately, my e-mail response reflected my anger more than my concern. Needless to say, bedlam broke loose. Christians were mad at non-Christians and vice versa, and everyone was angry at me. After 2 weeks of bedlam smoldered into silence, we broke for the semester for 2 weeks having had no holiday celebration.

Stage Two: Reconnecting

In reconvening as an office in early January 2001, we began a sort of informal dialogue that took various forms, and included varying configurations of the staff. Out of this informal dialogue emerged three parts of a process: (1) a recognition that we needed to address the conflict from December and work toward a positive resolution of it; (2) a general willingness to engage in a more formal dialogue toward that positive resolution; and (3) an understanding that we would eventually need help to realize that positive resolution. While the staff was unanimous about pursuing the first part, not everyone was as committed to pursuit of the second or third parts. But, the unilateral support for the first part, and substantial support for the other two, enabled us to move forward.

We began the process on our own, deciding to look at three questions we believed were *indirectly* related to the celebration conflict and, thus, questions we felt we could facilitate ourselves in discussion on. These questions were: (1) how do we talk about concerns we have in general?; (2) How do we talk about controversial issues in general?; and (3) What is the relationship between our answers to these first two questions and our social identity group demographics? In relationship to this last question, two secondary questions emerged: (a) What is the impact of the professional staff and graduate assistants' use of *academic language* and/or *jargon*?; and (b) What is the impact of discourse style, including silence (which may be related to race, ethnicity, national origin, language, socioeconomic class, and/or gender)?

Individual exploration of the first and second questions was uneventful, generating almost no discussion. Thus, we quickly agreed to move onto the third question, where it was clear everyone's attention and interest was already focused, and recognizing that in discussing it we would also be discussing the first and second questions in relationship to it.

The third question, along with its ancillary ones, generated the most discussion. It also generated the most active participation from support staff who asserted, very decisively, that professional staff and graduate assistants' use of *in discipline* language was not a barrier to their participation in discussions—they were quite capable of following discussions in which this language was used, and could clearly understand what was being said. Related to this, support staff wanted it known that their silence in discussions in which such language was being used (which was what had largely provoked this line of questioning in the first place), should be taken at face value—that they were actively listening but had no comment to make—nothing more, nothing less. It is important to mention that having this discussion not only generated the active participation from support staff in it but had the effect of substantially increasing their participation in all discussions from that point forward. Other aspects of discourse style were also addressed, specifically proclivities for or against conversation in which multiple speakers jumped into discussion to clarify, redirect, or challenge, as well as the pro's and con's of waiting for a speaker to stop talking, raising a hand to gain access to a conversation, or sitting with an expectation of being invited to chime in. Many associated the former discourse style with certain racial, ethnic, and socioeconomic experiences, but it was hard to reach consensus on which experiences these were. (For example, some thought jumping in was attributable to particular ethnic [i.e., Italian or African American] or working-class experiences in which people needed to be aggressive to be heard in large or hostile gathering contexts [i.e., family celebrations or community conflicts]. Others saw this as a manifestation of middle-class and/or white privilege, taking a conversation over because of an inflated sense of the importance of one's voice.) While it would have been impossible, as well as stereotypical, to come to a meeting of the minds on what motivated different people to participate differently—especially with respect to the possible role of social identity group memberships in this equation—what we were able to establish was that it was important that we were all more consciously aware of the range of differences in people's interaction norms and that we work, to the extent we were each able, to improve the degree to which everyone got to participate in the manner most comfortable for them. This meant monitoring our own behavior and each other's in a manner that facilitated participatory inclusivity.

After experiencing a degree of success with this first discussion, we continued the process on our own in deciding to look at one more question: How do we talk about religion, spirituality, faith, and secularity as both a concern and a controversy, while taking into account social identity group memberships? While we recognized that this question was, clearly, more *directly* related to the celebration conflict and, thus, could resurrect tensions toward an unproductive end, we agreed that we would focus our conversation on how we would talk about these things if we were going to talk about how to talk about the process, not the content. Discussion of this question led us to two major problematics.

Problematic One

If we have a discussion about our religion, spirituality, faith, and secularity, are we willing to have our knowledge of our own affiliations—especially religious affiliations, and, more especially, Christian affiliations—challenged with new, additional, and/or alternative views of those affiliations that may be more theologically, historically, or otherwise factually accurate? With little equivocation, the Christians in the office were pretty clear that this was not a challenge that they were open to experiencing. In addition to this point, however, four secondary problematics emerged:

1. What is the role that religion plays in defining other social identity group memberships? For example, how does being Catholic define Latina/o racial identity, or being Baptist define African American ethnicity? Or what about nonreligious Jews or Muslims who use the terms *Jew* or *Muslim* to define an ethnic or cultural, but not religious, identity?

2. What about the services that churches, synagogues, and mosques provide beyond religion? For example, social support to individuals who live alone, or social service support to the poor, disabled, and/or disenfranchised (i.e., battered women or ex-convicts). And, are these supports/services given *freely*, or is there a conversion string attached to their utilizations?

3. Can religions be liberatory? For example, liberation theology–oriented Protestantism in which the tenets of Christianity are directed toward the teachings, which emphasize self-determination and social justice.

4. If religions can be liberatory, then what is the implication of having something liberatory challenged? For example, what might be the consequences of confronting Christian privilege for a gay or female Presbyterian minister of a *Church of More Light?*[7]

Problematic Two

In identifying the first problematic and its subsidiaries, were we making assumptions about people's knowledge of their own affiliations—especially spiritual, faith-based, and secular ones—that are both inaccurate and that reinforce racial-, ethnic-, and socioeconomic class–based forms of discrimination and oppression? For example, are we assuming that working-class African American Christians are unaware of the ways in which Christianity was, and continues to be, used as a colonizing doctrine? Likewise, are we taking for granted that working-class African American Christians have no positive understanding of Pagan and/or Atheist traditions? Here, three secondary problematics arose:

1. Can people engage in a religion in a critically conscious way? For example, can a Muslim woman reconcile the passages in the Qur'an that sanction male violence toward their spouses by engaging a feminist point of entry to the religion? Or, can a lesbian Catholic resolve the Pope's position on homosexuality in order to maintain a positive self image as both lesbian and Catholic?

2. If people can engage religion in a critically conscious way, do we give people credit for being able to do this—to negotiate contradictions between their religion and self-determination and social justice— across demographics? For example, do we only assume well-educated, middle-class, and/or white people are capable of such kind of engagement?

3. What are the assumptions that we make about the devoutness of people's "practice" relating to their religious, spiritual, faith-based, and secular traditions? For example, do we assume religious, especially Christian, people are more disciplined and that their rituals are more legitimate, than Santeros or Atheists and their customs? What are the implications of religious, spiritual, faith-based, and secular legitimacy for a "Sunday Christian," a highly disciplined Yoruban, or a nonpracticing Jew?

Outcomes

While neither of these problematics nor their corollaries was actually discussed, simply raising them as a part of the discussion *process* exercise was instructive. That is, we didn't have to discuss them to *consider* them. Once they were raised, they entered our consciousnesses. It is important to point out that while we never discussed these points formally—as a whole group—in informal small group and pair configurations, we did. Some of us also reflected on them individually, and/or discussed them with people external to the office. So while the process focus may, at first glance, seem to have been of little value, upon closer examination it is clear just how assistive this focus was. In the end, our purpose in the raising of these problematics was never with an eye to resolving them. Rather, it was simply to explore, both as a group and interpersonally, what meaning various responses to them might have for ensuing more direct discussion on our celebratory conflict.

Stage Three: Reconceptualization

In having completed, on our own, what I have called "Stage Two" of this process by the end of January 2001, we found ourselves more or less ready to confront the celebratory conflict head on, but reacknowledged that because tensions surrounding that conflict persisted, we would need the help of a skilled facilitator, obviously from outside the office and, preferably, from outside the campus, to guarantee their professional detachment from our conflict and resolution process. With little effort, we identified a colleague at a neighboring university who we believed had the necessary content and process knowledge (in social justice education and group facilitation), and the right set of social identities (as an African American, gay, self-proclaimed *born-again* Christian, former Assistant Vice President of Student Affairs, choir director of a inner-city black church, and divinity school student). We contracted with this facilitator for a first session in February 2001, and, subsequently, for two additional sessions, in June and December 2001. All three sessions included some context setting by the facilitator, and then was comprised of one or more activities for us, as the participants, to engage in. In moving from session one to session three, the amount of dialogue that we engaged in increased through a combination of pair, small group, and whole group work. One particularly salient outcome emerged from each of the three sessions.

Session one led us to the development of the following *community learning norms*:

1. Develop the ability to acknowledge what you know, but don't pretend you do know;
2. Give others the benefit of the doubt;
3. Suspend judgment;
4. Take away titles/positions;
5. Stop making assumptions and go to a source;
6. This process is not an avenue for conversion;
7. Be sensitive to the closeness of the issue to the person and of the person to the issue;
8. Seek first to understand, then to be understood; and,
9. Make a commitment to your and others' individual readiness.

These norms were, and remain, posted in various locations around our workplace as ongoing, gentle reminders of *how* we, as a group, agreed to work toward the resolution of our celebratory conflict and the establishment of a more religiously, spiritually, faith-based, and secularly inclusive workplace.

In session two, we engaged in an activity entitled *Who Am I, and What Do I Bring? Understanding Our Religious and Spiritual Self,* which paired two Christians with two non-Christians in discussion of our own religious, spiritual, faith-based, and secular identities with respect to our responses to the following six discussion items:

1. I identify as _____on the issues of religion/spirituality;
2. What that means for me is…;
3. Things that I really celebrate about my spiritual/religious life are…;
4. Things that I really struggle with in my spiritual/religious life are…;
5. Commonly misunderstood things about my religion/form of spirituality are…; and,
6. My understanding of/experience with forms of spirituality/religions other than my own has been… (Washington, 2001).

At the conclusion of this session the facilitator directed us to repeat this activity with members of the staff with whom we had not been paired during the session. Some of us took this directive to heart, others of us did not. Despite this uneven follow-up, this activity was powerful, because it illustrated to us that, in large measure, our celebratory conflict was the result of us not knowing—by design, default, or a combination of both—each other's religious, spiritual, faith-based, and secular identities very well. Throughout the multicultural and social justice education literature bases, it is made clear that, absent strong personal relationships—especially along the lines of social identity group memberships in diverse environments—conflict is more likely to emerge and have at its core resentment for those social identity group membership categories (Banks, 1997; Banks & Banks, 1997; Nieto, 2000; Sleeter, 1996). While most of us knew this research, it took this activity to help us recognize our failure to act on our knowledge. It revealed this to us simultaneous with offering us a practice strategy aimed directly at strengthening relationships along the social identity group membership categories most at issue. In so doing, it also helped us to move one step closer toward the resolution of our celebratory conflict: if through it we learned more about each other's celebratory traditions, we could plan celebrations that took these traditions into account in meaningful ways.

Session three led us to a two-pronged approach for celebration that honored religious, spiritual, faith-based, and secular diversity. The first part of this strategy involved dedicating time during our biweekly staff meetings for people to share whatever they happen to be celebrating at that time. The second part of the strategy established that we would have three parties a year—one in May, one in September, and one in December (all three of which were piloted in 2002)—to which everyone would contribute a decoration, a piece of music, and a homemade food item, each commemorating something they celebrate at that time of year. This strategy was developed with three purposes in mind. The first purpose was to make celebration something that occurred year-round, instead of only when the Julian and academic calendars, reinforcing Christian privilege, dictated that it occur. The second purpose was to make celebration a community responsibility, instead of the responsibility of one or two people, to ensure both the inclusive spirit of celebration across religious, spiritual, faith-based, and secular affiliations, as well as to encourage officewide engagement and investment in celebration. Finally, the third purpose was to afford people the opportunity to teach others about their own celebrations, and learn about the celebrations of others—reinforcing the religious, spiritual, faith-based, and secular relationship-building objective of the activity from our second facilitated session. This enabled us to bring along those who resisted engaging this activity with coworkers after the session as directed by the facilitator, having the effect of more symmetrically augmenting our knowledge of each other's religious, spiritual, faith-based, and secular identities across the staff, thus strengthening our interpersonal relationships along these dimensions throughout the office.

Three important outcomes emerged from the facilitated sessions. The first was that we all became more aware of, knowledgeable about, and understanding of each other's religious, spiritual, faith-based, and secular identities and traditions. The second was that non-Christians could embrace expressions of Christianity by Christians in the office without feeling as though those expressions were an insult to them as non-Christians. Likewise, the third outcome led Christians to more consciously recognize their *Christianess,* and *Christianess* in general, and the *nonuniversality* of both for others in the workplace and society at large.

Stage Four: Realization

As alluded to in the previous discussion, the celebratory conflict that arose in December 2000 precluded our office from celebrating anything, other than birthdays, until the spring of 2002. In moving through stages one, two, and three between December 2000 and December 2001, by 2002 it was time for us to put our new strategies for celebration into action.

Our sharing about our celebrations during biweekly staff meetings began strong—especially non-Christians went to great lengths, typing up and distributing information sheets about their celebrations. Over that year this enthusiasm tapered off, partly because of the pace of work in the office, and partly because most Christians failed to invest reciprocal effort in the sharing process. Regardless of the current lower level of investment in this practice, it continues to be a part of every staff meeting agenda. As with other regular practices, I am certain that this one will experience periodic ebbs and flows of enthusiasm. In arriving at such a rhythm it will finally become an institutionalized practice of the office—a practice, like all practices, that is sometimes resented, sometimes taken for granted, and sometimes appreciated. Achieving commonplace status in the office culture, while seemingly an anticlimatic by-product of a great effort, is actually a positive accomplishment because it confirms that something that was once quite threatening, for Christians and non-Christians alike, to talk publicly with coworkers about, has become, at least, familiar, if not yet wholly comfortable.

The first of our triannual celebrations was held in May 2002. All of the full-time staff and many of the graduate students not only attended, but fully participated by bringing decorations, music, and food reflecting their celebratory focus at that time of year. Three staff members shared their musical talent with us through their voice, guitar, and harp. We also danced, talked—about our celebrations as well as about our work and our lives outside of work, and we laughed. This party was clearly a success, though it was somewhat obvious that we were all feeling our way around it. While we had a good time, there was an element of manufacturedness to the celebration—it did not flow naturally and/or effortlessly.

The second triannual celebration took place in September 2002. At this party we repeated all of the successes of the first one and added more. Everyone on the staff attended and almost everyone fully participated in the formal part of the celebration process. We also invited staff family members, OHRP alumni, and a few friends of the office to attend, which added to the climate of festivity. In addition to our staff's musical talent, guests shared their talents as well. The staff vocalist, a guest vocalist, and the staff harpist even teamed up for a couple of impromptu duets and trio numbers to rave reviews. We also played games. This party was truly a success. Everything we had worked to accomplish through celebration was realized in this party.

The third and final triannual celebration took place in December 2002. This party was very low key for several reasons. A number of staff members were absent, due to vacation or illness (both legitimately and less so to evade participation in the celebration). The majority of those in attendance were preoccupied with end of the semester deadlines and, thus, also very tired. And we had missed holding the staff meeting immediately prior to the party, at which we typically review the plan for the party, losing some of the momentum around it. Nonetheless, some people brought food, some brought decorations, and some brought music and we ate and talked, and then ate again and talked some more. A few OHRP alumni dropped by and joined in the conversation, offering the opportunity to reminisce about OHRP past, and learn about OHRP present and its plans for the future. Under the circumstances, the party was a success, though of a different ilk of success than the first two—more "natural" than the first, but less spirited than both the first and the second. There was also an undercurrent to this party that did not exist in the other two, related to its proximity to Christmas. In the weeks prior to this party, some Christians expressed uneasiness about the timing of it, suggesting that we should wait to have it in January, even though, as a part of our conflict resolution process, we had very clearly agreed to hold it in December precisely so Christians could embrace the celebration of Christmas. It was obvious from this uneasiness that it was going to take some time for the Christians in the office to figure out how to celebrate, and how to enjoy the celebration of, Christmas at a party that is not expressly a Christmas one.

Given the understated end to the year of celebrations, it was important for us to make our May 2003 party more upbeat to hang onto the positive momentum the parties earlier in the year generated—which we did. Yet, we have come to recognize that not every party can nor should be exactly the same, nor could it or should it seek to "top" the previous one. Over the long run, the same ebb and flow of enthusiasm described in relationship to our sharing of celebration at staff meetings has settled into this endeavor as well. Here again, as this has occurred, it has, ultimately, been viewed positively, as a true sign that we have finally resolved our celebratory conflict.

FOOD FOR CONTINUING REFLECTION AND ACTION

OHRP's celebratory conflict resolution process led us to a new way to celebrate. Key to this outcome was everyone's willingness to take some responsibility for arriving at it.

It is important to reiterate that, similar to some of the dynamics of resistance that existed throughout this process, the taking of partial responsibility in this process is still not engaged by everyone in the office unilaterally. As was the case in the beginning, the resistance hails from a small number of Christians and is directed toward this new way of celebration. It manifests itself in various forms of either compartmentalized participation or nonparticipation in the new celebration process. As previously suggested, people invent emergencies to avoid having to attend one of the triannual parties or to enable them to leave a biweekly staff meeting while others are sharing information about their current celebratory undertakings. Clearly, like every other multicultural and social justice educational issue, the struggle to achieve full and affirming religious, spiritual, faith-based, and secular inclusion is ongoing, and dependent on the degree to which the practice of democratic citizenship, by every member of the office community, is realized. To achieve this realization, we, as an office, but especially I, as its leader, must create a workplace climate in which people are able and motivated to participate—that the resistance persists is an indication that such a climate has not yet been adequately created to effectuate the motivation toward participation. Beyond individual and leadership responsibility to contribute to the creation of this climate, there is the responsibility of both those traditionally denied, and those traditionally afforded, access to full participation in democracy based on their religious, spiritual, faith-based, and secular social identity group memberships, as well as their racial-, ethnic-, national origin-, and socioeconomic class-based ones. Responsibility must be engendered and undertaken by everyone along all of the complex dimensions of individual and group identity if this climate is to become a reality.

Perhaps most important in this process was our goal to be more inclusive in celebrating, not less, and to be more celebratory, not less—ultimately, to engage the conflict toward inclusion, not retreat from it toward isolation. In the spirit of esteemed syndicated columnist, author, and lecturer Roberto Rodríguez, we must seek out joy in our lives to balance out our struggle for self-determination and social justice (Rodríguez, 2001). Absent that joy, our struggle reproduces the dehumanization it seeks to eradicate. Celebration is the key to joy, full and affirming inclusive celebration is the key to progressive multicultural- and social justice–oriented joy. It is toward increasing that joy that our ongoing celebration process is directed and dedicated.

Secularity, White Supremacy, and the Global Proliferation of Christian Capitalism

In his most recent book, *Democracy Matters: Winning the Fight Against Imperialism* (2004), preeminent scholar Dr. Cornell West discusses the rise of fundamentalism—be it Christian, Jewish, and/or Muslim fundamentalism—as the biggest deterrent to the practice of democracy in the United States and the world. While there are many people adopting more progressive views of their religious and secular identities, there are, perhaps, more people adopting increasingly reactionary orientations. In fact, the hegemony of fundamentalism is, indeed, so pervasive that there is even a recently documented surge in secular fundamentalism (Ahmed, 2004).

As laid out in the chapter introduction, fomenting this fundamentalism—Christian, Jewish, Muslim, or secular—serves the ultra-economically elite members of our society, nationally and internationally (West, 2004). Hip hop artist JadaKiss asks the question, *Why did Bush knock down the towers?* in his controversial song, *Why?* (JadaKiss, 2004). Many radio stations bleep out this line in his song, as they would profanity. This speaks volumes about the erosion of civil liberties in the United States, fanned by what, increasingly, appears to have been a highly coordinated and otherwise orchestrated act of terror on U.S. citizens in order to create a political climate in support of so-called massive *military spending*. Absent the events of September 11, 2001, the Bush administration would likely never have escaped the stigma of the first highjacked election. In the wake of these events, this administration has systematically filtered billions of public monies into private hands through the commodification of G–d—especially Christian G–d. These hands pat George W. Bush on the back as they line pockets (J. Moore, 2004; M. Moore, 2004). G–d is, in fact, big business these days. With the concoction of a Muslim fundamentalist terrorist threat looming large, the rationale for using the U.S. military to level mountains in Afghanistan in preparation for the privately owned Bush–Cheney oil pipeline was developed, packaged, mass-marketed, and sold in bulk (J. Moore, 2004). What would have taken years to accomplish through more legitimate corporate avenues took mere months—and so the scorecard reads, *Jesus 1, Allah 0* or, better, "Bush–Cheney one billion in petroleum revenues, U.S. citizenry zero in social security benefits and paying in excess of three dollars a gallon at the pumps while wearing those trendy fifty dollar *Jesus Rocks* t-shirts" (ABC, 2005). The U.S. public clings strongly to the tough-guy, you-can't-fool-me, street-smart image in proclaiming *Don't piss on me and tell me it's raining*, and yet sit idly by while national and international human rights laws are shattered under the auspices of doing G–d's—or, rather, Bush's—*goodwill* (ABC, 2005; J. Moore, 2004; M. Moore, 2004). It is increasingly difficult to distinguish one will from the other these days, as the attempted ousting of pro-Kerry Baptists from their church illustrates (Associated Press, 2005). It would seem that the struggle to extricate religion from state, was, in Hegelian fashion, turned on its head by Pastor Chan Chandler, of the East Waynesville Baptist Church, in his effort to extricate state from religion when he told congregants "who planned to vote for the Democratic nominee, Sen. John F. Kerry (Mass.), [to] either leave the church or repent" (p. 2). While the Patriot Acts are entrenched in the white supremacist, Christian privilege veil that the government claims to be using to blindfold the brown-skinned Muslim *enemy*, it is the U.S. populace—raped and impregnated by our abusive fathers and forced into a shotgun wedding—whom this veil is ultimately blinding. As the white supremacist and Christian privilege chickens come home to roost, the Patriot Acts will be turned against those U.S. citizens who, finally, dare to lift that veil in order to see clearly where democracy has been enslaved, with an eye toward its emancipation (J. Moore, 2004; M. Moore, 2004; West, 2004). Three important emancipation-related areas of struggle are: (1) the separation of religion and state;

(2) accommodating versus designating religious, spiritual, and faith-based public space; and (3) the United States as a Christian state: unacknowledged and uncontested. These struggles will be examined in relationship to public education and employment contexts.

The Separation of Religion and State

The laws governing the separation of religion and state in the United States require that public displays of a religious nature—practices and/or symbols—be limited by the parameters of time, place, and manner (Bayly, 2000; Clark, 2003a; Fineman, 2002; Schlosser, 2003; Schlosser & Sedlacek, 2001, 2003). This should mean, for example, that a Christmas concert at a public high school would be held at a specific time and place to afford individuals who want to attend the opportunity to do so, and those who do not wish to attend, the ability to avoid it, to *not* stumble upon it by accident in an open public space. Increasingly, however, not stumbling upon a "holiday" party—a Christmas party by another name—in a public educational and/or workplace setting, in which traditional Christmas decorations, food, music, and gift exchanges characterize the festivities, is harder and harder to do. While such a celebration might seem to violate the separation of religion and state, the laws regulating this separateness have been eroded in relationship to the rising commercialization of Christmas and, to a lesser extent, Easter (Bayly, 2000; Fineman 2002). While orthodox Christians express extreme disdain with commercial representations of Christianity—arguing that such are in fact misrepresentations of the faith and, thus, not Christian-like at all, many non-Christians experience Santa Claus and the Easter Bunny to infringe on secular space in equal measure as iterations of the words "one nation under God" in the Pledge of Allegiance or *In God We Trust* on currency—representations considered more religious and, thus, more authentic by even the most fundamentalist of Christians.

Ironically, there is a religiously, spiritually, and faith-based inclusive by-product embedded within the secularization of Christianity; that is, that aspects of non-Christian religions, spiritualities, and faiths are likewise secularized and, therefore, on occasion, also grace secular spaces (Clark, 2003b). The most common example of this is the Buddhist/Taoist Yin Yang symbol, often used as a logo for various Asian Studies programs at public higher education institutions. The extension of secularization to religious, spiritual, and faith-based belief systems other than Christian does begin to approximate something more multicultural (Banks & Banks, 1997; Nieto, 2000; Sleeter, 1996). But, in so approximating, this secularization also further violates the separation of religion and state, most marginalizing individuals who identify as agnostic or atheist.

Adding insult to injury, the extension of secularization beyond Christianity still privileges Christianity over other religions, spiritualities, and faiths, because its secularization penetrates the mainstream furthest and provokes the least controversy when it does. Said another way, Christianity is most readily accepted as more or less inevitable, status quo, standard, or even *normal* when it becomes visible. And this is only the case if it does, in fact, become visible, because part of *normalcy* is transparency; this is exactly why so much of the commercial proliferation of Christianity into the secular realm goes unchecked—because it is undetected (Clark & O'Donnell, 1999; McIntosh, 1988; McLaren, 1999). Practices and symbols of relatively well-known, though not always well-received, religions—like Judaism and Islam—while they permeate through public boundaries of secularity, when they do, they are not only noticed, but in so being are checked by both individual and institutional prejudice and discrimination (Schlosser, 2003; Schlosser & Sedlacek, 2001, 2003). The ongoing intermittent vandalism of Jewish synagogues is among the most readily apparent and, thus, most powerful example of this. Practices and symbols of lesser known or unknown religions, spiritualities, and faiths often enter into the public arena without raising an eyebrow because they are unrecognized. But lack of familiarity works against these belief systems when they are revealed—be that revelation partial or full—as mis- or disinformation is often what gets put forth about them first and, in many cases, forever. This occurs in part as a function of the novelty of these belief systems, but more so by the design of Christian privilege, which, by definition, must subsume other belief systems to not only lesser status, but to a status that evokes disdain, distrust, and even the fear by Christians of non-Christians if Christianity is to remain dominant (Clark, 2003b). Much in the same way that white privilege in its *purest* form demonizes all things brown and black, Christian privilege in its most *puritanical* form demonizes all things non-Christian, especially the indigenous, earth-based faiths known collectively by the name of Paganism (Ellerbe, 1995).

Pagans, long misunderstood to be *devil worshippers,* celebrate belief in a higher power through its manifestation in the natural world (Ellerbe, 1995). What is most telling about Paganism in relationship to Christian privilege, more specifically, about the emergence of Pagan practices and symbols in secular spaces, is the history of imposition of Christian practices and symbols virtually on top of Pagan ones. Such imposition served an important historical purpose in Christian proselytization, inserting new Christian practices and symbols alongside long-standing Pagan ones, eventually engulfing and extinguishing the Pagan ones and supplanting the Christian ones in their place. So, for example, while the Christmas tree, the holly wreath, and Easter eggs are Pagan symbols, and the practice of gift giving at Christmas is borrowed from the Pagan celebration of Yule, the prevalence of these traditions in the public sphere today is linked to the secularization of Christianity, not Paganism. Furthermore, if these traditions were still largely linked to Paganism, and to the extent that they have been relinked with Paganism by both Christian fundamentalist rejection and Pagan reclamation of them, their acceptability in the secular realm becomes more tenuous.

While the absolute separation of religion and state might fuel secular fundamentalism, a more clearly evident delineation between the two would advance the practice of democracy in the United States and, by virtue of U.S. influence internationally, the world over. Finding and maintaining a balance between our collective religious, spiritual, faith-based, and secular selves is the goal inherent in this struggle.

Accommodating versus Designating Religious, Spiritual, and Faith-Based Public Space

A particular aspect of the law governing the separation of religion and state in the public arena requires public institutions to make accommodations for the expression of religious, spiritual, and faith-based identity (Bayly, 2000; Fineman, 2002). Similar to disability law requiring public institutions to make *reasonable accommodations* for people with disabilities, religion and state separation laws require such institutions to accommodate religious, spiritual, and faith-based differences, though in far less permanent, concrete, and absolute ways than the Americans with Disabilities Act (ADA) does (Bayly, 2000; Fineman, 2002). Whereas Section 504 of the ADA can force a public institution to add ramps and elevators to buildings to increase their accessibility for people with physical disabilities, the body of religion and state law only requires an institution to accommodate to the degree it is able, and in nonpermanent, nonconcrete, and nonabsolute ways. So, for example, Muslim students in need of prayer space at a public university must be allocated such a space if there is space available for allocation; however, this space cannot be designated as Muslim space or even religious, spiritual, or faith-based space.

Yet, even in the context of the allocation versus designation of space parameters, Christian privilege emerges (Clark, 2003b). At one major public research institution, like many public colleges and universities, there is a chapel situated prominently on the campus. The chapel houses the offices of most of the university's *chaplains,* including the Muslim Imam, though not the director of the Jewish Hillel center. Both this center director and the Muslim Imam are identified as *chaplains*—a Christian term—in the university directory. And this is the case with the center director even though the person in this position does not have a religious title (e.g., Rabbi). (It should be noted that none of the so-called chaplains' salaries and/or program budgets are funded by state monies, but rather by private funds from their host communities of faith.) The chapel has an enormous steeple and a sanctuary with pews, a dais and lectern, and stained glass windows, but no cross. And, because the sanctuary has no cross, and is used for non-Christian and secular events, the argument is made that the chapel and the sanctuary are, like the Muslim prayer spaces (which often change from semester to semester), examples of space accommodation, not designated space (Clark, 2003b).

Just prior to the events of September 11, 2001, the Muslim students at this university lost the prayer space they had been using the previous semester (an unoccupied classroom) to an academic department's demand for increased instructional space. While the university looked for a new space for these students to pray—during which time the possibility that no space might be found was mentioned—a suggestion was made that they use the chapel sanctuary. In response to this suggestion, when the issue was raised of the sanctuary having pews (that face in a direction not toward Mecca) and that Muslims need to pray on the floor (facing Mecca), it was met with words to the effect of *beggars can't be choosers* by campus leadership. When the Muslim students offered to contribute funds to convert existing unused and uninhabitable space into a useable prayer space, this offer was met with the designation versus accommodation caveat and references to the separation of religion and state laws prohibiting the state from accepting money from religious sources. Yet, many Christian chaplains use money from their religious sources to fund programs, activities, and events on campus, and, certainly, religious monies support the university's Jewish Studies academic program. Perhaps most interesting to note in this quandary, when 300 Muslim students absent a noon prayer space (the time of day when the largest group of Muslim students come together to pray on this campus) gathered in stairwells and other open spaces in the university's libraries, a new prayer space was soon identified for them by university student affairs staff working in concert with space reservations personnel.

The struggle to negotiate balance between religious, spiritual, faith-based, and secular pluralism in the United States is directly related to the struggle to negotiate balance between accommodating and designating public space for religious, spiritual, and faith-based observances. Again, finding and maintaining a balance—in this instance between space accommodation and designation—is, likewise, the goal inherent in this struggle.

The United States as a Christian State: Unacknowledged and Uncontested

Clearly, the line between separation of religion and state—inclusive of the line between accommodating versus designating religious space—is hard to follow. But what tracks all too easily is the way in which both exactness *and* ambiguity in the law erode the integrity of secularity, and, in so doing, enable religion, spirituality, and faith to permeate public space to the clear advantage of Christians (Clark, 2003b). This should come as no surprise as the ability to change the rules of engagement midstream from exactness to ambiguity and back again, especially with respect to law and policy, serves the interests of the majority, in this case, Christians; in the context of race, white people; with regard to socioeconomic class, the rich; in relationship to gender, men; and in considering sexual orientation, heterosexual people.

It is the very *absence* of public discourse on religion, spirituality, and faith—inclusive of the separation of religion and state—that serves to strengthen the institutional power employed in shifting between exactness and ambiguity in continually reinforcing white Christian dominance (Clark et al., 2002; HBO, 2002; Schlosser, 2003; Schlosser & Sedlacek, 2001, 2003). In fact, separation of religion and state laws are often used *to prohibit* such discourse from unfolding on the one hand—erroneously used to bolster arguments that any discussion of religion, spirituality, and faith in public space is prohibited—while on the other they are eschewed when the issue of school prayer is raised. While it is clear to the rest of the world that the United States is a Christian state, both the U.S. government's and its Christian citizenry's unwillingness to affirm this reality and their utter avoidance of national dialogue on the topic of religion, spirituality, and faith works to strengthen Christian privilege. In much the same way that the secularization of Christian privilege in the public sphere leads to its unfettered proliferation, the unacknowledged—thus, at once, both undebated and indisputable—status of the United States as a Christian state guarantees its seamless progression as one. As mentioned in the chapter introduction, diversion of federal funds into *faith-based initiatives* and the President's request to a lower court to *reconsider* its decision declaring the recitation of the Pledge of Allegiance inclusive of its *under God* phrase unconstitutional are just two recent examples of how this proliferation and progression are made manifest.

To begin to dismantle white supremacy and Christian privilege in the United States and abroad, it is necessary to acknowledge the ways in which the United States operates as a racist Christian state despite claims to the contrary. Once acknowledged, concrete plans of action to move the United States from this state and toward a religious, spiritually, faith-based, and secularly inclusive and affirming commonwealth can be developed. Implementing these plans to dismantle U.S. racism, fundamentalism, and associated other forms of oppression is the goal inherent in this struggle.

CONCLUSION

The goal of opening up the multicultural educational conversation to extend to religion, spirituality, faith, and secularity is to become more inclusive, not less. Yet, the process of confronting and resolving Christian privilege will initially make participants involved in it want to abandon this goal. Once aware of the enormity of the task involved in trying to build religiously, spiritually, faith-based, and secularly inclusive community, the knee-jerk response is to say, *forget it, this is impossible!* What ensues is often a *false secularity* in which nothing is celebrated. As discussed throughout this chapter, some Christians often initially retaliate against the process, experiencing the discussion of Christian privilege as an attack on Christianity. Retaliation can manifest as protest toward recognition of Halloween as Pagan,[8] the emergence of Christian-oriented computer screen-savers, loud proclamations of plans to attend Christmas parties *elsewhere*, anonymous offerings of *Christmas* and *Easter* candy, among others. It is important to note that both false secularity and retaliation are developmental stages that most groups struggling with these issues will encounter. But, with time to adjust to the initial discomfort that broaching this new territory of social justice work causes, tension eases and the process continues toward the goal of how inclusivity can be achieved and, in achieving it, how celebration can be undertaken. The manner in which this process ensues and toward what outcomes will always be unique to the members of the groups who engage in it. Furthermore, outcomes are always temporary—that is, they may suffice with a particular group for a particular time, but as the group changes configuration and/or members' awareness, knowledge, and understanding of Christian privilege and of building religiously, spiritually, faith-based, and secularly inclusive community continues to develop, outcomes will necessarily change to reflect changes in group memberships and consciousness.

Drawing on the wisdom expressed by professor Patrick Slattery in his book, *Curriculum Development in the Postmodern Era* (1995), we must recognize that every individual's myriad social identities are present *all* the time—that is, we cannot check our race, gender, sexuality, and so forth at the door of our classrooms or work environments any more than we can check our religion, spirituality, faith, or secularity there. All of our identities influence and, in so doing, enrich how we move through our lives everyday. They influence and enrich how we teach, learn, supervise, and work. To suggest or, worse, try to require that we stop being all of who we are in certain contexts is not only unrealistic, but impossible. Our social identities not only inform how we engage the world, but how the world engages us. Denying that these identities exist or that they have no impact only guarantees that certain identities are allowed to manifest publicly uninterrupted, while others remain closeted. This practice ensures the persistence of social injustice.

Our nation's discomfort with the open and honest discussion of religious, spiritual, faith-based, and secular beliefs repeatedly emerges. In much the same way we have avoided thoughtful discourse on white privilege, meaningful dialogue on Christian privilege has likewise been scarce. While the value of cross-group interface as a community-building strategy has been long known, it is rarely practiced and certainly not with the sustained attention required to create intra- and inter-community understanding and action for the greatest collective benefit. It is only through education and professional development that the privilege–oppression dynamic can be confronted and, through open dialogue about it, resolved. In this way, public education and work environments and practices become increasingly socially just, building communities that are comprehensively inclusive across categories of social identity.

In light of recent and current global tensions and conflicts, now more than ever, the time is ripe for heads of nations—and, if not them, then nations of people—to lead in a new way, a way that challenges the privilege of one group over another on the basis of any category of identity, be it fixed or mutable. In the wake of September 11, 2001, the United States was poised, if only for a moment, to role-model such leadership, to not retaliate or seek retribution, but to consider the larger context that led to the tragic events of that day—and the thousands of other such days that have taken place around the world, many at the hands of U.S. intelligence forces in defense not of democratic ideals, but of corporate capitalism. These same forces fuel the secularization of Christianity for its colonizing and, thus, commercial value. The moment being squandered away, it is time for the people of all nations to call for, and act to, effectuate the global and national redistribution of resources along more equitable lines. It is in the spirit of this call that this chapter is directed.

NOTES

1. Portions of this chapter have been previously published as articles in the Winter 2002, Spring 2003, and Fall 2003 issues of *Multicultural Education*. These portions are reprinted with permission.

2. While this chapter focuses on the impact of Christian privilege in the public arena (for what should be obvious reasons related to the so-called separation of religion and state (see footnote 3, below), the discussion herein also has implications for private educational and workplace contexts to the extent that these contexts are impacted by Title VI. (Title VI of the 1964 Civil Rights Act requires that no person in the United States be excluded from participation in, or otherwise discriminated against, on the grounds of race, color, or national origin in any program or activity receiving federal financial assistance. Since many private educational and workplace settings receive federal funding, Title VI protections can extend beyond the public sphere.)

3. Usually referred to as *church*—a Christian place of worship—and state.

4. In the Jewish religion, writing out this word with the letter "o" intact is considered disrespectful. I have abided by this practice herein as a way of decentering the Christian norm in which the "o" is included. Clearly, there are still patriarchal, Western, and, largely, Christian implications in using this term even in this way (as opposed to using the terms Goddess, Allah, Jah, or the Great Spirit, among many others).

5. For example, Wiccans consider the new year to begin at the Final Harvest Festival of Samhain (Sah-wan), celebrated on October 31. Thus, for a Wiccan, the end of the year is at the end of October.

6. While there is irony in this, OHRP is clear that teaching by example is paramount to engaging its stakeholders in diversified education-oriented change processes. Thus, we use our own struggles, be they successfully resolved, ongoing, or at a stage of contentious impasse, as educational examples with our constituents. In so doing, we reinforce the reality that commitment to multicultural organizational development is commitment to life-long learning, not a static destination in which one day we will be able to proclaim that we have "arrived."

7. Churches of More Light are individual Presbyterian churches that, contrary to the national Presbyterian church, view homosexuality, like heterosexuality, as a normal sexual orientation.

8. Somewhat ironically, there is not equal retaliation toward the display of Christmas trees and wreaths, and Easter bunnies and eggs, among other things, which also have Pagan roots.

REFERENCES

ABC. (2005, May). "Under God" In *ABC World News*. New York: American Broadcasting Company.

Adams, M., Bell, L.A., & Griffin, P. (Eds.). (1997). *Teaching for diversity and social justice: A sourcebook*. New York: Routledge.

Ahmed, A. (2004). Muslim activists reject secular fundamentalism. *Islam on-line*. Retrieved April 22, 2004, at www.islam-online.net/english/News/2002-04/23/article17.shtml

Associated Press. (2005). N.C. vhurch kicks out members who do not support Bush. Retrieved May 8, 2005, at www.washingtonpost.com/wp-dyn/content/article/2005/05/07/AR2005050700972_pf.html

Banks, J. A. (1997). *Teaching strategies for ethnic studies* (6th ed.). Boston: Allyn & Bacon.

Banks, J. A., & Banks, C. A. M. (1997). *Multicultural education: Issues and perspectives* (3rd ed.). Boston: Allyn & Bacon.

Bayly, S. (2000). *Based on consultations with legal counsel.* Unpublished manuscript, University of Maryland, College Park.

Boston, R. (2004). *Religious groups are trying a back-door plan to evangelize public school students.* Retrieved August 28, 2004, at www.au.org/targetingschools

CBS. (2004, April). The greatest story ever told. In *CBS 60 Minutes II.* New York: CBS.

Chasnoff, D., & Cohen, H. (1996). *It's elementary: Talking about gay issues in school.* Cambridge, MA: Women's Educational Media.

Clark, C. (2003a). A case study of multicultural organizational development through the lens of religion, spirituality, faith, and secular inclusion. *Multicultural Education, 10*(3), 48–54.

Clark, C. (2003b). Secular aspects and international implications of Christian privilege. *Multicultural Education, 10*(4), 55–57.

Clark, C. (2005). From the results of a teacher action research survey conducted at the University of Maryland, College Park.

Clark, C., Brimhall-Vargas, M., Schlosser, L., & Alimo, C. (2002). It's not just "Secret Santa" in December: Addressing educational and workplace climate issues linked to Christian privilege. *Multicultural Education, 10*(2), 52–57.

Clark, C., & O'Donnell, J. (1999). *Becoming and unbecoming white: Owning and disowning a racial identity.* Westport, CT: Greenwood Press.

Cone, J. (1970). *A black theology of liberation.* New York: Lippincott.

Cone, J. (2000). *Risks of faith: The emergence of a black theology of liberation 1968–1998.* Boston: Beacon Press.

Daly, L. K. (1994). *Feminist theological ethics: A reader.* Louisville, KY: Westminster John Knox Press.

Ellerbe, H. (1995). *The dark side of Christian history.* New York: Morningstar Books.

Fineman, H. (2002, July 8). One nation, under...who? *Newsweek*, pp. 20–25.

Gutierrez, G. (1984). *We drink from our own wells: The spiritual journey of a people.* New York: Orbis Books.

Hair, J. (2004). *After Job.* Retrieved September 15, 2004, at www.poetrybay.com

Home Box Office (HBO). (2002, January). God's squad. In *HBO Real Sports with Bryant Gumbel.* New York: HBO.

Isasi-Díaz, A. M., & Tarango, Y. (1992). *Hispanic women: Prophetic voice in the church.* Minneapolis, MN: Fortress Press.

JadaKiss. (2004). Why? In *Kiss of death* [Album]. New York: Ruff Ryder/Interscope.

Lea, V., & Helfand, J. (Eds.). (2004). *Identifying race and transforming whiteness in the classroom.* New York: Peter Lang.

McIntosh, P. (1988). *White privilege and male privilege: A personal account of coming to see correspondences through work in women's studies.* Wellesley, MA: Wellesley College Center for Research on Women.

McLaren, P. (1999). Unthinking whiteness, rethinking democracy: Critical citizenship in Gringolandia. In C. Clark & J. O'Donnell (Eds.), *Becoming and unbecom-*

ing white: Owning and disowning a racial identity (pp. 10–55). Westport, CT: Greenwood Press.

Milem, J. (2000). The educational benefits of diversity: Evidence from multiple sectors. In M. J. Chang, D. Witt-Sandis, J. Jones, & K. Hakuta (Eds.), *Compelling interest: Examining the evidence on racial dynamics in higher education* (pp. 27–42). Palo Alto, CA: Stanford University Press.

Morrison, T. (1994). *The bluest eye.* New York: Penguin.

Moore, J. (2004). *Bush's brain: How Karl Rove made George W. Bush presidential.* New York: Wiley.

Moore, M. (2004) *Fahrenheit 9/11* [Film]. New York: Dog Eat Dog Films.

Mount, M. (2005). Air force probes religious bias charges at academy. Retrieved May 3, 2005, at www.cnn.com/2005/US/05/03/airforce.religion/index.html

Nieto, S. (2000). *Affirming diversity: The sociopolitical context of multicultural education* (3rd ed.). New York: Longman.

Quammen, D. (2004, November). Was Darwin Wrong? *National Geographic,* pp. 4–35.

Rodríguez, R. (2001, November). *Journey through hate.* Unpublished keynote address, University of Maryland, College Park.

Rorty, R. (1989). *Contingency, irony, and solidarity.* New York: Cambridge University Press.

Schlosser, L. Z. (2003). Christian privilege: Breaking a sacred taboo. *Journal of Multicultural Counseling and Development, 31*(1), 44–51.

Schlosser, L. Z., & Sedlacek, W. E. (2001). *Religious holidays on campus: policies, problems, and recommendations* (Research Report #02-21, 2-14). Office of the Vice President for Student Affairs, University of Maryland, College Park.

Schlosser, L. Z., & Sedlacek, W. E, (2003). Christian privilege and respect for religious diversity: Religious holidays on campus. *About campus: Enriching the student learning experience.*

Slattery, P. (1995). *Curriculum development in the postmodern era.* New York: Garland.

Sleeter, C. (1996). *Multicultural education as social activism.* Albany: State University of New York Press.

Takaki, R. (1994). *A different mirror: A multicultural history of multicultural America.* New York: Little, Brown.

Washington, J. (2001). From materials developed for the Social Justice Training Institute (SJTI), Baltimore.

West, C. (2005). *Democracy matters. Winning the fight against imperialism.* New York: Penguin.

Wolfe, T. (1967). *The electric kool-aid acid test.* New York: Bantam.

CHAPTER 9

TEACHERS' AND STUDENTS' EXPERIENCES WORKING WITH RELIGIOUS ISSUES IN U.S. SCHOOLS

**Binaya Subedi, Merry M. Merryfield,
Khadar Bashir-Ali, and Elvan Gunel**
Ohio State University

ABSTRACT

This chapter argues for the need to incorporate discussions about religion and religious identities within the research on diversity and equity in the United States. The authors contend that limited emphasis has been placed on religious dimensions of diversity and how it impacts the experiences of students who belong to marginalized religious groups in the United States. The discussion explores how teachers' beliefs, experiences, and perspectives shape the ways in which they work with students and how teachers' religious and spiritual beliefs influence their day-to-day classroom instruction. It similarly explores how teachers of diverse ethnic backgrounds negotiate their racial and religious identities in schools and how they collaborate with teachers to promote religious diversity. The chapter concludes by emphasizing the need to address religious dimensions of prejudice and the importance of infusing diverse religious knowledge in school curriculum.

Religion in Multicultural Education, pages 215–238

INTRODUCTION

One of the most controversial educational issues in the United States pertains to the role of religion in public, state-supported schools. High-profile court cases and frequent media attention testify to the tensions over the role of religion in state-funded institutions. Despite the constitutional ban on state-supported religion, the practice of *separation of church and state* has many interpretations in the nation's classrooms. This debate is especially significant in discussing local and global aspects of citizenship and identities, particularly in relation to students who come from diverse racial and ethnic backgrounds (Banks, 2001; Parker, 2002). Without knowledge about how religious history and politics have and continues to influence local and global events, it is difficult for students, particularly in middle and high schools, to understand complex issues such as imperialism, colonialism, and current local and global conflicts. Global and local cultures cannot be understood without insights into how religious and spiritual beliefs shape people's identity, everyday lives and cultures, and how individuals view people of diverse religious backgrounds (see Eck, 2000). In this chapter, by sharing Zine's (2001) call to emphasize discussions on religious diversity in schools, we examine how religion enters the U.S. schools through the beliefs, experiences, and perspectives of teachers and students. First, we begin with an overview on various debates over religion in schools and describe three teachers' experiences in religious schools. Second, we describe how European American social studies teachers perceive the effects of their own religious and spiritual beliefs in their day to day classroom instruction. Third, we explore the viewpoints of middle school Muslim American girls in relation to their schooling experiences. Lastly, we examine the religious identity and experiences of teachers of Indian American, Filipino/a American, and Pakistani American ancestry. We conclude this chapter by making recommendations in regard to the need to recognize students' religious identities and the importance of infusing diverse religious knowledge in curriculum.

WHY STUDY RELIGIOUS DIVERSITY

Discussions about religion in society have particular implications to the field of education in the United States since they help us further understand how the schooling process, including interpretations of curriculum, is shaped by dominant viewpoints of knowledge (see Diaz, Massialas, & Xanthopoulos, 1999; Hoffman, 1996; McCarthy, 1998; Merryfield, 2001; Sleeter, 2001; Smith, 1999; Subedi, 2003; Verma-Joshi, Baker, & Tanaka, 2004; Willinsky, 1998). Following the events of September, 11, 2001, in New York and the

U.S.-led invasions of Afghanistan and Iraq, many U.S. teachers and professional organizations have raised questions about how students are learning about world religions. An important topic of discussion includes how people's religious beliefs influence how they view ideas such as conflict and peace and the relationship between local and global identities. The passage of the Patriot Act has raised new questions over civil liberties, particularly on profiling people based on religion, race, or national origin (Ahmad, 2002). And because larger social events and policies affect schools, students of Muslim, Hindu, and Sikh backgrounds as well as people of South Asian, African, and Arab ancestry continue to face prejudice and harassment because they are often seen as embodying the identity of the Other (see Ahmad & Szpara, 2003; Elnour & Bashir-Ali, 2003; Peek, 2003).

Religion in the schools is, of course, more than mandated curriculum content. Students and teachers do not leave their personal beliefs at home; they enter the classroom with religious perspectives and assumptions that influence how they interact with their peers and interpret curriculum content. In many towns and cities in the United States, the cultural/religious practices of immigrants or refugees from Africa, Asia, Europe, or Latin America have come into conflict with those of teachers and mainstream students (Olsen, 1997). Religion adds a very sensitive dimension to the challenges of preparing young people to be effective citizens in a multicultural society, especially in relation to helping students understand about cultural differences. For example, religious aspects of stereotypes create inferior/superior or civilized/uncivilized notions of identity. Stereotyping is inextricably tied to issues of prejudice, domination, and racism, and is often used by people in power to describe the *deficient* intellectual abilities of people (Allport, 1954; Bhabha, 1993; Cortes, 2002; Steele, 1999). Religious stereotypes describe people belonging to a *different* religion in condescending or pejorative terms (see Mamdani, 2002). For example, stereotypes of Hinduism include images of cows, Hare Krishna, caste system, elephants, snake charmers, and arranged marriages (see Prasad, 2000). Similarly, dominant images reduce Islam into portraits of veiled women, men with turbans, camels in the desert, and so on (see Said, 1979). Buddhism is often described in relation to monks, meditation, and exotic temples (see Eck, 2000). Not only do such portrayals demean major world religions, they leave U.S. students unprepared to understand how religion influences people's everyday lives.

TEACHER BELIEFS, EXPERIENCES, AND INSTRUCTIONAL DECISION MAKING

Within the educational literature there are many studies of identity, beliefs, and experiences (Britzman, 1994; Neumann, 1998; Russell & Munby, 1992; Zeichner, 1995). Research on teacher thinking, personal theorizing, and teacher decision making identifies ways in which teachers' beliefs and values influence their practice (Clark & Peterson, 1986; Connelly & Clandidin, 1988; Cornett et al., 1992). Personal narratives and case studies take us into the dynamic process of teachers' beliefs influencing their instruction (Carter & Doyle, 1996; Clandidin, 1992; Gomez, 1996; Goodson, 1992; Schubert & Ayers, 1992; Wolk & Rodman, 1994). Within case studies of classrooms and schools, there are compelling stories on how teachers' and students' cultural experiences influence their perception of schools and how this impacts teaching and learning processes (Fine, 1991; Foster, 1997, Meier, 1995; Olsen, 1997; Taylor & Whittaker, 2003).

Recent discussions about religion in U.S. schools addresses issues such as teaching of evolution and prayer in schools (see Detwiler, 1999). In the majority of literature on educational equity and diversity (often referred to as multicultural education in the United States), limited attention has been given to how religious discourse influences curriculum development and the needs of students of diverse religious backgrounds. In the recent *Handbook on Research on Multicultural Education*, there is no chapter on religion (Banks & Banks, 2004). Even in books on cultural identity, such as Barbara C. Cruz's award-winning *Multiethnic Teens and Cultural Identity* (2001), religion is scarcely mentioned. In the literature devoted to religion, such as Diana L. Eck's *A New Religious America* (2000) or Rima Berns McGown's *Muslims in the Diaspora* (1999), limited attention is paid to public education or religious influences and conflicts in schools. In the past, research on immigrant education has focused largely on language acquisition and how immigrants can be assimilated into U.S. mainstream culture. And there is a lack of research linking immigrant educational struggles in relation to immigrant students' religious identities (Zine, 2000). Recent research on student identities documents immigrant educational experiences in relation to race, ethnicity, and language (see Olneck, 2004; Olsen, 1997).

There are some exceptions where religion does enter the multicultural literature. In *Multicultural Education: A Caring-Centered Reflective Approach* (2005), Valerie Ooka Pang describes culture and religion as being interrelated and discusses Somali immigrants' religious issues in U.S. schools. *Social Education*, the journal of the National Council for the Social Studies, ran numerous articles following the attacks of September 11, 2001, to help teachers teach about Islam and to develop a better understanding of diverse Muslim cultures worldwide. The 2003 *Social Education* article "Teaching Muslim Girls in American Schools" by Awatif Elnour and Khadar Bashir-Ali explains how U.S. educational journals are recognizing the need to educate teachers about the needs of Muslim students in the United States. There are also ethnographies that contribute significantly to our understanding of religion in schools. In *God's Choice: The Total World of a Fundamentalist Christian School*, Alan Peshkin (1986) takes us into the environment of a fundamentalist academy. Through observations of classes and interviews with teachers and students, the reader comes to understand the power of religion in a school where all adhere to the same religious beliefs. In *The Color of Strangers, the Color of Friends* (1991), Peshkin captures cross-cultural interaction in a town he calls Riverview and its only high school, which is made up of students of Sicilian, Mexican, African, and Filipino ancestry. Next, we highlight the experiences and practices of teachers of Muslim as well as of non-Muslim faith and explain its implications to teaching and learning about diversity in schools.[1]

Encountering Prejudice and Teachers Making Connections across Differences

Teachers' experiences in schools and classroom practices help us understand how religion is talked about in schools and society. Similarly, in our research, the experiences of the teachers illustrate ways in which religious aspects of culture and prejudice function in schools and how teachers continue to learn to work with students who come from religiously diverse backgrounds. The case of encountering prejudice based on religion is explained by two teachers, Dorina and Gabriella, who speak of the different ways religious bias operates in school and society, and which impacts the ways in which the teachers negotiate their identities. In the interview, Dorina, a Muslim American teacher of Arab descent, describes how she was assigned to teach at a local Catholic high school as part of her student teaching assignment and how she felt she was unwanted as early as the first day at the school. She explains that she was constantly stared at and hardly anyone spoke to her.

It was clear to me that the school was not ready for a person like me who wears her hijab[2] visibly. Although no one said anything to me, I had the distinct feeling that I did not belong there. I...asked to change my student teaching assignment as soon as I set foot in the school. I was later changed into a public school with diverse students, some of them were Muslims. I was successful there, and I am now working with the local school district.

Dorina's experience suggests how teacher education programs need to be sensitive to where preservice teachers are placed during their student teaching experiences so that students feel that they are welcomed at a particular school. Similarly, the case reminds us of the need to infuse the religious aspect of diversity to help students develop open-mindedness and respect of all religions (see Noddings, 1993). In Gabriella's case, her family shared their concern when Gabriella started teaching at an Islamic school, including asking her to be careful about working with *those people*. In the interview, she states: *My folks were concerned about me working here, but I told them not to worry. I would not work in a place where I know I am not safe.* And she told her parents that she felt that her students and their parents were very supportive of her teaching.

Teachers' practices also help us understand how, by recognizing students' cultural/religious identities, educators are infusing students' knowledge into school curriculum. The importance of making connections to students' identities is shared by Marina, a Christian woman of European American ancestry, a former social studies teacher, who currently teaches at a private Muslim school. During the interview, Marina speaks of how she continues to emphasize academic skills in her classroom so that students can understand history as emphasized in state-approved curriculum standards. For example, by recognizing the values students place on cultural/religious identities, Maria connects religious issues to teaching about history and current events. One example Marina shared was in relation to teaching about the Jewish Holocaust since many of her students had limited knowledge of the topic. As part of the lesson, she helped students understand how people can be persecuted because of cultural and religious beliefs, an issue she realizes her students would easily understand since students had shared how people looked at them differently in society. She also recognizes that there was limited emphasis placed in curriculum on issues pertinent to people of Jewish and Islamic faith and that there needed to be more dialogue among various religious groups to work for peace in the world. Marina's approach to teaching helps students understand historical concepts, particularly how history and identity are complexly intertwined (see Giroux, 1994).

Marina's experience also helps us understand how teachers can create a culturally and religiously appropriate environment for learning. For example, drawing upon her experience growing up in a Russian Orthodox community, which heavily emphasized rituals in religious activities, Marina felt that she had made a smooth transition in learning about Muslim rituals, except for the *practice of Muslims praying five times a day.* Nowadays, she takes pride in letting students know about the prayer schedule and *I remind them to get their prayer rugs out from the cubbies, line them up, and take them to the prayer place.* She also points out how she became accustomed to various Islamic holidays, and when students asked her if she prayed, she responds: *I tell them I pray all the time. I remember also when my students were fasting. It was my first experience to see children fast. I learned to eat my lunch in my room, so they would not see me eating in front of them.* Another instance of learning that she shares is when she mistakenly provided ice cream sandwiches to students and then realized later that the product contained pork by-products. During the interview, she pointed out how she continues to learn about the specific needs of her students and continues to ask them if *she is doing anything that is not religiously or culturally appropriate.* On one occasion, one student informed her how any kind of music was not appropriate to play during the class and then she heard another perspective from another student who suggested how music was fine to be used in classroom contexts. For this reason, she keeps an open mind and does not assume that everyone prefers a certain practice. Experiences such as these have helped her recognize that customs and beliefs vary across Muslim communities and that people who follow a certain religion have diverse opinions about specific practices.

How Social Studies Teachers Interpret and Teach Religion

In recent interviews with social studies teachers, we have found several ways in which the teachers describe how their religious beliefs and experiences influence their classroom practices. The various perspectives of the teachers reflect the ways in which they negotiate religion in their own lives, incorporate religion in curriculum, and work with students of diverse religious backgrounds. Some teachers describe that they recognize how their own religious background influences their teaching and how they develop relationships with students. One teacher describes growing up as a Presbyterian and attending a Catholic church since his marriage 2 years ago. *My beliefs haven't changed but now I am more interested in getting Catholic kids and Protestant kids to accept each other in my classroom.* Another teacher explains how he did not know much about Islam. *I haven't had any reason to learn about it before. But since I started getting Somalis in my classes I have tried to learn about their religion in order to understand them.* This is because *I need to teach the other kids about Somali customs so they won't make fun of the girls' covering their hair.*

Holistic Beliefs and Curriculum Expansion

Many teachers in the interview pointed out how their religious outlooks or beliefs were holistic, affecting everything they do from their commitment to the profession, the kinds of relationships they form with students, to curriculum planning and instruction. In day-to-day interactions, a number of teachers emphasize trying to treat their students according to the former's religious beliefs. The teachers' approaches to working with students are influenced by what they perceive as the positive forces of their religious influences, whether that be *Christian, Jewish,* or *Catholic* beliefs. Many teachers speak of modeling their religious beliefs everyday as they work with students: *My professional ethics come from my religious beliefs. I believe a higher power is directing me in the classroom. I try to interact with students as Jesus would.* Another teacher suggests: *It is a challenge to care about all students, not just the ones who are easy to work with. But a good Christian is fair and just. A Christian teacher loves each and every one.* These beliefs convey the *goodness* of sharing what the teachers have learned in relation to their religious beliefs. The teachers recognize that their religious knowledge may influence how they work with students who come from secular or from religious faiths that are different from the ones they practice (Islam, Hinduism, etc.). More research needs to be conducted on how teachers' beliefs may influence their ability to build rapport with students who come from different religious backgrounds. In the United States, research in multicultural education has emphasized the need to prepare future teachers who can understand issues related to race, ethnicity, and culture (Gay, 1993; Sleeter, 1993). And there is limited research on how teachers need to be prepared for religious diversity.

Many social studies teachers teach about the influence of religion or spiritual beliefs in their courses in U.S. or world history, world cultures, sociology, world geography, global issues, or contemporary events. Religion has been an important factor in the formation of imperialism and colonialism, local/global conflicts, and the settlement of the United States (see, e.g., Eck, 2000; Prasad, 2000). It would be difficult to understand critical issues in history such as immigration, the Jewish Holocaust, or the creation of the Israeli state without content knowledge on world religions. One teacher explains his rationale for incorporating discussions on religions: *I want them to have access to different kinds of information so they can make informed decisions.* He adds: *I want them to know how to demonstrate respect for other people's beliefs and conduct themselves well when they differ in the classroom.* Teachers' inclusion of diverse curriculum also attempts to create an open-minded atmosphere in the classroom when discussing various social issues. By recognizing the diversity of religious beliefs in their classes, teachers can create cross-religious dialogue. Being reflective about students' religious identities can lead teachers to examine how religious affiliations influence students' ways of being and knowing. And this recognition, as one teacher puts it, allows spaces to *deal with highly controversial issues, which always come up in my U.S. Government classes—abortion, gay rights, doctor-assisted suicide.*

Emphasizing Tolerance, Community Building, and Critical Thinking

Some teachers focus on the need to teach tolerance in general while others explain how they work at teaching students to respect religious beliefs that are different from the students' own religious values and practices. For example, one teacher explains how being Christian meant being respectful of other beliefs: *Christians are not the only people on the planet. Part of my Christian beliefs are in how I teach about the beliefs of others, how I teach kids to respect the beliefs of others, not make fun or put them down if they are Buddhists, Muslims, or Jews.* This is because *teaching respect and open-mindedness is my sacred trust.* The teacher is aware that:

> At times I have lost my faith in God. But I have never lost the goal of teaching kids to respect the rights of people who do believe. I am the son of a minister and that has affected how I deal with the world. I am veiled in my religious upbringing everyday. I teach my students to treat each other as they want to be treated—the Golden Rule.

Some teachers feel that they have benefited from knowledge of other religions and want their students to learn about and appreciate religions different from their own. One teacher explains: *I have been influenced by the spiritualism of Buddhism. Although I was brought up in another religion, I think Buddhism has ideas that students should learn about.* In other studies, researchers have found that students may influence the content of courses as teachers work to improve their teaching of a specific racial, ethnic, or religious group in relation to mandated courses in schools (Ladson-Billings, 1994). For example, when a Palestinian student enrolled in a teacher's fourth-grade classroom, the teacher expanded her instruction on Islam and consequently all students in her class that year had much improved coursework on understanding about Muslims (Merryfield, 1994).

Several teachers note that there was a need to protect students who were a religious minority within the local community or in the school community. Diverse religious groups were mentioned—Jehovah's Witnesses, Mormons, Jews, Sikhs, Bahá'ís, and Muslims. Since what is an acceptable and not acceptable religious identity varies across schools depending on demographics or the setting of schools, a number of teachers suggest the need to respect the rights of fundamentalist Christians while other teachers speak of the need to respect the rights of atheists or immigrant students' religious beliefs. *We had some Eastern Orthodox move in after the breakup of the Soviet Union. They were Christians but still quite different from our local Catholics and Methodists. Students didn't understand why these people have to have their own churches.* A number of teachers recognize that when students' religious beliefs influence their appearances (hair coverings of Sikhs or the conservative dress of Mennonites, for example) or participation in school events (Muslim girls not wanting to participate in after-school clubs), bias or harassment increase since such students are seen as *different.*

A recurring theme throughout many of the interviews was an emphasis on the teaching of critical thinking skills and the need for students to inquire into why people believe the way they do and how beliefs affect peoples' norms and perspectives. *I am deeply and profoundly aware that I don't know about higher powers. And I'm okay with that. I encourage questioning, exploration of beliefs as that is part of my religious orientation.* This concern can be seen both in the teaching of history and contemporary events. *They have to look critically at religions, at what is done in the name of religion, at why people hold certain beliefs. Why have so many people accepted their conquerors' Islam or Christianity? How have they changed the religion and their practices of it?* Perhaps it is the nature of common stereotypes that leads to the teaching of inquiry skills. *I have had kids come into my class thinking Hindus bow down and worship cows and idols. So I have them do some research online and then talk to some Hindus who live here.* Several teachers also note the fear and even hatred that students have of *foreign* religions and *foreigners,* and how students have overcome such prejudices through research projects.

UNDERSTANDING MUSLIM STUDENTS' EXPERIENCES

In this part of the chapter, we discuss the challenges Muslim girls encounter in schools and society. Our research parallels studies that describe how students of color face marginalization in schools because of the ways in which schools deemphasize students' racial and ethnic identities (Ferguson, 2000; Lei, 2003; Yon, 2000). Students may feel culturally marginalized because schools may not value the knowledge they bring to schools (Nieto, 1996; Olsen, 1997; Pizarro, 1997; Valdes, 2001). In schools, religious identity may play an important role depending on how students, for example Muslim or Hindu, identify themselves and how they express beliefs and values. Exploring the concept of accomodation without assimilation in her research with Sikh students, Gibson (1988) describes how Sikh students often acted the norms of the culture of the schools without giving up their religious and cultural values. Hall (1995) similarly illustrates how Sikh students in England negotiated when to express their own cultural/religious ways of being and when to perform mainstream identities depending on the particular context of their school experiences. Zine (2001) argues that Muslim Canadian students faced constant prejudice and felt isolated because of societal misrepresentation of their Muslim identity. However, despite the alienation they feel, and by being ambivalent about dominant social practices, they relied upon spiritual identities to resist marginalization. Research on, for example, Asian American and African American students' identities similarly suggest ways in which students resist assimilation and create safe spaces to cope in relation to being marginalized (Fordham, 1988; Lee, 1996). In this discussion, we highlight the ways in which Muslim American girls who attend a private middle school negotiate religious and gender identity.

Negotiating Appearances and Gender Issues

For many Muslim people, a *hijab* or headscarf is a way of expressing their religious identities and worldviews; however, people who have limited understanding of the cultural/religious significance of wearing a headscarf assume the practice as being oppressive (Ahmed, 1992). *Hijab* is a cloth that covers parts of the hair or head and also portions of the body. Depending on a person or community's cultural practices, which depends on economic, ethnic, and national affiliation, women cover portions of their hair, face, or the whole body to show their affiliations with Islamic values (Zine, 2000). Muslim women also defend the wearing of the *hijab* and consider the practice as their right to exercise free-choice and religious expression (Hashim, 1999; Rehman & Diziegielewski, 2003). In the schooling context, Muslim girls find it difficult to respond to multiple demands, ranging from the expectation that they follow family/community traditions to school practices that devalues their cultural/religious beliefs (Haw, 1998). The girls interviewed share that wearing the hijab or wearing long, full-sleeved, loose outfits represents honesty, integrity, and responsibility to their communities and to their faith. The girls also explain that the decision to wear the *hijab* was their personal choice, which was supported by their family, and they attribute the *hijab* as a symbol of their modesty as noted in Islamic faith. And because of the misconceptions that surround clothing issues, the girls describe how they have been treated differently in schools. Thus, in comparison to the girls who dress in mainstream ways, girls who wear a headscarf face prejudice in schools (see Pang, 2005). One girl explains how she was often asked questions such as: *Why are you wearing a scarf? Do you have hair?* Another girl notes how, in an elementary school, her headscarf was pulled off by a boy and how she remembers the incident quite vividly. *I remember I felt really embarrassed.* The girls also share how most of their teachers made attempts to understand Islamic cultural and religious beliefs. The girls suggest how they preferred women teachers because of their positive experiences with female teachers. One student explains how she felt women teachers were gentle and fostered a less competitive environment in class. This parallels Elnour and Bashir-Ali's (2003) argument that educators ought to be sensitive to the cultural context of the classroom. And, as Elnour and Bashir-Ali further note, practices such as talking softly, avoiding shaking hands, and not participating in classroom activities might be misunderstood by teachers as a lack of interest in learning or, worse, disrespectful of teachers. The girls interviewed in the study also recognize how in the past they had worked with male teachers who respected Muslim values and created a less competitive classroom environment.

The girls describe how the gender aspect of identity was similarly significant in relation to how they negotiate relationships with members of the opposite sex. The girls note how they were advised by their parents and communities to avoid interacting with boys. In many non-Western traditions, relationships between men and women develop not prior but after the marriage. And the concept of falling in love after marriage is quite new for many people in Western societies, which creates stereotypes about people's practices being backward or inferior (see Karp, 1996/97). The girls explain how their families believed, in accordance with Islamic values, that the roles of boys and girls ought to be separated to develop their own identities. One girl describes her situation: *I don't date at all. Sometimes I want to but it doesn't work with my religion. I know I can't date at all but if I knew I could then I would do it. It is easy for me not to eat pork but if it comes to dating and wearing I want to be like everybody else.*

For many girls, not being able to date means being invisible in some contexts and not being able to *be like everybody else.* Although not being able to act mainstream may be difficult for many girls who desire, on occasion, to act like mainstream adolescents, Muslim girls share how they have created outlets to socialize with Muslim girls, particularly by participating in various family or community events. Next, we examine how Asian American teachers negotiate their religious identities and how they have promoted religious diversity in their classrooms and in the school.

RELIGIOUS IDENTITIES OF ASIAN AMERICAN TEACHERS

Our research on the religious identities of Asian American teachers parallel studies on how teachers of color negotiate their cultural identities in schools (see Galindo, 1996; Gomez, 1996; King, 1993; Montecinos, 1994). Studies have described the challenges faced by teachers of color in relation to mentoring programs, curriculum issues, and in negotiating mainstream cultures of schools (Foster, 1990; Lipka, 1991).

A recurring experience the teachers share is being perceived as *different* in relation to their religious identity in U.S. society. Kiran, a Muslim American woman of Pakistani descent, an ESL (English as a second language) teacher, works in a racially and ethnically diverse high school where most of the teachers are of European American descent and none of whom are Muslim. Half of Kiran's class is comprised of Muslim students who are recent immigrants from Somalia, Eritria, and Ethiopia; the rest of the students are immigrants from Mexico, China, Laos, Cambodia, and Vietnam and identify themselves as either Buddhists or Christians. She points out that being a Muslim woman is often misunderstood in society as well as in her school. For example, she is often not thought of as an authentic Muslim since she does not wear a headscarf. She explains: *People ask me how can you be a Muslim? How can you be a real Muslim if you don't wear it?* This perspective interprets the *hijab* as the only symbol of being an authentic Muslim and discounts the multiple meanings the scarf represents in Muslim society (Ahmed, 1992). *It really puzzles people because there is the expectation that I be covered. When I say I don't wear a scarf, I am asked if I am a modern woman.* And furthermore, *then when I say I am divorced and dating, people think I am for sure not a Muslim.* Kiran pointed out that when her Muslim students ask her why she does not wear a headscarf she clarifies to students that there are a number of ways to being a Muslim. She explains to students that her *parents never asked me to wear one so I don't know what it means to wear a* hijab.

Mira, an elementary school teacher, similarly shares how exotic meanings are attached to her religious identity in society, yet she feels that students and teachers are respectful of her Hindu religious heritage. Mira works in a suburban school where most of the students and teachers are European Americans and she is the only teacher who affiliates with Hinduism. Mira noted that she is less inclined to talk about religion outside of the school unless it comes up in conversations and considers it a private topic. *I don't bring it up because people don't quite know what it means. But religious issues always comes up because people always ask where you are from and if you are a Hindu.* She points out that,

> I get asked two things the most. If it is really true that we don't eat cow or I have had an arranged marriage in a temple. I say of course you are right. I eat meat but I don't eat beef and my parents and I found my husband. For a lot of people, the idea of having an arranged marriage is so backward like in medieval times. And we have been married for more than 25 years.

Mira's experience reveals how stereotypes devalue people's identity. In her school, by developing positive relationship with teachers, she feels quite comfortable talking about her cultural and religious values with teachers. She adds: *Teachers here respect me because I explain to them what the practices are in Hinduism and I feel that helps getting to know each other better. In the beginning there were misconceptions and it is all about dialogue and coming to certain understandings.* Similarly, *I ask a lot of questions about Jewish traditions and Christianity from the teachers here, which I know little about.*

Anil, a male teacher of Indian American ancestry, is a high school biology teacher in an urban school, where most of the students are African Americans. He considers himself a secular person and noted that his racial identity was more significant than his religious identity; however, Anil pointed out that he has been learning about Hinduism from his parents and the local Indian American community. *The problem is that most people ask me if I am a Hindu and ask where I was born and this means in what country. And when I say rural Ohio, people say they are sorry for asking the question.* It is useful to consider how Anil's identity as an Indian American is often defined through his *foreign* appearances and which conveys his not being an authentic U.S. citizen (see Lee, 1996). He further explains: *A lot of people have misconceptions about Hinduism and people think of idolatry and think of it as a superstition. And when I explain to people that Hinduism has a lot of gods, sometimes people get curious.* Anil attributes the stereotypical viewpoints about Hinduism to the way in which people have been educated. *Most people are not taught about religions in an open-minded way so it is hard for people to even understand the basic concepts. People mostly ask me about yoga and reincarnation.* Anil does not feel invisible in the school despite being the only teacher of Asian origin, which he credits to the strong relationship he has built with teachers, most of whom are African American. He feels that his colleagues validate his racial identity and his Hindu heritage. *I don't get jokes about snakes and magic carpets here.* Similarly, he has come to recognize the values of spirituality by observing how African American teachers and students affiliate with Christianity. *I have learned a lot about black Christianity and this has helped me in understanding religious issues better.*

Maria, a Filipina, teaches social studies at an urban middle school where the student population is comprised of African American, European American, and immigrant students from China, Somalia, Mexico, Cambodia, and so on. Teachers in the school, with the exception of one Kenyan immigrant male teacher and a male African American principal, are of European American descent. Maria is often perceived as a foreigner because *of how I look and because of my accent.* Maria explains about religious identity: *Some people get confused when I say I am a Christian since people think I am Buddhist. I explain to people how a lot of Filipinos are Catholic and they are quite devoted.* And she finds herself reasserting her religious identity when there is a discussion about religion in her school. Maria realizes that there is often the assumption that she is not an authentic Christian: *I get the feeling sometimes that I am less of a Christian for people because of my Asian identity.* Maria's perspective helps us understand how societies often create insider/ outsider versions of religious identities and how certain racial or ethnic groups are perceived as being more legitimate followers of a religion.

In sum, the teachers' perspectives help us understand not only the extent to which the teachers value spirituality but also the heterogeneous religious identities they express. The teachers share how they have felt as well as responded to religious stereotypes and how religious identities intersect with racial and gender identities. The teachers' experiences also speak of how some of the teachers have been able to collaborate with other teachers in the school to create a more supportive cultural/religious environment for themselves. Next, we describe the ways in which the teachers (Kiran, Maria, and Mira) attempt to infuse religious diversity in their classrooms and in the schools. The teachers' practices also help us understand the challenges educators face in promoting nonmainstream cultures in school settings (Banks, 2001; Pang, 2005).

RECOGNIZING THE SPIRITUAL NEEDS OF STUDENTS

To promote a better cultural climate for her diverse ESL students, most of whom are immigrants from Asia, Africa, and Latin America, and who are of Muslim, Buddhist, and Christian backgrounds, Kiran serves as a liaison between ESL students and teachers. To meet the academic needs of her students, she makes efforts to collaborate with teachers on infusing students' knowledge, particularly on cultural and religion issues, into curriculum. *I wish all teachers would be sensitive to students' experiences and I get frustrated when that does not happen.* Similarly, Kiran continues to work with administrators and teachers on creating a more culturally supportive atmosphere for her students, particularly in regard to school functions that are supportive of students' cultural and religious identities. And, to make lessons culturally relevant for her students, Kiran heavily incorporates discussions on Islam, Buddhism, Christianity, and so on. In her classroom, she often asks students to emphasize cultural and religious issues they are familiar with when writing daily journals, which are designed to improve students' writing skills. In one of the group research projects, students researched how cultural and religious customs impact the life of people in a particular country.

The challenges Kiran faced in creating a more culturally supportive atmosphere for her students reflects the contradictory messages schools send when attempting to incorporate religious diversity in schools. For example, school officials responded positively when Muslim students requested a separate dining space for students who were fasting or students who did not eat beef or pork. This was after Kiran and her students notified and met with school officials on how the lack of space hindered students' spiritual and cultural needs. Kiran also feels that school officials were receptive about resolving tensions between ESL students and non-

ESL students in schools. She recognizes that *it was mostly about misunderstanding since students know very little about each other and name-calling and jokes made it more tense.* And also *when you have students of the same racial yet different ethnic backgrounds, misunderstandings take place.* She continues: *A lot of time it is about who is more Asian or black or what religion is more valid.* And Kiran felt that there were some contradictions on how the school was dealing with religious diversity, which impacted her on a personal level. For example, when she requested 5 days of absence during the month of Ramadan, she was asked to provide an official letter from the mosque indicating that she would be attending religious ceremonies at the mosque. She wondered: *Would teachers of various religious faiths be asked to do the same on specific holidays?* Thus, the act of requesting a letter not only sought to ascertain the validity of her religious identity but also attempted to see/monitor if the religious activities were legitimate. Similarly, she came to the understanding that the school was *doing small things here and there but there is not a schoolwide program to talk about the needs of Muslim and ESL students.*

TEACHERS COLLABORATING TO PROMOTE RELIGIOUS DIVERSITY

Maria, a Filipina American middle school teacher, feels that there is more dialogue about religion in the urban school where she teaches now. And she is optimistic that, in general, there is a positive attitude in her school toward religious diversity. She points out that *on occasion we have students telling other students like "go back to where you came from" or "speak English-only here" or "if you eat pork you will go to hell."* Although there have been misunderstandings among African American and immigrant students, she feels that much progress has been made through talking about religions and cultures in the school. She attributes the positive climate to the willingness of educators, teachers of color as well as white teachers, who see the benefits of collaborating on classroom lessons as well as in school programs. For this reason, in virtually every classroom, upcoming religious/spiritual events such as Christmas, Ramadan, Kwanza, and the Sabbath are posted as items of discussion. Similarly, to teach cultural and religious differences, Maria assigns students to conduct two mini-interviews with students who come from a different cultural background. *When Somali and African American students gather to talk about similarities and differences it helps them see issues of religion and history in a different way.* Maria points out that students taking international trips, particularly to the continent of Africa, has also helped them understand about religions. *When students return from Kenya or Tanzania, we talk about cultures and religions and how people who live in the two countries are Hindus, Muslims, and Christians and also have local aspects of religious beliefs.* To expand their knowledge about global issues, students in Maria's sixth-grade world culture class take part in mini-research to investigate the history and everyday lives of people in a specific country. Maria noted during the interview: *I feel quite good about this project because it takes students to a new place and opens their minds. I have found that students are very willing to accept the ideas talked about in many religions.*

Mira, a third-grade teacher of Indian American ancestry who has been teaching in public schools for close to 10 years, became more aware of how religious issues impacted her classrooms when she realized that many of her students of Jewish, Hindu, and Muslim heritage did not often attend the programs the school organized prior to winter and summer holidays. She attributes this to the ways in which holidays are taught and discussed in the school. After she contacted parents on the students' lack of participation, she began to realize that the absence was a reflection of how the school incorporated cultural and religious issues overall. *I would also invite parents of Jewish, Hindu, and Muslim students and only a few would come and some shared the concern over the programs not being balanced. Parents alluded that Christmas and Easter were talked about in the functions and other religions were not emphasized.* Mira attributes the parents' input as being an important factor that helped make the subsequent school functions religiously diverse. However, Mira points out that not everyone at her school or not all of the parents of her students were unanimous on how to incorporate religious diversity at the school. She notes: *One viewpoint was to completely get rid of religion and actually some parents voiced that perspective. The idea was to be religiously neutral.* She added: *But luckily we did not go that route. Otherwise students would not have learned anything.* Similarly, Mira describes that there was some opposition from a couple of families about the change of format on *how this was changing the tradition of the school.* Yet, many teachers and school administrators voiced opposition to *keeping tradition* as well as the *neutral* approaches to religious diversity. Since the change, Mira feels that more teachers are collaborating on teaching about cultural as well as religious diversity in her school.

IMPLICATIONS FOR EDUCATORS

Similar to racial, ethnic, or linguistic prejudices, religious dimensions of prejudice produce stereotypes. And to overcome discriminations based on religion, educators should incorporate discussions about religion and religious identities when teaching about diversity and equity. For many students and teachers, the combination of religious and racial prejudices negatively impacts their experiences at school and marginalizes the knowledge they bring to classrooms. To promote discussions about religion and religious identities, educators can do the following:

- Be informed of current events since local and global events influence how religiously underrepresented students are treated in schools. For instance, U.S. involvement in Vietnam, Somalia, Iraq, and so on, has impacted students who trace their ancestries to these countries or those students who may appear to be from Asia, Africa, or the Middle East since such students are often seen as the *enemy* (see Pang, 2005). Similarly, in post-9/11 context, because of the perception of Muslims or Sikhs being terrorists and Islam being perceived as a new threat for Western countries, students of Arab, Asian and African descent have become targets of cruel stereotypes and racial and religious profiling (Ahmad & Szpara, 2003). Educators ought to openly discuss historical and contemporary issues relevant to religion in an age-appropriate manner so that students do not develop bias.

- Examine how one's religious viewpoints may influence teaching about a specific subject area. This is particularly relevant in teaching about topics in science (e.g., evolution), literature, world history, religions, U.S. history, and current events. What might be the limits of teaching one religion (Christianity) more extensively while treating other religions (Hinduism, Judaism, Islam, etc.) superficially?

- Critically examine how one's religious perspective may influence everyday interaction with students, parents, and students' larger communities. What ethical obligations would a teacher with very strong religious convictions have when working with students who come from either secular or different religious backgrounds?

- Continue to emphasize how religion influences people's ways of life since, historically, topics on religious history and the diversity of religious practices have been less emphasized in schools. Marginalized people in society have often utilized spiritual beliefs to advocate peace, freedom, love, and justice (Hanh, 2001; hooks, 2000; Menchu, 1984). There is often the belief that there is no need to discuss various religions in schools since, according to the argument, students will learn about religion at home. This viewpoint marginalizes the need to learn about religions students may not be part of or may not be familiar with. Moreover, the culture of most U.S. schools often privileges one religion (mostly Christianity) and this is reflected in observed holidays, which are based on Christian calendars. And various school functions (plays, musicals, etc.) similarly emphasize Christian beliefs.

- Recognize that students' identities are diverse since they are shaped by factors such as national origin, racial, and ethnic differences, and this may influence how students identify themselves in schools. For example, the tendency to homogenize all Muslims, Hindus, or Sikhs as having certain characteristics or attributes creates stereotypes. Would all followers of a specific religion fit into a neat category of habits and behaviors? Similarly, for example, being Muslim is a part of an individual's identity since the person may also identify as being a woman, an American, an Indonesian, an Asian , or an African American.

- Make efforts to change the culture of the school if it does not validate the religious identities of students of color or other disadvantaged populations (Amish, Jewish, etc.). Educators should advocate that schools hold diverse functions that highlight the histories, cultures, and religions of various people.

- Create a meaningful classroom climate in which racially and religiously underrepresented students can express their knowledge. Recognize that students might be sensitive to specific teaching and learning styles.

- Advocate that the school hire people of diverse religious backgrounds. For example, as U.S. schools continue to become more diverse in regard to student population, teachers and administrators in most schools continue to be racially/ethnically and religiously less diverse. And this lack of diversity of the teaching and administrative workforce influences how schools implement curriculum and work with religiously diverse students and parents.

Similarly, educators ought to develop culturally relevant curriculum that validates students' identities in school (Gay, 2000; Ladson-Billings, 1994). By developing relationships with parents and community members and learning about students' cultural and religious identities, educators can help students academically succeed in school. Lastly, we believe that research on religious differences and religious identity is marginalized in the field of education and more research is urgently needed.

When examining the significance of religious diversity in schools and society, it is critical to move away from perspectives that treat religions, similar to the concept of culture, as being static and unchanging. For example, what it means to be a Hindu or Christian has changed over time since religious identities are influenced by political, historical, and cultural events. And because of continued migration of communities across international borders, cities in Western nation-states are becoming increasingly diverse. For example, people of Muslim faith who migrate from Asia, the Middle East, or Africa to Europe or North America influence religious debates in their new places of residence. Although nation-states are often viewed as being religiously homogenous, educators can help students recognize how countries in the world are religiously and culturally heterogeneous. For example, countries such as Egypt, India, and the United States have historically been religiously diverse since they have been populated by people of multiple religious beliefs. By emphasizing the need to respect differences, schools can play a critical role in helping students understand the cultural and religious diversity that exists in their communities as well as in the world.

NOTES

1. Data on the experiences of a Muslim American teacher teaching in a Catholic school and the two European American teachers working in Muslim schools was collected in the fall of 2004. (2) Data for Muslim students in the middle school (four students participated in the research) was collected in the fall of 2004. In both research, data was collected via informal interviews. (3) Similarly, data on the beliefs and practices of European American teachers was collected in the fall of 2004 by interviewing 32 teachers in 12 U.S. states. The teachers were selected from those who demonstrated expertise in global education either through taking global education courses or working in a professional development school network in global education. The interviews took place either online or over the telephone. The majority of the participants were middle and high school public school teachers. (4) Lastly, the research with Indian American, Pakistani American, and Filipina American teachers is part of a larger research project on immigrant teachers and was collected in 2001 and 2002 via interviews and observation in schools.

2. A *hijab* is a headscarf or clothing worn by Muslim women to convey respect to Islamic values. Depending on specific cultural traditions and practices, a *hijab* may cover portions of the hair or head or segment of the body.

REFERENCES

Ahmad, I., & Szpara, M. Y. (2003). Muslim children in urban America: The New York City schools experience. *Journal of Muslim Minority Affairs, 23*(2), 295–301.

Ahmad, M. (2002). Homeland insecurities: Racial violence the day after September 11. *Social Text, 20*(3), 101–115.

Ahmed, L. (1992). *Women and gender in Islam.* New Haven, CT: Yale University Press.

Allport, G. (1954). *The nature of prejudice.* Reading, MA: Addison-Wesley.

Banks, J. A. (2001). *Cultural diversity and education: Foundations, curriculum, and teaching.* London: Allyn & Bacon.

Banks, J. A., & Banks, C. A. M. (Eds.) (2004). *Handbook of research on multicultural education.* London: Allyn & Bacon.

Bhabha, H. (1993). *The location of culture.* London: Routledge.

Britzman, D. P. (1994). Is there a problem with knowing thyself? Towards a post-structuralist view of teacher identity. In T. Shanahan (Ed.), *Teachers thinking, teachers knowing* (pp. 53–75). Urbana, IL: NCRE.

Carter, K., & Doyle, W. (1996). Personal narrative and life history in learning to teach. In J. Sikula (Ed.), *Handbook of research on teacher education* (pp. 120–142). New York: Macmillan.

Clandinin, D. J. (1992). Narrative and story in teacher education. In T. Russell & H. Munby (Eds.), *Teachers and teaching: From classroom to reflection* (pp. 124–137). New York: Falmer Press.

Clark, C. M., & Peterson, P. L. (1986). *Teachers thought processes: Research in teaching and learning.* New York: Macmillan.

Connelly, F. M., & Clandinin, D. J. (1988). *Teachers as curriculum planners.* New York: Teachers College Press.

Cornett, J. W., Chase, S. K., Miller, P., Schrock, D., Bennett, B. J., Goins, A., & Hammond, C. (1992). Insights from the analysis of our own theorizing: The viewpoints of seven teachers. In E. W. Ross, J. W. Cornett, & G. McCutcheon (Eds.), *Teacher personal theorizing: Connecting curriculum practice, theory, and research* (pp.137–157). Albany: State University of New York Press.

Cortes, C. E. (2002). *Children are watching: How the media teach about diversity.* New York: Teachers College Press.

Cruz, B. C. (2001). *Multiethnic teens and cultural identity.* Berkeley Heights, NJ: Enslow Publishers.

Diaz, C. F., Massialas, B.G., & Xanthopoulos, J. H. (1999). *Global perspective for educators.* Needham Heights, MA: Allyn & Bacon.

Detwiler, F. (1999). *Standing on the premises of god: The Christian rights' fight to redefine America's public schools.* New York: New York University Press.

Eck, D. L. (2000). *A new religious America.* New York: Harper San Francisco.

Elnour, A., & Bashir-Ali, K. (2003). Teaching Muslim girls in American schools. *Social Education, 67*(1), 62–64.

Ferguson, A. A. (2000). *Bad boys: Public schools in the making of Black masculinity.* Ann Arbor: University of Michigan Press.

Fine, M. (1991). *Framing dropouts: Notes on the politics of an urban public high school.* Albany: State University of New York Press.

Foster, M. (1997). *Black teachers on teaching.* New York: New Press.

Fordham, S. (1988). Racelessness as a factor in black students' school success: Pragmatic strategy or pyrrhic victory. *Harvard Education Review, 58*, 280–298.

Galindo, R. (1996). Reframing the past in the present: Chicana teacher role identity as a bridging identity. *Education and Urban Society, 29*, 85–102.

Gay, G. (1993). Building cultural bridges: A bold new proposal for teacher education. *Education and Urban Society, 25*(3), 285–299.

Gay, G. (2000). *Culturally responsive teaching: Theory, research, and practice.* New York: Teachers College Press.

Gibson, M. (1988). *Accommodation without assimilation.* Ithaca, NY: Cornell University Press.

Giroux, H. (1994). Living dangerously: Identity, politics, and the new cultural racism. In H. Giroux & P. McLaren (Eds.), *Between borders: Pedagogy and the politics of cultural studies.* New York: Routledge.

Gomez, M. L. (1996). Telling stories of our teaching, reflecting on our practices. *Action in Teacher Education, 18*(3), 1–12.

Goodson, I. F. (Ed.). (1992). *Studying teachers lives.* New York: Teachers College Press.

Hall, K. (1995). There's time to act English and a time to act Indian: The politics of identity among British-Sikh teenagers. In S. Stephens (Ed.), *Children and the politics of culture* (pp. 243–264). Princeton, NJ: Princeton University Press.

Hanh, T. N. (2001). *Anger: Wisdom for cooling the flames.* New York: Riverhead Books.

Hashim, I. (1999). Reconciling Islam and feminism. *Gender and Development, 7*(1), 7–14.

Haw, K. (1998). *Educating Muslim girls.* Buckingham, UK: Open University Press.

Hoffman, D. M. (1996). Culture and self in multicultural education: Reflections on discourse, text, and practice. *American Educational Research Journal, 33,* 545–569.

hooks, b. (2000). *All about love.* New York: HarperCollins.

Karp, S. (1996/97). Arranged marriages, rearranged ideas. In B. Bigelow, B. Harvey, S. Karp, & L. Miller (Eds.), *Rethinking our classrooms: Teaching for equity and justice* (Vol. 2, pp. 188–193). Milwaukee, WI: Rethinking Schools.

King, S. H. (1993). Why did we chose teaching careers and what will enable us to stay? Insights from one cohort of the African American teaching pool. *Journal of Negro Education, 62*(4), 475–492.

Ladson-Billings, G. (1994). *The dreamkeepers: Successful teachers of African American students.* San Francisco: Jossey-Bass.

Lee, S. L. (1996). *Unraveling the "model minority" stereotype: Listening to Asian American youth.* New York: Teachers College Press.

Lei, J. L. (2003). (Un)necessary toughness?: Those "loud black girls" and those "quiet Asian boys." *Anthropology and Education Quarterly, 34*(2), 158–181.

Lipka, J. (1991). School failing minority teachers: Problems and suggestions. *Educational Foundations, 8*(2), 57–80.

Mamdani, M. (2002). Good Muslim, bad Muslim. *American Anthropologist, 104*(3), 766–775.

McCarthy, C. (1998). *The uses of culture.* New York: Routledge.

McGown, R. B. (1999). *Muslims in the diaspora.* Toronto: University of Toronto Press.

Menchu, R. (1984). *I, Rigoberto Menchu: An Indian woman in Guatemala* (A. Wright, Trans.). Verso: London.

Merryfield, M. M. (1994). Shaping the curriculum in global education: The influence of student characteristics on teacher decision-making. *Journal of Curriculum and Supervision, 9*(3), 233–249.

Merryfield, M. M. (2001). Moving the center of global education: From imperial worldviews that divide the world to double consciousness, contrapuntal pedagogy, hybridity, and cross-cultural competence. In W. B. Stanley (Ed.), *Critical issues in social studies research for the 21st century* (pp. 179–208). Greenwich, CT: Information Age.

Meier, D. (1995). *The power of their ideas: Lessons for America from a small school in Harlem.* Boston: Beacon Press.

Montecinos, C. (1994). Teachers of color and multiculturalism. *Equity and Excellence in Education, 27*(3), 34–42.

Neumann, A. (1998). On experience, memory, and knowing: A post-holocaust (auto) biography. *Curriculum Inquiry, 28,* 425–442.

Nieto, S. (1996). *Language, culture and teaching: Critical perspectives for a new century.* Hillsdale, NJ: Erlbaum.

Noddings, N. (1993). *Educating for intelligent belief or unbelief.* New York: Teachers College Press.

Olsen, L. (1997). *Made in America: Immigrant students in our public schools.* New York: New Press.

Olneck, M. (2004). Immigrants and education in the United States. In J. A. Banks & C. A. Banks (Eds.). *Handbook of research on multicultural education* (pp. 381–403). San Francisco: Jossey-Bass.

Pang, V. O. (2005). *Multicultural education: A caring-centered reflective approach.* Boston: McGraw-Hill.

Parker, W. C. (Ed.). (2002). *Education for democracy.* Greenwich, CT: Information Age.

Peek, L. A. (2003). Reactions and response: Muslim students' experience on New York City campus post 9/11. *Journal of Muslim Minority Affairs, 23*(2), 271–283.

Peshkin, A. (1986). *God's choice: The total world of a fundamentalist Christian school.* Chicago: University of Chicago Press.

Peshkin, A. (1991). *The color of strangers, the color of friends.* Chicago: University of Chicago Press.

Pizarro, M. (1997). Power, borders, and identity formation: Understanding the world of Chicana/o students. In J. Gracia (Ed.), *Perspectives in Mexican American studies* (pp. 142–167). Tucson, AZ: Mexican American Studies & Research Center.

Prasad, V. (2000). *The karma of brown folk.* Minneapolis: University of Minnesota Press.

Rehman, F. T., & Diziegielewski, S. F. (2003). Women who choose Islam. *International Journal of Mental Health, 32*(3), 31–49.

Russell, T., & Munby, H. (Eds.). (1992). *Teachers and teaching: From classroom to reflection.* New York: Falmer Press.

Said, E. (1979). *Orientalism.* New York: Random House.

Schubert, W. H., & Ayers, W. C. (Eds.). (1992). *Teacher lore: Learning from our own experience.* New York: Longman.

Sleeter, C. E. (1993). How White teachers construct race. In C. McCarthy & W. Crichlow (Eds.), *Race, identity and representation in education* (pp. 157–171). London: Routledge.

Sleeter, C. E. (2001). Preparing teachers for culturally diverse schools: Research and overwhelming presence of whiteness. *Journal of Teacher Education, 52*(2), 94–110.

Steele, C.M. (1999). A threat in the air: How stereotypes shape intellectual identity and performance. In E. Y. Lowe, Jr. (Ed.), *Racial diversity and higher education* (pp. 92–128). Princeton, NJ: Princeton University Press.

Subedi, B. (2003). Inventing the Other: The geographical production of racial difference and capitalist desires. *Inquiry: Critical Thinking Across the Disciplines, 12*(2), 75–82.

Taylor, L. & Whittaker, C. (2003). *Bridging multiple worlds: Case studies of diverse educational communities.* Boston: Allyn & Bacon.

Smith, L. T. (1999). *Decolonizing methodologies: Research and indigenous people.* London: Zed Books.

Valdes, G. (2001). *Learning and not learning English: Latino students in American schools.* New York: Teachers College Press.

Verma-Joshi, M., Baker, C. J., & Tanaka, C. (2004). Names will never hurt me? *Harvard Education Review, 74*(2), 175–208.

Willinsky, J. (1998). *Learning to divide the world.* Minneapolis: University of Minnesota Press.

Wolk, R. A., & Rodman, B. H. (Eds.). (1994). *Classroom crusaders.* San Francisco: Jossey-Bass.

Yon, D. (2000). *An elusive culture: Schooling, race, and identity in global times.* New York: State University of New York Press.

Zeichner, K. M. (1995). Reflections of a teacher educator working for social change. In T. Russell & F. Korthagen (Eds.), *Teachers who teach teachers: Reflections on teacher education* (pp. 11–24). Washington, DC: Falmer Press.

Zine, J. (2000). Redefining resistance: Towards an Islamic subculture in schools. *Race Ethnicity and Education, 3*(3), 293–316.

Zine, J. (2001). Muslim youth in Canadian schools: Education and the politics of religious identity. *Anthropology & Education Quarterly, 33*(4), 399–423.

CHAPTER 10

BLESSED COMMUNION

Antiracism, Cultural Competence, and Theological Education in the United States

Sheryl A. Kujawa-Holbrook
Episcopal Divinity School

ABSTRACT

As the population within our religious institutions and the United States grows increasingly diverse, the need for a greater awareness of cultural and racial differences is a challenge facing theology students who will live and work within a changing context. For European American students this challenge includes an understanding of the power dynamics inherent in *whiteness* and how the resultant social power affects persons of other races and cultures. This chapter focuses on the need for cultural competence among current theology students, and outlines a five-stage developmental process whereby they have an opportunity to enhance their understanding of multiculturalism and antiracism within their own context. This chapter also directly addresses the importance of antiracism and cultural competency within the religious community and how religion can help or hinder such efforts.

Religion in Multicultural Education, pages 239–258
Copyright © 2006 by Information Age Publishing
All rights of reproduction in any form reserved.

INTRODUCTION

As the population within our religious institutions and the United States grows increasingly diverse, the need for a greater awareness of cultural and racial differences is a challenge facing theology students who will live and work within a changing context. This challenge includes an understanding of the power dynamics inherent in *whiteness* and how the resultant social power affects persons of other races and cultures. This chapter focuses on the need for *cultural competence* among current theology students, and outlines a five-stage developmental process whereby they have an opportunity to enhance their understanding of cultural diversity and racism oppression within their own context.

Theologian Fumitaka Matusoka writes about the need for Christians to reclaim *redemptive traditions* and speaks to the need for all religious institutions to become transformative communities amid a culture that often sees racial differences as negative and oppositional. Matusoka asserts that "blessed communion" is central to the gospel, and yet it is experienced within the midst of the erosion of human relationships in our broader society. "We Christians come to the communion table in our yearning, hollow in our loss, to see if there is any speech and act that can take us again into communion that is genuinely blessed, communion for which we have been made, and in which we live in freedom" (Matsuoka, 1998, p. 8). Furthermore, Matsuoka argues the need for religious institutions to emulate the *embodiment of God's reign in the community:*

> Life cannot be lived in separation and isolation. The church's ministry, then, is to witness in its own life and society a vision of life that transcends those barriers that divide persons from one another. Our baptism into Christ and our celebration of his presence at the Table mark us as people whose shared experience of grace is stronger than any dissimilarities among us.... The embodiment of God's reign in this community, the church, is meaningful precisely because it comprises the full diversity of peoples, cultures, traditions, races, and languages.... We are tied together not by our own blood, but by Christ's blood. (p. 103)

In this context, theological education then becomes an attempt to embody human yearnings witnessed by Christian communities in multicultural and pluralistic societies. Yet while many theological schools suggest the need for cultural awareness, such efforts often serve to reinforce homogeneity, rather than promote genuine multiculturalism and advocate for social change. Though organizational theories differ slightly, most suggest a five- or six-stage change process leading to a fully inclusive multicultural organization, with full participation and shared power at the final stage. Application of several schema suggest the following stages of change that characterize theological schools on the pilgrimage to transformational community (Kujawa-Holbrook, 2003, pp. 20–22).

The exclusive institution perpetuates the domination of one racial group over another. Such congregations intentionally exclude or segregate racial groups on all institutional levels, including decision making, policies, religious teaching, and so on. Leaders of such schools maintain that either one race is inferior to the other, or that to challenge the racism of the church would be to hinder the life of the congregation or jeopardize their own position in it.

The passive institution maintains the privilege of those who have traditionally held power within theological education and the church, with the exception of a very limited number of people of color, with *the right* credentials and who do not threaten the established order. The organizational model of this congregation resembles that of a private club. The fear in this school is that it will have to change to accommodate persons of other races and cultures if they join. In other words, the majority culture's history, worship, language, or other cultural forms will be lost if those outside *the club* are allowed in.

The compliant institution values multiculturalism on a symbolic level, yet essentially reflects an assimilation model. That is, the school may welcome persons from various racial backgrounds, and it may even hire a staff member in order to identify with an incoming racial group. However, most other aspects of the school and curriculum remain the same, and there is often an unconscious assumption that the incoming group should make the effort. This model is essentially conflict avoidant, and though often nominally antiracist, has put *fit in* the burden for change on the marginalized group. One fairly common manifestation of this model is to invite *ethnic* students to share a facility or occasionally participate in educational programs. Though the invitation is usually expressed to demonstrate a desire for more cross-cultural relationships, it does not necessarily also include an invitation to share in the power and ownership of the institution. Another scenario in this category is theological schools that claim to be multicultural, but will only address race from the perspective of *racial unity* in the belief that to do otherwise is contentious and divisive. The limitation of this approach is that the racism and prejudice of the members are not addressed, but are suppressed for the sake of an artificial *unity* that only exists on a superficial level.

An antiracist institution is one that has grown in its understanding of white privilege and of racism as a barrier to multicultural community. Such schools benefit from specific antiracism training on all levels of the institution, and have developed an increasing commitment to eliminate racism in the congregation. At the same time such schools begin to develop relationships with communities of color, as well as increasing sensitivity to the effects of other forms of oppression. An antiracist congregation can envision an alternative community, but its institutional structures continue to maintain white privilege and white culture.

A *redefining institution* makes intentional choices to rebuild its institutional life according to antiracist analysis and identity. By this stage schools are prepared to recognize and acknowledge: (1) that racism is inherent in all institutions; (2) that racism is instrumental in both historic and current institutional contexts; (3) the need for a commitment to change; (4) the need to put mechanisms in place to facilitate change; and (5) that action is a necessary step in the change process. Institutions engaged at this stage of the change process understand that the purpose of antiracism education and training is not only to enhance individual awareness, but to enable multiracial community. In these schools, members acquire the educational support and challenge they need, while at the same time keeping the focus appropriately on sustainable community action. This type of school seeks to address issues and differences so they can be processed in a healthy manner. Schools at this stage of development undertake regular racism *audits* of all aspects of institutional life in order to ensure full participation of people of color. Here the school has transformed their means of organizing structures, policies, and practices in order to distribute power among all of the diverse groups in the institution. Furthermore, through their commitment to antiracist action, such schools are intentionally accountable to communities of color and work to dismantle racism in their wider community.

A *transformed institution* upholds a *future* vision of a new reality where racial oppression no longer sets limits on human growth or potential. A transformed school is a fully multicultural organization that has overcome systemic racism and all other forms of oppression. A congregation within this context would reflect the contributions and interests of diverse racial and cultural groups in its mission, ministries, and institutional structures. Here people of color are full participants throughout the institution. Moreover, the boundary between the wider community and the school is *porous*; the institution works to form alliances and networks in support of efforts to eliminate social oppression and to educate others to do the same.

Certainly, the fact that an institution has a religious mission does not automatically make it more inclined to embrace transformation. Religion is deeply ingrained in identity, culture, and history. Religion can be use as an instrument of oppression, as well as an instrument of transformation. For some, particularly those unsure about their own beliefs, an encounter across religious differences may cause them to feel threatened in their own identity, and lead them to withdraw from or attack those with different beliefs. Realistically, those who most easily embrace religious differences are those who are clear about their own commitment and convictions and draw deeply from the resources of their faith.

Theologian Kortright Davis speaks to the birth of a "new and surprising spirituality" and asserts that as faithful Christians "we are all in this search for meaning and struggle for wholeness together" (1999, p. 145). One of the reasons why so many attempts at multiculturalism in theological education fail is that white American culture often does not recognize or strive to correct the deep power imbalance that exists in many institutions. While some theological schools have made attempts at incorporating diverse cultural sources into their spiritual practice, they have not seriously struggled with the impact of racism on their communities. Thus, multicultural, antiracist theological schools emanate from the collective concern that we are all, despite the divisions we perpetuate, part of one human community; if life is improved for one person, all benefit. Justice does not admit of partitioning. In the Jewish tradition this practice is known as *tikkun olam,* or the healing and reparation of the world. In the Christian tradition this sense is conveyed in the belief that we are called to live in communion with one another, to be transformed for the sake of one another and the world. Theological schools committed to breaking from the status quo often develop a sense of *radical hospitality.* Rather than seeking out like members for mutual support, they seek to form community across the boundaries of difference, and in doing so include people who often consider themselves beyond the reach of organized religion. Rather then limiting their public theology to outreach that maintains the unjust distribution of power and resources, theological schools formed in radical hospitality exercise a commitment to justice. They seek to transform both the believer and society as a whole.

For the purposes of establishing some common terminology, an understanding of the following definitions are important for theological faculty and students interested in the exploration of multiculturalism and racism in the United States (Batts, 1998, pp. 6–12; *The National Dialogues on Anti-Racism,* 1999, 2003, pp. 17–20).

Diversity—Differences among people or peoples reflected in a variety of cultural forms, included but not limited to race, ethnicity, gender, age, religion, class, etc.

Prejudice—A prejudgement that is directed against others before one has all the facts. Prejudice can be positive or negative.

Race—A social (rather than biological) construction based on differences in skin color and facial features imposed by Europeans in North America in order to justify colonization.

Racism—The systematic oppression of one race over another. In the United States, racism operates on the personal, interpersonal, institutional, and cultural levels, and as a system differentiates between whites and people of color. Because the social systems and institutions within the United States are controlled by whites, whites have the social power to make and enforce decisions and have greater access to resources.

Power—The capacity to have control, authority, or influence over others. In the context of cultural competence and white racism awareness, social power refers to the capacity of the dominant (white) culture to have control, authority, and influence over people of color. Social power + prejudice = oppression.

The 21st century is a global society with a high degree of mobility. Educators should keep in mind when sharing definitions in the classroom that not all the persons in any context are necessarily from the United States in terms of national origin. While racial and ethnic oppression exists worldwide, how it impacts persons living in a specific context varies. For instance, racism as it is experienced in the United States is a result of a particular set of historical circumstances that may be similar to, but not identical to, the oppression experienced by others elsewhere. Moreover, students of color who come to the United States to study from other countries will face racism in this context even if it is not their experience in their home countries. Diversity in national origin and religious background can greatly enrich classroom discussions, but only if there is an openness to information and critique from those who are from the majority culture.

Until fairly recently much of the American history written either minimized or denied racial differences. The *melting pot* theory envisioned that racial, ethnic, economic class, regional, and other cultural differences could be subsumed under the inclusive identity, *American*. Although the theory has proved untenable, its assumptions continue to exercise influence over the way racial differences are approached. Many Americans of European descent are raised to believe in the well-intentioned but misinformed *melting pot* vision of American society. That is, those racial differences are negative and that the ideal American society would not consist of discreet racial groups. Rather, all such groups would somehow become melted into one coherent whole. Recent work by educators in multicultural studies has pointed to the limitations of this perspective, including its racist bias. As Edward W. Rodman notes:

> All this adds up to a situation in which the so-called majority in this country is really to be understood as a coalition of European ethnic groups who have dropped their ethnic identity, and have chosen to become that homogenized *American* that we call white. This in turn is then portrayed as the norm for the society, and is identified as the melting pot. The only problem is that those who are not European cannot melt, and that the numerically average person in the world is an eighteen-year-old Asian woman. (Rodman, 1995, p. 14)

The effect of this racist perspective on whites is illustrated by Mary Elizabeth Hobgood in *Dismantling Privilege.*

> The race system is a complex web of social institutions that devastates people of color economically, politically, and culturally. The race system, which gives whites dominance over other racialized groups, also restricts whites emotionally and damages us morally. White dominance, or white supremacy, harms people socially constructed as white in ways most whites neither see nor understand. That said, the truth is that whites gain at the expense of communities of color, which is the primary reason for the construction of whiteness and the racial system. (2000, p. 36)

The automatic privileges received by Americans of European descent within United States' culture was the topic of an influential study by Peggy McIntosh titled "White Privilege: Unpacking the Invisible Knapsack." McIntosh argues that she was taught about racism as a phenomenon that puts others at a disadvantage, but not taught how it gave her, as a white person, personal and societal advantages. These advantages are what McIntosh calls *white privilege.* McIntosh uses the metaphor of white privilege as an invisible, weightless knapsack of special provisions, maps, codebooks, visas, tools, and blank checks (1990, pp. 31–36). White people in the United States are socialized, according to McIntosh, "to think of themselves as mentally neutral, normative, and average, and also ideal, so that when we work to benefit others, this is seen as work that will allow *them* to be more like us" (p p. 31–32). The impact of white privilege on people of color in the United States is so pervasive that it is experienced even when no white people are present. As bell hooks illustrates:

> Nowadays, it has become fashionable for white and black folks alike to act like they do not have the slightest clue as to why black folks might like to separate, to be together in some corner, or neighbourhood, or even at some dining table in a world where we are surrounded by whiteness. It is not a mystery. Those of us who remember living in the midst of racial apartheid know that the separate spaces, the times apart from whiteness, were for sanctuary, for re-imagining and remembering ourselves. In the past separate space meant down time, time for recovery and renewal. (1995, pp. 5–6)

Many of the privileges McIntosh (1996) lists in her study are that which white Americans living in the United States—including theology students—can and do take for granted. For instance, white students can arrange to be in the company of people of their own race most of the time. They can avoid studying theology written from the perspective of people of color and still be considered *educated.* They are educated knowing that the accomplishments of those of their race will not only be included in the curriculum, but determines the canon. They can live within church and seminary communities that feature music and worship indicative of European American culture. American theology students of European descent have a choice of mentors and role models, while it is still possible for students of color not to have access to role models of their same racial, cultural, or religious background within the immediate community. It is not yet a given that a theology student of color will learn anything from the perspective of their own culture within the classroom or through assigned texts.

Since liberalization of United States' immigration legislation in 1965, even relatively remote communities have fairly diverse student populations and religious communities. Increasing mobility and access through international travel and electronic communication have opened the way to increased cultural diversity throughout the United States. All theology students will be better prepared for ministry in multicultural contexts if they are challenged to become culturally competent. The term *cultural competence* is used here because it suggests a long-term developmental process rather than such terms as *cultural awareness* or *cultural sensitivity*, which suggest knowledge gained in a more limited way about particular cultural groups. The ability to recognize and respond to varying aspects of cultural difference is an integral step toward the eradication of white racism. Cultural competence is a *learned* skill, not an automatic part of the educational process, thus it is important to be intentional to evaluate theological curricula from a multicultural perspective.

Though often left unincorporated into practice, research has shown that sound mental health is correlated to strong ethnic identification (Pinderhughes, 1989). One of the most rewarding aspects of theological education for students can be to learn about other cultures. Such work provides opportunities for lasting relationships between individuals of diverse racial and ethnic backgrounds and confronts the isolation of those outside the dominant culture. Many of these groups have a history of courage in the midst of racism that can strengthen communities when recognized. Furthermore, inadequate understanding of how race and ethnicity work within a religious context hampers multicultural coalition building. African Americans, Asian Americans, Latino/a Americans, American Indians, or European Americans bring to their study of theology their distinctive cultures and contributions to the larger community.

Promoting cultural competence among theology students requires a commitment on all levels of institutional life. For instance, the theological school I serve has made a course on racism a requirement for all entering master's-level students. In addition, the school offers an additional course as an elective, and provides antiracism training opportunities for all faculty and staff. While workshops on *diversity* may assist students in gaining a greater knowledge of other cultures, as well as their own, *cultural competence* suggests a long-term educational process, as well as a systemic intervention into the life of the institution. Before work with students can even begin, theological faculty and religious leaders must be prepared to make a long-term commitment to become culturally competent themselves. Institutional change will only occur when theological faculty and religious leaders take responsibility to end the monocultural bias that underlies the racism within our divinity schools and seminaries.

Cultural competence is the outcome of engaging in a multilevel change process of multicultural and antiracism awareness, which enables persons to (*The National Dialogues on Anti-racism*, 1999, 2003, p. 127, appendix):

1. *Know the difference between race, ethnicity, and culture; that culture is more than race and ethnicity, and can apply this competency within theological contexts.* While the focus of this chapter is on racism, which to a large degree remains the most divisive issue in United States' society, other dimensions of our culture include ethnicity, religion, gender, geography, age, ability, economic class, sexual identity, and so on. We need to acknowledge that cultural differences are real. On a personal level, this means students understand how culture shapes identity, how whiteness dominates our culture, and how the reshaping of our identities is a lifelong process. We also need to recognize the multitude of cultural differences between people of color. Here students may be assisted through exercises designed to get in touch with their cultural backgrounds with the goal of building a common experience through a process of sharing pride in commonness and differences. Person-to-person sharing of stories, as well as exercises designed to elicit experiences of *belonging* and *otherness*, are helpful.

2. *Get in touch with their own issues of prejudice and stereotypes.* Cultural competence requires each person to examine their own personality traits and to develop an understanding about how these characteristics impact relationships with persons of different cultures. When dealing with issues of race and culture, feelings of anxiety, awkwardness, fear, and discomfort are natural. Some students have had little opportunity to develop expertise in cultural issues. Often there is a lack of a multicultural vocabulary, or uncomfortable feelings discussing cultural differences. Biases about different racial and cultural groups are often based on a feeling level, rather than on a cognitive level. At this stage it is important to share with students the definitions on race and culture offered here, as well as provide them with an opportunity to discuss the effects of racism and prejudice in their own lives. Here students may benefit from a discussion about their families of origin and what their own background taught them about racial and cultural differences.

3. *Challenge the myth of color blindness, and be aware of the reality of color consciousness as it pertains to race and theological institutions.* Here we need to realize that people of color have suffered many injustices, continue to do so within our institutions, and that these factors of oppression are present, whether we choose to recognize them or not. Thus, we need to be aware of how our racial identity informs the power relationships within our institutions. Furthermore it is important for students to learn how to communicate accurate information on behalf of communities of color, as well as when and how it is appropriate to advocate on behalf of persons from different cultural and religious groups. Here students benefit from inventories designed to evaluate their multicultural skills. For instance, the *Skills in Cultural Competence Inventory.*

4. *Understand that race, ethnicity, gender, economic class, sexual identity, age, ability, religion, and so on are organizing principles for good or ill in everything they do.* It is important for those working for systemic change within theological institutions to have a grasp of the "interlocking" nature oppressions. That is, oppression, the use of power by one group against another, is expressed in many different contexts. Racism, religious oppression, sexism, classism, homophobia, ableism, and ageism are terms used to describe various types of oppressions. All too frequently persons concerned with social inequities focus on only one or two of these *-isms,* often at the price of disregarding the others. *Everyone* has experienced some form of oppression, and all forms of oppression damage not only those in the target group (people of color, non-Christians, women, etc.), but those in the dominant culture as well. Cultural competency suggests a knowledge of the complex nature of interlocking oppressions, rather than focusing on all forms of oppression through a lens of a single issue. Here students would benefit from case studies that examine multiple forms of oppression, and force them to make decisions and name their own biases.

5. *Recognize that there are multiple centers of truth, whose legitimacy is often determined by the amount of power any given perspective may have in a particular context.* The human tendency to universalize our own experience notwithstanding, it is important to understand that what we value as truth may not be perceived the same way by persons of different cultures who have their own versions of truth. Humility means that we can never *really* know what it means to be anyone other than a white person, and that part of the skills needed are those that help us identify how to be an effective ally to people of color given our own experience, attributes, and limitations. Here it is important for students to come to terms with questions such as: What experiences

have you had in changing your perception of a person from another culture or racial group? How did this happen? How did your relationship change with people from other groups? Out of this discussion where are you most challenged?

Over 15 years of teaching about racism and culture in churches and theological schools has suggested to me that students who are introduced to the concepts of cultural competence and make a commitment to racism awareness undergo a five-stage change (internal and external) process. The examination of racism and culture in a classroom context elicits emotional responses in students that range from guilt and shame to anger and despair. Yet, when students are given the opportunity to examine issues related to race in an environment where both their affective and intellectual responses are acknowledged, the possibilities for understanding and change expand (Tatum, 1996, pp. 321–322) Although the complexities of individual culture suggest that no two students experience a stage in exactly the same manner, the steps in the process correlate according to the following frameworks (*The National Dialogues on Anti-Racism,* 1999, 2003)"

1) *Appreciating Diversity–Deconstruction.* At this step students learn not only to recognize difference as valid, they also learn to trust and value diversity as a positive dimension of human society. Students here learn that the present, unparalleled shifts in the impact of various cultures in our communities are a sign of healthy, positive growth. *People are equal, but not the same.* Though human difference does involve managing conflict, in many cases this conflict is due to resistance on the part of the dominant culture—in racial and ethnic terms, white culture—to the influence of other, often newer cultures. Here it is important for students to stay beyond conflict to the point of realization that diversity enhances our lives.

The key to this stage of the change process is deconstruction; that is, students must first "unlearn" the misinformation that they have absorbed, which serves to reinforce their biases and prejudices. Deconstruction addresses the fundamental basis of prejudice, and how misinformation has been passed on through the generations about particular groups. In order for this deconstruction to occur, the falsehoods of the misinformation need to be exposed, along with the realities of the oppression that have been endured. For real appreciation to occur, students need to be aware of the levels of diversity that impact their lives. This can only be accomplished *in relationship* with people from other racial, ethnic, and/or cultural groups.

2) *Prejudice Reduction–Behavior Analysis.* Students enter this stage of cultural competency with an appreciation of diversity and with some cultural sensitivity. They are aware that there is much to *unlearn* about the nature of prejudice and the misinformation upon which it is based. At this stage students begin to develop an understanding of how misinformation is passed

along from one generation to another and is used to justify prejudice, discrimination, and bigotry. It is at this point in the change process where students are first able to distinguish between *appreciating diversity* and *racial justice* because it is the behaviors that justify prejudice and reinforce white privilege that support the perpetuation of racism. Thus, an analysis of the behaviors that perpetuate racial oppression are important if students are eventually going to be able to construct new behaviors to counter it. Here students need a supportive environment to examine their prejudices in an effort to change their oppressive attitude and behaviors. It is not uncommon for white students to feel guilt and/or shame at this stage of the process, along with a sense of hopelessness about doing anything to change the situation. In such cases, students need clarity: Though none of us who are white is personally to blame for creating racism, we all benefit from racist structures (Hobgood, 2000, pp. 41–42). Additionally, students should be encouraged to explore an alternative vision. If the status quo reinforces white privilege and racism, then what would our communities look like if these were no longer present realities? This last step is perhaps one of the most difficult for those on the road to cultural competence, for it challenges students to go beyond identifying the negative and urges them to construct a reality in which European Americans are no longer a racially privileged group.

3) *Power Analysis–Social Constructivism.* Power, both personal and corporate, is a necessity for all persons to feel truly human. It is integral for shaping self-identity and healthy self-esteem. "Powerlessness breeds a sense of anomie which is a major source of psychological distress among those who lack power" (Chinula, 1997, p. 43). The third step in the change process moves the student beyond the realm of personal and interpersonal beliefs and behaviors and introduces them to power analysis. Racism is ultimately a social construct, and it is important for those interested in change to realize that while personal and interpersonal change is positive, without structural change racism will continue to be perpetuated through our religious and educational institutions, and indeed through society as a whole. In other words, racism is bigger than any one of us alone. Here it is emphasized that the institutionalization of racism occurs at a *structural* level when the beliefs and behaviors of the dominant culture are reinforced through social power. Social power is that which allows members of one group to maintain a system of disadvantages against another. However, reason suggests that if racism is a negative social construct, it can also be *deconstructed*. Here skills in social analysis can assist students to make the connections between the sources of power that have historically maintained the status quo—defined as access to basic human needs and rights—and those that continue to do so. Ultimately students should identify those social structures that need to be challenged in order to change the status quo.

Not surprisingly, it is this stage of the change process that can be the most difficult for individuals and institutions committed to social change; it is here where personal experience meets historical context. Indeed, many educational efforts directed toward multiculturalism and/or antiracism stop at what would be considered stage two of this change process and never enter into an arena of power analysis. However, racism exists in diverse and multicultural contexts. It is quite possible to have the presence of persons of different races and cultures in our classrooms, but not address who has the power to control the curriculum and who does not. During stage three in this change process, students are faced with the idea that what they have learned as history is not in fact objective truth, but shaped by the dominant culture. It becomes apparent that what may be respected beliefs and traditions for some are also the source of degradation and oppression for others in the same context.

Obviously, there are many implications for students at this stage in the change process. As members of the dominant culture we are often reluctant and ill equipped to give up power, and our forays into *sharing* power often remain within our own context—where we comfortably control the outcome. After all, white privilege often remains invisible to those who benefit from it. If the majority culture controls the curriculum in our theological institutions, what impact does this have on white students, as well as students of color? How do white faculty, trained in white institutions, equip themselves to teach in multicultural settings? How do white students educated within the limitations of white experience respond to the changing communities they will encounter in their professions? How does the way we have historically defined our disciplines oppress those who are of different races and cultures? And lastly, how can we use our social power for the good within our educational institutions, as well as within the contexts of religion and theology?

One test to determine whether or not a student has an integrated understanding of the first three models of the change process and is to ask them to envision an alternative to the status quo: What would a school, church, or society without racism look like? Such an exercise not only leads into stage four of the change process, but it also measures whether or not students have the skills to identify where oppression exists and analyze what needs to be done to counter it.

4) *Visioning–Anti-Oppression.* While the opportunity to envision a reality free of racism gives students the opportunity to utilize their skills in power analysis, the experience often brings with it a degree of fear. It can be much more difficult to envision a positive alternative to racism than it is to imagine a situation where current power relationships are simply reversed; that is, power relationships realigned to the detriment of the former oppressors and the advantage of the formerly oppressed. Resistance to

racial justice is not borne entirely out of misunderstanding. Much of modern bigotry and racism are fueled by the underlying fear of those in the dominant culture that as white people become the statistical minority we may lose our social power and open ourselves to the kind of oppression we have perpetrated on people of color for centuries. While often unarticulated, this fear of reverse victimization is a fundamental part of the resistance to racial justice. However, the concept of racial justice is not rooted in revenge, but in equal access to human needs and rights. The heart of the question is: What would racial justice look like, and how might we overcome our history of violence and oppression?

Stage four in the change process focuses on the interrelationship of numerous forms of oppression. While groups of white students might easily use a discussion of the *interlocking* nature of oppressions to avoid further work on racism, it is important here to underscore that the common roots of all forms of oppression are prejudice and power. In other words, racism = racial prejudice + social power. To use another example, sexism = prejudice against women + social power.

Here it is important to emphasize that *everyone* has experienced some form of oppression, and both the oppressor and the oppressed are harmed. For instance, while sexism oppresses women, men are also harmed through the imposition of rigid sex roles. In the case of racism, people of color are oppressed, yet white privilege also harms those who benefit from it by limiting the cultural awareness, relationships, and experience of the dominant group. Stage four instructs the student about the role of members of dominant groups in perpetuating oppression, and also emphasizes how the oppressed are complicit with that oppression. This complicity with that which oppresses us, or *internalized* oppression, suggests that in regard to racism and other forms of oppression both groups need to change in order to achieve justice (Batts, 1998, pp. 9–14). In other words, in the case of racism, white Americans need to understand the affects of their racial privilege and bring about change; people of color who suffer the effects of racism and who are unaware of the self-defeating behaviors that reinforce it must also change. The reality of internalized oppression is an important part of the change process, and is often ignored in classroom discussions on racism, just as interracial discussions of racism are often avoided. However, without an analysis of the learned behaviors of the oppressed that perpetuate racism, these behaviors can continually be used by the dominant culture as a justification for racism. Also, it is important for students at this stage to learn about the reality of internalized oppression in order to cure any *romanticism* they may have for other cultures. Such romanticism can inadvertently reinforce negative stereotypes and encourage group isolation. Rather, students who have reached this step of understanding are equipped to envision a new reality where racial oppression no longer sets limits on human growth and potential.

5) *Reconstruction–Institutional Racism.* This final stage of the change process is focused on the implementation of a new vision in concrete terms. The new vision may be as diverse as the students, yet with the understanding that change occurs only when *action* follows commitment and dialogue. White racism cannot be changed purely through education. Good intentions must be translated into action. By this stage of awareness, students are prepared to recognize and acknowledge: (1) that racism is inherent in our institutions; (2) that racism is instrumental in both historic and current institutional contexts; (3) the need for a commitment to change; (4) the need to put mechanisms in place to facilitate change; and (5) that action is a necessary step in the educational process. Students engaged at stage five of the change process understand that the purpose of white racism education is not only to enhance individuals, but to enable a true multicultural community. By using a developmental process that is based in a paradigm of change, students acquire the personal support and challenge they need while learning, while at the same time keeping the focus appropriately on sustainable action.

Educators engaged in the teaching of religion and theology would by necessity adapt any process designed to enhance the cultural competency of students to the work of the particular discipline. However, in terms of teaching methods, this change process is best facilitated by keeping in mind several key elements whenever introducing cultural competence or white racism into the curriculum: (1) build on an analysis of power and privilege; (2) continually tie together action and reflection; (3) create a *democratic* place for the healthy expression of emotion; (4) reserve time for cultural sharing and discovery; (5) discourage discussion that suggests polarities (e.g., *good people and bad people*); (6) encourage the study of history; (7) show how oppression harms everyone; (8) resist attempts to define one objective reality and hold multiple truths; (9) be gentle, but uncompromising throughout. Lastly, for those who teach in settings where religious belief and vocational formation are part of the discussion, make connections between racial justice as envisioned through the change process and the curriculum, community and church life, and faith practice. While religious institutions are racist like all other institutions, theological discourse upholds the possibility of another vision of reality. "The starting point is not to find ways of uniting people divided by fear and violence, but to recognize, celebrate, and learn from God's gift of one creation embodied in varied cultures, languages, religions and races. It is to restore moral integrity in the midst of the culture of decay by restoring freedom and dignity to the captives we held" (Matsuoka, 1998, p. 104).

How to introduce these elements into teaching practice will varying according to context. There is a great deal of debate over many of these issues. However, it is the goal of the change process to move students from debating each other to a place where they can listen to each other's dialogue. *Dialogue* emphasizes the desire to understand myself and others, while *debate* focuses on the successful promotion of one argument over an opponent. Ultimately, racial justice work cannot be learned wholly on a theoretical level; it is advanced when persons of diverse groups discuss their similarities and differences and are accountable to each other. No two groups will respond the same way. Yet, in most situations, it is important to assess the level of the students' listening skills to ascertain if preliminary work in this area should be done before addressing racial and cultural issues. In all cases, teachers and students alike should be encouraged to speak only from the perspective of their own experience using *I* statements; allow only one person to speak at a time; and listen to what others have to say with openness and understanding. No person should be demeaned or trivialized for their experiences. Rather, other's experiences should be respected as real and valued for them. Silence should be honored as well as the expression of emotion. In some contexts it may be appropriate to request that teachers and students alike respect the confidentiality of the group.

We live at a time when the demographics of the world are rapidly changing; our societies are becoming increasingly pluralistic in cultural, racial, and religious terms. Culturally competent theological students should feel more adept at working in contexts in which the dynamics of race, as well as other forms of oppression, underlie the situation at hand. The fact remains that, unless theological students become culturally competent they will remain unable to meet the needs for intercultural and interracial dialogue within religious institutions, our local communities, and American society as a whole. Furthermore, they will continue to consciously and unconsciously perpetuate the racism that inhabits our educational and religious institutions. Theological schools interested in evaluating their institutional life from the perspective of racism and multiculturalism can explore the assessment questions in Appendix B.

As people of faith, we are called to respond to a world that is groaning under the weight of injustice and broken relationships. Our differences and our interdependence are intended to be a source of strength and a gift from God. As people of faith, we also know that the reign of God will not ultimately be built on separatism or political arguments, but on the transformation of hearts—*new* life, not just reordered life. As the people of God who believe in justice, forgiveness, and reconciliation, we can resist the temptation to stop at superficial levels of racial awareness. Through building multicultural, antiracist worshipping communities we can work toward the healing and wholeness that the whole world craves.

REFERENCES

Batts, V. (1998). Modern racism: New melody for the same old tunes (*Episcopal Divinity School Occasional Paper*). Cambridge, Massachusetts.

Chinula, D. (1997). *Building King's beloved community: Foundations for pastoral care and counseling with the oppressed.* Cleveland, OH: United Church Press.

Davis, K. (1999). *Serving with power: Reviving the spirit of Christian ministry.* New York: Paulist Press.

Hobgood, M.E. (2000), *Dismantling privilege: An ethics of accountability.* Cleveland, OH: Pilgrim Press.

Hooks, b. (1995). *Killing rage: Ending racism.* New York: Henry Holt.

Kujawa-Holbrook, S. A. (2003). *A house of prayer for all peoples: Congregations building multiracial communities.* Bethesda, MD: Alban Institute.

Matsuoka, F. (1998). *The color of faith: Building community in a multiracial society.* Cleveland, OH: Pilgrim Press.

McIntosh, P. (1990, Winter). White privilege: Unpacking the invisible knapsack, *Independent School,* pp. 31–36.

The national dialogues on anti-racism: Expanded version. (1999, 2003). New York: Episcopal Church Center.

Rodman, E. (1995). Why we need culturally/racially specific youth programs. In S. A. Kujawa-Holbrook, *Resource for ministries with youth and young adults.* New York: Episcopal Church Center.

Tatum, B. D. (1996). Talking about race, learning about racism: The application of racial identity development in the classroom. In T. Beauboeuf-Lafontant & D. S. Augustine (Eds.), *Facing racism in education* (pp.321–322). Cambridge, MA: Harvard Educational Review.

APPENDIX A

In addition to the definitions found in the text, educators may find the following additional definitions helpful. Sharing definitions with students during the educational process, as well as giving them time to respond to them, is often a helpful way to enable the appropriation of this information into the *culture* of a classroom situation.

African American or Black (not of Hispanic origin)—Persons who are of African descent or who have African ancestry. Though the terms are used interchangeably, some prefer reference to geographic origins rather than skin color.

Asian American/Pacific Islanders—Persons who have origins in the people of the Far East, South Asia, or the Pacific Islands.

Cultural identity—The part of us that relates to what we have learned and internalized from the cultural groups to which we belong.

Culture—The body of learned beliefs, traditions, behavior patterns, communication styles, concepts, values, institutions, and standards that are commonly shared among members of a particular group, and that are socially transmitted to individuals and to which individuals are expected to conform. Persons belong to a variety of cultural groups simultaneously, for example, ethnic groups, racial groups, regional groups, etc.

Dominant culture—That which is considered mainstream American culture; the historic and institutionally recognized set of cultural patterns.

Ethnic—Refers to a people who share a sense of group identity because of common racial, national, tribal, religious, linguistic, or cultural characteristics.

European American—Persons who are of European descent or who have their origins in the people of Europe.

Latino/Latina or Hispanic American—Persons of Spanish-speaking cultures of origin such as Mexico, Puerto Rican, Dominican, Central or South American. Latino/Latinas or Hispanic Americans are from a variety of racial groups.

Multicultural—The coexistence of a variety of distinct cultures within a given context.

Native American/Alaskan Native—Persons who have descended from or with ancestral connections to any of the original (indigenous) peoples of North America.

People of color—A collective term, including African Americans, Asian Americans, Native Americans, Hispanic Americans. Though commonly used, the term "minorities" is a misnomer when used in referring to people of color within the United States; persons within these groups are the numerical majority in the world and in parts of the United States.

Pluralism—A state where members of diverse groups maintain autonomous participation in both a common society and separate cultural groups.

White—A political (rather than cultural) construction used to describe the racial identity of European Americans. It was first used in 17th-century Virginia by upper-class persons in an effort to have lower-class "white" persons identify with themselves, rather than with blacks or indigenous persons seeking freedom. Previously, legal documents referred to ethnic identities: England, German, Dutch, etc. In a racist system, white standards of behavior are considered superior and are the standards by which other groups are judged.

APPENDIX B

Assessment Questions
Characteristics of Multicultural, Antiracist Theological Institutions

Does your institution respect the dignity of all human beings, treat all people with respect, and encourage relationships based on mutuality?

Has your institution investigated its history from the perspective of people of various races and cultures? Who is reflected in the historical discourse and who is not? What has the institution learned from its history, and how does this learning impact the future?

Does the worship of your institution include a diversity of cultures in language, symbols, music, readings, and content? Is there an openness to work in languages other than English? Are worship planners respectful and inclusive of other cultures, but also avoid appropriating others' traditions out of context? Is racism challenged through sermons and worship?

Do people from different racial, ethnic, and cultural groups share their stories openly in the institution? Does the educational process include material reflective of and relevant to people of various races and cultures? Does the pastoral care of the institution blend both the pastoral and the prophetic?

Is your institution genuinely grounded in the local community? Are projects planned with, rather than for, the local community? Are there opportunities for dialogue between members of the school and local community leaders? Does the school seek new staff and students from the local community through outreach, including notices in targeted media? Does the institution participate in community celebrations and events related to diverse cultures?

Does the institution provide structured opportunities to explore racism for all members? Are those in leadership required to participate in antiracism training? Does the institution utilize denominational and community resources and networks in this area? Does the institution have relationships with organizations for people of color for information, referrals, and support? Does the institution advocate at the judicatory and denominational level for racial justice for all persons? Are the institution's leaders in antiracism well chosen and is there provision for their continuous training?

Is the institution's commitment to a multiracial community evident in all publications, including newsletters, websites, etc.? How is the "sacred space" of the institution reflective of different races and cultures?

Are the governance structures of the institution reflective of people of various races and cultures in leadership positions? Do the hiring practices and by-laws of the congregation explicitly state that no one should be denied access due to race, cultural, or religious background? Are the ordained leadership of the institution diverse racially, ethnically, and culturally? Is the institution's committee membership reflective of all identity groups?

Does the institution regularly monitor and evaluate its antiracism efforts? Are there clear indications of long-term commitment? Does the school utilize the media to make its commitment to multiracial community and racial justice known?

CHAPTER 11

RECONSIDERING MODERATE SECULARISM

Constructing a Language of Possibility for Religion in Public Education

Barbara K. Curry
University of Delaware

Neil O. Houser
University of Oklahoma

ABSTRACT

People often resist that which they fear or misunderstand. When this resistance precludes the reflection and compromise is needed to promote societal well-being, it becomes a legitimate focus of social education. Nowhere has the fear been greater or the resistance more rigid than in the debate over religion in public education. This chapter examines the current status of religion in education and considers the implications for policymaking and practice. A brief history of religion in education and two recent cases challenging educational policy are used to frame the discussion. The chapter concludes with a proposal for a "moderate secularism," an alternative approach to pol-

Religion in Multicultural Education, pages 259–277
Copyright © 2006 by Information Age Publishing
All rights of reproduction in any form reserved.

icy and practice based on a language of possibility for addressing religion in public education.

INTRODUCTION

People often resist that which they fear or misunderstand (Berger & Luckmann, 1966). When this resistance precludes the self-reflection and personal compromise needed to promote societal well-being, it becomes a legitimate focus of social education (Baldwin, 1988; Banks, 1987; Kohl, 1988). Nowhere has the fear been greater—or the resistance more rigid—than in the debate over the role of religion in public education (Kaplan, 1994; Marzano, 1993/ 1994; McQuaide & Pliska, 1993/1994; Noddings, 1992; Provenzo, 1990; Rippa, 1992; Slattery, 1995). As with many controversial problems, addressing the fear and resistance related to religion in education requires new forms of thought and discussion (Giroux, 1985; Greene, 1988). In the words of Giroux, it requires "a discourse that combines the language of critique with the language of possibility" (1985, p. 379).

This chapter examines the current status of the debate over religion in education and considers the implications for policymaking and practice. The critique begins with a brief review of the history of religion in American education. It continues with two examples of challenges to educational policy in Pennsylvania and New York. The discussion concludes with a proposal for a *moderate secularism*, an alternative approach to policy and practice based on a language of possibility for addressing religion in public education.

A BRIEF HISTORY OF RELIGION IN EDUCATION

Throughout our nation's history, the relationship between religion and education has been complex, multifaceted, and continuously evolving. Among other factors, it has been influenced by prevailing religious doctrines, varying cultures and social conditions, competing political and economic interests, and legal precedents and parameters established by the courts. Many public policies and current educational practices are grounded in the views of early American leaders, the Constitutional laws that emerged from those views, and subsequent judicial decisions. The separation of church and state, for example, is rooted in the determination to maintain, in the words of Thomas Jefferson, "eternal hostility against every form of tyranny over the mind of man" (quoted in Rippa, 1992, p. 68).[1] To that end, the First Amendment was framed: *Congress shall make no law respecting an establishment of religion, or prohibiting the free exercise thereof.*

Although general parameters have been established by the legal system, these guidelines are often insufficient to address the countless, complicated issues that arise each day within particular educational contexts. Even seemingly unambiguous doctrines such as the separation of church and state have failed to provide clear consensus on the role of religion in American education (Rippa, 1992). The nature of the problem can be more clearly understood by briefly examining historical issues and recent developments related to religion in public education.

Debates over the role of religion in public education have existed for centuries (Rippa, 1992; Zinn, 1990). Even before the founding of the United States, opinions regarding religion and education varied among European colonists. While many northern colonists viewed education as a vehicle for evangelism, southern colonists typically believed religion was a private matter for church and family rather than a civic or governmental responsibility (Rippa, 1992). Although a variety of factors (e.g., internal migration, changing economic conditions) have blurred the boundaries, ongoing social relationships, prevailing religious activities, and persistent political trends nonetheless indicate that significant regional distinctions continue to exist even in the waning years of the 20th century.

In addition to regional differences, the debate over religion in education has been fueled by increased population growth, the cultural diversification of the nation, industrial and technological developments, increased urbanization, a shrinking middle class, and so forth. In response to these changing conditions, both religious and educational institutions have sought to assimilate diverse populations into the prevailing structures, norms, and practices of society (Baldwin, 1988; Banks, 1987; Kohl, 1988; Ogbu, 1987; Rippa, 1992). Insofar as these efforts have imposed religious ideologies and denied religious freedoms, they have often met with fierce opposition.

Finally, ideological divisions have slowly increased through gradual shifts from religion to reason (Rippa, 1992), evolving theories of multiple intelligences and diverse ways of knowing (Belenky, Clinchy, Goldberger, & Tarule, 1986; Gardner, 1985; Sternberg, 1987), and a growing belief that reality, *morality*, and even spirituality may be socially constructed rather than absolute (Berger, 1967; Berger & Luckmann, 1966). The gradual evolution of the Age of Reason, emphasizing the need and ability of humans to understand, control, and improve themselves and their environment, has posed a significant threat to those who advocate complete faith in (a particular interpretation of the will of) God and the relinquishing of personal control over one's own life in favor of (a particular version of) God's will (Peshkin, 1986; Provenzo, 1990).

In addition to the growing emphasis on human ability to understand, interpret, and improve oneself and one's environment through rational thought, some scholars have begun to develop theories of multiple intelligence and alternative ways of knowing. For example, theorists such as Belenky and colleagues (1986) have argued that women's ways of knowing are often qualitatively different (e.g., private, intuitive, connected) but no less important than the rational, technocratic approaches to understanding that have long been privileged in our society. Similarly, individuals such as Gardner (1985) and Sternberg (1987) have described multiple forms of intelligence based on differing natural propensities and varying sociocultural experiences and conditions. An important implication of this work is that, since different forms of intelligence serve different but equally important functions, primacy should not be accorded to any particular way of knowing. To the extent that these views seem to challenge the existence of an ultimate source of truth and authority, they too are seen by many as a threat to religion.

One of the greatest challenges to the religious right is the assertion that reality itself is socially constructed and context specific rather than predetermined and absolute (Berger, 1967; Berger & Luckmann, 1966). The assumption that ideas (including the concept of *God*) are created by people rather than people by ideas poses a clear challenge to creationist beliefs, ideologies based on salvation through divine grace, and so forth.

Scholars such as Peshkin (1986) and Provenzo (1990) have argued that ultra-fundamentalist perspectives constitute closed belief systems that intentionally shut out external influences that they perceive as a threat to their versions of *Absolute Truth*. In his ethnographic study of a Christian fundamentalist school, Peshkin (1986) demonstrated that the educational approach was not intended to promote balance and inquiry. Rather, within this setting, schooling was designed to provide students with absolute values and a rigid point of view. Provenzo (1990) explains that ultra-fundamentalists have increasingly imposed their views on the public schools largely in an effort to regain the status and respect that have gradually eroded over the last several decades: "Although the Social Revolution of the 1960s empowered many individuals, it also diminished the influence and authority of those whose cultural and social values had predominated up until that time" (p. 88).[2]

Thus, gradual social changes related to the Age of Reason, the prospect of multiple intelligences, and socially constructed realities have posed a steadily growing threat to narrowly defined religious doctrines. In combination with the demographic and structural changes occurring since the colonization of America, these factors have fueled renewed resistance from the religious right (Kaplan, 1994; Marzano, 1993/1994; McQuaide & Pliska, 1993/1994; Peshkin, 1986; Provenzo, 1990; Slattery, 1995). To the extent that educators have dared address these developments in public schools, opposition has neared the breaking point.

As a result of the volatility and complexity of the debate over religion in public education, many philosophical arguments and legislative actions intended to clarify the issue have actually exacerbated the overall confusion. Depending on where they position themselves, for example, some people currently contend that the First Amendment prohibits all attention to religion in public education. Others argue that the restriction of religious practice, such as organized prayer in school, violates *the free exercise thereof.* The debate has intensified and captured wider interest in the midst of the conservative shift in Congressional power and new promises (e.g., the Contract with America) vying for public trust.

To the extent that particular religious perspectives have served the interests of some while restricting opportunities for others, the role of religion in education has become increasingly contentious (Kaplan, 1994; Marzano, 1993/1994; Peshkin, 1986; Provenzo, 1990; Rippa, 1992; Slattery, 1995; Zinn, 1990). And to the extent that the debate has itself exacerbated initial ideological and practical divisions, it is apparent that American educators need to develop new ways of thinking and talking about the relationship between religion and education.

RECENT DEVELOPMENT ON RELIGION
IN PUBLIC EDUCATION

Although most public educators have maintained a distance between sectarian doctrines and public educational systems, this separation has perhaps never before been so vocally and forcefully challenged. Dialogue about the possibility of maintaining the separation of church and state as it relates to the school curriculum has been all but lost in the distance between groups that support the infusion of Christianity in education and those who believe public education must be responsive to a multiplicity of needs. Nowhere has this debate resounded more loudly than in Pennsylvania's recent furor over outcomes-based education.

Pennsylvania became a forum for debating these issues when the State Board of Education revised its statute, focusing on educational *outcome* rather than clock hours. Other states intending to implement similar changes watched the drama unfold as educators and citizens debated the meaning and merit of outcomes such as *tolerance of differences* and *respect for diversity* (McQuaide & Pliska, 1993/1994). Christian fundamentalist organizations from around the country organized to establish a presence at Pennsylvania's public hearings on school change (Kappan, 1994; McQuaide & Pliska, **XXXX**).

In a less prominent but equally significant case, the Board of Education for the State of New York joined the debate when it permitted the creation of a district *co-terminus* with a Hasidic religious community. The community, and therefore the district, was bound to a particular gender-related religious doctrine. This orthodoxy became an issue when a school bus driver brought charges of discrimination because she was not permitted to pick up and transport male students to school (*Board of Education of Kiryas Joel Village School District v. Grumet*, 114 S. Ct. 2481). The case sparked a vigorous debate over the constitutionality of public support for a system in which the community, and therefore the district, was bound to a particular religious doctrine. Unlike other prominent cases, the Hasidic community represented a minority religious perspective within the United States. Therefore, rather than the familiar issue of protecting minority groups from dominant forms of religious imposition, this case addressed the responsibility of the general public to provide educational environments that do not prohibit religious freedom.

Like other social and philosophical developments, recent cases such as these have contributed to the debate over religion in education. On the one hand, the religious right has denounced the left for advocating "immorality, situation ethics, outcomes-based education, sex education without moral values, school-based clinics promoting birth control and abortion, euthanasia, child rights and on and on" (Martin, 1994, p. 7, quoted in Slattery, 1995). On the other hand, the left derides the Christian right as "the self-appointed conscience of American society. Without its unique brand of divinely inspired goading, its leaders believe, the nation is destined to sink into the compost heaps of atheism and secular humanism" (Kaplan, 1994).

Based on cases such as those in Pennsylvania and New York, many states have begun to ask with renewed concern: Is secularism always the best approach for providing educational services to the general public? Although policy and practice in public education have been heavily influenced by the United States Constitution and subsequent court decisions, it has become increasingly clear that the relation between religion and education is too complex and controversial to be managed by legislation alone.

A SECTARIAN CURRICULUM IN PENNSYLVANIA

Each year for more than a decade Pennsylvania's Board of Education has reviewed its public school regulations (Chapters 3, 5, and 6 related to student testing, curriculum, and vocational education, respectively). Few modifications other than those influenced by a continuous flow of federal changes attached to titled funding resulted from that review. The state's last attempt to substantially change its regulations was in 1983, following the publication of *A Nation at Risk*. At that time, the state added high school graduation requirements, vocational education requirements, and the monitoring of skills development to its statutes. The requirements included 120 hours of courses, and the monitoring process included basic skills testing in the third, fifth, and eighth grades.

The 1983 changes were later described by the State Board as isolated and without thoughtful connections to other parts of the curriculum. There was a 50% decline in vocational education enrollments, a modest increase in higher level mathematics in the curriculum, and significant increases in attempts to develop lower level cognitive skills. The majority of students graduated unprepared for college or work. Based on these and related observations, the 1983 modifications were deemed largely ineffective, and in 1989 the board began a statewide attempt to revise the curricular components of its regulations. It combined Chapters 3, 5, and 6 under a new chapter. The new chapter, Chapter 5, included curriculum, student assessment, and vocational education related to curriculum and assessment.

According to its executive director, the Pennsylvania Board of Education spent the first year of the 3-year process listening to what people had to say about education in general, and education in Pennsylvania in particular. After reviewing the state's regulations, the Board asked: What should states regulate? What should be regulated elsewhere? Is it possible to define what constitutes an educated citizen and then design regulations to help produce those citizens?

After extensive internal review and careful consideration of several other states (e.g., Minnesota, New Hampshire, New York, and Virginia) in the process of change, the Board decided to delineate related learning outcomes for its students. It saw this as a much-needed attempt to influence teaching as well as curriculum. The changes were consistent with the state's tradition of home rule and local control of schools. The Board convened meetings throughout the state to gather public commentary on its new regulations. At those meetings, constituencies with divergent interests began to emerge. One of the major criticisms of the State Board's learning-outcomes was that they contained values that many parents and religious groups believed were un-Christian or that should be addressed at home rather than in school.

While the Board believed it was appropriate and timely to codify the responsibilities of schools, groups opposing the proposed legislation argued that many of the specified goals represented values that should be optional, decided locally, or taught at home according to parental predilection. They charged the state with attempting to establish a curriculum based on religious *secular humanism.* Several community groups (e.g., Citizens for Excellence in Education; Pennsylvania Conference for Academic Excellence; Pennsylvania Parents Commission) took aggressive social and political action on behalf of the people they claimed to represent. For example, the Citizens for Excellence in Education disseminated a document containing the following excerpt:

> We are Citizens for Excellence in Education in Pennsylvania. We are parents, teachers, businessmen and business women. In short, we are a representative sample of citizens and taxpayers from across the Commonwealth.... After analyzing the proposals, we realized the changes suggested by the Board of Education would, in effect, remove local control of our schools from our elected representatives and put it in the hands of the State Board....*Ethical Judgment* and *Adaptability to Change* do not address the lack of literacy skills. Enforcing politically correct views through *Appreciating and Understanding Other* will not assist students acquiring the skills necessary to fill out a job or college application.... (excerpted from a document distributed by Citizens for Excellence in Education/Erie, 1992, pp. 1–11)

Another quotation from the same source addressed the issue of secular humanism more directly. It also represents the kind of powerful and menacing images of the Board that were being constructed.

> The educational system is an efficient means of turning this generation's thinking toward a world community. Can you think of a better way to break the foundations of the family, national sovereignty and belief in God, which, if left in place, would destroy any hope for the fulfillment of a New World Order? Why deal with the wise-to-the-world adult when there are innocent, naive hearts to be had? (excerpted from a document distributed by Citizens for Excellence in Education/Erie, 1992, p. 11)

Thus, acting on what they believed were religious and spiritual imperatives, parent and religious groups lobbied under the banner of home rule for school prayer and the infusion of Christian values in the curriculum. Finally, in January 1993, after a 3-year development process, the Pennsylvania Board of Education adopted the outcome-based education regulations (see also Curry, 1994; Zahorchak & Boyd, 1994). In the end, the outcomes most closely related to values, such as *respect* and *tolerance* for others, had been significantly modified to comply with the pressures brought to bear by the religious right.

The essential point of the Pennsylvania case is that a relatively small but highly vocal and well-organized group of citizens was able to make problematic—and to an extent, modify—the secular education proscribed by the state. In the next case, the challenge to the separation of church and state came from citizens on both sides of the debate over the role of religion in schooling.

A SECTARIAN SCHOOL DISTRICT IN NEW YORK

A less prominent but equally significant case involved a disagreement between the Kiryas Joel Village School District and the New York State School Boards Association. This dispute has a substantial history. The Kiryas Joel Village, located in Orange County, New York, is a religious community of Satmar Hasidim, practitioners of a strict form of Judaism. Yiddish is the principal language of the Kiryas Joel; television, radio, and English-language publications are not generally used. The dress and appearance of the Hasidim are distinctive. Young men wear side curls, head coverings, and special garments. Both men and women follow prescribed dress codes. The group lives apart from other members of the Monroe–Woodbury School District, and young men and women are educated separately in parochial schools.

From the perspective of the Kiryas Joel, the community's religious practices were jeopardized by secular education. The community needed special education services for its children; however, it maintained that its children could not be sent to public schools where those services were available. To do so violated their religious tenants. To resolve the long-standing dispute over the special needs of the children of Kiryas Joel, the 1989 New York Board of Education established Chapter 748; a compromise was reached between this group and the state legislature. A statute was created that permitted the Hasidic community to form the Kiryas Joel Village School District, a public school district whose boundaries were coterminous with the Hasidic religious community.

This action was expected to quiet the dispute; however, it created another. Citizens outside that community believed their rights, ordinarily protected by a government neutral in its treatment of religion, were abridged by this statutorily created parochial school district. Several months before the new district began operation, the New York State School Board Association, along with two individuals named Grumet and Hawk, brought legal action against the state education department and state officials challenging the new statute (114 S. Ct. 2481). The parties charged that the statute violated the national and state constitutions as *an unconstitutional establishment of religion* (114 S. Ct. 2481).

On November 29, 1993, the Supreme Court agreed to hear the case of the *Board of Education of Kiryas Joel Village School District v. Grumet* (114 S. Ct. 2481). The court's decision to hear the case was viewed as *an opportunity to revamp the strict church–state separation rules it set down in 1971* (*Lemon v. Kurtzman*, 403 U.S. 602, 91 S. Ct. 2105, 29 L. Ed. 2d 745) (NPR, 11, 1993). Although the court questioned the law as set forth in the *Lemon* decision, there had previously been insufficient agreement to overturn it. Social commentators predicted that with judiciary retirements and the appointment of more conservative judges, the court would eventually overturn the decision.

The *Lemon* decision provided a three-pronged test in order to determine whether the establishment clause of the First Amendment of the United States Constitution had been violated. The test questioned whether laws or actions had a secular *purpose*, whether their *principal or primary effect advanc[ed] or inhibit[ed] religion*, and whether they resulted in *excessive governmental entanglement with religion* (187 A.D. 2D 16, 592 N.Y.S. 2D. 123). The court ruled in favor of the Association, Grumet and Hawk, upholding the doctrine of the separation of church and state.

Attorneys for Kiryas Joel appealed the decision, but it was affirmed on the ground that Chapter 748, in effect, advanced religion and violated the doctrine of the separation of church and state. Because the district's student population and board members were exclusively Hasidic, "the statute created a symbolic union of church and state that was likely perceived by the Satmar Hasidim as an endorsement of their religious choices, or by nonadherents as a disapproval of their own" (114 S. Ct. 2481).

The United States Supreme Court granted certiorari and ruled that the statute creating a district coterminous with the village lines violated the establishment clause of the First Amendment (114 S. Ct. 2481). The Court's decision was based on a vote of six to three, with Justices Scalia, Rehnquist, and Thomas casting the dissenting votes. Therefore, for the majority of the court, the expectation that governmental institutions and religious establishments operate in different spheres of public life remains a guiding tenant of American democracy (114 S. Ct. 2481). Government cannot legislate in favor of a particular group, and state and federal roles in the lives of the citizenry are to remain neutral regarding matters of religion that do not violate civil codes. The message from the court was clear—the separation between church and state will not be bridged in favor of a particular religious sect.

For the purposes of this discussion, the key point of the New York case is that even though the Kiryas Joel constituted a majority within their district (unlike the religious right in Pennsylvania), their religious practices nonetheless excluded some of their neighbors from full and equal participation in educational services provided through public funds. By rejecting the coterminous status of the Kiryas Joel Village School District, the Court once again upheld the prevailing principle of separation of church and state.

Although the Pennsylvania and New York cases differed in many respects, they were congruent in at least two important ways. First, both cases focused on the central tension between the right of free worship for all citizens and the restriction of those rights by particular groups. In Pennsylvania, the challenge came from Christian fundamentalist groups who believe secular curriculum practices have taken schooling far from their own religious doctrines. While the Kiryas Joel did not attempt to impose their beliefs upon their neighbors, the exclusion of their neighbors from the district brought local and state government into religious affairs and technically jeopardized the education of any citizen whose religious practices were not represented.

The second similarity is that a concerted and highly effective effort was made in each case to use the state's policy venues to question the role of religion in public education. In essence, both cases served to politicize and once again direct public attention to the issue of religion in education. Although the principle of separation of church and state was ultimately upheld in each of these cases, the tensions have not subsided and the debate remains clearly unresolved. The debate is further complicated by President George W. Bush's faith-based initiatives where Federal funding may be granted to social service providers while maintaining their religious identity.

CURRENT CHALLENGES AND QUESTIONS

While the religious right may envision the development of an immoral society created by the imposition of undesirable values such as *tolerance* and *secular humanism*, others from the left fear a future in which our country, like other nations, may be divided along religious rather than political party lines. In such a time, new liberals would be individuals advocating religious freedom for all Americans. Such concerns continue to grow today as the vocal and ever present group to the right of the American mainstream is courted by conservative politicians such as the proponents of the *Contract with America.*

Although the Contract with America does not specifically include school prayer, a school prayer amendment has been developed as a collateral proposal (*USA Today,* November 15, 1994, p. 3A). In the meantime, silent prayer is the preferred forum for challenging the separation of church and state. While these mandates come at high costs (e.g., a teacher in Georgia was fired for ignoring his district's silent prayer statute, and a principal in Mississippi was fired for his efforts to support school prayer, *USA Today,* November 15, 1994, p. 3A), the larger point is that challenges to the separation of church and state persist in spite of recent court cases such as those in Pennsylvania and New York.

Significant considerations crowd the discussion on secular education. Who will pray? How will they pray? What happens to individuals who choose not to pray or to bear witness to others' acts of prayer? And, how can advocates on both sides safeguard against distilling the act to an essential Americanism akin to saluting the flag with refusal considered an act of treason? National moments of prayer have been observed during both domestic and international crises.

If schools educate for citizenship, one must ask, who defines citizenship in contemporary American society? Historically, that definition has included general education content areas, the focus of the standards movement of the past decade, and more recently the subject of the George W. Bush administration's legislation titled No Child Left Behind. Does that definition include tolerance for differences? Where do lessons of citizenship and tolerance begin? Whether they begin at home or at school, schools eventually play an important role in those lessons.

In summary, the current debate over religion in education is grounded in a long history of controversy on the issue and appears to represent polar extremes. On the one hand, fear of the inculcation of particular religious views has justifiably reinforced the doctrine of the separation of church and state in cases such as those in Pennsylvania and New York. However, precisely because the issue is so intense, complex, and socially embedded, the debate over the role of religion in public education cannot simply be legislated away. Given the pervasiveness of the problem, the relationship between religion and education must ultimately be addressed in a language that leads to the consideration of new possibilities. Thus, the final section of this chapter offers a framework for a language of possibility for addressing religion in public education. For more discussion and a well-developed historical perspective, see DelFattore (2004. See also Wallis (2005).

TOWARD A MODERATE SECULARISM:
IMPLICATION FOR POLICY AND PRACTICE

Among the numerous approaches that might be used to address the relationship between religion and education, neither of the extreme alternatives (i.e., inculcation of particular religious values or complete separation of church and state) seems to be acceptable. On the one hand, it is inappropriate to use public education within a democratic and pluralistic society as a forum for inculcating morality. On the other hand, in a nation of citizens whose lives have been deeply influenced by varying religious perspectives, it seems that spirituality should be addressed in *some* capacity. Within such a society, it is difficult to imagine any credible program of social education (e.g., history, sociology) that does not include thoughtful examination of the role of religion on human lives. The challenge is to develop an approach equally responsive to those who believe religion must be included in public education and those who view religion in school as potentially dangerous.

Beyond modifying school curricula and instruction and beyond even the restructuring of governance and management systems, the problem of addressing religion in education calls for a fundamental restructuring of the debate itself. Like all substantive reformations, reforming the policies and practices of religion in education will require the development of a *language of possibility* (Giroux, 1985).

Between the extremes of sectarian indoctrination and *hands-off* secular alternatives, it is possible to conceive of a third possibility that might be referred to as a *moderate secularism*. This becomes more of a possibility in light of the recent Supreme Court decision on religious icons such as tablets of the Ten Commandments on display on federal property. Such an alternative would neither be sectarian (insofar as it would not be partisan) nor secular (insofar as it would not abstain from meaningful spiritual investigation and religious inquiry). A *moderate secularism* could serve to initiate a dialogue of possibility for policy and practice.

Recognizing the fundamental importance of spiritual life to many Americans, a moderate secularism would embrace rather than avoid discussions about religion in the classroom. New York City's *Rainbow Curriculum* is an example of a recent educational reform effort that pushed toward a more rigorous and comprehensive critique of the dominant social norms underlying religious (and other) traditions without actually *teaching* religion. Similarly, Noddings (1992) has addressed the possibility of investigating various aspects of religion and spirituality through the social studies curriculum. Consistent with these examples, a moderate secularism would reject the advocacy of specific religious perspectives while promoting critical investigation into the nature of spirituality itself and authentic inquiry into the philosophical aspects of various forms of religion.

Several highly interrelated themes are central to the notion of a moderate secularism. First and most important, a moderate secularism in public education would include spiritual inquiry. Rather than sanitizing the curriculum with politically safe and unambiguous (and therefore unchallenging) information, substantive religious inquiry would be an essential part of public education. This would be reflected in policy and practice deliberations extending from daily instruction to state-level board meetings.

This first theme, the *inclusion* of religious inquiry in the school curriculum, cannot exist without four additional themes—*plurality, equality, inquiry,* and *authenticity*—that contextualize and support the original premise. A moderate secularism recognizes that *pluralistic* societies such as our own reflect a variety of needs and concerns as well as multiple intelligences and ways of knowing. Within such a society, it is necessary to address the needs of all groups and individuals. This is perhaps best achieved by valuing and nurturing rather than seeking to standardize (e.g., through cultural assimilation, Banks, 1987; Ogbu, 1987) the multiple intelligences and perspectives represented in our society. Just as a plurality of perspectives and abilities in community polity can provide a basis for national strength and mutual well-being, serious academic inquiry into a variety of religious perspectives can broaden, strengthen, and otherwise facilitate social development and personal growth.

In addition to investigating different religious views and issues from a variety of perspectives, moderate secularism is also *egalitarian*. Therefore, no religious perspective should be more heavily represented than the others. A moderate secularism would reject from the outset the assumption that religious representation in the curriculum should be commensurate with the given community, school, or classroom population.

Consistent with the principles of constructivist learning theory, a moderate secularism assumes that psychological development involves contemplating ideas that differ from one's existing beliefs (Kamii, 1984; Piaget, 1972). Applied to the study of religion, this suggests that Christians, Jews, Muslims, agnostics, atheists, and so forth would each benefit by struggling to understand the arguments of the others. Insofar as the goal is education through critical inquiry rather than uncritical indoctrination, a moderate secularism would strive for a balanced representation of religious perspectives regardless of the prevailing religious orientations within the local community.

Beyond advocating balanced investigation of a variety of religious issues and orientations, a moderate secularism would focus on *inquiry* rather than application. The overall focus would be academic in nature. Rather than learning particular practices, the explicit focus would be to gain a better understanding of the philosophical orientations, premises, histories, and struggles of a variety of religious traditions. Instead of concentrating on specific rituals and routines, educators would help their students examine broader concepts of spirituality and historical religious developments across varied social and cultural settings.

Finally, moderate secularism is *authentic*. It is not an attempt to debunk religion through scientific investigation or to ridicule one orientation while exalting another. A moderate secularism must operate from a position of humility rather than certainty. In the words of Giroux (1985), a moderate secularism would seek to balance a language of critique with a language (and attitude) of possibility. Diverse perspectives would be presumed meritorious based on the insights they provide about the beliefs and actions of various individuals and groups in society. To the extent that religion influences the views and actions of countless members of society, meaningful education requires attention not only to a variety of social, cultural, and political perspectives, but to alternative religious orientations as well.

Thus, a moderate secularism embodies at least five fundamental themes, including: (1) inclusion rather than the avoidance of religion in education, (2) plurality of religious orientations based on the premises of constructed realities and multiple ways of knowing, (3) equal representation and investigation of these approaches regardless of the particular makeup of the community, (4) explicit focus on philosophical investigation rather than practical application, and (5) a standard of authenticity that balances the attitudes of critique and possibility. Each of these themes represents a necessary part of the whole. In the absence of any of these, *moderate secularism* would not exist.

SUMMARY AND CONCLUSION

The moderate secularism we have described differs from typical approaches in public education. Rather than omitting religion from the curriculum as is usually the case, moderate secularism advocates serious and sustained attention to the study of religion. Unlike existing situations such as outcomes-based education in Pennsylvania and Kiryas Joel in New York in which religious preferences and biases are perpetuated through acts of omission and commission, moderate secularism advocates thoughtful and balanced inquiry into a variety of spiritual issues and perspectives. No local perspective would be excluded (as the opponents of outcomes-based education sought to do by omitting discussions of *values*), nor would public funds be used to support the privileging of one orientation over another (as was the case with the Kiryas Joel Village School District). Authentic, academic inquiry into a variety of religious perspectives, histories, and social conditions would serve as the basis for the religious curriculum in public education.

Each of the themes: inclusion, plurality, egalitarianism, inquiry, and authenticity, is significant for policymaking and practice in public education. For example, the principle of inclusion implies that religion should be considered both in governance meetings and in curriculum development and lesson planning. Based on the principles of inclusion and authenticity, religious fundamentalists (such as the opponents of outcomes-based education) could be assured that many of their views would be addressed in meaningful ways in the curriculum. On the other hand, the principles of plurality and equality would help assure that the same groups could not veto the inclusion of perspectives (e.g., tolerance) that diverge from their own ideals. While their *Absolute* belief systems might prevent many ultra-fundamentalists from choosing to participate in any form of public education that affirms diversity and mutual respect, the essential point is that they *could* choose to participate and that their views would be examined with the same care and scrutiny as any other religious orientation.

The issue of religion in education is as important today as it was during the settlement of the New World. As the nation has gradually evolved, the issue has become progressively complex and ideological divisions increasingly intense. The escalation of the debate over religion in public education suggests that educators can ill-afford to ignore this important issue. Although court decisions establish important parameters, they cannot address the countless differences in perspective and practice that characterize a nation such as our own. The alternative to ignoring the situation is to address it, and the alternative to endless oppositional debate is the development of a language of possibility for addressing religion in education.

Moderate secularism, as a framework for philosophical inquiry and a mechanism for policymaking and practice, allows for the development of a more comprehensive approach for coping with the difficult religious issues facing our changing society. A moderate secularism acknowledges the need to study rather than avoid the influence of spirituality upon the lives of Americans. At the same time, it recognizes that a democratic society must never concede to the imposition of particular religious perspectives and practices upon its pluralistic body. Like all proposals addressing difficult educational issues, the views we have expressed will require further dialogue. It is our hope that the concept of a *moderate secularism* will help generate such dialogue and promote a meaningful exploration of new possibilities for the role of religion in public education.

END NOTE ON THE 21ST CENTURY DILEMMA AND POST-9/11 AMERICA

From the mid-20th century controversy over whether or not America should have a Catholic president during John F. Kennedy's election campaign, religion has moved forward into the public spotlight as more than a matter of private concern. Although it receives high regard as more than spiritual guidance used to shape the moral character and fiber of individuals, religion and spirituality incorporated in the rhetoric of morality is now openly part of civil rules of engagement. It has been used to delineate territories as well as a means to blur demarcations such as Democrat and Republican.

No longer closeted or speculative in the influence it has on social interaction, religion is enjoying wider acknowledgment as playing a central role in personal and social identity. Any and all holy or sacred places factor into both continental and global political processes.

Religion often used synonymously with moral learning and development is still very much idealized. However, in its ability to guide the righteous it is much more earthbound and complex as an uncompartmentalized part of people's lives (Pargament, 1997). Good and evil, good deeds or harm face a process of reconciliation that children must figure out early and not just at home. Moral development, to harm or to do no harm—indeed the very definition of harm is one of the complexities to be sorted out in civil process, sacred places, and in moral education.

We acknowledge that the secular and religious coexist in unease and close quarters in public schools. We do not provide an answer as to how to aide in reconciliation of this tension in the classroom apart from a curriculum that involves that study of religion and moral positioning in academic exercise. This is a controversy that will be resolved by school districts. However, Durkheim, in his treatise on *Moral Education,* presents this much more to the point in his consideration of the students' motivation to affiliation with others' verses their affiliation with orienting society as an example of classroom context and a teacher's dilemma in the following:

> Since the aim of the school is to prepare for life it would fail in its task if it made the child develop habits that the conditions of life would someday contradict. If patterns of school life accustom the child to count on a reward for every good thing he does, what great disenchantment he will experience when he discover that society itself does not reward virtuous behavior with such punctuality and precision! He will have to reconstruct a part of his oral self and learn a disinterestedness that the school will not have taught him. ... For it is important that behavior absolutely indispensable for the moral life be rigorously required and if, as a result, any breach of the rules must have a specific sanction, conversely, anything that goes beyond the strictly necessary minimum of morality resist all regulations. For this is the domain of liberty, of personal endeavour and free initiative, which cannot be foreseen—much less regulated. (2002, p. 205)

The social need to cope with an emerging redefinition of civility joining secular and nonsecular in the identity formation of children that becomes the persona of the citizen imbued with the responsibilities of citizenship is the dilemma for public schools. Following Durkheim's reasoning, in schools, at home in our civic arrangements and codes, we come full circle to reasoning through the tensions that make us citizens and moral individuals.

NOTES

1. It is important to note that Jefferson considered himself a religious person. His concerns had more to do with the potential for governmental abuse of religion than with the mere existence of religious perspectives and practices.

2. While acknowledging the problems "Absolute" belief systems pose for public education within a pluralistic and democratic society, both Peshkin and Provenzo contend that the continued existence of alternative perspec-

tives—even closed perspectives such as those of the ultra-fundamentalist—
is a important testimony to the health of the ideological plurality within
our nation.

REFERENCES

Baldwin, J. (1988). *A talk to teachers.* In Simonson, R. & S. Walker (Eds.), *The Gray-wolf Annual Five: Multicultural literacy.* St. Paul, MN: Graywolf Press.

Banks, J. A. (1987). The social studies, ethnic diversity, and social change. *The Elementary School Journal, 87*(5), 531–543.

Banks, J. A. (1989). Integrating the curriculum with ethnic content: Approaches and guidelines. In J. A. Banks & C. A. Banks McGee (Eds.). *Multicultural education: Issues and perspectives.* Boston: Allyn & Bacon.

Belenky, M. F., Clinchy, B. M., Goldberger, N. R., & Tarule, J. M. (1986). *Women's ways of knowing: The development of self, voice, and mind.* New York: Basic Books.

Berger, P. L. (1967). *The sacred canopy: Elements of a sociological theory of religion.* New York: Anchor Books.

Berger, P. L., & Luckmann, T. (1966). *The social construction of reality: A treatise in the sociology of knowledge.* New York: Anchor Books.

Board of Education of Kiryas Joel Village School District v. Louis Grumet et. al. Board of Education of Monroe-Woodbury Central 114 S. Ct. 2481, 129 L. Ed. 2d 546, 62 USLW 4665, 91 Ed. Law Rep. 810, 187 A.D. 2D 16, 592 N.Y.S. 2D

Contract with America: The bold plan by Rep. Newt Gingrich, Rep. Dick Armey, and the House of Republicans to change the nation. (1994). The Republican National Committee: Times Books.

Curry, B. K. (1994). The dissident voice and school change. *Educational Planning: The Journal of the International Society for Educational Planning, 9*(4), 3–13.

DelFattore, J. (2004). *The fourth R: Conflicts over religion in American public schools.* New Haven, CT: Yale University Press.

Durkheim, E. (2002). *Moral education.* New York: Dover Publications.

Gardner, H. (1985). *Frames of mind: The theory of multiple intelligences.* New York: Basic Books.

Giroux, H. A. (1985, May). *Teachers as transformative intellectuals. Social Education,* pp. 376–379.

Greene, M. (1988). *The dialectic of freedom.* New York: Teachers College Press.

Hasson, J., & Manuro, T. (1994, November 15). GOP targeting school prayer. *USA Today,* p. 3A.

Kamii, C. (1984, February). Autonomy: The aim of education envisioned by Piaget. *Phi Delta Kappan,* pp. 410–415.

Kaplan, G. R. (1994). Shotgun wedding: Notes on public education's encounter with the new christian right. *Phi Delta Kappan, 75*(9), K1–K12.

Kohl, H. (1988). *Thirty-six children.* New York: Penguin Books.

Lemon v. Kurtzman, 403 U.S. 602, 91 S. Ct. 2105, 29 L. Ed. 2d 745

Marzano, R. J. (1993/1994). When two worldviews collide. *Educational Leadership, 51*(4), 6–11.

Martin, E. B. (1994). Left has its zealots too [Letter to the editor]. *The Times of Aca-diana.*

McQuaide, J., & Pliska, A-M. (1993/1994). The challenge to Pennsylvania's education reform. *Educational Leadership, 51*(4), 16–21.

Molnar, A. (1993/1994). Fundamental differences? *Educational Leadership, 51*(4), 4–5.

Noddings, N. (1992). *The challenge to care in schools.* New York: Teachers College Press.

Ogbu, J. (1987). Opportunity structure, cultural boundaries, and literacy. In J. A. Langer (Ed.), Language, literacy and culture: Issues of society and schooling (pp. 149–177). Norwood, NJ: Ablex.

Pargament, K (1997). *The psychology of religion and coping.* New York: Guilford Press.

Peshkin, A. (1986). *God's choice: The total world of a fundamentalist Christian school.* Chicago: University of Chicago Press.

Piaget, J. (1972). *The principles of genetic epistemology.* New York: Basic Books.

Provenzo, E. F. (1990). *Religious fundamentalism and American education: The battle for the public schools.* Albany: State University of New York Press.

Rippa, S. A. (1992). *Education in a free society: An American history.* New York: Longman.

Slattery, P. (1995). Understanding political-religious resistance and pressure. *Child-hood Education, 20*(10), 266–269.

Sternberg, R. J. (1987). Second game: A school's-eye view of intelligence. In J. A. Langer (Ed.), *Language, literacy, and culture: Issues of society and schooling.* Nor-wood, NJ: Ablex.

Wallis, J. (2005). *God's politics: A new vision for faith and politics in America.* San Fran-cisco: HarperCollins.

Zahorchak, G. L., & Boyd, W. L. (1994). *The politics of outcome-based education in Penn-sylvania.* Paper presented at UCEA, Philadelphia.

Zinn, H. (1990). *A people's history of the United States.* New York: Harper & Row.

ABOUT THE CONTRIBUTORS

Khadar Bashir-Ali is Visiting Assistant Professor at Ohio State University. Her research looks at discourses of educational access and issues on linguistic empowerment of newcomer second language learners.

Christine Clark is the Executive Director of the Office of Human Relations Programs at the University of Maryland, the equity compliance and diversity education arm of the Office of the President. Clark is also affiliate Associate Professor in the Department of Education Policy and Leadership and affiliate faculty in the Department of Curriculum and Instruction and in the Maryland Institute for Minority Achievement and Urban Education.

During the 1998–1999 academic year, Clark was a Fulbright Senior Scholar at La Universidad Autónoma de Ciudad Juárez, where she conducted research with graduate students on violence in schools. Clark is currently on the editorial board for the National Association for Multicultural Education's journal, *Multicultural Perspectives* and also is Associate Editor for the Higher Education section of Multicultural Education.

Elizabeth Conde-Frazier is Associate Professor at the Claremont School of Theology. As a religious educator she seeks to integrate the discipline of religious education with theology, spirituality and the social sciences. She has written on multicultural issues, Hispanic theological education, and the spirituality of the scholar. Conde-Frazier also teaches at the Latin American Bible Institute in La Puente and has taught in Kazakhstan. Her scholarly passions involve her in doing participatory action research with communities working on justice issues. She seeks to do collaborative research and teaching in the areas of immigration and ecumenism as they relate to religious education. Conde-Frazier is an ordained American Baptist minister with more than 10 years' experience in the local church.

Religion in Multicultural Education, pages 279–282
Copyright © 2006 by Information Age Publishing

Barbara K. Curry is Professor in the College of Human Services, Education, and Public Policy at the University of Delaware. Her research has focused on leadership and organizational change incorporating models of adult identity development.

Kimberly Franklin is Assistant Professor and Director of Professional Education Programs at Trinity Western University in Langley, British Columbia, Canada. She teaches courses in curriculum studies and teaching and learning language arts. Franklin is currently completing her dissertation about diversity leadership and the choices beginning teachers make with regard to integrating their spiritual identity with their professional identity in public education settings.

Gerald W. Fry is Professor of International/Intercultural Education at the University of Minnesota. He has also taught at the University of Oregon, Stanford University, and numerous universities in Southeast Asia, especially Thailand. He has spent over 12 years living and working in Southeast Asia. Among Fry's many publications are *Thailand and Its Neighbors: Interdisciplinary Perspectives, Synthesis Report: From Crisis to Opportunity, The Challenges of Educational Reform in Thailand,* and *International Cooperative Learning: An Innovative Approach to Intercultural Service.*

Elvan Gunel is a PhD student in the School of Education at Ohio State University. Her research looks at Muslim American students' cultural and religious identities.

Elaine Hampton is Associate Professor at the University of Texas at El Paso. She has 11 years' experience teaching science in middle schools in commuities near the U.S. border with Mexico, and provides a critique to traditional science educational experiences from the views of feminism and multiculturalism. Hampton's research interests also focus on the social and educational changes occuring in Mexico as the United States and other nations locate large factories there to mine the labor resources. In addition, she has studied and documented the impact of high-stakes testing programs in the border communities on the curriculum and on the students' opportunities.

Rumjahn Hoosain is Professor of Psychology at the University of Hong Kong. His interests are in cognitive psychology, including psychological aspects of the Chinese language, bilingualism, and the learning of language.

Neil O. Houser is Associate Professor in the Department of Instructional Leadership and Academic Curriculum in the College of Education at the

University of Oklahoma. She teaches social studies, global education, multicultural education, and qualitative research.

Sheryl A. Kujawa-Holbrook is the Academic Dean and the Suzanne Radley Hiatt Professor of Feminist Pastoral Theology at the Episcopal Divinity School is Cambridge, Massachusetts. An Episcopal priest, Kujawa-Holbrook is the author of numerous books and articles, including *A House of Prayer for All Peoples: Congregations Building Multiracial Community*, and the forthcoming *God Beyond Borders: Congregations Building Interreligious Community*.

Michael S. Merry is Visiting Associate Professor in the Department of Education at Beloit College. His interests include multicultural education, identity formation, religious epistemology, and political theory.

Merry M. Merryfield is Professor of social studies and global education at Ohio State University. Her research looks at global education, cross-cultural experiential learning, and online communication.

César Augusto Rossatto is Associate Professor at the University of Texas at El Paso. He is committed to dialogical education and praxis for the liberation of disenfranchised groups. Rossatto is also well versed on Paulo Freire's work, critical temporal theory, social context of education, organizational politics, and urban education with deep familiarity with U.S. and Latin American cross-cultural issues, Brazilian culture in particular.

Farideh Salili is Honorary Professor in the Department of Psychology at the University of Hong Kong. Her research interests are in cross-cultural differences in student learning and motivation, bilingual learning, and multicultural education.

Binaya Subedi is Assistant Professor at Ohio State University where he teaches social studies and global education. His research examines the intersection of post-colonial theory and race discourses in education.

Harro Van Brummelen is Professor and Dean of the School of Education at Trinity Western University in Langley, British Columbia, Canada. Most of his research has involved curriculum studies and educational issues relating to culture and religion, with much of his writing focusing on how worldview thinking and ideologies affect curriculum development and implementation. His best known books are *Walking with God in the Classroom* (available in eight languages) and *Steppingstones to Curriculum*.

Harry S. Wilson is a presbyter of the Church of South India. He is currently the H. George Anderson Professor of Mission and Cultures and Director of the Multicultural Mission Resource Center at the Lutheran Theological

Seminary in Philadelphia. Prior to this he served as Wilhelm Loehe Associate Professor of World Mission at Wartburg Theological Seminary in Dubuque, Iowa; as Executive Secretary for the Department of Theology of the World Alliance of Reformed Churches in Geneva, Switzerland, and taught at United Theological College, in Bangalore, India.

INDEX

A

Religion in Multicultural Education, pages 283–292
Copyright © 2006 by Information Age Publishing
283

Printed in the United States
201376BV00021B/35/A